Christology
From the Margins

Thomas Bohache

scm press

British Library Cataloguing in Publication data

A catalogue record for this book is available
from the British Library

978 0 334 04058 3

First published in 2008 by SCM Press
13–17 Long Lane,
London EC1A 9PN

www.scm-canterburypress.co.uk

SCM Press is a division of
SCM-Canterbury Press Ltd

Typeset by Regent Typesetting, London
Printed and bound in Great Britain by
CPI William Clowes Ltd, Beccles, NR34 7TL

Contents

Dedication

Always to Tom Laughingwolf Simmons,
my husband and partner in life and ministry:
what could be more queer than for two lovers to
read theology to one another in their leisure time?

And to Jane Carl, my first pastor:
who knew what you would unleash when you
dared to tell me that God loved me?

And
In Memory of

Charles Edward Strait
(1948–2007)

Friend. Brother. Christ-Bearer.

Acknowledgements

Many people have helped me in the process of writing this book and bringing it to publication, and I acknowledge them with all my love and appreciation.

The book has its origins in a Master of Arts thesis I wrote at Georgetown University. I was enriched by the careful supervision of Professor Chester Gillis, one of the finest teachers I have had the privilege to study with during my more than 30 years of university work. Chester not only pushed me toward more careful and precise scholarship; he also demonstrated to me that heterosexual males can be pretty queer themselves!

Subsequent to writing the first draft of this book, I had the good fortune to take my doctoral degree at the Episcopal Divinity School, where my que(e)rying of scholarship was greatly enhanced by the courses I took from Professors Kwok Pui-lan and Carter Heyward. Both of these feminist women scholars gave me bread for my journey, the results of which are reflected in these pages. Working with Pui-lan as my thesis advisor strengthened and challenged me to continue to ask hard questions and not settle for easy answers. Carter's pedagogical style in her 'Liberating Jesus' course allowed me to find Jesus all over again and affirm what I had already written in these pages.

Colleagues and fellow travellers along the theological path have aided me tremendously. I thank the Revd Dr Robert Goss for his ongoing mentorship of nearly 15 years and his unfailing graciousness and generosity to a beginning scholar. Likewise, I thank my good friend the Revd Wayne Schwandt for reading the text and sharing with me his own extensive scholarship on the historical Jesus; I 'picked and chose' from among what he shared and any oversights are entirely my own. Classmates Alex Hivoltze-Jimenez and the Revd B. K. Hipsher affirmed my own queer sensibilities by gracing me with their own. Sadly, I learned during the editing of this book for publication that Alex had passed away quite suddenly, at the age of 33; I will always regret that we were unable to have our long-anticipated 'scholarly summit meeting', which would have included copious martinis and episodes of 'Project Runway'! Cheers to Alex, who would have been the next great queer theologian.

I owe a tremendous debt of gratitude to the Revd Dr Emily Robertson, whose beautiful 'Christa' graces the cover of this volume. Emily is a practitioner of the art of New England rug-hooking and submitted Christa as her final project for Carter Heyward's aforementioned 'Liberating Jesus' class at EDS. As soon as I saw it I knew that it was so beautiful and so boundary-pushing that it must, if at all possible, be the first impression people receive of a Christology from the Margins.

My experiences with SCM Press have been phenomenal. I thank my initial editor, Barbara Laing, for submitting this project for approval and for carrying it forward. I am extremely grateful to her successor, Dr Natalie Watson, for bringing the project to completion and for her availability and dedication, her quick responses to emails from across the Atlantic, her attention to detail, helpful suggestions, and, most of all, patience with one who is trying to juggle many plates in the air at one time. I would also like to express my appreciation to SCM's editorial staff, particularly Lawrence Osborn and Jill Wallis, and to Mary Matthews for her overall coordination of this endeavour.

I am forever grateful that I have such a supportive and accepting family: my father, Lewis Bohache, about to celebrate his ninetieth birthday, is a marvel to me for his deep faith and unconditional love for his children, no matter what paths we choose; my sisters Jacquelyn Faucette and Patricia Strait have taught me so much for so many years that all I can say is 'thank you!' During the preparation of this book for publication, my brother-in-law Charles Strait left this life (and our family) much too early; I will always cherish him, the example he set for me, and the respect I always felt from him.

Finally, I acknowledge with gratitude the permission of Sage Publications to reprint in different form portions of Chapters 9–11, which initially appeared in my essay 'Embodiment as Incarnation: An Incipient Queer Christology', in *Theology and Sexuality* 10:1 (October 2003), pp. 9–29.

Introduction

Why Another Christology?

For 2,000 years, theologians have developed a wide-ranging variety of Christologies – articulations of the person and work of Jesus as Christ.[1] This book seeks both to map what has gone before and to explore uncharted territory in order to add to this plurality of Christologies a perspective that has either been silenced or gone unheard – that of those who self-identify as 'queer'.[2]

Queer people join other groups who are situated 'at the margins' of Church and society, theology and social theory. Women and non-white people of both genders have created significant and vibrant theologies from their contexts of gender, race, ethnicity and class. What each group has in common is that they exist in contradistinction to the dominant voices that have shaped religious tradition in Church and academy, voices that have been predominantly white, European/ American, male and presumptively heterosexual. In decades gone by, those who did not fit into the majority were made to feel that they had to join 'the centre' in order to be taken seriously; a heteropatriarchal logic informed them that to be 'objective' one had to leave behind one's origins, uniqueness and individuality. However, in recent years, theologians who locate themselves away from the centre have claimed the margins as a legitimate place for doing theology.

Thus, Korean-American theologian Jung Young Lee points out that

---

1 Following the example of Roger Haight, I will use the designation 'Jesus' to refer to the human person Jesus of Nazareth and 'Jesus Christ' or simply 'Christ' to refer to the object of the Church's Christologies. See Roger Haight, *Jesus Symbol of God* (Maryknoll, NY: Orbis Books, 1999), p.14.

2 I define 'queer' as those who identify themselves as gay, lesbian, bisexual, and transgendered, as well as supportive heterosexuals who, in a homophobic world, are truly 'queer'. See my definition of 'queer' as an inclusive term in my essay, '"To Cut or Not to Cut": Is Compulsory Heterosexuality a Prerequisite for Christianity?' in *Take Back the Word: A Queer Reading of the Bible*, eds Robert E. Goss and Mona West (Cleveland: The Pilgrim Press, 2000), p. 236, n.1; as well as the discussion of 'queer' in Chapter 9 below.

twenty-first-century multiculturalism demands a new way of doing theology since '[n]o theology is free of personal bias'.[3] Claiming and living into one's own bias reveals theological nuances that would remain invisible if one adhered rigidly to what is considered normative or traditional (the centre). Moreover, according to Lee, those at the margins think differently from those at the centre precisely because they coexist in both worlds. They live what he calls an 'in-between' and 'in-both' existence in which the margins and centre influence one another in a dialectical process. He concludes, 'By stressing marginality over centrality, we can restore the balance between the two poles. Such a balance, which creates harmony, finds a new center, the authentic center, which is no longer oppressive but liberative to the people located at the center or the margin.'[4]

This volume, by investigating in detail the various Christologies that have been done 'from the margins', seeks to contribute to the finding of a new, authentic centre vis-à-vis thinking about the Christ figure, with a view toward making Christology more inclusive and accessible to everyone, whether they self-locate in the centre or at the margins.

Part I discusses what I call 'mainstream' or 'traditional' Christologies – that is, theological interpretations of Christ that were developed within their historical contexts and not from the various social locations of the contemporary world. Chapter 1 describes differing views of Christ created by the authors of the New Testament based upon their remembrances of Jesus of Nazareth, as well as the work of the early Church Fathers that led to the writing of the creeds at the Councils of Nicaea and Chalcedon. Chapter 2 surveys theologies of the Christ that have developed from the medieval period to the present day, with special attention to some major contemporary Christologies, both Protestant and Catholic, that expand the doctrine of Christ for a pluralistic world. Chapter 3 examines post-Enlightenment attempts to reconcile the 'Jesus of history' and the 'Christ of faith' and concludes with a discussion of recent attempts to locate the 'historical' Jesus.

Part II analyses what I call 'contextual' Christologies – views of the Christ that have developed out of late twentieth-century liberation movements from the specific context of social location, marginalization and oppression. Thus, Chapter 4 summarizes the Christologies of African-American, African and Asian interpreters, who articulate a

---

3 Jung Young Lee, *Marginality: The Key to Multicultural Theology* (Minneapolis: Fortress Press, 1995), p. 2.

4 Lee, *Marginality*, pp. 30–31.

INTRODUCTION

vision of Jesus Christ based upon race, inculturation and marginalization by the predominant white culture. Chapter 5 describes Latin American liberation Christology, as it has developed in the overall discipline of liberation theology, which approaches religious discourse in the context of class from the vantage point of the majority of the earth's population – the suffering poor. Chapter 6 discusses how feminist Christology employs the context of gender to articulate a vision of Christ for women and post-patriarchal men. Chapter 7 broadens the discussion to include the voices of women of colour (Black, Hispanic and Asian), recognizing that their unique experience as triply marginalized people (on the basis of race/ethnicity, gender and class) has been absent from the other liberation Christologies.

Each of the Christologies discussed in Parts I and II, in its own way, contributes to the articulation of a 'queer' Christology in Part III. By examining the social location of sexual orientation, as well as its similarities with other contexts, Part III presents elements of how queer people of faith might follow Christ in today's world. Chapter 8 begins by first acknowledging hostility and oppression on two fronts: on the one hand, a heteropatriarchal logic manifested in both individual and institutionalized homophobia has influenced the Christian Church and much of Christian theology, due to the unexamined assumption of heteronormativity and compulsory heterosexuality as the divine plan. On the other hand, many queer people display what I call 'Christophobia' – the often internalized, sometimes externalized conviction that Jesus Christ is a 'holy terror' who has nothing to offer those who are of a non-normative sexual orientation. Such Christophobia goes beyond mere 'ecclesiophobia' (aversion to the Church) and strikes at the very heart of queer persons' views of what it means to be created in God's image, to be 'saved', or to be 'in right relation' with God and with one another. Once this intersection of homophobia and Christophobia has been named, Chapter 9 will examine whether sexual orientation or 'queerness' is a legitimate social location from which to do theology. This chapter also analyses the use of the word 'queer' in more detail, as well as recent efforts toward a gay/lesbian or queer theology. Chapter 10 introduces my reasons for articulating a specifically queer Christology and then examines some other Christologies one might consider queer and which have influenced my own. Chapter 11 concludes this study by offering my own queer Christology, a suggestion of how the Christ figure might be appropriated by the queer community as example, saviour and guide to wholeness. By looking at the story of Jesus of

Nazareth, I seek commonality between his story and our own so that every queer person may recognize that in Jesus they have met a brother who can lead them further on their journey toward enlightenment, wholeness and fulfilment – to the discovery of their very 'Christ-ness'. Thus, an explicitly queer Christology will also suggest a queer anthropology (theology of personhood), soteriology (theology of salvation) and ecclesiology (theology of community).

I hope that this work will contribute to understanding among and between the queer and non-queer communities. I pray that it may serve as a bridge between those who are seeking to follow Christ as fully authentic persons and those who may until now have taken their place in Christianity for granted and not realized the exclusionary nature of much Christian theology and practice.

Part I

Traditional Christologies

I

From Jesus to Christ:
Incipient Christology

Introduction

Every Christology has its origin in the story of Jesus of Nazareth. Any doctrine of the person or the work of Christ can be traced ultimately to the life of this Jewish man who lived and died in Palestine in the first century of the Common Era. Over the past few hundred years, scholars have debated how much we can know about this actual historical person, Jesus; yet, for 2,000 years, the paucity of information about his life has not hindered countless people from developing theologies about who Jesus was in relation to the God of his understanding and what Jesus did for the people of his time and for humankind in perpetuity.

Although beliefs in Jesus' saving power as the Christ began to develop within ten years of his death,[1] the first stories of Jesus' life are contained in the Gospels of the New Testament, which began to be composed some 40 years after his death. Thus, one can see that from the start Christology (literally, 'talk about Christ') did not necessarily depend on the historical events of the life of Jesus, but originated rather from the effect his life had on those around him, as they began to believe that in this Jesus they had encountered the Divine.

Every articulation of 'Christ' – from the earliest letter of Paul to the most recent postmodern thesis – is an example of theorizing and theologizing about characteristics that are inseparably linked to a physical human being, Jesus of Nazareth, and seeks to answer two basic questions:

---

1 For dating of the New Testament materials, I rely on Bart D. Ehrmann, *The New Testament: A Historical Introduction to the Early Christian Writings*, second edition (Oxford and New York: Oxford University Press, 2000); and Marinus de Jonge, *Christology in Context: The Earliest Christian Response to Jesus* (Philadelphia: The Westminster Press, 1988).

1 How did the human manifest the Divine?
2 How did the Divine come to reside in the human?

Some have tried to say too much, while others have said too little. This chapter sketches the beginning of Christological thought from its New Testament origins to its doctrinal formulation by the early Church councils.

The New Testament

The doctrine of Christ as established by the Nicene Creed – that Jesus Christ is both fully human and fully divine – has dominated contemporary Christological thought among Christians. Because the creed's language is so definitive and succinct, one may be tempted to think that belief in Jesus as Christ was always simple and clear-cut, though nothing could be further from the truth. On the contrary, New Testament scholars have concluded that 'from the first the significance of Christ could only be apprehended by a diversity of formulations which though not always strictly compatible with each other were not regarded as rendering each other invalid'.[2]

The letters of Paul (from the 50s CE), contain the earliest Christology of the New Testament, while the Gospel of John and the Epistle to the Hebrews (from the early part of the second century CE) reflect the latest Christology of the New Testament. Surprisingly, both the earliest and the latest Christologies reveal what is termed a 'high' Christology, that is, an emphasis upon the 'God-ness' of Jesus Christ, while the intervening New Testament compositions (specifically, the so-called 'Synoptic' Gospels of Matthew, Mark and Luke, composed between 65 and 90 CE) reflect varying degrees of what is termed a 'low' Christology, that is, an emphasis upon the humanness of Jesus Christ.[3] This dichotomy has been accounted for in a variety of ways.

Paul, the great apostle to the gentiles, who is often credited with the

---

2 James D. G. Dunn, *Christology in the Making: A New Testament Inquiry into the Origins of the Incarnation*, second edition (London: SCM Press, 1980, 1989; Grand Rapids, MI: William B. Eerdmans Publishing Company, 1996), pp. 266–7.

3 For a more detailed discussion of the nuances of high and low Christologies, see Roger Haight, *Jesus Symbol of God* (Maryknoll, NY: Orbis Books, 1999), Chapter 6.

geographical spread of Christianity,[4] did not concern himself in his writings with the details of Jesus' life. This has resulted in some uncritical speculation that Paul did not know much about the human Jesus[5] but instead was acquainted with the divine Christ through his supernatural experience of conversion (Acts 9.4–5; Galatians 1.11–2, 15–16; 1 Corinthians 15.8); thus, some contemporary scholars involved in historical Jesus research discount the Pauline corpus entirely as a source of knowledge about Jesus.[6] However, Paul is *the* primary witness for what the earliest Christians believed about the identity of Jesus as Christ in the first years after his death; therefore, he cannot be summarily dismissed in any discussion of Christology. I believe that Paul's world-view was so shaken by his experience of the resurrection that he was at pains in his letters to account for this experience theologically; thus, his writings attempted to stimulate belief in the risen Christ who had been Jesus of Nazareth and should be seen in this context.[7] Moreover, Paul may not have needed to provide a biography of Jesus if his audience was already familiar with the basic facts of Jesus' life and death.[8]

For a human person to rise from the dead was unheard of; the Jews had no expectation that their awaited Messiah would die and then rise.[9] So when individuals and groups of Jesus' followers experienced their friend and teacher after his execution and burial (1 Corinthians 15.5–8), it would have caused a great deal of speculation and consternation. Paul's earliest and most important writings are attempts (a) to confirm the early Christian belief that Jesus was in fact the Messiah (Greek

---

4 Ehrmann, *The New Testament*, Chapter 18.

5 For example, Bishop John Shelby Spong in a series of books throughout the 1990s. See, for example, *Resurrection: Myth or Reality? A Bishop's Search for the Origins of Christianity* (New York: HarperCollins, 1994), Chapter 4.

6 For example, John Dominic Crossan and the Jesus Seminar. (See Bibliography.) A notable exception is Luke Timothy Johnson in *The Real Jesus: The Misguided Quest for the Historical Jesus and the Truth of the Traditional Gospels* (New York: HarperCollins, 1996), pp. 158–65. For a fuller discussion of research into the historical Jesus, see Chapter 3 of the present work.

7 Rudolf Bultmann, *Theology of the New Testament*, trans. Kendrick Grobel, 2 volumes (New York: Charles Scribner's Sons, 1951, 1955), Vol. 1, pp. 293–4.

8 This argument is predicated on the scholarly form-critical assumption that there was a 'floating' Jesus tradition, which circulated around the Mediterranean in various forms (miracle stories, groups of sayings, parables, etc.) and then was gathered into organized texts, which became our canonical Gospels. See Ehrmann, *The New Testament*, Chapter 3.

9 John Macquarrie, *Jesus Christ in Modern Thought* (London: SCM Press, Harrisburg, PA: Trinity Press International, 1990), pp. 38–9.

christos, 'Christ') expected by the Jews, and (b) to reconcile this Messiahship with the Jewish scriptural tradition that one who had been killed as Jesus had been ('on a tree') would have been 'cursed' (Galatians 3.13, quoting Deuteronomy 21.23). This is the 'stumbling block' (Greek *skandalon*, 'scandal') that Paul alludes to in 1 Corinthians 1.23–24 and seeks to overcome by developing a *resurrection Christology* in which God rewarded the crucified Jesus for his faithfulness and exalted him by raising him from the dead. Paul thus creates one type of New Testament Christology, when he proclaims this exaltation (for example, Romans 8.34; Philippians 2.9). Apparently related to this *exaltation Christology* is an *eschatological Christology*, which described the resurrection of Jesus as the 'first fruits' of a general resurrection to occur at the end of time (1 Corinthians 15.20).

Alongside these nascent Christologies stands the *kenosis Christology* of Philippians 2.6–7, in which Paul quotes an early Christian hymn about the Christ figure: 'who, though he was in the form of God, did not regard equality with God as something to be exploited, but emptied himself, taking the form of a slave'.[10] Many scholars interpret this as an extremely high Christology and have thus attributed to Paul a belief in the pre-existence of Jesus as God's Son and Christ before his human life.[11] Recently, however, Roger Haight has explained this type of Christology by analogy to a strain of Jewish wisdom thought that personified and manifested the Divine Wisdom (Hebrew *hochmah*, Greek *sophia*) in the human life of Jesus. Haight sees the Philippians hymn as an example not of a high Christology but a low Christology that sees Jesus in human terms but with an 'infusion of God's Wisdom'.[12] The earliest Christological thought, then, represented a sort of 'apology' for the resurrection in order to explain how the crucified Jesus was not only beloved by God but possessed the very qualities of this God.[13]

---

10 Unless otherwise indicated, Hebrew Testament quotations are from the New Revised Standard Version of the Bible (National Council of Churches of Christ in the USA, 1989) and are rendered in inclusive language. Greek Testament quotations are the author's own translations.

11 For example, Paula Fredricksen, *From Jesus to Christ: The Origins of the New Testament Images of Jesus* (New Haven and London: Yale University Press, 1988), p. 56.

12 Haight, *Jesus Symbol of God*, pp. 168–73. See also Elizabeth A. Johnson, 'Wisdom Was Made Flesh and Pitched Her Tent Among Us', in *Reconstructing the Christ Symbol: Essays in Feminist Christology*, ed. MaryAnne Stevens (New York/Mahwah: Paulist Press, 1993), pp. 95–117.

13 Another early Christological hymn, Colossians 1.15–20, need not be

The next step in Christological thought in the New Testament occurred with the composition of the Gospels, written with the purpose of expressing and inspiring belief in Jesus as the Christ – the expected Messiah. Jesus, as portrayed in all four of the canonical Gospels, is at once a human being but more than a human being, because the authors sought to interpret the events of his life using the hermeneutical key of the resurrection. Post-resurrection ways of speaking about Jesus Christ (Christology) are thus intermingled with remembrances of his life. In many ways, then, it becomes virtually impossible to separate the human Jesus from the Christian proclamation of Christ. As soon as the belief arose that God had raised Jesus from the dead to become Messiah/ Christ, all of the stories of his life would have taken on the imprint of this theological belief, leading to their retelling with mythological embellishments.

Although Paul did develop a Christology, he did so in order to express how *the Risen One* could be Christ, not how the human Jesus became Christ. Therefore, the very first self-conscious Christological statement appears in Mark 8.29, when Jesus asks, 'Who do you say that I am?' The evangelists – unlike Paul – because they were providing details of Jesus' life, had to contend with the issue that would become the crux of all future Christology: how did this human life manifest the Christ, or, what did it mean to say that Jesus was the Christ?

In discussing the Christologies of the Gospels, New Testament scholars have taken two sometimes overlapping approaches. One approach classifies each evangelist's Christology according to when that evangelist believes Jesus 'became' Christ,[14] while the other approach seeks to extract Christological belief from the evangelists' use of titles to refer to Jesus.[15] The titular approach was highly regarded in New Testament studies for many years; through the examination of the various titles used for Jesus, scholars attempted to classify these titles according to their origins among select groups of early Christians by ethnic

---

considered when discussing Pauline Christology, inasmuch as it is now widely believed that Colossians was the later work of a disciple of Paul (Ehrmann, *The New Testament*, pp. 346–50). It can be argued that this Colossians hymn, even if it is Pauline or pre-Pauline, does not necessarily assume pre-existence but, like Haight's view of Philippians, could be merely an articulation that Jesus, because he was made Christ by God, possessed divine qualities ('the image of the invisible God') by virtue of his identification with God.

14 This is the approach taken by Marinus de Jonge in *Christology in Context*.

15 This is the approach taken by Reginald H. Fuller in *The Foundations of New Testament Christology* (New York: Charles Scribner's Sons, 1965).

background or geographical location. More recent scholarship, however, has shown that the Christological titles of the New Testament do not lend themselves to such easy categorization, noting that each of the Gospels – which can be traced to different parts of the Mediterranean and to different target audiences – uses the same titles for Jesus, although sometimes preferring one to another for theological and contextual reasons.[16]

Nevertheless, the titles used for Jesus in the Gospels to connote his status vis-à-vis God and other human beings still convey worthwhile information about incipient Christology, regardless of whether or not they can be traced to specific groups of Christian believers. For example, the title *Son of Man*[17] seems to have been one of the earliest titles used to refer to Jesus and may have even been used by Jesus to refer to himself.[18] This title seeks to interpret the figure of Jesus by recourse to the book of Daniel in the Hebrew Scriptures, where Daniel has a vision of 'one like a son of man' (Daniel 7.14) who appears to be an intermediary between God and humankind, one who is to come in the last days to announce God's judgement and favour. For the first Christians to use this designation for Jesus indicated that they had begun to associate Jesus with this heavenly being who was to come from God at the end of time. It thus can be situated within the eschatological Christology that Paul had enunciated previously; its context is the apocalyptic fervour that characterized much of Jewish intertestamental preaching and writing and, by extension, the earliest Christian proclamations about salvation in

---

16 The nuances of this discussion are beyond the scope of the present essay. I refer the interested reader to the following works, which discuss these approaches: John Macquarrie, *Jesus Christ in Modern Thought*; and Raymond E. Brown, *An Introduction to New Testament Christology* (New York/Mahwah: Paulist Press, 1994).

17 Greek *huious tou anthropou*, literally 'son of a human being': the ancient languages had separate words for generic humanity and for male and female creatures; unfortunately, English translation until a very short time ago was dominated by androcentric language and interpretative bias, resulting in the use of the so-called generic 'man' to represent all of humanity. Although I have a strong commitment to the use of gender inclusive language, I also recognize that 'Son of Man' has become a term of art in New Testament studies and to refer to 'Son (or Child) of Humanity' would risk awkwardness and misunderstanding.

18 The difficulty here is determining whether sayings of Jesus are his *ipsissima verba* or creations of the early Church retrojected into the mouth of Jesus for polemical and/or evangelistic purposes. See Brown, *Introduction to New Testament Christology*, Part II.

Christ.[19] Use of this title indicates that the earliest Christians had made the Christological connection between Jesus of Nazareth and one who had a special ministry from God and would impact human history forever. Calling Jesus 'Son of Man' betrays a 'low' Christology, for the human Jesus is not yet seen as a divine figure; Son of Man Christology sees Jesus as undergoing some sort of transformation *after* his death to become God's eschatological representative.[20]

Messiah is another title the first Christians used to indicate a special relationship between God and Jesus. The Jews had expected this messiah for generations, specifically in a political context as one who would overthrow foreign oppression.[21] Its etymological meaning is 'one anointed' for service; Hebrew prophets and kings were anointed, and special mention is made in the Gospels of Jesus having been anointed (for example, John 12.1–8).[22] Nevertheless, because Jesus did not appear to have demonstrated strong political aspirations, this title seems to have become spiritualized, and its Greek translation, *Christos*, becomes so associated with Jesus that it functions as a sort of surname ('Christ') rather than a title.[23]

Son of God as a title for Jesus at first glance would appear to indicate a high Christology. However, this is not so, for this title was used in the ancient world to refer to those who had a special relationship with God (prophet or king)[24] or through whom God's deeds of power were made manifest (healers or wonder-workers).[25] Philosopher of religion John

---

19 Fuller, *Foundations of New Testament Christology*, pp. 34–42.

20 An exception to this generalization is the use of Son of Man language in the Gospel of John, for example, 'The fact is that no one has ascended into heaven except the one who has descended from heaven, the Son of Man' (John 3.13). The Johannine community seems to have used the Son of Man image as one more example of Jesus' ontological difference from common humanity. See John Ashton, *Understanding the Fourth Gospel* (Oxford: The Clarendon Press, 1991), Chapter 9. (The translation of John 3.13 quoted here is from Ashton, p. 349.)

21 Fuller, *Foundations of New Testament Christology*, pp. 23–31.

22 This concept of 'anointedness' is essential to my queer Christology; see Chapter 10.

23 Related to the title Messiah is the designation 'Son of David', for the Jews had been told that this Messiah would come from the Davidic line. Once Jesus is associated with the messianic figure, his Davidic lineage is highlighted and emphasized. See Fuller, *Foundations of New Testament Christology*, pp. 33–4.

24 Macquarrie, *Jesus Christ in Modern Thought*, p. 42, citing the work of German New Testament scholar Martin Hengel.

25 Morton Smith, *Jesus the Magician: Charlatan or Son of God?* (New York: Harper & Row, 1978; Berkeley: Seastone Press, revised edition 1998), Chapter 3.

Hick has noted that to call Jesus 'Son of God' was not the same thing as delineating him 'God the Son' as the Second Person of the Trinity.[26] On the contrary, the earliest Christians seem to have referred to Jesus as Son of God to demonstrate their belief that the divine power flowed through him, not that he was metaphysically divine himself.

Lord is a sort of hybrid, as it were, in the categorization of low or high Christology. On the one hand, to refer to Jesus as Lord did not originally connote any sort of divinity, since etymologically the Greek word *kyrios* ('lord') was used as an epithet of respect for one of a higher status than the speaker, as we would call someone 'sir' with whom we were not intimately acquainted;[27] additionally, *kyrios* could be used in the sense of 'master' by one who was enslaved or indebted to another.[28] On the other hand, *kyrios* was also used by Greek-speaking Jews as a designation for the Hebrew God ('the LORD') to translate Hebrew *Adonai*, a substitution for the divine name YHWH, which Jews regarded as too holy to be spoken aloud.[29] Realizing the twofold nuance of the term 'Lord', one can easily recognize how important this title became in the transition from a low Christology that regarded Jesus as human to a high Christology that portrayed Jesus as ontologically divine.

I believe that it is much more productive to examine each Gospel as a whole, in order to ascertain how each evangelist viewed Jesus as Christ and described him for the particular community for whom that evangelist was writing. When this is done, the titles employed by that particular evangelist may then be examined in the context of that evangelist's overall Christology, rather than looking at the title in isolation from the text. Thus, one finds that Mark, the first Gospel to be written, sees Jesus as one who was designated by God for a mission at his baptism: '[Jesus] saw the heavens torn apart and the Spirit descending like a dove on him; and a voice came from heaven, "You are my Son, the Beloved; with you I am well pleased"' (Mark 1.10–11). This has been termed *adoptionist Christology*.[30] (Subsequently, when Adoptionism was being declared heretical by the Church, the Markan Christology would be downplayed in favour of the higher Johannine Christology.) The Gospel of Mark

---

26 John Hick, *The Metaphor of God Incarnate: Christology in a Pluralistic Age* (Louisville: Westminster/John Knox Press, 1993), pp. 4–5.

27 Gerald O'Collins, *Christology: A Biblical, Historical, and Systematic Study of Jesus* (Oxford and New York: Oxford University Press, 1995), p. 138.

28 De Jonge, *Christology in Context*, p. 184.

29 Fuller, *Foundations of New Testament Christology*, pp. 67–8.

30 Macquarrie, *Jesus Christ in Modern Thought*, p. 144, citing the designations employed by New Testament scholar John Knox.

emphasizes Jesus as one who preached the kingdom or reign of God. In Mark, the reign of God becomes actualized in Jesus' ministry of healing and exorcism, by virtue of which he is called 'Son of God'. Mark's Gospel records the story of a life that is extraordinary because of its connection to the Divine; it is not, however, the story of a divine life. The Markan Jesus is very definitely a human being; his 'Christ-ness' begins at his baptism and culminates in his being raised from the dead. Mark does not feature resurrection appearances, but merely describes an empty tomb (Mark 16.5–6[31]). Reminiscent of Paul's exaltation Christology, Mark implies that God has raised Jesus as a reward for his faithfulness. To explain why Jesus was not lauded as Christ until after his death and resurrection, Mark crafts the literary device of 'the messianic secret' (for example, Mark 8.30), whereby Jesus' Christic nature is known to some but deliberately kept secret until after his glorification.[32] It is thus apparent that Mark formulates his Christology under the influence of post-resurrection beliefs, which is what makes it Christology and not biography. Mark theologically interprets the life of Jesus Christ through the lens of his belief that Jesus the crucified has been exalted by God.

Matthew and Luke, writing some 15–20 years later, used Mark's Gospel to craft their own. However, in the intervening years, the Christ Event had so captured the first Christians' imaginations that many began to view Jesus' Christ-ness as a basic part of his existence from his very conception. Once these communities believed that Jesus was so unique that an 'ordinary' human life could not contain him, a higher Christology resulted: Jesus' very origin was from God.[33] He was 'Son of God' not solely because of God's power flowing through him in the healings and exorcisms; he became 'God's Son' in some ontological way that set him apart from others and made him able to be God's representative more fully. Nevertheless, Matthew and Luke do not yet recognize Jesus as 'God'; the Gospel of John took that step.

---

31 It is commonly agreed in New Testament scholarship that the Gospel of Mark originally ended at Mark 16.8; subsequently, a 'shorter' ending and a 'longer' ending were added to make Mark's version similar to Matthew's and Luke's. See Ehrmann, *The New Testament*, pp. 72–3, 446.

32 Ehrmann, *The New Testament*, p. 68. The concept of a 'messianic secret' was originally developed by German scholar William Wrede in 1901; see Albert Schweitzer, *The Quest of the Historical Jesus: A Critical Study of Its Progress from Reimarus to Wrede*, trans. W. Montgomery (1906; New York: Collier/ Macmillan, 1968), Chapter 19.

33 See Raymond E. Brown, *The Birth of the Messiah* (New York: Doubleday, 1979).

Matthew, writing for a predominantly Jewish audience, appropriately portrays Jesus as the 'new Moses'.[34] Much of Jesus' life is recapitulated according to the narrative of Moses' life in the Hebrew Scriptures. Jesus enunciates a 'new Torah', just as Moses delivered the Torah to the Hebrews; Matthew divides Jesus' teaching into five blocks of material to correspond to the five 'books of Moses'. In this sense, Matthew develops what may be called a *prophetic Christology*: Jesus is interpreted Christologically as being the successor of the Hebrew prophets; yet, he is the quintessential prophet who could succeed where even Moses could not because Jesus' origin was not exclusively human. He could lead humanity away from oppression into the promised land – first the Jews and then the gentiles – because he was not only a prophet and not only the promised Davidic Messiah, but also the personification of the Hebrew epithet *Immanuel*, 'God-with-us'. Matthew includes dramatic resurrection appearances to demonstrate that in this Jesus – the Christ – God interacted and intervened definitively in human history in a new way.

Luke, not only writing for a gentile audience, but also seeking to demonstrate that Jesus Christ is the midpoint of salvation history, which continues on in the Christian Church,[35] articulates a *spirit Christology*, whereby God's Spirit is made manifest in the entire life of Jesus – from conception through the public ministry and death all the way up to the resurrection and ascension and beyond into the life of the first Christians. God's Spirit makes Jesus the Christ in Luke's Gospel, and empowers the early Church to be the body of Christ in Luke's companion work, the book of Acts. Luke's Christology is perhaps the most inclusive of the Christologies of the New Testament, because Luke sees the Spirit as uniting all the nations of the world (Acts 2.5–11) in a new covenant (Luke 22.20).

Matthew and Luke, because they incorporate a great deal of teaching material recognized as originating in the so-called 'Q' Gospel or 'Sayings Source',[36] also articulate what may be called a *wisdom Christology*, whereby Jesus personifies the divine wisdom that appears throughout the Hebrew Scriptures in, for example, the books of Proverbs,

---

34 David E. Garland, *Reading Matthew: A Literary and Theological Commentary on the First Gospel* (New York: Crossroad, 1995), pp. 51–2.

35 Pheme Perkins, *Reading the New Testament*, second edition (1978; New York/Mahwah: Paulist Press, 1988), p. 235.

36 Perkins, *Reading the New Testament*, pp. 62–5. See also Burton L. Mack, *The Lost Gospel: The Book of Q and Christian Origins* (New York: Harper Collins, 1993).

Ecclesiastes and Job. Wisdom Christology dominated the Gnostic Scriptures, of which much has been made in recent years,[37] especially the Gospel of Thomas, regarded by some contemporary biblical scholars as including earliest sayings of the historical Jesus.[38]

By the time the Gospel of John was written some 20 years later, the early Christians had split from Judaism and differentiated themselves as a new religion and not just another Jewish sect. John's Christology thus connotes a polemical and exclusive tone. Moreover, in John's high Christology, Christological development reached its ultimate fulfilment, for John portrays Jesus as a fully divine being (the *Logos* or 'Word' of God) who always existed with God but 'pitched a tent' among humanity (John 1.14) for a time before returning to God. In John, therefore, one finds the fully formulated Christological language of the divinity of Christ (John 20.28), of Jesus' self-identification with God (John 10.30), and of Jesus' absolute essentialness for human salvation (John 14.6). Some scholars detect in John a *logos Christology* that Christianity shares with other religions to describe communion between the human and the divine.[39]

With the high Christology of John, we have come full circle. Paul's Christology constitutes a high Christology because it is not concerned with Jesus' humanity; I accounted for this above due to Paul's concern with relating the one who had been raised by God with the Christ figure who represents God to humanity. John's Christology does have something in common with Paul's, but, in my view, does not express a high Christology but rather a lack of concern with the human trappings of Jesus Christ. Paul was distracted from Jesus' humanity for his own tangible reasons, while John was distracted for other reasons: by the time John was writing his Gospel, Christianity was moving into the mainstream of Greco-Roman culture; Jesus was no longer perceived as an exclusively Jewish Messiah figure, but rather as one who had transnational significance. In turn, this transnational significance for John took on a 'cosmic' significance (to use a somewhat overworked contemporary term). The relevance of Jesus as Christ had to extend beyond his narrow historical context; pre-existence permitted him to play a univer-

---

37 See, for example, Elaine Pagels, *The Gnostic Gospels* (New York: Random House, 1979).

38 John Dominic Crossan, *The Historical Jesus: The Life of a Mediterranean Jewish Peasant* (New York: HarperCollins, 1991), pp. 427–8.

39 See, for example, Raimundo Panikkar, *The Unknown Christ of Hinduism: Towards an Ecumenical Christophany* (Maryknoll, NY: Orbis Books, 1981), pp. 45–61.

sal role. The later books of the New Testament express this universality soteriologically (for example, Hebrews) and eschatologically (for example, Revelation), as Jesus Christ came to be seen as God's decisive revelation to the world, through whom the world could be reconciled to God. Once this theological mindset became the official religious view of the Roman Empire in the early fourth century CE, the stage was set for theological development resulting in the Christological affirmation of the Nicene Creed.

The Early Church Fathers

As demonstrated above, the New Testament contains a diversity of Christologies. This diversity is not as apparent in the canon as it has come down to us as it would be if the materials had been arranged chronologically. If that were the case, one would see the so-called 'higher' Christologies, stressing Jesus Christ's relation to the Divine, at the beginning and the end, while the 'lower' Christologies, highlighting the humanity of Jesus, would be arranged in the middle. Moreover, one must keep in mind that the authors of the New Testament were not attempting to compose systematic theology. The evangelists were seeking to inspire faith through the telling of the life of Jesus Christ, while Paul was using his faith in Christ to address specific situations in the early Church. The biblical information was as complete as it needed to be at the time and in the context for which it was written; however, as time went by, statements about Jesus required elaboration and inconsistencies and omissions had to be corrected, as new generations of believers brought their own contexts and questions to the biblical witness; that is, the texts and tradition invited a 'move from narrative to theological Christology'.[40]

As Christianity became a religion of its own, separate from Judaism, the early Christians had to protect themselves on two fronts: first, since they claimed to be a 'fulfilment' of Judaism, they had to articulate a theology which showed that, in their revering of Jesus as Christ, they were neither violating the monotheistic heritage of Judaism, nor were they 'atheists' in the parlance of their pagan neighbours. Second, as they determined Christianity's unity in the midst of diversity, they needed to articulate a view of exactly how God had come near to humanity in the

---

40 O'Collins, *Christology*, p. 160.

figure of Jesus the Christ that could be acceptable to an educated, non-Jewish audience.[41]

There was no problem as long as there was 'acceptable' diversity; however, certain sects developed, which, at one extreme, saw Jesus as merely a human being who had no connection with the Divine (the Ebionites) and, at the other extreme, believed Jesus had only 'seemed' to be human but was actually a divine figure who took up residence in a human body (the Docetists).[42] The first Christian theology, therefore, had two aims: on the one hand, it was *apologetic*, seeking to show how Christianity was not antithetical to Judaism; and, on the other, it was *descriptive*, seeking to delineate the person and the work of Jesus Christ in a way that was true to his multifaceted portrayals in the canonical Gospels and yet had coherence in the Greco-Roman philosophical milieu. It fell to that group of theologian-philosophers known as 'the Church Fathers' to articulate an apologetic, descriptive Christianity that would come to be known as orthodox ('right-believing').

Roman Catholic theologian Gerald O'Collins points out that the Christological thinking and debating that resulted in dogmatic language about the true humanity and true divinity of Christ took place in two stages: (a) evaluation of the significance of Jesus' death, and (b) speculation on who Jesus must have been in relation to God in order to give his death that significance.[43] Both of these articulations have been the subject matter of Christology ever since, even though, strictly speaking, one should speak of 'Christology' as theology about Christ's person and 'soteriology' as theology about Christ's work.[44]

The Work of Christ

Before believers could begin to dialogue about who Christ was, they had to have some recognition of his importance; in other words, they had to believe that he *did* something worth discussing. Thus, Roger Haight states:

> Jesus was and is significant because in his lifetime he raised, and confronted people with, the religious question of the nature of God and the meaning of human existence. . . . But the religious question is none

---

41 Macquarrie, *Jesus Christ in Modern Thought*, p. 149.
42 Macquarrie, *Jesus Christ in Modern Thought*, pp. 144, 153.
43 O'Collins, *Christology*, pp. 154, 172.
44 Haight, *Jesus Symbol of God*, p. 155.

other than the question of salvation. Although salvation is conceived specifically in a variety of ways, generally it consists in a positive response to the negativities that threaten the existence, meaning, purpose, and destiny of human life. This involves God or the equivalent of God. *The reason why people were and are interested in Jesus is that in some experiential manner he mediates salvation from God. Thus the fundamental structure of Christian faith and christology is soteriological*, and, from an anthropological perspective, the whole of christology rests on soteriology.[45]

The New Testament makes some soteriological statements about Jesus, but does not explain them in detail. For example, Paul states that Jesus undid the disobedience of Adam through his righteousness (Romans 5.18–19), becoming obedient to the point of death (Philippians 2.8); that Jesus is a 'sacrifice of atonement through his blood' (Romans 3.25); and that Jesus was sent to redeem humanity so that it might receive adoption as God's children (Galatians 4.5). The Synoptic Gospels speak of the Son of Man giving his life as a 'ransom for many' (Mark 10.45; Matthew 20.28). The Jesus of the Gospel of John asserts that he will be 'lifted up from the earth [to] draw all people to myself' (John 12.32). The Epistle to the Hebrews declares that Jesus 'made purification for sins' (Hebrews 1.3) as a 'high priest . . . to make a sacrifice of atonement for the sins of the people' (Hebrews 2.17). This, then, is the 'raw material', as it were, with which the early Church Fathers worked. (Nevertheless, it would not be until nearly 1,000 years after Christ that a systematic doctrine of the work of Christ was developed.[46])

The Apostolic Fathers of the early second century organized their theories of Christ's work around two themes: first, they viewed Jesus' very life as salvific through his revelation of God and God's law and the opportunity for immortality for humankind through a recognition of God's sovereignty through Christ. Second, they focused on Jesus' passion, death and resurrection as occurring 'for our sakes' in order to

---

45 Haight, *Jesus Symbol of God*, pp. 178, 181 (emphasis added).

46 Macquarrie, *Jesus Christ in Modern Thought*, pp. 169–72. But note also the opinion of patristics scholar J. N. D. Kelly: '[W]hile the conviction of redemption through Christ has always been the motive force of Christian faith, no final and universally accepted definition of the manner of its achievement has been formulated to this day'; *Early Christian Doctrines*, fifth edition (1960; New York: HarperCollins, 1978), p. 163.

challenge persons to repentance. These Apostolic Fathers (Clement of Rome, Polycarp, Barnabas and Ignatius of Antioch) saw Jesus primarily in terms of his humanity as a great lawgiver and example, as described in the Synoptic Gospels.[47]

The Apologists of the late second century were more concerned with developing an anthropology, or doctrine of the human person, as the motivating factor for Christ's salvific work, based upon the cultural influence of Greek philosophy and its delineation of body–soul dualism. According to Justin Martyr's soteriology, humanity had been created with free will but had fallen from divine grace and been cursed; Christ was sent to overcome this curse by imparting saving knowledge and shedding his blood as purification for those who believe in him.[48] Tertullian of Carthage supplemented this soteriology with the idea that God and Satan were in a battle over the souls of humankind. According to his scenario, which Augustine later developed into the doctrine of original sin, the sin of Adam infected the entire human race, thus requiring that God send Jesus Christ to die as an expiation for this sin.[49]

At the turn of the third century, Irenaeus of Lyons developed his theory of recapitulation to explain the work of Christ. According to Irenaeus, humanity was created in the image and likeness of God, but had fallen from this image due to sin. Following Paul in Romans 5, Irenaeus asserted that humankind may be saved from the effects of the sin of the first Adam through belief in the last Adam, Christ; thus, Christ as Redeemer recapitulates the history of the human race in his life and work and restores it to unity with God.[50] Irenaeus called this unity with God humanity's 'deification', an idea that came to fruition in the fourth-century theology of Athanasius, who asserted that Christ 'became man that we might become God'.[51]

Once these early attempts to explain Jesus Christ's saving work were formulated, however, the Church Fathers realized that they would be insufficient unless they also explained who this Jesus had been, that he was able to save humankind. The most important theologizing of the

---

47 Kelly, *Early Christian Doctrines*, pp. 163–5. It is my opinion that these authors' lack of concern with a high Christology is because the Gospel of John had not yet achieved wide circulation at the time they were writing.

48 Kelly, *Early Christian Doctrines*, pp. 166–70.

49 Kelly, *Early Christian Doctrines*, pp. 175–7.

50 Kelly, *Early Christian Doctrines*, pp. 171–2.

51 Macquarrie, *Jesus Christ in Modern Thought*, pp. 154, 159, quoting Athanasius' *De Incarnatione*.

first five centuries, then, was devoted to explaining the person of Christ, to which we now turn.[52]

The Person of Christ

British historical theologian J. N. D. Kelly states as the basic problem behind the Church's earliest Christological development that it had inherited certain elements from Judaism, yet had to integrate with it, intellectually, the fresh data of the specifically Christian revelation.[53] Its roots were in the monotheism of Judaism, yet its adherents were being drawn more and more from those who were steeped in the polytheism of the Greco-Roman religions and in the metaphysical philosophy of Plato and Aristotle. These pagan converts thus had the twofold task of, on the one hand, accepting the foundational tenets of Judaism and Jesus Christ's primary role as the Jewish Messiah, and, on the other, reconciling these notions with what they believed about the world and its origins. In the religious atmosphere of the Roman Empire, people performed rituals to the various gods of the Roman pantheon and the emperors. However, this was mere lip-service to tradition; the real religious beliefs were those of Greek philosophy and its various schools. This philosophical basis, then, and not Greco-Roman polytheism, was what the first Christian thinkers relied upon to explain the nature of the Godhead.[54]

The most important development for the formation of Christology proved to be the authority accorded the Gospel of John in the Christian Church beginning in the second century. 'The Jesus who was the subject matter of christology ceased to be the Jesus of the synoptics.'[55] Why this occurred remains a matter of speculation; however, I suggest that the non-Jewish audience affected by the Christ Event would have seen in the

---

52 I realize that it is an artificial distinction to discuss the doctrines of the work and person of Christ as though they developed separately, for they did not. The writings of the Church Fathers on these two doctrines are complex and intertwined and do not lend themselves to neat chronological discussion. However, as stated previously, I do believe that before any thought could be given to who Jesus was, there had to be some appreciation of what he did.

53 Kelly, *Early Christian Doctrines*, p. 87.

54 For a detailed discussion of Greco-Roman philosophy as a background to Christology, see Kelly, *Early Christian Doctrines*, pp. 14–22; and Everett Ferguson, *Backgrounds of Early Christianity*, second edition (Grand Rapids, MI: William B. Eerdmans Publishing Company, 1993), Chapter 4.

55 Haight, *Jesus Symbol of God*, p. 247.

Jesus of John's Gospel a figure who resembled in his discourses a Greek philosopher and who engaged the very stuff of their culture. Moreover, the 'three-stage Christology' of pre-existence, descent and ascent[56] found in the Prologue to John accorded in many ways with Platonic mythology (and, negatively, with the Gnostic redeemer myth[57]).

The Christological image that served as the 'bridge' between Judaism and Greek philosophy was the figure of the *Logos* ('Word'). The Prologue to John's Gospel (1.1–3, 13) portrays this Logos as a pre-existent divine being who was with God at creation, was God, and became flesh. Reminiscent of the figure of Wisdom in the Hebrew Bible,[58] the Logos was explained to a Hellenistic Jewish audience by Philo of Alexandria, who saw the Logos as the divine principle revealed in various theophanies throughout the Hebrew Bible. Perhaps most importantly, religious interpreters saw in the Logos an integral notion of Stoic metaphysical philosophy.[59] It was thus 'ready-made', as it were, for transferring idea about the person of Christ from a Jewish environment to a Greco-Roman milieu.

John Macquarrie describes Justin Martyr, the first to write extensively on the Logos in his *First and Second Apologies* and in the *Dialogue with Trypho the Jew*, in this way:

> He had been a pagan philosopher, and even after his conversion to Christianity, he still regarded himself as a philosopher, and regarded Christianity as the true philosophy. . . . Inevitably he was attracted by the description of Jesus Christ as the Word or Logos, and this was understood by him in the way in which the term was employed in Greek philosophy. The Logos had existed from eternity, and it mediates God's activity to the world.[60]

---

56 Haight, *Jesus Symbol of God*, p. 247.

57 See Bultmann, *Theology of the New Testament*, Vol. 2, pp. 6, 12–13, 66–67.

58 For example, Proverbs 8.22–31; Sirach 1.9–10; Wisdom 7.22. See the work of Elizabeth A. Johnson: 'Wisdom Was Made Flesh'; *Consider Jesus: Waves of Renewal in Christology* (New York: Crossroad, 1992), pp. 111–12; and *She Who Is: The Mystery of God in Feminist Theological Discourse* (New York: Crossroad, 1992), pp. 94–100. The role of Wisdom in Jesus Christ is foundational in much feminist Christology; see Chapter 6 of the present work.

59 William G. Rusch, *The Trinitarian Controversy* (Philadelphia: Fortress Press, 1980), p. 4.

60 Macquarrie, *Jesus Christ in Modern Thought*, pp. 151–2.

Justin, in accordance with the prevailing philosophy of his time, understood God as unapproachable and remote, wholly 'other', and utterly transcendent; however, the Logos could bring God closer to humanity and make God utterly immanent.[61] This was fused, for Justin, in the person and work of Christ: because he had always been a part of God, the Logos or Christ, within the person of Jesus, could make God manifest to humankind without threatening the monotheistic basis of the Christian faith.

However, this idea, which evidently seemed simple to Justin based upon his background, nevertheless precipitated Christological controversies of several centuries' duration. Moreover, Justin precipitated the questions that still engage our interest today: how could Jesus be both God and human? Could Jesus be a true human being if he had the divine Logos within him? Could God take the form of a human being while still remaining true God?

The Apologists who followed Justin (Tatian, Athenagoras and Theophilus) interpreted the Logos not as God's very self but as a creature of God who nevertheless possessed true divinity: God the Father was the source of all that existed and from this Godhead sprang forth the Logos, an emanation or manifestation of Godself who could be called God the Son; yet this Son was undifferentiated from the Father ('I and the Father are one.' John 10.30).[62]

Irenaeus viewed Christ as one who manifests the 'economy' (Greek *oikonomia*, Latin *dispensatio*) of salvation, that is, God's self-disclosure to the world, so that all might be reconciled to God. In what would become known as economic Trinitarianism, Irenaeus insisted that there was only one God, but that this God has been manifested in different ways for the sake of our salvation.[63] According to Tertullian, prior to creation there was no need for differentiation within the Godhead; it was in the act of creation that God spoke God's Word (Logos), and then the Spirit became the Word's representative to humanity after the Son returned to the Father. In this way, Tertullian became the first to articulate the three 'persons' of God and to use the term 'Trinity'.[64] In the next

---

61 Macquarrie, *Jesus Christ in Modern Thought*, p. 152.

62 Kelly, *Early Christian Doctrines*, pp. 98–100.

63 Kelly, *Early Christian Doctrines*, pp. 104–05, 108.

64 Kelly, *Early Christian Doctrines*, pp. 112–13. Various heresies originated in connection with the Trinitarian formulation: for example, *monarchianism* or *adoptionism* stressed that Jesus was a mere human being whom God 'adopted' and occupied for a time (using the low Christology of Mark's Gospel), while

century, Origen of Alexandria, influenced by middle Platonism, stressed that the Godhead manifested in Jesus Christ (the Son) was derived from the Father, even going so far as to refer to Christ as a 'secondary God' (Greek *theos deuteros*),[65] the first articulation of *subordinationism*, a major Christological heresy.

Up until this time, the Church Fathers had concentrated on the divine aspect of Christ, that is, what 'degree' of God was he? However, they then had to address how this divine figure was related to the Jesus of the Gospels; this required them to develop further the doctrine of the incarnation, whereby the divine Son became human through birth of the Virgin Mary. Tertullian stressed that the spirit remained spirit and the flesh remained flesh (citing Jesus' statement to Nicodemus in John 3.6), and thus developed the notion of the two substances or natures within the one person.[66]

The Church Councils

Speculation about Jesus' relationship to God dominated Christianity during the fourth century. Emperor Constantine called the first ecumenical council of the Church at Nicaea in 325 CE to deal with the so-called 'Arian controversy', which had begun when a certain Arius, fuelled by subordinationism, relegated Jesus Christ to the status of a creature, arguing that because the Son was 'begotten' from the Father, there must have been a time when he was not. This council developed a creed that stated, in opposition to Arius, that there was never a time when the Son was not; the Arian subordinationist position was labelled a heresy. The Nicene Creed as we know it today was finalized at the Council of Constantinople in 381 CE, at which Jesus Christ's relationship to God was said to be 'consubstantial' (Greek *homoousios*).[67]

However, the composition of the Nicene Creed did not stop dialogue among Christians about the person of Christ, and divisiveness characterized the Church of the fifth century, as bishops and theologians

---

modalism described the one God as acting in different 'modes' at different times. Kelly, *Early Christian Doctrines*, pp. 115–17.

65 Kelly, *Early Christian Doctrines*, p. 128.

66 Kelly, *Early Christian Doctrines*, p. 151.

67 Macquarrie, *Jesus Christ in Modern Thought*, pp. 157–9. Rusch, *The Trinitarian Controversy*, pp. 19–20, notes that the term *homoousios* was 'unscriptural and employed with some reluctance', but adopted because different groups could 'interpret it in ways compatible with their own theology'.

debated whether, if Jesus Christ was *homoousios* with God, he could still be fully human, or, more properly, 'how the union between his divinity and humanity [is] to be understood and interpreted'.[68]

In this respect, there developed two rival Christologies, one from Alexandrian theologians including Athanasius and Apollinaris, and another from Antiochene theologians including Theodore of Mopsuestia and Nestorius. The Alexandrian Christology (known as *logos–sarx*, 'word–flesh', Christology) postulated that the entire fleshly body of Jesus was taken over by the divine Logos, that Christ had but one nature (that of the Logos); whereas the Antiochene Christology (known as *logos–anthropos*, 'word–human being', Christology) asserted that the divine Logos took the place only of the human soul in Jesus, thus preserving two natures within Jesus Christ, one human and one divine.[69]

Church councils declared both of these Christologies in their extreme forms (for example, those of Apollinaris and Nestorius) heretical; nevertheless these theories precipitated a discussion of Jesus' personhood that has endured to this day. The major danger of the extreme Alexandrian view was that it so stressed the divinity of Christ that it verged on Docetism; by denying Jesus a human mind or soul, Apollinaris was 'denying an essential element in his humanity', leading Gregory of Nazianzus to declare, 'That which he [Jesus] has not assumed, he has not healed.'[70] The Council of Constantinople eventually condemned Apollinaris' view. On the other hand, the extreme Antiochene view segregated the Logos' divinity from the life of Jesus to such an extent that Nestorius refused to honour Mary with the title *Theotokos* ('God-bearer'), since she had only given birth to the human Jesus. The Council of Ephesus declared this view heretical in 431 CE.[71]

Nevertheless, 'the paradox of the divine and human in Jesus Christ remained', and so the Council of Chalcedon effected a compromise in 451 CE, by condemning another form of the doctrine of one nature (the Monophysitism of Eutyches), in favour of the enduring statement that

---

68 O'Collins, *Christology*, p. 183. Some, most notably Gregory of Nyssa and Gregory of Nazianzus, preferred to say that the Son was 'of similar substance' (Greek *homoiousios*) with the Father. Rusch, *The Trinitarian Controversy*, p. 23.

69 Richard A. Norris, Jr, *The Christological Controversy* (Philadelphia: Fortress Press, 1980), pp. 19–25.

70 Macquarrie, *Jesus Christ in Modern Thought*, p. 160, quoting Gregory's *Epistle 101*.

71 O'Collins, *Christology*, pp. 186–7.

in the one person of Jesus Christ there coexist both a human and a divine nature.[72] Thus, Gerald O'Collins concludes:

> In confessing that the unity of Christ exists on the level of person and the duality on that of his natures, the Council of Chalcedon proved a lasting success in regulating language about Christ. Its terminology of 'one person in two natures' became normative down to the twentieth century. Its teaching effected a brilliant synthesis between the Alexandrians, who highlighted Christ's unity, and the Antiochenes, who championed the duality of Christ's distinct natures.[73]

However, despite O'Collins's optimism, one may nevertheless speculate as to the 'normative' character of the Christological statement crafted at Chalcedon. What does it mean to say that Jesus Christ is both human and divine in a postmodern world in which Greek philosophical terms are no longer as influential as they once were? I believe John Macquarrie provides a fitting answer, while at the same time warning us that there really is no answer:

> [T]he purpose of a dogmatic statement like the formula of Chalcedon is not – or, at any rate, ought not to be – to put an end to all further discussion of the matter. *The church never reaches final truth.*[74]

As we shall see in the following chapters, theologians have continued for over 1,500 years to speculate about the person and the work of Jesus Christ. Some have sought to elucidate 'the Christ of faith', while others have searched for 'the Jesus of history', leading to contemporary attempts to articulate Christologies grounded in the historical person of Jesus while nevertheless speaking to present-day social contexts.

---

72 Macquarrie, *Jesus Christ in Modern Thought*, p. 164.
73 O'Collins, *Christology*, pp. 193–4.
74 Macquarrie, *Jesus Christ in Modern Thought*, p. 165 (emphasis added).

2

Jesus as Christ: The Development
of Christology

Subsequent to the Council of Chalcedon, the Christian Church seemed
willing to live with the compromise that the bishops had reached there.
Jesus Christ was fully divine and fully human, one person in two
natures; although, as we shall see, most of the Christology which developed among theologians from the sixth century until the early twentieth
century was concerned not with the human side of Jesus Christ, but
rather with his divinity – how God had united Godself with the human
race and for what purpose. In this development, as Roger Haight
reminds us,[1] Christology was inseparably intertwined with soteriology.
Jesus Christ had been determined to be the God-human; how and why
that occurred remained the new task for theologians, the subject matter
of this chapter. It would fall to biblical scholars and historians of
Christian origins to deal with the human side of Jesus, the focus of the
next chapter.[2]

---

1 Roger Haight, *Jesus Symbol of God* (Maryknoll, NY: Orbis Books, 1999), p.
181.

2 Although Christological developments and the quest for the historical Jesus
will be discussed in separate chapters, it should not be implied that these studies
took place 'in a vacuum'. On the contrary, the work of theologians of the middle
to late twentieth century was greatly informed by the work of New Testament
scholarship. Nevertheless, biblical scholars have prided themselves on their historical objectivity and have attempted in their enquiries to keep themselves from
drawing theological conclusions, whereas those who have articulated
Christological concepts have been quite clear that they are doing theology. See
John P. Meier, *A Marginal Jew: Rethinking the Historical Jesus*, 3 volumes (New
York: Doubleday, 1991–2001), Vol. 1, pp. 4–6. Thankfully, some of this artificial
separation has dissolved in recent years, especially among the contextual
Christologies that will be discussed in Part II of the present work.

Patristic and Medieval Soteriology

The Nicene Creed formulated at the Councils of Nicaea and Constantinople and affirmed by the Council of Chalcedon stated the following about the work of Christ:

> Who *for us [human persons] and for our salvation, came down* from heaven, and was incarnate by the Holy Ghost of the Virgin Mary, and was made [hu]man; he was *crucified for us* under Pontius Pilate; and suffered and was buried, and the third day he rose again (Articles 3, 4, and 5).[3]

The councils were preoccupied with addressing the various opinions on who Christ was and how he was incarnated, that is, what his relationship was to the God who sent him. In their discussions of why this took place, the Council Fathers did not move much beyond the earliest belief that Jesus Christ had come to earth and suffered and died 'for us' and 'for our salvation'. These simple statements were never in dispute in the Trinitarian and Christological controversies. The crux of the dispute concerned whether an ordinary human being could achieve what had been accomplished 'for our salvation,' and the definitive answer was no, that it had to be God's very self who did this. It was not until some 500 years had passed that theologians in the West began to formulate doctrines as to the 'why' of the incarnation, and the results of their discussions still engage students of Christology 1,000 years later.

Before turning to the soteriology that developed in Western Christianity, let us briefly summarize what occurred in the East. The Greek Fathers (Irenaeus, followed by Athanasius) stressed Christ's work among us as '*deification*' (Greek *theosis*), whereby the human person grows more and more into its 'God-ness' through the example of Jesus Christ, who *recapitulates* all of creation in his person and work.[4] During the Byzantine period, Maximus Confessor developed it further, and it remains the prevailing soteriology of the Eastern Orthodox Churches. Maximus used the Pauline imagery of the first and second Adam to develop a Christology and soteriology in which the Logos quintessentially revealed in Jesus Christ was an essential part of Adam

---

3 Philip Schaff, ed., *The Creeds of Christendom*, 3 volumes (New York: Harper and Row, 1931; Grand Rapids, MI: Baker Book House, sixth edition, 1993), Vol. 1, p. 28 (emphasis added).

4 Haight, *Jesus Symbol of God*, p. 217.

that had been muted by the fall. The supreme Logos of Christ was able to overcome the fall through his life and death so that once again the Logos is potentially a part of every human being.[5]

The Latin Fathers went beyond this exemplary notion of Christ's work. As noted in the last chapter, the apologist Tertullian had seen Christ's death as the result of a battle between God and Satan which began when Satan triumphed through the fall of humanity. The doctrine of original sin was developed by such late patristic theologians as Ambrose and Augustine, who saw every human creature as tainted by the sin of the first humans, thus requiring a redeeming sacrifice through the mediator Jesus Christ.[6] This soteriology stressed the concept of *substitution*, whereby Jesus Christ paid the price (the 'ransom') required by Satan through the shedding of his blood.[7] This was the major soteriological doctrine in the West for some 700 years.[8]

Anselm of Canterbury developed the next major theory of salvation in 1098 CE. in *Cur Deus Homo?* ('*Why a God-Human?*'); many modern scholars accept this *satisfaction* theory as the classic statement of the doctrine of the atonement.[9] According to Anselm, the incarnation and death of Jesus took place in order to render satisfaction to God for the sin of the human race. According to Anselm's satisfaction theory, God's honour is damaged by sin and must be restored by something greater than what was diminished, the sacrifice of Jesus Christ who, in his divine capacity, is able to give more than the human who did the original damage to God's honour.[10] The necessity of satisfaction is why God cannot simply forgive human sin, according to Anselm; the work of Christ returns humanity to a state of 'at-one-ment' with God.

It is noteworthy that this view of salvation could only have originated

---

5 John Macquarrie, *Jesus Christ in Modern Thought* (London: SCM Press, Harrisburg, PA: Trinity Press International, 1990), pp. 167–8. In this sense, Maximus reiterates the *substitutionary* nature of Christ's death as articulated by Athanasius. Haight, *Jesus Symbol of God*, p. 221.

6 J. N. D. Kelly, *Early Christian Doctrines*, fifth edition (1960; New York: HarperCollins, 1978), pp. 353–4.

7 Haight, *Jesus Symbol of God*, pp. 224–6.

8 The notion of a price paid to Satan was also found in the East in the writings of Gregory of Nyssa, who described Jesus Christ as 'hiding' his divinity under his humanity so as to 'trick' Satan when he was resurrected. Gerald O'Collins, *Christology: A Biblical, Historical, and Systematic Study of Jesus* (Oxford and New York: Oxford University Press, 1995), p. 199.

9 For example, James Wm. McClendon, Jr, *Doctrine: Systematic Theology, Volume II* (Nashville: Abingdon Press, 1994), p. 203.

10 Haight, *Jesus Symbol of God*, pp. 227–9.

in Western Christianity, inasmuch as it is tied to the Latin Fathers' notion of original sin. Clearly, according to this view of salvation, the incarnation was a result of sin and would not have occurred otherwise; it concentrates solely on the suffering and death of Jesus, to the exclusion of the life of Jesus and his subsequent resurrection.[11] Conversely, Eastern soteriology suggests that the incarnation would have occurred whether or not humanity had sinned, since Jesus Christ's life and example was a means for humanity's ultimate deification. This distinction must be emphasized, for this is where certain of the contemporary contextual Christologies (discussed in Part II) and my own queer Christology (described in Part III) take issue with traditional articulations of the work of Christ: Oppressed people are not able to 'swallow' the notion that God demands suffering and death; to state that Christ 'paid the price once and for all' trivializes current suffering and blames the oppressed person for her/his circumstances. Consequently, liberation Christologies portray Jesus Christ's work as seeking to improve the human situation rather than restoring an otherworldly satisfaction to a God who is more concerned with 'his' damaged dignity than compassion toward a hurting humanity.[12]

The Enlightenment

With Anselm, the doctrine of the work of Christ took its place alongside the Chalcedonian doctrine of the person of Christ. In this way, Christology was to remain relatively intact for roughly 600 years, even surviving the Reformation, which was more concerned with the nature of sin and grace and a return to biblical authority than with the person or work of Christ.

It is with the Enlightenment, or the 'Age of Reason' as it is sometimes

---

11 O'Collins, *Christology*, p. 201.

12 '[A]s a piece of theology, *Cur Deus homo?* has repelled many readers because its legalistic God has seemed to them sub-Christian.' Macquarrie, *Jesus Christ in Modern Thought*, p. 169. In this regard, liberation Christology was perhaps anticipated by the Christology of Peter Abelard, whose view is diametrically opposed to that of Anselm, for Abelard sees God as a vehicle of pure love, who sent to humanity the Logos in Jesus Christ as a gift of incarnate love; Haight, *Jesus Symbol of God*, p. 231. Gerald O'Collins notes that Abelard's Christology inspired much of the mystical contemplation of Christ as Lover and Mother in the Middle Ages: 'At all events he rightly appreciated love as the key to the story of salvation'; O'Collins, *Christology*, pp. 202–03.

called,[13] that theology becomes inseparably linked with – and differentiated from – the philosophy of religion. Already in the Middle Ages, scholastics such as Thomas Aquinas and Albertus Magnus had begun to reintegrate Greek philosophical notions into their theologies, while the Renaissance stimulated a further re-examination of the Greco-Roman heritage, including observations on cosmology and the human body. Fuelled by rediscovered metaphysical traditions and disheartened by the political battles that seemed to have taken over Christendom, many thinkers began to look outside the Church for spiritual and moral answers.

Thus in seventeenth-century France, René Descartes, beginning from an assumption of universal doubt, believed that one could find solutions to one's doubts – including the existence of God – by recourse to reason (Cartesian *rationalism*). Meanwhile, in Great Britain philosophers such as John Locke and Thomas Hobbes were developing Aquinas' theory of *empiricism*, that all knowledge derived from experience. Empiricism taught that God's existence could be proved through examination of the effects that lead back to the cause. David Hume in the next century discounted this belief by pointing out that what the empiricists were labelling effects of a cause were only attributes through which one is unable to get at the ultimate cause.

Hume's scepticism influenced the philosophy of Immanuel Kant, who proposed a radical alternative to both rationalism and empiricism, by pointing out that the mind gives us perceptions which mould our experiences; however, we are never able to grasp 'the thing in itself' (German '*das Ding an sich*'), but only our perceptions of it. Thus, Kant concluded that there is no such thing as pure objective knowledge, only human interpretation of that knowledge. This line of thinking reached its culmination about sixty years later, when nineteenth-century philosopher-theologian Søren Kierkegaard asserted that one can never prove religious matters such as God's existence through a resort to pure reason; one must always at some point take a 'leap of faith'. The Christian Church, however, neither taught nor exemplified this faith.

---

13 For this brief summary, I am indebted to the following sources: Justo L. Gonzalez, *The Story of Christianity, Volume 2: The Reformation to the Present Day* (New York: HarperCollins, 1985), Chapters 14, 21 and 28; and *A History of Christian Thought, Volume III: From the Protestant Reformation to the Twentieth Century*, revised edition (Nashville: Abingdon Press, 1975, 1987), Chapters 12 and 13. For primary sources, see John Hick, ed., *Classical and Contemporary Readings in the Philosophy of Religion*, third edition (Englewood Cliffs, NJ: Prentice Hall, 1990), pp. 63–107, 121–49, 164–9.

For Kierkegaard, true faith involved a 'risk' of cost or pain and was not merely a topic of intellectual contemplation; rather, it must be felt from the very core of one's existence. (Hence, Kierkegaard is credited with founding modern *existentialism*.)[14]

These developments in epistemology would have wide-ranging ramifications for all of theology, but especially, as we shall see, for Christology and the study of the historical Jesus. The Enlightenment's legacy for theology was that people began to question what had been preached by the Church unchallenged for centuries.[15] The Enlightenment's call to reason and experience still affects people of faith today, such as those participants in contemporary liberation movements who are learning to critique theological presuppositions from the standpoint of rationality and their own experience of the world and of a power greater than that world.

Post-Enlightenment Christologies

As a result of the Enlightenment, religious studies devised a new concept of history and developed the 'historical-critical method,' applying it to the Scriptures of Judaism and Christianity.[16] The so-called 'quests' for the historical Jesus that have consumed the interest of biblical scholars from the eighteenth century to the present will be the subject of the next chapter. The remainder of the present chapter will examine the effect of the Enlightenment upon articulations of 'the Christ of faith'.[17]

A major development in biblical studies during this period, which affected the discipline of Christology, was the theory that Christianity as it had been preached was essentially a religion developed not by Jesus Christ but by Paul. Thus, theologians sought to rediscover the message of Jesus himself as a clue to who he was and what he had sought to

---

14 For a detailed discussion of the Christologies that resulted from the Enlightenment, which is beyond the scope of this study, see Macquarrie, *Jesus Christ in Modern Thought*, Chapters 8–12.

15 Jaroslav Pelikan, *The Christian Tradition: A History of the Development of Doctrine, Volume 5: Christian Doctrine and Modern Culture (Since 1700)*, (Chicago and London: University of Chicago Press, 1989), p. 60.

16 Gonzalez, *Story of Christianity* 2, p. 291.

17 Again, the reader should note that this is in many ways an artificial division of a single topic into two separate discussions. However, I believe that when the discussion is presented in this way, one is able to detect much more easily the differing aims and results of theologians, biblical scholars and historians.

accomplish. In this way, the language of the creeds, while not discounted in any way, was set off to one side, as it were, in favour of descriptions of Christ that had more relevance to a modern world of thinking people.[18]

> The nineteenth century opened with a deep and widespread sense that 'the disbelief of revealed religion' had become well-nigh universal, at least 'among the people of education' in Christian lands. A German Protestant pastor, 'the gifted, noble' Friedrich Daniel Ernst Schleiermacher . . . [s]haring the conviction of many of his contemporaries that skepticism was 'the problem of the age' and 'one of the characteristic plagues of the epoch,' . . . called upon his skeptical contemporaries to look beyond the superficialities of conventional piety and official doctrine, to . . . find deep within themselves the wellsprings of an authentic religion.[19]

Schleiermacher's Christology has been called 'anthropocentric' and 'massively subjective' because it draws upon the turn to self that Descartes had pioneered;[20] nevertheless, his view of Christ may be characterized as the first fully modern Christology, inasmuch as it takes into account the human person's relation to God in the context of the human's overall relation to the cosmos, past, present and future. Schleiermacher's primary lens for doing Christology was the human self-consciousness of absolute dependence on God, which he calls '*God-consciousness*'. The Church had created its creeds in order to explicate the God-consciousness found in the revelatory Scriptures; the Scriptures' focus upon Jesus was as a mediator of Christian revelation and redemptive experience. Redemption for Schleiermacher was the retrieval of one's God-consciousness. The role of the Christ-figure was to point humanity toward its proper God-consciousness, and Jesus was an example of one who was fully in touch with his own God-consciousness; this ideal or perfect God-consciousness is what made Jesus 'Christ'. For Schleiermacher, Jesus Christ is fully human, by virtue of being a historical human being; he is what humanity can become. But Jesus Christ is fully divine as well, by virtue of his perfect God-consciousness which came 'from above', rendering him incapable of sin.[21]

---

18 Pelikan, *Christian Tradition 5*, pp. 99–102.
19 Pelikan, *Christian Tradition 5*, p. 174 (citations omitted).
20 O'Collins, *Christology*, p. 213.
21 Haight, *Jesus Symbol of God*, pp. 304–08.

Nevertheless, Schleiermacher did not see Jesus Christ as 'God' in the sense of being final and ultimate, and in this he anticipates contemporary pluralistic theories of soteriology and world religions; for him, Christ is a mediator, but 'never maintained he was the only Mediator', thus calling his followers to be mediators as well, allowing for the truth of other religious paths.[22] Schleiermacher inspired the liberal Christologies of the nineteenth and twentieth centuries which focused upon Jesus not as a divine figure but as a human (even if *the* human) who was 'the teacher of wisdom, and the perfect example of moral perfection', thereby denying or marginalizing the doctrine of the Trinity as lying outside the realm of rational discussion.[23]

At the other end of the spectrum from Schleiermacher's 'anthropocentric' liberal Christology is the 'theocentric' conservative Christology of Karl Barth.[24] Whereas Schleiermacher approached Christology 'from below' through the lens of human experience of the world, Barth's Christology is 'from above', with little importance given to subjective human experience; rather, the Christ Event is seen as God's objective disclosure of the Word to humanity:

> This Word reveals God's perspective on things; . . . Barth's theology envisages and presupposes God coming to human beings in revelation, judgment, and self-disclosure. There is utterly no ascent or even point of contact between human nature or experience and God. God comes in total freedom and surprise to human existence.[25]

Unlike Schleiermacher, who had seen the coming of Jesus Christ as always a part of God's plan for the world so that humanity could become perfected (similar to the deification soteriology of Irenaeus), Barth sees the work of Christ in strictly Anselmian terms: Christ came as a substitution for fallen humanity, to undo the sin of Adam and suffer punishment on humanity's behalf and to reconcile the world to Godself

---

22 Macquarrie, *Jesus Christ in Modern Thought*, p. 200.

23 O'Collins, *Christology*, pp. 216–17, thus characterizing the nineteenth-century Christology of Albrecht Ritschl, and labelling as 'neo-Ritschlian' the contemporary work of John Dominic Crossan and Burton L. Mack (see Bibliography). For a more sympathetic view of Ritschl, see Gonzalez, *Christian Thought III*, pp. 374–7.

24 Haight, *Jesus Symbol of God*, p. 301, analogizes the differences of the Christologies of Schleiermacher and Barth to those of the Alexandrian and Antiochene schools discussed in Chapter 1.

25 Haight, *Jesus Symbol of God*, pp. 309–10.

through his passion and death. By this God's glory is revealed, without any participation whatsoever on the part of humankind.[26]

Twentieth-Century Christologies

The twentieth century has seen a proliferation of works devoted to the study of Christology. Indeed, every Christian theology, because it is Christian, includes a Christology; because Jesus Christ is normative for Christian theology, it must, if only superficially, take some account of the person and work of Christ. The following discussion of twentieth-century Christology is quite selective, by intention. I have chosen to focus on some of the more recent Christologies which, while they do not themselves come from any particular social location or context, nevertheless have influenced or share some commonality with the contextual Christologies of Parts II and III.

Although primarily a biblical scholar, Rudolf Bultmann had important ramifications for Christology in the first half of the twentieth century. His work, coming after the so-called 'first quest' for the historical Jesus, was significant for many reasons, perhaps because the subsequent quests largely reacted to Bultmann's theories.[27] Bultmann maintained that it was fruitless to try to reach the historical Jesus at all; he preferred to discuss the effects of the Christ of faith, about whom the earliest Christian *kerygma* (proclamation) had been developed.[28] In frequently quoted language, Christ's importance was his 'that-ness' (German *dass*) and not his 'what-ness' (German *was*); essential to Bultmann's Christology was the fact that Christ had become part of the world and brought God's salvation, however that managed to occur.[29] His message could be taken to heart by every individual without knowing who it was who delivered that message or what the messenger's relationship was to

---

26 Haight, *Jesus Symbol of God*, pp. 312–13.

27 See Chapter 3.

28 Rudolf Bultmann, *Theology of the New Testament*, trans. Kendrick Grobel, 2 volumes (New York: Charles Scribner's Sons, 1951, 1955), Vol. 1, pp. 35–6: '[T]he personality of Jesus has no importance for the kerygma either of Paul or of John or of the New Testament in general. . . . Nor did the faith in him as Messiah rest upon understanding the historical phenomenon of Jesus . . . Jesus' importance as Messiah-Son-of-Man lies not at all in what he did in the past, but entirely in what is expected of him for the future.'

29 Macquarrie, *Jesus Christ in Modern Thought*, pp. 349–50, quoting Bultmann's essay 'The Primitive Christian Kerygma and the Historical Jesus'.

God. In this way, Bultmann formulated what has been called an *existential Christology*, concerned solely with the individual's turn to faith in God through Jesus Christ.[30]

As part of his overall systematic theology, the great Roman Catholic theologian Karl Rahner made a substantial contribution to twentieth-century Christology. Influenced by the Enlightenment but remaining faithful to the creeds of the Church,

> Rahner's Christology of human self-transcendence within an evolutionary view of the world interpreted the incarnation not only as the divine self-communication in the person of the Son but also as *the* limit-case in what is possible to humanity in its dynamic openness to the Absolute.[31]

Rahner sees Christ as the eternal Word of God; yet, because he interprets the world as constantly changing and progressing, he understands this Christ-Word as God 'progressively communicating himself both in and to the creation'.[32] Rahner's Christology is thus cosmic in its dimensions; nevertheless, it remains grounded in anthropology due to his insistence that the human person and Christ are connected. This is part of Christ's soteriological significance: he shows us 'what humanity can be when brought to the fulness of its possibilities' while at the same time demonstrating how 'everyday humanity falls short of its archetype in Jesus Christ'.[33] Thus, Rahner's is what may be called an *exemplary Christology*, whereby humans see in Christ their potential as beings created in the image and likeness of God.[34]

Similar to Rahner's Christology but of more recent vintage and in many ways more traditional is the Christology of Daniel Helminiak, who enunciates a 'Catholic dogmatic view', keeping in tension the

---

30 Macquarrie, *Jesus Christ in Modern Thought*, p. 294.

31 O'Collins, *Christology*, p. 214, citing Rahner's *Foundations of Christian Faith* (1978). For a discussion of 'limit' language as regards Christology, see David Tracy, *Blessed Rage for Order: The New Pluralism in Theology* (New York: The Seabury Press, 1978), pp. 218–37.

32 Rahner, *Foundations*, as quoted by O'Collins, *Christology*, p. 214.

33 Macquarrie, *Jesus Christ in Modern Thought*, pp. 306–07. One of the most important aspects of Rahner's Christology is his belief that Jesus Christ is God's full and final revelation; this will be addressed below in the discussion of Christology and other religions.

34 Haight, *Jesus Symbol of God*, p. 326, although Haight prefers to call Rahner's Christology an 'apotheosis of human existence'; the term 'exemplary Christology' is my own.

results of a historical-critical reading of the New Testament with the dogmatic decrees of the early Church councils.[35] Both of these elements are needed for a proper Christology, he believes, for the councils developed a systematic Christological statement based upon kerygmatic statements made about Jesus Christ 'from above' and 'from below'.[36] Neither vantage point can be eliminated without undoing the doctrine of Jesus' humanity and divinity.[37] Therefore, Helminiak's purpose is to develop a 'new model' that would 'give full emphasis both to Jesus' eternal divinity and to his historical humanity'.[38] His method, which is not really new at all, seeks to articulate *Christology in two movements*: the first movement, from above, is Jesus Christ's eternal divinity, which is 'set aside' (*kenosis*) to become human; the second movement, from below, is the human Jesus' absolute fidelity to God through which he becomes divinized (*theosis*). Salvation comes from this divinization and gives to every human that possibility through sanctification by the Holy Spirit.[39] The attractiveness of Helminiak's work is that his is one of the few recent Christologies that attempts to keep the Chalcedonian balance between divinity and humanity without jettisoning the full divinity of Jesus Christ. The weakest point of his Christology is that Helminiak risks self-contradiction, for, in his desire that Jesus Christ remain fully divine, he states that Jesus must be divine in order to save, while elsewhere he states that the Holy Spirit saves humanity by assisting the process of divinization made available by the work of Christ.

A much more nuanced Christology is that of German Protestant theologian Jürgen Moltmann, which is in direct contrast to Bultmann's existentialist Christology of the individual, for Moltmann's theology is always done with the community in mind.[40] Moltmann's Christology begins with the Jesus of history, but specifically with the crucifixion, for only when we are reminded of the crucified Christ can we be set free from the power of present circumstances.[41] In this sense, Moltmann has

---

35 Daniel A. Helminiak, *The Same Jesus: A Contemporary Christology* (Chicago: Loyola University Press, 1986), pp. xii, 19.

36 Helminiak, *The Same Jesus*, pp. 62–3.

37 Helminiak, *The Same Jesus*, pp. 45–6.

38 Helminiak, *The Same Jesus*, p. 157.

39 Helminiak, *The Same Jesus*, pp. 164–79.

40 Jürgen Moltmann, *The Crucified God: The Cross of Christ as the Foundation and Criticism of Christian Theology*, trans. R. A. Wilson and John Bowden (London: SCM Press, 1974), p. 4.

41 Moltmann, *The Crucified God*, p. 1: '[O]nly the crucified Christ can bring the freedom which changes the world because it is no longer afraid of death.'

been very influential for Latin American liberation Christologies that approach Christ from the context of the suffering poor, for Moltmann's own theological work derives from his experience of suffering as a prisoner-of-war in World War Two. Thus, one of the merits of his Christology is his positioning of the death of Jesus Christ as the defining moment for salvation: the cross makes the resurrection possible; a theology of the cross is thus linked to a theology of hope and resurrection; one is the 'flip-side' of the other, as it were. For the Jesus who rose was the *crucified* Jesus.[42] In this sense, Moltmann articulates what might be called an *eschatological Christology*, for it looks ahead at what is yet to come as a result of the work of Christ.[43] This is confirmed by his insistence on the 'unfinished' nature of all Christology: he notes that the question of Jesus' identity is never answered unambiguously in the New Testament; the importance of Jesus' identity always hinges on his question, 'Who do *you* say that I am?' (Mark 8.29) 'Thus, Christology is essentially unconcluded and permanently in need of revision.'[44]

Moltmann's Christology is of course contingent upon his notion of soteriology. He reminds his readers that the original soteriological statements in the New Testament were interpretations not of Jesus' resurrection but of his death. Christ's resurrection was the way in which the humiliation and horror of the crucifixion was rehabilitated, but the major scandal which the New Testament writers addressed was not that someone had been raised from the dead, but that this someone was Jesus who had been *crucified*. For Moltmann, this means going further than what the crucifixion meant for the first believers or even what it means for us; he radicalizes the question and asks, what did the crucifixion mean *for God*?[45] The conclusion he reaches is that God suffered in the crucifixion – it was an event that occurred 'within the Trinity', when the love of Jesus Christ which allowed him to give himself up to death coincided with the grief of the Father. God's unconditional love was contradicted by the cross of Christ, even as it was fulfilled by Jesus' outpouring of love from the cross toward his enemies. Suffering is thus stronger than hate and thereby becomes salvific; belief in the cross of

---

42 Moltmann, *The Crucified God*, p. 5.

43 In the wake of the events of September 11, 2001, this is a Christology that can have definite relevance for today's world, as people grapple with the theological meaning of this tragedy.

44 Moltmann, *The Crucified God*, pp. 104–06.

45 Moltmann, *The Crucified God*, pp. 177–8, 201.

Christ leads to belief in the power of love and ultimate openness to the future.[46]

When Moltmann turns from the crucifixion to the incarnation as an articulation of Christology, he follows very much in the footsteps of Rahner, for he calls it the 'eternally self-communicating love of God'.[47] A way for humans to commune with God was always intended; thus, the incarnation as God's self-communicating love must have preceded creation (the Logos).[48] He sees Jesus Christ's 'Sonship' as a three-step process, very similar to Johannine Christology: the sending, the suffering (or surrender) and the exaltation.[49] Yet, because his Christology is directed toward the future and toward the community, Moltmann reminds us that Jesus Christ is the 'firstborn of many brethren [sic]' and that Jesus' Sonship to God is inseparable from his brotherhood with humanity; his resurrection leads to the outpouring of the Spirit at Pentecost that facilitates ongoing fellowship and communication.[50] Thus, his eschatological Christology may also be characterized as a *pneumatic Christology*.

This is quite evident in his most recent work, which Moltmann describes as Christology 'on the way' for men and women who are 'on the way', since Christology must always remain 'provisional knowledge'.[51] Seeking to highlight Christianity's ties with Judaism, Moltmann articulates a *messianic Christology* that blends his previous eschatological and pneumatic Christological language. Since messianic hope links Jews and Christians, the appropriate title for Jesus Christ in what Moltmann calls a 'holistic integral' Christology is not true God or true human being but rather 'the One who will come'.[52] This Christ is a restorer of brokenness in the cosmos; but, in keeping with Moltmann's

---

46 Moltmann, *The Crucified God*, pp. 248–9, 255. Moltmann notes that the God of Greek philosophy had been apathetic, whereas the Christian God was sympathetic. *The Crucified God*, pp. 270–2.

47 Jürgen Moltmann, *The Trinity and the Kingdom: The Doctrine of God*, trans. Margaret Kohl (London: SCM Press, New York: Harper & Row, 1981), p. 114.

48 Moltmann, *The Trinity and the Kingdom*, p. 117.

49 Moltmann, *The Trinity and the Kingdom*, pp. 61–88.

50 Moltmann, *The Trinity and the Kingdom*, pp. 120, 124.

51 Jürgen Moltmann, *The Way of Jesus Christ: Christology in Messianic Dimensions*, trans. Margaret Kohl (New York: HarperCollins, 1990), pp. xiii–xiv.

52 Moltmann, *The Way of Jesus Christ*, pp. 2–4. One foreseeable problem in this line of thinking which Moltmann does not address is that Jews do not see Jesus as 'the One who will come'.

focus on community, there are three ways of perceiving Jesus Christ: prospective (revealing the coming glory of God), retrospective (remembering the exaltation of Christ and thereby legitimizing the life of Jesus) and reflexive (recognizing one's own call to share in the work of Christ).[53] The Christ of God is revealed through examination of the life of Jesus in three dimensions: eschatological (the One to come), theological (the Son of God) and social (the Lover of all).[54] Nevertheless, the Christ's 'history' goes well beyond the life of Jesus; it is 'essentially the vertical history between God and human beings', beginning not with Jesus but with God's Spirit (Hebrew *ruach*), which 'soared' over the waters at creation (Genesis 1.1). The power of this same Spirit anointed Jesus, bestowing upon him his Christness and revealing to him God as *Abba* ('Papa'), and allows us in the present day to understand the messianic mission of both Christ and the Church.[55] Recalling his earlier work, Moltmann focuses on the necessity of Christ's suffering, and suggests that in the theologically diverse and questioning atmosphere of the first century, God was put on trial. Moltmann disputes the traditional doctrine of the atonement by pointing out that if God and Jesus are one, as the creeds assert, then God would not have 'killed himself' by engineering the death of Jesus. Rather, the cross allows us to articulate a theology of surrender, that is, a theology of the pain of God in confrontation with human evil.[56] Thus, Moltmann, especially in his late work, is an important resource for Christologies seeking to grapple with the reality of human oppression and the evil confronted in this life.

I believe that the work of British process theologian Norman Pittenger has important ramifications for contextual Christologies, for his Christology explores the dialectical nature of divine self-expression and human response.

Jesus Christ . . . is that One in whom God actualized in a living personality the potential God-[hu]man relationship which is the divinely intended truth about every [hu]man. . . . [Christ is the] fulfilment of man's [sic] capacity for God, [but first he is the] fulfilment of God's purpose in man [sic]. He is *the* Man.[57]

---

53 Moltmann, *The Way of Jesus Christ*, p. 220.
54 Moltmann, *The Way of Jesus Christ*, p. 149.
55 Moltmann, *The Way of Jesus Christ*, pp. 52, 72–4.
56 Moltmann, *The Way of Jesus Christ*, pp. 171, 176–9.
57 W. Norman Pittenger, *The Word Incarnate: A Study of the Doctrine of the Person of Christ* (New York: Harper and Brothers, 1959), p. 285.

In common with other process theologians, Pittenger sees the world in a state of becoming; this carries over into his portrayal of *process Christology*. He notes that present-day Christology should not be bound to the creeds, but rather to the interpretation of the historical record; our aim remains the same as the patristic thinkers – to elucidate thinking about Christ – but our context is different, thus leading to new language about Christ.[58] Consequently, a process Christology derives from Christ's abiding significance, situated in our own historical context; just as Jesus in his own day pointed toward God, any subsequent Christological language must also point toward God.[59]

As we have seen in other Christologies, Pittenger's Christology is informed by his soteriology. The salvation of humanity in a process Christology consists of human becoming, a process of self-actualization or self-realization. (Pittenger thus adapts the Irenaean model of divinization for the work of Christ.) Becoming is love in relationship. The reality of love is the key to our understanding of God, for love is 'God's root attribute' and 'because God is Love, the love in Jesus is the human reflection, mediation, manifestation . . . of God himself'.[60] Pittenger believes that Christ, in reflecting the love of the Godhead, did save humanity from sin, but his definition of sin differs significantly from most traditional theologians. He sees sin as 'distortion or deviation of aim', that is, 'sin means the refusal to play one's part in the total expression of love-in-action'; it is a failing to become, a saying 'no' to God's love in Christ. The opposite of sin is participating in goodness, and this is how Jesus was unlike us in sin, for he always empowered the good (similar to Schleiermacher's notion of Jesus' perfect God-consciousness).[61]

The beauty of Pittenger's Christology is its utter accessibility in a postmodern world. He accounts for the interpenetration of divinity and humanity in Jesus Christ in such a way that it is understandable in a contemporary context: Jesus Christ was divine in his absolute revelation of what God is like, but was human in the very act of his becoming, his self-realization and his ability to be comparable to every other human being in their process of becoming.[62]

---

58 Norman Pittenger, *Christology Reconsidered* (London: SCM Press, 1970), pp. 4–6.

59 Pittenger, *Christology Reconsidered*, pp. 8, 26.

60 Pittenger, *Christology Reconsidered*, pp. 20, 41–2, 47–9.

61 Pittenger, *Christology Reconsidered*, pp. 53–7.

62 Pittenger, *Christology Reconsidered*, p. 87.

I conclude this discussion of twentieth-century Christology by examining briefly the Christologies of three scholars whose work I have used extensively throughout these two introductory chapters because they have done such an extraordinary job of summarizing the history of Christological thought. Nevertheless, in addition to recapitulating and critiquing what has gone before, these theologians have also made their own significant contributions to contemporary Christology.

John Macquarrie articulates a *representative Christology* in which Christ is the 'representative human being' who sums up in his being both human possibility and human actuality. This is demonstrated in Macquarrie's description of the Godhead as a dialectic of immanence and transcendence;[63] the difficulty in the Christological and Trinitarian debates was that they saw God's nature as an 'either/or' situation. When one sees the dialectic cohering in Jesus Christ, one is able to see God represented as both immanent and transcendent.

> Only if there is *in all human beings* a possibility for transcendence and a capacity for God, can there be such a possibility and capacity in the man Jesus; and only if God makes himself present and known in and through the creation generally can there be a particular point at which he is present and known in a signal way. Jesus Christ could not be a revelation if he was only an anomaly in the creation. He is revelation because he sums up and makes clear a presence that is obscurely communicated throughout the cosmos.[64]

Gerald O'Collins describes a *Christology of personal presence*, whereby we see God whenever we see Jesus Christ. Jesus Christ's incarnation as one of us assures us of our creation in the image and likeness of God.[65] This personal presence infuses O'Collins' description of salvation, for if Jesus Christ is God's constant reminder of personal presence, then God could neither have sent Jesus to die a horrific death, nor could God have abandoned Jesus to that death:

> Rather, . . . we should think of the passion and crucifixion as the inevitable consequences of Jesus' loving fidelity to his mission which he lived out for us in a cruel and sinful world (see Galatians 1.4).[66]

---

63 Macquarrie, *Jesus Christ in Modern Thought*, pp. 372–9.
64 Macquarrie, *Jesus Christ in Modern Thought*, p. 381 (italics in original).
65 O'Collins, *Christology*, pp. 233, 309.
66 O'Collins, *Christology*, p. 285.

Finally, we come to the magisterial work of Roger Haight, who simply describes Jesus Christ as 'Symbol of God'.[67] I believe that the significance of Haight's Christological work lies in his ability to show that prior Christologies both ancient and modern have made the subject needlessly difficult, when it is quite simple:[68] God empowered Jesus as a symbol for who Godself was, is, and will be.

> By being a symbol of God, by mediating an encounter with God, Jesus reveals God as already present and active in human existence. Historically he does this both by being and by making God present in a thematic way through his words, actions, and whole person. Jesus reveals by causing in the persons who come to him in faith an analogous reflective awareness of the presence of God to them. . . . The church, by remembering Jesus, continues the causality of his revelatory salvation through history by drawing people into the historical community of the force-field and impact of Jesus.[69]

Haight thus enunciates what I propose to call a *revelatory Christology*: 'Jesus saves by revealing and making God present. . . . He is God's Word about God, the world, and human existence.'[70]

Haight concludes his study, however, with the proviso (and warning) that an integral Christology for today must 'balance faithfulness to the tradition and present interpretation that actually engages today's questions',[71] the most pressing of which is the pluralism which characterizes contemporary existence.

Contemporary Christology and the World Religions

Thus, a new 'cutting edge' in Christology is the Christological thought generated by recent discussion concerning the relationship of Christianity to other religions of the world. This discussion centres on the salvific

---

67 Haight, *Jesus Symbol of God*, passim.

68 As articulated in his very dense book, Christology comes across as anything but simple; my point is that Haight is able to engage the topic in such a lucid and down-to-earth way that in the end it does not appear complex or mysterious at all.

69 Haight, *Jesus Symbol of God*, p. 359.

70 Haight, *Jesus Symbol of God*, p. 440.

71 Haight, *Jesus Symbol of God*, p. 490. See the Epilogue of the present work for further discussion of Haight's requirements for a constructive Christology.

significance of Jesus Christ (indeed, his very uniqueness[72]), challenging the traditional Christian assumption that it was through the person and work of Jesus Christ that God definitively saved the entire human race.

Dialogue among the world's religions is certainly nothing new; it has been going on for quite some time. Nevertheless, what is new on the contemporary landscape is the coexistence of so many different faiths in such close proximity to one another, as is the current state of affairs throughout the world, but especially in North America and Europe, where the majority of Christian theology is developed. The problem which such a pluralistic environment has raised has been articulated well by theologian Chester Gillis:

> Given the extensive knowledge available about the religions, and the increased dialogue among them, it is less and less credible that Christianity is either the only path to God, or the superior path that co-opts all other ways. The increasingly more accurate information about the religions available to the Christian theologian and community now makes it difficult for us to dismiss the other religions as misdirected or as uninspired by the divine. . . . Only a Christianity that sees itself in the context of the world religions will makes sense in the twenty-first century.[73]

As we have seen before in discussions about Christ, the major question in this regard involves soteriology, that is, how are people saved? In the past, there have been two major ways of articulating Christian salvation: the *exclusivist* position has held that 'those, and only those who explicitly express faith in Jesus Christ' are saved, while the *inclusivist* position has maintained that 'those who are saved are saved by the merits of the death and resurrection of Jesus Christ, whether or not they are aware of, or acknowledge, Christ's role in their salvation.'[74] Exclusivism is quite emphatic in stating that those of other religions must be converted to Christianity in order to attain salvation. Inclusivism, as its name suggests, seems at first glance more accepting of other

---

72 See, for example, Leonard Swidler and Paul Mojzes, eds, *The Uniqueness of Jesus: A Dialogue with Paul F. Knitter* (Maryknoll, NY: Orbis Books, 1997).

73 Chester Gillis, *Pluralism: A New Paradigm for Theology* (Louvain: Peeters Press; Grand Rapids, MI: William B. Eerdmans Publishing Company, 1998), pp. 26, 28.

74 Gillis, *Pluralism*, p. 18.

religions;[75] however, in its assertion that Christ is still the only means of salvation – even for those who embrace and practise their non-Christian faith to the best of their ability – the inclusivist stance has been called, rightly I believe, 'a form of Christian imperialism'.[76] Nevertheless, inclusivism is the soteriological position of most of mainstream Protestantism and Roman Catholicism; exclusivism survives only in the most conservative evangelical and fundamentalist Protestant denominations (although Pope Benedict XVI seems to be leading Catholicism towards exclusivism).[77] However, the reasonableness of these positions has been rightly contested.

> Requiring explicit recognition of the Lordship of Jesus Christ in order to be eligible for salvation implies that all who do not know, or who do not follow, Jesus, are not saved. Since approximately twenty-eight percent of the world's population is Christian, this means that seventy-two percent of humanity is not on the proper path to salvation. Is it reasonable to think that God, who, in Christian theology, is the creator of all persons, would permit the vast majority of them to come to their end being separated from their creator?[78]

Consequently, a third soteriological possibility has been proposed. The *pluralist* position suggests that 'those who are saved are saved by their own religion, independent of Christ and Christianity'.[79] Essential to the pluralist paradigm is the understanding of an 'axial age' in the history of religions, when God (or the Ultimate or the Divine or the Real) revealed itself to different peoples in different places on the earth and at different moments in history; thus, one may visualize a 'family tree' of religions deriving from a single source.[80] Those who advocate this pluralist position believe that there can be no valid dialogue among

---

75 Karl Rahner has contributed greatly to the discussion, with his notion of the 'anonymous Christian', a righteous person of whatever faith tradition who is still saved by the merits of Jesus Christ. John Hick, *The Metaphor of God Incarnate: Christology in a Pluralistic Age* (Louisville: Westminster/John Knox Press, 1993), p. 87. See also Haight, *Jesus Symbol of God*, pp. 412–15.

76 Gillis, *Pluralism*, p. 21.

77 For a detailed discussion of the views held by the various churches, see Paul F. Knitter, *No Other Name? A Critical Survey of Christian Attitudes Toward the World Religions* (Maryknoll, NY: Orbis Books, 1985), Chapters 5–7.

78 Gillis, *Pluralism*, p. 168.

79 Gillis, *Pluralism*, p. 19.

80 John Hick, *An Interpretation of Religion: Human Responses to the Transcendent* (New Haven: Yale University Press, 1989), pp. 22–32.

the world religions as long as Christianity is viewed as God's final, decisive and complete revelation, and as long as the figure of Jesus Christ as God's only Son is seen as not only normative but mandatory for salvation as well.[81] Pluralism has been vilified by many critics, both Catholic and Protestant, who have charged that pluralism relativizes Christianity, rendering it just another religion among many, and undermines the uniqueness of Jesus Christ as the quintessential saviour figure.[82]

In response to these critics, theologians of the new pluralism have sought to articulate a *pluralistic Christology*, for many of the difficulties between exclusivists, inclusivists and pluralists stem from a reifying of traditional Christology: 'Simply to repeat the doctrines as they have been formulated classically is not adequate. . . . [T]raditional doctrine must be open to reinterpretation and revision.'[83] Thus, Paul Knitter has suggested a *theocentric Christology*, which looks at the historical Jesus to ascertain Jesus' message. Knitter concludes that Jesus himself was theocentric (God-centred); it was his disciples who made Christianity and the message of Jesus Christocentric (Christ-centred). Jesus' central message was that the reign (Greek *basileia*, 'kingdom') of God was at hand, whereas the Church's message was that Jesus Christ, incarnate Son of God and future Son of Man, had saved humanity through his death and resurrection. If we can articulate a Christology which is centred on the reign of God and not on the reign of Christ, Knitter maintains, then we can be in a better position vis-à-vis the other religions of the world.[84] Moreover, Knitter reminds his audience that the New Testament featured a plurality of views of who Christ was (Christologies); thus, contemporary theology cannot afford to adhere to only one doctrinal view of Christ.[85] He also notes that much of the New Testament's exclusivist rhetoric regarding Jesus can be seen as less severe if one understands it in its original polemical context.[86] He con-

---

81 Paul F. Knitter, 'Five Theses on the Uniqueness of Jesus,' in *The Uniqueness of Jesus*, ed. Swidler and Mojzes, pp. 5–7.

82 Paul F. Knitter, *Jesus and the Other Names: Christian Mission and Global Responsibility* (Maryknoll, NY: Orbis Books, 1996), Chapter 3.

83 Gillis, *Pluralism*, pp. 71–2.

84 Knitter, *No Other Name?*, Chapter 8, passim, but especially p. 173. This concentration on the reign of god is a central feature of Latin American liberation Christology; see Chapter 5 of the present work.

85 Knitter, *No Other Name?*, pp. 178–9.

86 Knitter, *Jesus and the Other Names*, pp. 67–69.

cludes that Jesus can be the 'true' but not the 'only' bearer of God's salvation.[87]

John Hick believes that the best way to see the Christ figure in a pluralistic age is metaphorically. Thus, he has articulated what I call a *metaphorical Christology*, maintaining that the incarnation that Christianity has described, debated and made doctrine need not be seen in literal, physical terms as God taking on human flesh; rather, for the incarnation to be understood today, it must be interpreted as a metaphor of God uniting with humankind – something which has happened more than once.[88]

Surprisingly, many of the contextual Christologies to be examined in Part II do not take into account the pluralistic nature of our contemporary world – to their detriment.[89] A queer Christology, the subject of Part III, must not be so myopic as to exclude the relevance of other faiths besides Christianity, especially since many refugees from a brutalizing Christianity have sought solace in other religions. Where the Christologies of various oppressed groups do coincide is in their realization that the historical Jesus cannot be divorced from the Christ of faith; that is, in articulating a theology of the Christ suited to individual contexts such as race, gender, class or sexual orientation, the life and ministry of the physical Jesus of Nazareth must be taken into account, along with his death and resurrection. Therefore, the next chapter will examine the so-called 'quests' for the historical Jesus that have occupied biblical scholars for several hundred years.

87 Knitter, *Jesus and the Other Names*, pp. 72–83. See also Haight, *Jesus Symbol of God*, p. 411: 'I propose . . . that Christians may regard other world religions as true, in the sense that they are mediations of God's salvation.'

88 Hick, *The Metaphor of God Incarnate*, pp. 12, 98. The idea of other incarnations of the 'Christ-Spirit' in other religions is not new. It has been proposed by Raimundo Panikkar, who articulated a 'universal Christ' – the Logos – who could take on the physicality of avatars such as Jesus and others; Raimundo Panikkar, *The Unknown Christ of Hinduism*, completely revised and enlarged edition (1964; Maryknoll, NY: Orbis Books, 1981), pp. 50–61. The difficulty with Panikkar's language, however, is that it seems inclusivist rather than pluralist in its selection of Christian terms such as Christ and Logos to refer to the Divine's interaction with humanity.

89 Gillis, *Pluralism*, pp. 82–8.

3

From Christ to Jesus: Historical Jesus Studies as New Christology

No contemporary Christology can ignore the extensive work on the historical Jesus that has occupied many New Testament scholars for the past decade. However, this concentration upon Jesus' human life is not really new, for there have been three such 'quests' for the historical Jesus. Each has had its triumphs and its setbacks; each has been judged both a success and a failure, as the subsequent discussion will show.

The First Quest

As noted in the last chapter, during the Enlightenment, people of faith, in their quest for religious meaning, began to turn to reason and experience as ways of knowing important truths. Nowhere was this more apparent than in biblical studies, which began applying the historical-critical method to the Scriptures. This method sought to situate the biblical text in its historical and cultural context; events that did not seem credible in the light of human experience were dismissed as mythology or accounted for by scientific explanations. These scholars very quickly turned their lens upon the accounts of Jesus' life as contained in the Gospels. Thus, the Enlightenment was the catalyst for the so-called First Quest of the historical Jesus.[1]

The First Quest, which took place primarily in Continental Europe, began in the late eighteenth century and continued through the nineteenth century; in the context of modernity, countless books and articles sought to make sense of the seemingly fantastic Gospel stories about Jesus. In 1906, Albert Schweitzer's *The Quest of the Historical Jesus*

---

1 James M. Robinson, 'Introduction', in Albert Schweitzer, *The Quest of the Historical Jesus: A Critical Study of Its Progress from Reimarus to Wrede*, trans. W. Montgomery (1906; New York: Collier/Macmillan, 1968), p. xi.

both summarized prior scholarship and added Schweitzer's own theory of the historical Jesus. One of the most important contributions of this book was that it made available to an English-speaking audience the results of research published at that time only in German and French.[2]

Hermann Samuel Reimarus, a German Deist, may be credited with the inception of the quest, even though his writings were published anonymously after his death due to their incendiary content. Reimarus believed that Jesus had been a simple teacher whose wisdom could be summarized by the notion of the kingdom of God, which Reimarus asserted was a thoroughly Jewish notion, inasmuch as Jesus had no intention of founding a religion. Thus, according to Reimarus's thesis, anything that seemed incredible to a rational eighteenth-century person, such as miracles or resurrection from the dead, must have been added by Jesus' followers after his martyrdom, as they sought to give their dead master the sort of 'larger-than-life' quality that befits the founder of a religion. Reimarus, verging upon disbelief in the divinity of Jesus Christ, concluded that whatever supernatural elements appeared in the Gospel accounts of Jesus' life must have been later accretions, from a Church that desired to create an aura around Jesus as Christ.[3] Reimarus even went so far as to propose that the resurrection was an elaborate hoax planned and carried out by the disciples, who stole and disposed of Jesus' corpse, lest his mission appear a failure and the incipient Church be discredited.[4]

Many 'lives' of Jesus began to be written as the new rationalism took hold. These lives had in common a suspicion of the miraculous, a distrust of anything contained in the Gospel of John, and a newfound preference for the brevity of the Gospel of Mark.[5] These lives are of two kinds – the rational and the fictional. The rational stressed logic above all else and looked for reasonable explanations for the miracles attrib-

---

2 Many of these works have subsequently been translated into English; however, I will be relying primarily upon Schweitzer's synopses unless otherwise noted.

3 Schweitzer, *Quest*, pp. 13–26. See also Stephen J. Patterson, *The God of Jesus: The Historical Jesus and the Search for Meaning* (Harrisburg, PA: Trinity Press International, 1998), pp. 29–30; and Charles H. Talbert, ed., *Reimarus: Fragments*, trans. Ralph S. Fraser (Philadelphia: Fortress Press, 1970).

4 Schweitzer, *Quest*, p. 21. This view has been repeated on and off ever since, especially in popular works such as *The Passover Plot*.

5 Schweitzer, *Quest*, pp. 34–6. Scholars began to favour Markan priority over Matthean, rejecting the prevailing theory that Mark was an 'epitome' of Matthew and Luke, in favour of the new Two-Source Hypothesis. See Patterson, *The God of Jesus*, pp. 18–22.

uted to Jesus. For example, Heinrich E. G. Paulus believed that Jesus' cures were effected by some sort of medicine unknown to others, that the nature miracles could be explained by the unreliability of eyewitnesses, and that Jesus' raising of people from the dead was the result of premature burial.[6] The fictional lives, on the other hand, also rejected what was illogical, but substituted instead the authors' own fanciful suggestions. For example, German theologian Karl Friedrich Bahrt asserted that Jesus, under the influence of an Essene plot, pandered to the superstitions of the uneducated Jewish masses and therefore staged his miracles: the feeding of the multitude resulted from disciples hiding behind Jesus in a cave and passing him food to be distributed; Jesus walked on a submerged barge so as to appear to be walking on the sea; Jesus only seemed to be dead because he had been drugged by Luke the physician and his body hidden; when Jesus recovered from the drug, he appeared to select followers, who spread the story of a miraculous resurrection.[7] None of these attempts succeeded in revealing the 'real' Jesus, however; on the contrary, they only muddied the waters and removed Jesus even further from reach.

The first scholar to deal constructively with the historical Jesus was David Friedrich Strauss, whom Schweitzer regarded as the most important of his predecessors. Strauss applied the concept of myth to Christianity, for which he was persecuted his entire life both personally and professionally.[8] Applying the Hegelian method, Strauss saw the early supernatural interpretation of Jesus as the thesis, which was confronted by the antithesis of the rationalistic interpretation, resulting in the synthesis of Strauss's own mythological interpretation. For Strauss, myth was the clothing of religious ideas in historical form; thus, like some contemporary liberation theologians, Strauss saw a basic truth underlying fictional events in the Gospels. Noting that the Gospel accounts group events by theme, he rejected the possibility of obtaining a true chronology of the life of Jesus. Further, Strauss pointed out that the New Testament reiterated Old Testament prototypes such as birth narratives, prophetic callings and healings, casting doubt as to whether they really occurred at all.[9] Indeed, Strauss's contribution to the quest for the historical Jesus is that he raised the issue of whether one can ever recover the historical Jesus.

---

6 Schweitzer, *Quest*, pp. 52–3.
7 Schweitzer, *Quest*, pp. 41–3.
8 Schweitzer, *Quest*, pp. 71–6.
9 Schweitzer, *Quest*, pp. 78–83.

In Strauss' view, the gospels are mythic narratives that bear in them-selves the universal idea of God's incarnation in humanity. To histori-cize them is to miss their point. . . . But Strauss had planted the seed of an idea: that perhaps the gospels had not been written with the intention of recounting a history at all. It was this basic idea that turned out to be the undoing of the first quest.[10]

Up to this time, discussions of the historical Jesus had taken place primarily in Protestant German universities. Ernest Renan was to change this with the publication of his *La Vie de Jésus*, which revealed the problem of the historical Jesus to Catholics and non-Germans alike. Schweitzer was quite disparaging of Renan's work, noting his poor taste, sentimentality and strictly historical, non-Christian approach.[11] Renan's major contribution was his suggestion that the life of Jesus falls into two parts: the gentle teacher and the eschatological prophet. Heretofore, scholars had not focused upon the eschatological nature of Jesus' message due to their zeal for reconstructing the chronology of his life. Renan asserted that Jesus changed from an idealist teacher to a preacher of the end times due to his disillusionment with his audience's lack of response;[12] whether he was right or wrong about this 'change', he nevertheless introduced into the discussion the issue of eschatology, which would become crucial for all subsequent discussions of the historical Jesus.

Renan's work met with disappointment and rejection by the scholarly community. Instead, late nineteenth-century New Testament scholars turned their attention to formulating so-called 'liberal lives' of Jesus that sought to import Jesus into the society of their day and age. Schweitzer was dismissive of these liberal lives, believing that they cast Jesus in the mould of a nineteenth-century liberal theologian-philosopher rather than a teacher and healer in first-century Palestine.[13]

Schweitzer emphasized that in the post-Enlightenment quest of the historical Jesus there were three major controversies.[14] First, the degree of historicity of the Gospels, a question raised by Strauss; second, the priority of the Synoptic Gospels over the Gospel of John, which was and

---

10 Patterson, *The God of Jesus*, p. 33.
11 Schweitzer, *Quest*, pp. 180–1.
12 Schweitzer, *Quest*, pp. 184–7.
13 Schweitzer, *Quest*, p. 208.
14 Schweitzer, *Quest*, pp. 4–11.

has continued to be an ongoing discussion;[15] and third, the importance of eschatology in the message and ministry of Jesus, an issue introduced by Renan but more thoroughly analysed by Johannes Weiss. Weiss looked at Jesus' 'messianic consciousness' and concluded that the figure of Jesus makes no sense unless one sees him as a prophet looking toward the future and not the present: 'All modern ideas, he insists, even in their subtlest forms, must be eliminated from it; when this is done, we arrive at a Kingdom of God which is wholly future.'[16] Schweitzer, prior to beginning his own examination of Jesus, noted that, subsequent to Weiss's work, New Testament scholars devoted themselves to dispelling the notion of an eschatological Jesus. For example, Wilhelm Bousset portrayed Jesus as one whose inner *joie de vivre* was in contradistinction to the rest of the world, which he sought to remould according to his notion of God.[17]

Schweitzer's own contribution to the First Quest is contained in the final chapter of *The Quest of the Historical Jesus*, entitled 'Thoroughgoing Scepticism and Thoroughgoing Eschatology'. In this conclusion to his scrutiny of the Jesus scholarship of the past 150 years, Schweitzer contrasts his own insistence on eschatology as the hermeneutical key for Jesus' identity with the scepticism of William Wrede. Both of these men view the Gospel of Mark as the most credible witness to the historical Jesus; both of them see that two representations of Jesus (the natural and the supernatural) have been telescoped into one in Mark, who superimposes a dogmatic element (the Messianic Secret) on to the natural elements of Jesus' life.[18]

Their interpretation begins to differ at this point, however. Wrede believes that Jesus' Messiahship has been injected into his life by the early Church and that the Messianic Secret is a literary device, whereas Schweitzer sees the Messianic Secret as historical.[19] The discontinuity of

---

15 See, for example, John P. Meier, *A Marginal Jew: Rethinking the Historical Jesus*, 3 volumes (New York: Doubleday, 1991–2001); Meier disputes the outright dismissal of the Gospel of John as a source of information on the historical Jesus. As noted in Chapter 11, I agree that the Gospel of John should not be dismissed; however, I see it not as a record of the historical Jesus but as a testimony of remembrances about Jesus. Unlike Meier, I believe that non-canonical gospels such as Thomas can be helpful in constructing a more complete portrait of the Christ figure.

16 Schweitzer, *Quest*, p. 239.

17 Schweitzer, *Quest*, p. 248.

18 Schweitzer, *Quest*, pp. 330–2.

19 Schweitzer, *Quest*, pp. 338, 349.

the natural and the supernatural need not be explained away by resorting to a literary device, if one realizes that there was discontinuity in Jesus' own historical situation. Schweitzer uses the category of eschatology to account for this discontinuity, noting that 'the atmosphere of the time was saturated with eschatology'.[20]

Schweitzer thus views the historical Jesus through the lens of what he calls 'thoroughgoing eschatology'. Everything in the Gospel looks forward to the end times, the apocalyptic kingdom of God which Jesus believed would come in his own lifetime. Once Schweitzer makes this decision as to Jesus' consciousness, he analyses everything in the Gospels using this lens: the miraculous feedings become eschatological sacraments; baptism is a prerequisite for entering the eschatological kingdom; suffering and death are seen as messianic tribulation.[21] Schweitzer was one of the first scholars to place Jesus within the context of late Second-Temple Jewish apocalyptic, which some contemporary historians continue to do.[22] Ultimately, however, Schweitzer went too far with this thesis, for he forced the final events of Jesus' life to fit his own preconceived idea by concluding that Jesus engineered his own death when he saw that the apocalyptic end had not arrived.[23]

Albert Schweitzer chronicled the First Quest in a masterful way, but, ironically, he was also responsible for bringing it to a close, for he realized its ultimate failure.

> There is nothing more negative than the result of the critical study of the Life of Jesus. . . . The historical Jesus will be to our time a stranger and an enigma. . . . The mistake was to suppose that Jesus could come to mean more to our time by entering into it as a man like ourselves. That is not possible. . . . Jesus as a concrete historical personality remains a stranger to our time.[24]

Two others scholars were to place the nails in the coffin of the First Quest. Martin Kähler asserted that the historical Jesus was irrelevant for Christian faith because (1) the gospels were not intended to be read as

---

20 Schweitzer, *Quest*, p. 350.

21 Schweitzer, *Quest*, pp. 376–80.

22 For example, Dale C. Allison, *Jesus of Nazareth: Millenarian Prophet* (Minneapolis: Fortress Press, 1998); Bart D. Ehrman, *Jesus: Apocalyptic Prophet of the New Millennium* (Oxford and New York: Oxford University Press, 1999); and E. P. Sanders, *Jesus and Judaism* (Philadelphia: Fortress Press, 1985).

23 Schweitzer, *Quest*, pp. 389–91.

24 Schweitzer, *Quest*, pp. 398, 399, 401.

history in the first place, and (2) the Christian Church is not really interested in the historical Jesus but rather that which makes Jesus significant to human lives ('the historic Jesus').[25] For Kähler, that significance resided in the death and resurrection of Jesus, leading him to make his famous declaration that the Gospels were nothing more than 'passion narratives with extended introductions'.[26]

Rudolf Bultmann was the other scholar who pronounced the First Quest finished. Bultmann asserted that the life of Jesus is not particularly important for Christian faith. Rather, the *kerygma* (proclamation) developed by the early Church after Jesus' death and resurrection is important, for it helps one encounter God.[27] Thus, Bultmann, following in Strauss's footsteps, called for a 'demythologizing' of the New Testament materials so that each person could enter more fully into that encounter.[28] Moreover, he sought through form criticism to detect the *Sitz im Leben* (setting in life) of the individual sayings or pericopes contained in the Gospels in order to detect how the kerygma of the early Church was formulated.[29] In this way, Bultmann, using an existentialist hermeneutic, bypassed reconstruction of the life of the historical Jesus in order to recover Jesus' effect upon his followers then and now.

The Second Quest

The students of Rudolf Bultmann were dissatisfied with their mentor's dismissal of the historical Jesus. What is now referred to as the Second Quest of the historical Jesus began with a talk delivered by Ernst Käsemann to a group of Bultmann's former students, who themselves were now New Testament scholars in their own right.[30] While noting

25 Patterson, *The God of Jesus*, pp. 33–4.

26 Martin Kähler, *The So-Called Historical Jesus and the Historic, Biblical Christ*, trans. and ed. Carl E. Braaten (1896; Philadelphia: Fortress Press, 1964), p. 80, n.11.

27 Roger Haight, *Jesus Symbol of God* (Maryknoll, NY: Orbis Books, 1999), pp. 32, 34.

28 See, for example, Rudolf Bultmann, *New Testament and Mythology and Other Basic Writings*, trans. and ed. Schubert M. Ogden (Philadelphia: Fortress Press, 1984).

29 See Rudolf Bultmann, *The History of the Synoptic Tradition*, trans. John Marsh (Oxford: Basil Blackwell, 1963).

30 This talk was delivered in 1953 and subsequently published as 'The Problem of the Historical Jesus' in Ernst Käsemann, *Essays on New Testament Themes*, trans. W. J. Montague (London: SCM Press, 1964), pp. 15–47.

that the term 'historical Jesus' is not necessarily 'appropriate or legitimate' because it suggests that one can 'nourish the illusion of a possible
and satisfying reproduction of [Jesus'] "life story",' Käsemann nevertheless asserted that the Gospel traditions should not be dismissed
entirely,[31] for there is more to be gleaned about Jesus than Bultmann
was willing to admit.

> The Gospel is always involved in a war on two fronts. . . . Primitive
> Christianity is obviously of the opinion that the earthly Jesus cannot
> be understood otherwise than from the far side of Easter, that is, in his
> majesty as Lord of the community and that, conversely, the event of
> Easter cannot be adequately comprehended if it is looked at apart
> from the earthly Jesus.[32]

Käsemann went on to state, against Bultmann, that Jesus' death and
resurrection alone were not sufficient to account for his importance to
the earliest Christian community. Käsemann therefore suggested that
the preaching of Jesus must be examined and its content used to interpret his other activities and his ultimate destiny: 'My own concern is to
show that, out of the obscurity of the life story of Jesus, certain characteristic traits in his preaching stand out in relatively sharp relief.'[33]

Käsemann's talk spurred others to embark upon what came to be
known as 'the New Quest'.[34] While the First Quest had sought to separate Jesus from his followers' impressions of him, the New Quest
attempted to ascertain how Jesus' message was similar to the preaching
of the early Church.[35] The New Questers therefore developed some
methodological tools which are still used in today's Jesus quest: for
example, they employed the principle of dissimilarity to examine the
continuity between Jesus and the Church and the principle of multiple
attestation to gauge the significance of the sources of Jesus material. The
New Quest faded from sight after a decade or so; commentators have
proposed various reasons for its demise – that the need for accessing

---

31 Käsemann, 'The Problem of the Historical Jesus', pp. 17, 23.

32 Käsemann, 'The Problem of the Historical Jesus', p. 25.

33 Käsemann, 'The Problem of the Historical Jesus', pp. 44, 46.

34 James M. Robinson, *A New Quest for the Historical Jesus* (London: SCM
Press, 1959).

35 The most significant work in this regard was Günther Bornkamm, *Jesus of
Nazareth*, trans. Irene and Fraser McLuskey with James M. Robinson (New York:
Harper & Row, 1960).

Jesus' importance for one's own walk with God evaporated as the interest in existentialism waned,[36] or that biblical scholars grew disheartened with their inability to locate anything like a full picture of Jesus, but only fragments.[37]

The Third Quest

We are currently in the midst of the Third Quest of the historical Jesus. Beginning in the 1980s, New Testament scholars, in an effort to elucidate the 'real' Jesus, began to ask different questions as they examined the biblical texts and the ancient world that produced them. Unlike the first two quests, however, these scholars are primarily from North America and Great Britain.[38] In my opinion, there are two characteristics that distinguish this quest from the previous two. First, contemporary New Testament scholars, in an effort to discover more about the historical Jesus, have begun to take an interdisciplinary approach to the topic. That is, rather than relying exclusively upon the traditional tools of biblical scholarship (the historical-critical method and literary criticism), these scholars have broadened their scope to include data from such social sciences as anthropology, sociology and economics, in order to construct a picture of what Jesus' total world would have looked like. Second, these questers do not restrict themselves to the canonical Gospels, but examine in addition the entire range of intertestamental and first-century writings. Thus, in recent studies of Jesus, one finds a greater reliance upon the so-called Gnostic Scriptures (especially the Gospel of Thomas), the writings of Second-Temple and rabbinic Judaism, and the work of non-Christian historians of the period, for example, Tacitus and Josephus.

The product of this Third Quest has been voluminous; if one does a computer search at a university library or at an on-line bookstore for works on Jesus published in the last 20 years, the result is a listing of hundreds of books aimed at both scholarly and popular audiences, and this does not even include the countless articles published in academic journals. Thus, the following discussion will be selective, both by inten-

36 Ben Witherington, III, *The Jesus Quest: The Third Search for the Jew of Nazareth* (Downers Grove, IL: InterVarsity Press, 1995), p. 11.

37 Patterson, *The God of Jesus*, p. 42.

38 Mary M. Knutsen, 'The Third Quest for the Historical Jesus: Introduction and Bibliography', in *The Quest for Jesus and the Christian Faith*, ed. Frederick J. Gaiser, *Word and World* Supplement Series 3 (September 1997), p. 13.

tion and of necessity. I shall examine the major trends in this newest quest, with a particular view toward those techniques and strategies which inform the liberation Christologies discussed in Part II.

Both the earliest and arguably the most important book in this newest quest is *Jesus and Judaism* by E. P. Sanders. Sanders, in a very careful and thorough treatment of the life of Jesus, places Jesus within the Judaism of his time. His major contribution is that he demonstrates that Jesus was in continuity with a strand of Judaism that he calls 'Jewish restoration eschatology',[39] and that Jesus' message and activity was not dissimilar from the Old Testament prophets. Sanders demonstrates effectively that we can know a great deal about Jesus; unlike other contemporary scholars, Sanders, in order to reconstruct Jesus' life, places more emphasis upon his deeds than his words.[40] He concludes that Jesus was an eschatological prophet who believed he was inaugurating the kingdom of God that he preached.[41] Sanders places particular importance upon the clearing of the Jerusalem temple by Jesus, asserting that this was a symbolic act of protest intended by Jesus to provoke the Roman and Jewish authorities into moving against him.[42] In his emphasis upon eschatology, Sanders follows in Schweitzer's footsteps; nevertheless, he goes beyond Schweitzer by disputing, in his minute examination of the characteristics of the Judaisms of Jesus' day, Schweitzer's belief that the Jesus of history must remain an enigma to us. The Jesus who emerges from Sanders's work is a powerful and incendiary Jewish prophet who was in control of his environment and absolutely convinced that the end times were at hand. The major weakness of Sanders's work is that he does not give enough importance to Jesus' preaching in developing his view of Jesus; his confrontational Jesus is at odds with the gentle wisdom teacher who is also found in the Gospels.

This is the view of Jesus espoused by Marcus Borg in his many works. Borg is noteworthy among Jesus scholars, for several reasons. First, he has devoted his career to elucidating a Jesus who is 'a Spirit person'.[43] Thus, unlike other historians who see Jesus as just another teacher or

---

39 Sanders, *Jesus and Judaism*, pp. 91–116. For example, Sanders sees Jesus' selection of twelve disciples (assuming that this is historical) as an indication of this restoration eschatology, for the number 'twelve' would have signified the twelve tribes of Israel, pp. 95–8.

40 Sanders, *Jesus and Judaism*, pp. 10–13.

41 Sanders, *Jesus and Judaism*, p. 319.

42 Sanders, *Jesus and Judaism*, pp. 61–76.

43 Marcus J. Borg, *Jesus, A New Vision: Spirit, Culture, and the Life of Discipleship* (New York: Harper & Row, 1987), p. 25.

social critic, Borg acknowledges that there was something supernatural about Jesus, namely, his ability to access the Spirit as a visionary subject to trances, as revealed in his healings and exorcisms.[44] Second, Borg believes that Jesus was interested in his contemporary world and not the world to come. He thus disputes any eschatological view of Jesus that is based in Jewish apocalypticism and has surveyed other New Testament scholars in order to announce a supposed consensus that the eschatological Jesus is 'dead'.[45] His non-eschatological Jesus is a teacher of wisdom involved in criticizing the prevailing Jewish 'politics of holiness' in favour of a 'politics of compassion'.[46] Third, unlike other scholars who try to divorce the quest for Jesus from the Christian faith, Borg is quite open about his theological agenda – to empower other people of faith to find Jesus 'again for the first time'.[47]

Probably the best-known scholar involved in contemporary Jesus research is John Dominic Crossan, whose book *The Historical Jesus*[48] has been widely read and generally well received among both scholarly and popular audiences; this was actually the first book to bring the quest of the historical Jesus to popular attention and has been the catalyst for the widespread interest in other books which heretofore would have been considered too academic for popular interest. The most distinctive and controversial aspect of Crossan's work is his methodology. Unlike Sanders, Crossan is interested almost exclusively in the sayings of Jesus and believes that it is possible to discover what Jesus actually said. Comparing his method to archaeological excavation, Crossan identifies various 'strata' of tradition and assigns each ancient text to a stratum; he then uses the criterion of multiple attestation to determine how many independent attestations there are of a given saying. He then 'cross-references' the number of attestations with the stratum in the tradition to determine what is most 'genuine' among the sayings attributed to

44 Borg, *Jesus, A New Vision*, pp. 65–7.

45 Marcus J. Borg, 'A Temperate Case for a Non-Eschatological Jesus,' in *Jesus in Contemporary Scholarship*, ed. Marcus J. Borg (Harrisburg, PA: Trinity Press International, 1994), pp. 59–60.

46 Borg, *Jesus, A New Vision*, pp. 86–93, 131–41. See also Borg, *Conflict, Holiness, and Politics in the Teachings of Jesus*, second edition (Harrisburg, PA: Trinity Press International, 1998).

47 Marcus J. Borg, *Meeting Jesus Again for the First Time: The Historical Jesus and the Heart of Contemporary Faith* (New York: HarperCollins, 1994), pp. 1–3. See also Borg, *Jesus, A New Vision*, pp. 190–200.

48 John Dominic Crossan, *The Historical Jesus: The Life of a Mediterranean Jewish Peasant* (New York: HarperCollins, 1991).

Jesus.[49] His method has been both lauded for its ingenuity and condemned for its selectivity. Crossan seems to make random judgements about the dating of documents, and this determines both the rest of his process and his end result; he also requires multiplicity of attestation on an arbitrary basis rather than in a uniform fashion.[50] Once his method has been thoroughly applied, the image of Jesus that emerges is that of an itinerant Jewish preacher, a peasant who wandered on the fringes of society, entertaining the landless poor with feats of magic and open meals.[51] A major weakness in his approach is his dismissal of the eschatological content to Jesus' message; he sees this element added to Jesus' original preaching by the early Church in later layers of the Jesus tradition. A major strength is his willingness to consider other texts outside the New Testament in formulating his assessment of Jesus,[52] unlike more conservative scholars who restrict themselves to the canonical Gospels.[53]

A second element of Crossan's work that has rendered it distinctive is his use of the social sciences in his quest for the historical Jesus. In order to locate Jesus within Mediterranean peasant society, Crossan draws upon the work of social anthropologist Gerhard Lenski, who has described and categorized the social classes of the ancient world.[54] Crossan uses a cross-cultural analysis in order to deduce information about Jesus' everyday life; a major drawback to this type of cross-cultural analysis, however, is that it assumes uncritically that all ancient societies were alike and thus are subject to comparison.

Another scholar who employs the methods of sociology is Richard Horsley, who has done extensive work on messianic figures and peasant

---

49 Crossan, *The Historical Jesus*, pp. xxviii–xxxiv. For a discussion of Crossan's methodology, see also Marcus J. Borg, 'Portraits of Jesus in Contemporary North American Scholarship (with Addendum)', in *Jesus in Contemporary Scholarship*, ed. Borg, pp. 32–6.

50 Witherington, *The Jesus Quest*, pp. 77–9.

51 Crossan, *The Historical Jesus*, Chapter 13. As noted by Witherington, *The Jesus Quest*, p. 70, Crossan's argument stands or falls on this extremely dense chapter.

52 For example, Crossan assigns the first version of the Gospel of Thomas to his 'First Stratum' (from the years 30 to 60 CE). Crossan, *The Historical Jesus*, p. 427.

53 For example, after an exhaustive discussion (100 pages) of the potential sources, John Meier states that he is nevertheless going to use only the canonical Gospels; Meier, *A Marginal Jew: Rethinking the Historical Jesus*, Vol. 1, p. 140.

54 Crossan, *The Historical Jesus*, pp. 43–6.

unrest at the time of Jesus.[55] Horsley examines Jesus' actions in the context of colonial oppression of the Jewish people by the Roman Empire. He concludes from his analysis of social groups in first-century Palestine that Jesus was a radical social prophet standing in the tradition of the Hebrew prophets and that Jesus' intention before he was stopped was to enact a social revolution.[56]

> Jesus' overall perspective was that God was bringing an end to the demonic and political powers dominating his society so that a renewal of individual and social life would be possible. . . . Jesus preached that the kingdom of God was at hand. . . . The divine activity of the kingdom of God is focused on the needs and desires of people. . . . In fact, Jesus' preaching generally, and particularly his announcement of the kingdom of God, rarely calls attention explicitly to God, but concentrates on the implication of the presence of the kingdom for people's lives and on how people must respond.[57]

This social emphasis, according to Horsley, is what differentiated Jesus from the other messianic figures of his day, who were more interested in political revolution.[58] Nevertheless, Horsley notes that such a distinction between the political and the social is actually a recent one, for in Jesus' time the social and the political were one. He cautions that we must not be so quick to distance Jesus from politics, for to do so would be ahistorical; he suggests that this tendency stems from the Bultmannian existentialist interpretation of Jesus as a preacher of inner transformation because that was who Bultmann needed him to be.[59]

Moreover, Horsley also disputes prior understandings of eschatology, noting that the Greek *eschaton* need not mean 'final' in the sense of 'end' (as in the end of the world), but can also mean 'final' in the sense of 'ultimate' (as in the fulfilment of God's rule on earth). Thus, according to Horsley, Jesus' eschatological orientation need not be dispensed with entirely (as Borg would advocate), but can be contextualized to

---

55 See, for example, Richard A. Horsley, *Jesus and the Spiral of Violence: Popular Jewish Resistance in Roman Palestine* (New York: Harper & Row, 1987); Horsley, *Sociology and the Jesus Movement* (New York: Crossroad, 1989); and Horsley and John A. Hanson, *Bandits, Prophets, and Messiahs: Popular Movements at the Time of Jesus* (Minneapolis: Winston, 1985).

56 Horsley, *Jesus and the Spiral of Violence*, pp. 173–4.

57 Horsley, *Jesus and the Spiral of Violence*, pp. 157–8, 169.

58 Borg, 'Portraits of Jesus', pp. 28, 29.

59 Horsley, *Jesus and the Spiral of Violence*, pp. 152–3.

reveal Jesus' congruence with the social resistance movements of his time.[60]

Both Borg and Crossan have been 'fellows' in the Jesus Seminar, a group of scholars called together and presided over by Robert Funk.[61] Their original purpose was to gather periodically to share the results of their research on the historical Jesus, with the intention of compiling a multi-volume work about the authenticity of the sayings and actions of Jesus.[62] Their controversial method was to vote on specific portions of the Jesus tradition, using different coloured beads, and thus arrive at a consensus as to the *ipsissima verba* and the *ipsissima acta* of Jesus. The members of the Jesus Seminar have been praised for their vision and their boldness in sharing their findings with the general public[63] and have been criticized for their lack of recognized scholarship and the fallacious premise of their method – that one can in fact arrive at a consensus about Jesus by voting.[64] Additionally, their selection of sources upon which to rely for the 'authentic' Jesus is rather arbitrary, leading to the criticism that the resulting portrait of Jesus has been manipulated by the data consulted.[65] In my opinion, the most glaring weakness in the Jesus Seminar's work is their implication that whatever does not come from Jesus' very mouth is somehow unimportant or lacking in truth. I believe that what the early Christian believers may have 'retrojected' into the mouth of Jesus is an important witness to what they thought about Jesus, how they were affected by him, and what lasting truth their departed Lord had for their lives.[66]

Nevertheless, despite controversy and criticism, the Jesus Seminar has

---

60 Horsley, *Jesus and the Spiral of Violence*, pp. 168–9.

61 For descriptions and discussion of the Jesus Seminar, see (pro) Marcus J. Borg, 'The Jesus Seminar and the Church', in *Jesus in Contemporary Scholarship*, ed. Borg, pp. 160–181; and (con) Luke Timothy Johnson, *The Real Jesus: The Misguided Quest for the Historical Jesus and the Truth of the Traditional Gospels* (New York: HarperCollins, 1996).

62 These books are: Robert W. Funk, Roy W. Hoover and the Jesus Seminar, *The Five Gospels: The Search for the Authentic Words of Jesus* (New York: Macmillan Publishing Company, 1993); and Robert W. Funk and the Jesus Seminar, *The Acts of Jesus: The Search for the Authentic Deeds of Jesus* (New York: HarperCollins, 1998).

63 Borg, 'The Jesus Seminar', p. 168.

64 Johnson, *The Real Jesus*, pp. 1–5; Witherington, *The Jesus Quest*, pp. 42–5.

65 Witherington, *The Jesus Quest*, pp. 46–52; and Arland J. Hultgren, 'The Use of Sources in the Quest for Jesus: What You Use Is What You Get', in *The Quest for Jesus*, ed. Gaiser, pp. 33–48.

66 See Johnson, *The Real Jesus*, p. 81, for a similar view.

gone on to publish its findings on a continuous basis; indeed, the Seminar has sought to rise above the harsh and sometimes excessive criticisms levelled at its work. In responding to critics, one member of the Seminar warns:

> So in the Jesus Seminar we too need to be careful not to . . . argu[e] that we are right because our Jesus is earlier, and therefore more authentic and pure. To do so would again allow those who wish to, to claim for themselves the power to say who are true Christians and who are heretics, the power to define the terms of the discourse.[67]

Another member of the Jesus Seminar, who has written both independently and under the auspices of the Seminar, is Stephen Patterson, whose book *The God of Jesus* makes a significant contribution to the literature in the field by virtue of Patterson's willingness to 'take the next step' and explore the Christological ramifications of the historical quest.[68] New Testament scholars usually leave this task to theologians; it is to Patterson's credit that he recognizes that the New Testament itself is full of Christological interpretation that can be explored and supplemented by contemporary study. For Patterson, the key to understanding Jesus – and what ultimately makes Jesus important – is his view of God; through Jesus, others 'had come to know what God is really like'.[69] For Patterson, the entire purpose of Jesus' life and ministry and the entire content of his preaching is summed up in the phrase 'the love of God'.

> When early Christians claimed Jesus as their Savior, they were claiming that the love of God was to be found around the open tables of the Jesus movement. It was there that they experienced care. It was there that they experienced love. It was there that they experienced the safety and security that comes only from knowing experientially that there is a God who cares about me personally. Jesus created an experience of the unmitigated love of God for those in the world who had experienced it least: the poor, the blind, the lame, the homeless. They in turn confessed him as 'Savior.'[70]

---

67 Karen L. King, 'Back to the Future: Jesus and Heresy', in The Jesus Seminar, *The Once and Future Jesus* (Santa Rosa, CA: Polebridge Press, 2000), p. 87.

68 Patterson, *The God of Jesus*, pp. 274–8. Patterson seeks to elucidate the 'essence' of Jesus, which he labels 'the love of God'; he calls this an 'existential Christology', p. 278.

69 Patterson, *The God of Jesus*, p. 57.

70 Patterson, *The God of Jesus*, p. 50.

Thus, unlike many in the Jesus Seminar, Patterson values the testimony of the early Church; their thoughts about Jesus tell us what he awakened in them. For Patterson it is not an 'either/or', but a 'both/and': 'So the historical Jesus is important. And so are the confessions of the early church.'[71]

Burton Mack has made a name for himself among Jesus scholars by suggesting that Jesus was a cynic preacher whose message was recorded by the 'Q community' in the Q document, which scholars have sought to reconstruct from sayings which occur in both Matthew and Luke but not Mark.[72] Mack asserts that the 'Q Gospel', which contains no passion narrative, demonstrates that, amid the diversity of earliest Christianity, there was a community for whom Jesus' importance lay in his wisdom teachings and not his death and resurrection.[73] Mack's critics point out that one can only hypothesize a Q document, let alone a particular community behind it;[74] moreover, most New Testament scholars, including Crossan, have been adamant that the passion narratives – found in all four canonical Gospels – were probably the earliest stories circulated about Jesus.[75]

Mack's most recent book is significant for a different reason. Returning to the topic of his earliest work,[76] Mack suggests that the early Christian communities used various 'myths' to explain and evangelize Jesus.[77] He asserts that there are two pictures of Jesus that are in sharp contrast to one another in the New Testament materials, and that we may better understand these two pictures by seeing that they are the product of two different 'myths' about Jesus:

---

71 Patterson, *The God of Jesus*, p.50.

72 On Q, see Pheme Perkins, *Reading the New Testament*, second edition (1978; New York/Mahwah: Paulist Press, 1988), pp. 62–5.

73 Burton L. Mack, *The Lost Gospel: The Book of Q and Christian Origins* (New York: HarperCollins, 1993), p. 4.

74 'It seems highly unlikely that there ever was a "Q community," if by that is meant a Christian community that possessed as their sacred tradition only the Q collection of Jesus' sayings, without some form of passion and resurrection traditions.' Witherington, *The Jesus Quest*, p. 50.

75 See Raymond E. Brown, *The Death of the Messiah*, 2 volumes (New York: Doubleday, 1994); and John Dominic Crossan, *The Cross That Spoke: The Origins of the Passion Narrative* (New York: Harper & Row, 1988).

76 Burton L. Mack, *A Myth of Innocence: Mark and Christian Origins* (Philadelphia: Fortress Press, 1988).

77 Burton L. Mack, *The Christian Myth: Origins, Logic, and Legacy* (New York and London: Continuum, 2001), pp. 13–18.

The myth of Jesus *christos* was based on the logic of a martyrdom that merged the Greek notion of the noble death with a hellenistic version of an old Semitic wisdom tale about the trial and vindication of an innocent victim. The *christos* myth was a very early development within a Jesus movement that had spread to northern Syria, as reflected in the letters of Paul, but it does not document the earliest or the most characteristic form of cultivating the memory of Jesus . . . [which] consist mainly of the 'teachings of Jesus'.[78]

Thus, Mack believes that sayings sources such as Q and Thomas memorialize the other myth about Jesus – that he was a wandering cynic philosopher.[79] In this most recent work, Mack has left the quest of the historical Jesus behind, calling it 'hoopla'.[80] He believes that the only way to 'get at' the figure of Jesus is by acknowledging once and for all that he may only be approached through mythical categories (à la Bultmann). It is too early to tell whether Mack's newest take on Jesus will have lasting ramifications for Jesus studies, but I seriously doubt that it will.

The majority of scholars doing Jesus research, however, are unconnected with the Jesus Seminar and are sometimes overtly critical of the Seminar's work. Luke Timothy Johnson believes that those involved in the Third Quest are either amateurs (such as A. N. Wilson and John Shelby Spong) or undisciplined scholars (such as Marcus Borg and Barbara Thiering).[81] His own solution to the problem of the historical Jesus is to reiterate the opinions of Kähler and Bultmann: 'Christians direct their faith not to the historical figure of Jesus but to the living Lord Jesus.'[82] Thus, Johnson prefers to sidestep the issue entirely and fall back upon the 'Christ of faith', reverting to the state of affairs which prevailed at the end of the First Quest. I think this is unfortunate, for it ignores the social scientific material that can enrich our faith images of Christ.

Ben Witherington, III, while critical of many of the Third Questers (especially the Jesus Seminar), makes his own contribution to the Third Quest. He sees Jesus as a sage, the very embodiment of God's Wisdom.

---

78 Mack, *The Christian Myth*, p. 41. (Citations omitted.)
79 Mack, *The Christian Myth*, pp. 49–51.
80 Mack, *The Christian Myth*, p. 28; 'The current furor about the historical Jesus and the historicity of the gospels, both in the guild and in the media, will runs its course without resolution,' p. 74.
81 Johnson, *The Real Jesus*, pp. 32–7, 39–44.
82 Johnson, *The Real Jesus*, p. 142.

He carefully distinguishes his position from that of Elisabeth Schüssler Fiorenza, who sees Jesus as the prophet of Sophia (Wisdom), a non-androcentric image of the Godhead.[83] For Witherington, this Wisdom not only sent Jesus but was personified in Jesus. Witherington makes a good case for using Wisdom as the 'heuristic category that comes closest to explaining the most about who Jesus thought he was and what he said and did'.[84] He thus is able to show that many of the characteristics of Jesus that are highlighted by contemporary Jesus studies – such as Jesus' wisdom sayings, his eating and drinking, and his persecution and death – make absolute sense and cohere nicely when Jesus is seen as God's Wisdom and juxtaposed with the wisdom literature of the Hebrew Bible.[85]

Gregory Riley has made a major contribution to the study of Jesus in a recent book.[86] Riley, who approaches the topic from his roots as a classicist, seeks to locate Jesus in the atmosphere of the Greco-Roman world. Thus, he asserts that the best way to image Jesus in an ancient context is according to the myth of the hero. Riley asserts that the earliest Christians, living in a classical milieu, would have been well acquainted with the myth of the classical hero (such as Herakles), who is born from a union of the human and the divine, undergoes trials and sometimes death, and is rewarded with everlasting divinity.[87] At first glance, this might seem like a recycling of Burton Mack's notion of myth. However, the genius of Riley's theory is that he neither casts doubt upon the historicity of Jesus, nor does he state that Jesus' life story was a myth. Rather, he suggests that the earliest Christians would have

83 Witherington, *The Jesus Quest*, pp. 161–5. See also Elisabeth Schüssler Fiorenza, *Jesus, Miriam's Child, Sophia's Prophet: Critical Issues in Feminist Christology* (New York: Continuum, 1994), as well as my discussion of her work in Chapter 6.

84 Witherington, *The Jesus Quest*, p. 185. See also Ben Witherington, III, *Jesus the Sage: The Pilgrimage of Wisdom* (Minneapolis: Fortress Press, 1994), and *The Christology of Jesus* (Philadelphia: Fortress Press, 1990).

85 Witherington, *The Jesus Quest*, pp. 186–9. See also Elizabeth A. Johnson, 'Wisdom Was Made Flesh and Pitched Her Tent Among Us', in *Reconstructing the Christ Symbol: Essays in Feminist Christology*, ed. Mary Anne Stevens (New York/Mahwah: Paulist Press, 1993), pp. 95–117.

86 Gregory J. Riley, *One Jesus, Many Christs: How Jesus Inspired Not One True Christianity, But Many* (New York: HarperCollins, 1997).

87 Riley, *One Jesus, Many Christs*, pp. 39, 41, 46–7. Riley outlines the typical story of the hero (Chapter 3) and then applies it to the Jesus story (Chapter 4), concluding, 'His resurrection was the authentication of his status,' p. 92.

used this concept as the hermeneutical key for interpreting the events of Jesus' history.[88] Riley's thesis is particularly important for understanding the various liberation Christologies and their reliance upon both traditional Christian and ethnic or racial types, as we shall see in subsequent chapters.

Ramifications of the Quests for Contemporary Christology

I believe that contemporary Christologies can benefit a great deal from the quests for the historical Jesus. From the First Quest, we can learn the dangers of creating a Jesus who looks just like us. From the Second Quest, we can ascertain the importance – and the limitations – of comparing Jesus to the Church founded in his name. However, it is the current Third Quest that has the greatest impact on Christology.

First, contemporary Jesus research, through cross-cultural analysis, situates Jesus in his own time. This is extremely important, for the Christologies of the New Testament were born in that culture, and all subsequent Christology is based on the New Testament texts. Moreover, knowing the social and cultural factors that affected Jesus in his own context dissuades us from wresting Jesus out of that context to become a universal Christ with no roots in the world; we then will be less likely to formulate a Christology based exclusively on modern agendas. Thus, Jesus' response to his own cultural situation allows the contemporary liberation Christologies to compare Jesus' attitudes to today's pressing questions of discrimination and liberation and develop a view of Christ's person and work that is historically grounded and socially relevant.

Second, the work of Marcus Borg and Stephen Patterson in particular demonstrates how important it is to develop a Christology based upon the Jesus of history, rather than merely stopping once a satisfactory portrait of Jesus has emerged. In this way, contemporary people of faith are able to know more about the God to whom Jesus pointed, through knowing more about the human Jesus. His human responses to the God of his understanding aid us in our quest for the God of our understanding, and at the intersection of the two lies an authentic Christology, rather than one in which the 'Christ of faith' is at odds with the 'Jesus of history'.

---

88 Riley, *One Jesus, Many Christs*, pp. 14, 19–20.

Third, the current quest reveals to us the diversity that was present in earliest Christianity, and this empowers diversity in today's world. Contemporary scholars' use of the Gospel of Thomas and other non-canonical texts, whether or not they are from Crossan's 'first strata', are able to demonstrate to us that there were, in Gregory Riley's words, 'one Jesus, but many Christs'[89] in earliest Christianity. This has important ramifications in a world where fundamentalism is on the rise, when people in churches are led to believe that there is only 'one way' to God and one view of Jesus' Christological importance. Moreover, in recovering voices from the past that were silenced by the early Church Fathers, perhaps we can learn to hear voices from our present that some would seek to silence because they offer a view different from the mainstream.

---

89 Riley, *One Jesus, Many Christs*, p. 4.

Part II

Contextual Christologies

4

A Saviour Just Like Me: Black, African and Asian Christologies

This chapter will examine Christologies that define themselves by their focus upon the effects of racism and inculturation – the Christologies of those of African and Asian descent. I discuss these Christologies together because race and culture are linked in contemporary society, especially in Christianity. Christians of African and Asian descent are colonized people, whose earliest experiences of Christ and Christianity came from white colonial oppressors, missionaries and slave-traders. Thus, their view of Christ is different from that of mainstream (white) Christology. The defining context of African-American, or black,[1] Christology is race, while the defining context of African and Asian Christology is culture. Therefore, I shall treat the Christology of African-American blacks separately from that of blacks on the continent of Africa; the latter bears more similarity to the Christology of Asian peoples due to their common concern with Christ in culture.

Black Christology

Black Christology has developed within the discipline of black theology, which arose in the 1960s as a religious response to the white racism confronting American blacks that gave rise to the Civil Rights Movement in the United States.[2] Black Christianity of course developed first in slave churches and then in the black Christian denominations,[3] but a

---

1 Although of course both African-Americans and Africans are black, the terms 'black theology' and 'black Christology' are usually used to refer to the scholarship of African-Americans, while 'African theology' and 'African Christology' are used to refer to the scholarship of Africans.

2 Kelly Brown Douglas, *The Black Christ* (Maryknoll, NY: Orbis Books, 1994), p. 6.

3 For a discussion of the history of black religion, see Gayraud S. Wilmore,

specifically black 'theology of liberation' was first articulated by theologian James Cone, who believed that not only was the ongoing enslavement of black people an ongoing theme throughout American history, but, more importantly, traditional theologies had been complicit in its continuation. Consequently, he saw an intentional 'black theology' as the only hope for ameliorating the plight of black Americans by means of the Christian gospel.[4]

In his early work, Cone seriously wonders whether it is even possible for blacks to be Christian, inasmuch as the Christian faith has been mediated to blacks through their white oppressors.[5] Thus, his theology has much in common with both feminist and queer theology, for each of these theologies also asks whether it is possible for women or gays and lesbians to be Christian, since, in their view, Christianity has been formed and handed down by a patriarchal and homophobic Church.[6] As a result, each of these theologies is truly a 'liberation' theology, since they seek to liberate Christian theology from the often narrow and exclusive interpretation of white, heterosexual males.

Cone is adamant that any theology that calls itself 'Christian' must be a theology of liberation, for Jesus Christ was involved in liberation for all people.[7] Using traditional Christian imagery, Cone speaks of Christ freeing human persons from sin, but then, in the style of every liberation theology, names that sin in terms of the context of a particular oppressed people: for Cone, this is the sin of racism; thus, in his theology, Jesus Christ came to liberate blacks from racism.[8] Today, Cone still believes that Christian theology is in the grip of this sin, asserting that racism is 'America's original sin'.[9]

When one turns to black Christology and its notion of a 'Black Christ',

----

Black Religion and Black Radicalism: An Interpretation of the Religious History of Afro-American People, second edition (Maryknoll, NY: Orbis Books, 1983).

4 James H. Cone, *Black Theology and Black Power*, 20th anniversary edition (1969; New York: Harper & Row, 1989), p. 31.

5 James H. Cone, *Black Theology and Black Power*, p. 33.

6 See Chapters 6 and 8 of the present work.

7 'Any interpretation of the gospel in any historical period that fails to see Jesus as the Liberator of the oppressed is heretical.' James H. Cone, *God of the Oppressed* (New York: The Seabury Press, 1975), p. 36.

8 James H. Cone, *A Black Theology of Liberation*, 20th anniversary edition (1970; Maryknoll, NY: Orbis Books, 1990), pp. 104–07. Cone notes that in a white society, sin for black people takes the form of wanting to be white, thus denying their own self-identity.

9 James H. Cone, 'Theology's Great Sin', plenary address at the American Academy of Religion Annual Meeting, 18 November 2001, Denver, CO.

it is significant that as early as 1963, Malcolm X asserted, 'Christ wasn't white. Christ was a black man.'[10] There are even earlier references to a black Christ in early twentieth-century African-American literature.[11] Nevertheless, the first theological work on a specifically black Christ did not appear until 1968, when Albert Cleage published *The Black Messiah*, a collection of sermons that sought to inspire black Christians to stronger faith in the midst of oppression.[12]

The most controversial assertion in this book is that Jesus was histori-cally, ethnically black. Whereas most black Christology articulates Christ's blackness in metaphorical terms, Cleage saw his blackness as literal, resulting from black blood that the Israelites had acquired dur-ing their sojourn in Egypt.[13] Cleage believed that the Synoptic Gospels portrayed a black Jesus whose radical message was then 'spiritualized' by the apostle Paul, who 'modified his [Jesus'] teachings to conform to the pagan white gentiles'.[14] The Romans were white oppressors of Black Israel, and Judas Iscariot was an 'Uncle Tom'.[15] Although one may dis-pute much of Cleage's thesis (for example, that Jesus was 'a revolution-ary black leader, a Zealot'[16]) on the basis of traditional historical and anthropological research, recent study has suggested that there may be some truth to his claim that Jesus came from a tribe of mixed Israelite-African ancestry.[17]

Moreover, Cleage was boldly prophetic in daring to assert, 'Black people cannot build dignity on their knees worshipping a white Christ.'[18] Throughout his sermons, one sees the primary characteristic

10 Quoted in Douglas, *The Black Christ*, p. 1.

11 For example, Langston Hughes asserted, 'Christ is a nigger, beaten and black,' while Countee Cullen wrote a poem entitled 'The Black Christ' and John Henrik Clarke a short story called 'The Boy Who Painted Christ Black'. See Douglas, *The Black Christ*, pp. 32–3. W. E. B. DuBois also discussed the blackness of Jesus, fancifully describing 'Mary Black', a black woman whom God chooses to bear the Messiah for blacks; racism forces her to have her child in a stable, and this child grows up to be lynched by whites. See Dwight N. Hopkins, *Shoes That Fit Our Feet: Sources for a Constructive Black Theology* (Maryknoll, NY: Orbis Books, 1993), pp. 156–9.

12 Albert B. Cleage, Jr, *The Black Messiah* (New York: Sheed and Ward, 1968), p. 3.

13 Cleage, *The Black Messiah*, p. 3.

14 Cleage, *The Black Messiah*, p. 4.

15 Cleage, *The Black Messiah*, pp. 75, 83.

16 Cleage, *The Black Messiah*, p. 4.

17 Douglas, *The Black Christ*, p. 79, citing the work of Cain Felder and Martin Bernal.

18 Cleage, *The Black Messiah*, p. 3.

of black Christology – a concern for nurturing black self-esteem and fostering their self-identification with the *imago dei*, a common element in the theological discourse of oppressed people. He warns his black audience against the dangers of assimilation to a white agenda, comparing it to Paul's altering of the black Messiah to fit into the white gentile world. In fact, Cleage charges Paul with formulating a 'slave religion' that eschewed the message of the real (black) Christ, urging politically active blacks such as Stokely Carmichael and those who are turning to Islam not to give up on Christianity, but to re-evaluate it in the context of the black Messiah.[19] In Cleage's estimation, the historical Jesus was not racist, but was a black man who sought liberation for his people then and now; his very resurrection was a foreshadowing of the resurrection of the black nation that he started.[20] In this way, black Christology, like other liberation Christologies to be discussed, as well as the contemporary quest for the historical Jesus, emphasizes the importance of returning to the actual message of Jesus and rejecting the accretions of the later Church.

In contrast, James Cone favours a metaphorical approach to the black Christ,[21] noting that the quest for the historical Jesus has eroded the theologian's ability to wrest Jesus out of his context and create Jesus in his or her own image.[22] Cone stresses that Jesus 'is who he was'[23] and cannot be otherwise, but that, once Jesus is established in his context, parallels may be drawn and comparisons made between his context and the contemporary situation of oppressed blacks; for example, Cone compares Jesus' cradle in a stable to 'a beer case in a ghetto alley'.[24] For Cone, the most important characteristic of the historical Jesus is his identification with the poor of his time, and therefore he is able to interpret Jesus' solidarity with the poor and oppressed Christologically as the hermeneutical key for imaging Jesus as black: 'If he is not black as we are, then the resurrection has little significance for our times. Indeed, if he cannot be what we are, we cannot be who he is.'[25]

Thus, for Cone, the question is not '*Was* Jesus black?' but '*Why couldn't* Jesus be black?' Once he makes the connection between Jesus'

---

19 Cleage, *The Black Messiah*, pp. 89, 98.
20 Cleage, *The Black Messiah*, p. 99.
21 Cone, *A Black Theology of Liberation*, p. 123: 'It seems to me that the *literal* color of Jesus is irrelevant.'
22 Cone, *A Black Theology of Liberation*, pp. 111–13.
23 Cone, *A Black Theology of Liberation*, p. 119.
24 Cone, *A Black Theology of Liberation*, p. 114.
25 Cone, *A Black Theology of Liberation*, pp. 119–20.

historical actions and the metaphorical blackness of Christ, Cone is able to interpret God's act in becoming human in Jesus as a taking-on of blackness by God, thus disclosing to a white racist world that 'blackness is not what the world says it is'[26] and confirming, as Cleage did, the black person as the *imago dei*. The resurrection confirms this, for the risen Lord transcends time and is present today, linking the present struggle for liberation with the struggles that the earthly Jesus engaged in his own day and time.[27]

Joseph Johnson, a bishop of the Christian Methodist Episcopal Church, in a speech at Andover Newton Theological School in 1969, also lifted up the view of Jesus as the great liberator of humankind.[28] However, with a stridency reminiscent of Malcolm X, Johnson asserted that it is imperative that blacks read the Jesus story through the lens of their own experience, a prerequisite for any liberation Christology. Johnson demanded that one seek out the absolute humanity of the historical Jesus in order to strip away the Christ of faith who has been portrayed as 'white, straight-haired, blue-eyed, Anglo-Saxon', to the exclusion of non-white peoples from full Christian fellowship.[29] The radicality of the human Jesus has been distorted by the white Christ; once his ability to 'address, probe, disturb, and challenge us'[30] is restored, Christians will once again be able to experience the Jesus Christ who is liberator and not oppressor.

J. Deotis Roberts agrees with Johnson and incorporates much of his argument; but, whereas Cone and Johnson counsel a revolutionary Christology which removes Christ from the possession of whites and makes him black, Roberts advocates a theology of reconciliation, noting that 'separation, however rewarding to set the record straight, cannot be an ultimate Christian goal. Separation must give way to reconciliation.'[31] Surveying the historical landscape, Roberts asserts that blacks must not become like white racists, for hatred has not served them

---

26 Cone, *A Black Theology of Liberation*, p. 121.

27 Cone, *God of the Oppressed*, p. 120.

28 This speech was subsequently published in Johnson's *The Soul of the Black Preacher* (Philadelphia: United Church Press, 1971) and is reprinted as Joseph A. Johnson, Jr, 'Jesus the Liberator', in *Black Theology: A Documentary History*, 2 volumes, ed. James H. Cone and Gayraud S. Wilmore (Maryknoll, NY: Orbis Books, 1993), Vol. 1, pp. 203–13.

29 Johnson, 'Jesus the Liberator', p. 204.

30 Johnson, 'Jesus the Liberator', p. 211.

31 J. Deotis Roberts, *Liberation and Reconciliation: A Black Theology*, revised edition (1971; Maryknoll, NY: Orbis Books, 1994), p. ix.

well.[32] The solution to the sin of racism, which has shattered relations between the races, is reconciliation, which requires both repentance on the part of whites and forgiveness on the part of blacks: '[I]t is sinful not to be able to forgive, just as it is sinful not to be able to repent.'[33] Blacks and whites are aided in this endeavour by the Holy Spirit that was in Christ; Christ the Liberator is also Christ the Reconciler.[34]

In articulating his theology of reconciliation, Roberts both affirms and dismisses the necessity of a black Christ. On the one hand, he sees the black Christ as integrally related to the growing of blacks toward wholeness and esteem;[35] on the other hand, he sees any particularization of Christ as counter-productive to the work of reconciliation. That is, the black Christ can work as a symbol,[36] but once he becomes literal, he acts as a stumbling block to the unification of the races. Roberts thus categorically denies the literal blackness of Christ as articulated by Cleage[37] in favour of a 'universal Christ' who can only be embraced once the 'skin color of Christ' has been overcome through mutual respect among equals.[38]

Roberts is an important voice in black Christology; however, his view is a conservative, minority opinion, which reflects generational differences.[39] Roberts approaches the subject from the context of the 1954 Supreme Court school desegregation decision and the subsequent non-violent protest of Martin Luther King, when black leaders believed that civil rights would come gradually and were happy with whatever small progress was made. In contrast, Cone and younger contemporary black scholars see the issue through the lens of the turbulent 1960s, the rhetoric of Malcolm X and the resulting black radicalism, and are consequently less willing to 'settle' for slow progress. These positions are analogous to stances in the women's and gay rights movements that have pitted assimilationists or revisionists on one side against radical reformers on the other.

---

32 Roberts, *Liberation and Reconciliation*, pp. 51–2.

33 Roberts, *Liberation and Reconciliation*, pp. 59–61.

34 Roberts, *Liberation and Reconciliation*, pp. 67, 80.

35 Roberts, *Liberation and Reconciliation*, pp. 68, 72.

36 Roberts, *Liberation and Reconciliation*, p. 70.

37 Roberts, *Liberation and Reconciliation*, p. 70. He specifically takes issue with Cleage's assertion that the Black Madonnas are 'proof' of Christ's literal blackness, noting that these Black Madonnas involve artistic and aesthetic portrayals and not actual skin colour.

38 Roberts, *Liberation and Reconciliation*, p. 73.

39 Roberts, *Liberation and Reconciliation*, p. xii.

The scholars discussed thus far have carved out a place for the black Christ in today's religious landscape, explaining why a black Christ, whether literal or symbolic, is necessary for African-Americans. More recently, black systematic theologians have sought to explain this Christ's relationship to God and to humanity in more theological language. Thus, Major Jones stresses that in Jesus Christ God entered the world 'fully and explicitly' to reveal Godself to humans as 'God's ultimate purpose for human life'.[40] According to Jones, black Christology does not debate *how* God was in Christ but rather *what* God was doing in Christ – saving and liberating the people through revelation of God's actual nature; the message of Jesus is the proclamation not of himself but of God.[41] Jesus Christ is not abstract but is there with the people ('in yo' face'); this is why black Christians can say Jesus was black, because '[i]n Jesus Christ God has entered the battle for human wholeness'.[42] Jones contrasts black Christology with mainstream (white) Christology, noting that whites have had the 'leisure' to opt out of striving for a balance between the Jesus of history and the Christ of faith. Thus, black Christology fuses the Jesus of history together with the Christ of faith to form a 'third, new man – the Black Messiah of liberation'.[43] Jesus Christ is 'the continual evidence that God is forever at one with the human condition. . . . This is the Black doctrine of the "at-one-ment."'[44] The crux of Jones's Christology is that Jesus' experience of humiliation and oppression not only saved humankind but helped *God* to become different, for the incarnation made possible God's participation in humanity and thus points toward the very blackness of God.[45]

Finally, James Evans notes that contemporary African-American Christology relies upon messianic themes of deliverance and in-gathering of God's people, derived from African-American spirituals that

40 Major J. Jones, *The Color of God: The Concept of God in Afro-American Thought* (Macon, GA: Mercer University Press, 1987), p. 75.

41 Jones, *The Color of God*, pp. 76, 82–3. This is similar to the Christology of Stephen Patterson, discussed in Chapter 3.

42 Jones, *The Color of God*, pp. 85–6.

43 Jones, *The Color of God*, pp. 85–6.

44 Jones, *The Color of God*, pp. 91–2. In similar rhetoric, Gayraud Wilmore has called Jesus 'the Nigger of Galilee'. See Gayraud S. Wilmore, 'Blackness as Sign and Assignment', in *Black Preaching: Select Sermons in the Presbyterian Tradition*, ed. Robert T. Newbold, Jr, (Philadelphia: The Geneva Press, 1977), pp. 165ff.

45 Jones, *The Color of God*, pp. 97–9. Jones notes, 'God's Blackness does not negate his [sic] Whiteness or his [sic] Brownness. In African myth, the divine is sometimes referred to as the Chameleon.'

depict Jesus as both epic hero and revolutionary.[46] Evans disputes the notion that black Christology is 'Jesusology', asserting that there is emphasis on both the humanity and the divinity of Jesus Christ in black Christology.[47]

One can see that, despite their diversity, the Christologies examined above have several things in common. First, they emphasize that blackness is good, that it is part of God's very self, and that, because Christ united God and humanity, Christ was black. Second, they stress the importance of the historical Jesus for a liberation Christology; Jesus' actual life, suffering and death are important indicators of how God is in solidarity with the plight of suffering blacks. Third, they demonstrate that previous traditional Christologies have been lacking because they have not involved the experience of the black segment of humanity; this experience enriches and deepens Christology.

But do these black Christologies go far enough? Is it enough to say that God is on the side of oppressed blacks and therefore God's Christ has the characteristics of blackness? Theologian and historian of black Christianity Kelly Brown Douglas says no.

> Such a Christ challenges Black churches to be prophetic in relation to issues of race, but has little impact beyond that. . . . Yet in order for the Black Christ to be effective and prophetic in relationship to the contemporary Black quest for freedom, it must have meaning in relation to issues beyond White racism.[48]

Therefore, Douglas and other black women scholars have criticized black theology and Christology for focusing on racial oppression alone, at the expense of oppression based upon gender, class and sexual orientation.[49] Douglas points out that '[n]ot everything that is Black is sustaining or liberating for the Black community',[50] noting that much oppression exists within the black community. She concludes that a truly black Christ must empower blacks not only to throw off white racist oppression but to end the self-destructive attitudes and activities

---

46 James H. Evans, Jr, *We Have Been Believers: An African-American Systematic Theology* (Minneapolis: Fortress Press, 1992), pp. 79–82.

47 Evans, *We Have Been Believers*, p. 77.

48 Douglas, *The Black Christ*, p. 5.

49 See Chapter 7.

50 Douglas, *The Black Christ*, p. 84.

of blacks against other blacks:[51] 'A vital and effective Black Christ must reflect the complexities of black reality.'[52]

African Christology

Black reality is different on the continent of Africa from what it is in America. Africa is huge and diverse; one might even say that there are many 'Africas', for the social problems that produce Christological reflection there are different, depending upon what part of Africa one is discussing. Thus, African Christologies are formulated in light of the effects of colonialism, AIDS, drought and famine, and apartheid.[53]

The major purpose of African Christology is to find a view of Christ based in African reality and not merely taken over from European or North American missionaries. Thus, Justin Ukpong lists five ways in which *inculturation Christology* can be articulated in the indigenous cultures of Africa:[54]

1   *Incarnational*: God's Word is incarnated in human cultures; thus one can look for Christ in culture.
2   *Seeds of the Word*: The eternal Logos pervades all cultures, even if it is not known as such.
3   *Functional analogy*: Jesus is redemptive for Africans according to other African deities' patterns.
4   *Paschal mystery*: The resurrection allowed the historical Jesus to escape his cultural limitations, thus allowing him to be inculturated elsewhere.
5   *Biblical*: Since Jesus is God incarnate ('I and the Father are one,' John 8.58), then Jesus was present in Africa before the Christian missionaries; he has thus been one with African culture since pre-Christian times.

Ukpong's purpose in naming these five approaches is to show that one need not dismiss African Christology as exclusively the product of non-

---

51 Douglas, *The Black Christ*, pp. 85–6.

52 Douglas, *The Black Christ*, p. 116.

53 Robert J. Schreiter, 'Introduction: Jesus Christ in Africa Today', in *Faces of Jesus in Africa Today*, ed. Robert J. Schreiter (Maryknoll, NY: Orbis Books, 1991), p. vii.

54 Justin S. Ukpong, 'Christology and Inculturation: A New Testament Perspective', in *Paths of African Theology*, ed. Rosino Gibellini (Maryknoll, NY: Orbis Books, 1994), pp. 41–3.

African missionaries; one may find Christological meaning in African culture itself.

Efoe Julian Penoukou advocates a *functional Christology* that concentrates less on Jesus the person and more on his relationship with people: 'Jesus is really someone for me.'[55] This Christology sees Christ in radical solidarity with African people, thus becoming their Saviour. The Christ Event comes from the 'radical fidelity of God's love for human beings'.[56]

Charles Nyamiti discusses *African traditional (non-Christian) Christology* (similar to Ukpong's principle of functional analogy) by describing how Africans may image Christ as the Chief, the Healer and the Ancestor, categories from pre-Christian African religion.[57] Anselme Sanon adds the category of the Master of Initiation,[58] while François Kabasele notes that Christ can be the Son of the Great Chief (God) and thus the Elder Brother who serves as Mediator.[59]

Perhaps the most important way of seeing Christ in African culture is as the Ancestor, since the 'veneration of ancestors is the cornerstone of the African worldview'.[60] In this way, Africans take seriously their faith in Christ and their own cultural and historical situation, which is quite similar to how Asians have begun to look at Christology.

Asian Christology

Contemporary Asian Christologies examine Christ in the context of Asian culture. However, R. S. Sugirtharajah of India reminds us that the true context of Asian Christology is Christ's importation by colonists from outside Asian culture. Therefore, a hermeneutic of suspicion must be applied, inasmuch as these bearers of Christ were in many cases

---

55 Efoe Julien Penoukou, 'Christology in the Village', in *Faces of Jesus*, ed. Schreiter, p. 25.

56 Penoukou, 'Christology in the Village', pp. 47–8.

57 Charles Nyamiti, 'Contemporary African Christologies: Assessment and Practical Suggestions', in *Paths*, ed. Gibellini, pp. 63, 70. See also Nyamiti, 'African Christologies Today', in *Faces of Jesus*, ed. Schreiter, pp. 3–23.

58 Anselme T. Sanon, 'Jesus, Master of Initiation', in *Faces of Jesus*, ed. Schreiter, pp. 85–102.

59 Francois Kabasele, 'Christ as Ancestor and Elder Brother', in *Faces of Jesus*, ed. Schreiter, pp. 116, 122–3. Mary is said to have taken the place of the chief female ancestor, p. 117.

60 Kabasele, 'Christ as Ancestor and Elder Brother', p. 69.

opposed to Asian culture.[61] Heretofore, Asians were content with accepting European notions of Christianity; in the past 20 years, however, Asian Christians have begun to reconcile their Christianity with their culture, rather than embracing the one at the expense of the other.[62]

Choan-Seng Song of China believes that Asians must develop their own theology and not simply perpetuate that of Europe.[63] In order to do this, Asian Church leaders and theologians have sought to incorporate the stories of people (*minjung*) into theology, thus breaking a Western theological taboo against mingling Christianity with indigenous spirituality out of fear of syncretism.[64] Song notes that Asia is an overcrowded space and yet Christians make up only 3 per cent of the population, and so he warns, 'As long as Christian theology is incapable of dealing with indigenous resources of Asia . . . Christianity will always remain a stranger.'[65] He urges both Western and Eastern theologians to engage in 'third eye theology', that is, using the context of Asian poverty, injustice and exploitation as a lens for doing theology.[66]

The first Asians to interpret Jesus were Hindus, who welcomed him and incorporated him into their pantheon alongside other deities, under various aspects – 'one who has attained liberation while alive', 'lover and fighter for truth' and 'one who has realized destiny with Brahma (God)'. Some Indian Christians subsequently began to interpret him according to Hindu models – 'Lord of creatures', 'consciousness', 'eternal *om*'.[67] Indians noted the similarities between Christ and Krishna and

61 R. S. Sugirtharajah, 'Prologue and Perspective', *Asian Faces of Jesus*, ed. R. S. Sugirtharajah (Maryknoll, NY: Orbis Books, 1993), pp. viii–xii.

62 Douglas J. Elwood, 'Asian Christian Theology in the Making: An Introduction', in *Asian Christian Theology: Emerging Themes*, ed. Douglas J. Elwood (Philadelphia: Westminster Press, 1980), p. 26.

63 Choan-Seng Song, *Third Eye Theology: Theology in Formation in Asian Settings*, revised edition (1979; Maryknoll, NY: Orbis Books, 1990), p. 6.

64 Song, *Third Eye Theology*, pp. 10–11; Elwood, 'Asian Christian Theology in the Making', p. 24.

65 Song, *Third Eye Theology*, pp. 2, 5, 8. A Catholic missionary has suggested that it might be easier to capture the notion of Jesus' kingdom of God in Asia, where Christians are in the minority. Sebastian Kappen, SJ, 'Orientations for an Asian Theology', in *Asian Christian Theology*, ed. Elwood, p. 314.

66 Song, *Third Eye Theology*, pp. 26, 42. See also Elwood, 'Asian Christian Theology in the Making', p. 26: 'Contextualization . . . is . . . "the capacity to respond meaningfully to the gospel within the framework of one's own situation"' (quoting the Theological Education Fund Committee).

67 R. S. Surgirtharajah, 'An Interpretive Foreword', in *Asian Faces of Jesus*, ed. Sugirtharajah, pp. 3–4.

explained it according to their view of multiple incarnations of the Divine:

> Krishna . . . incarnates himself in the world 'whenever the law of righteousness withers away and lawlessness arises.' . . . [I]t is God who takes the initiative in reconciling us to Godself by becoming incarnate.[68]

Buddhists throughout Asia have likened Jesus to the Buddha because both religious leaders saw the problem of human arrogance that gives rise to pain (Buddha) or sin (Jesus), the overcoming of which leads to *dharma* (Buddha) or the reign of God (Jesus).[69] Many Asian Christians thus take a theocentric approach to Christology that sees God becoming one with humanity in many ways and at many times and places, not exclusively in Jesus.[70] Moreover, Asian consciousness understands the intersection of humanity and divinity in Jesus by analogy to the Asian concept of *yin* and *yang*, 'perfect complementarity'.[71]

The major work in Asian Christology has been done by Choan-Seng Song, in his three-volume work *The Cross in the Lotus World*.[72] The lotus is the Asian symbol of comfort and peace, serenity in the midst of turbulence; it represents for Buddhists the deliverance that the cross represents for Christians.[73] Thus, Song uses the lotus as a way of incorporating Asian culture into Christological discourse. Song situates his Christology in a world where 'the poor do christology with an empty stomach', noting that there are more hungry, homeless, unemployed

---

68 Ovey N. Mohammed, 'Jesus and Krishna', in *Asian Faces of Jesus*, ed. Sugirtharajah, pp. 9–11, 22 (quoting *Bhagavad Gita* 4:7).

69 Seiichi Yagi, 'Christ and Buddha', in *Asian Faces of Jesus*, ed. Sugirtharajah, p. 28.

70 See the discussion of the pluralistic paradigm for salvation in Chapter 2.

71 Jung Young Lee, 'The Perfect Realization of Change: Jesus Christ', in *Asian Faces of Jesus*, ed. Sugirtharajah, p. 71.

72 Choan-Seng Song, *Jesus, the Crucified People: The Cross in the Lotus World, Volume I* (1990; Minneapolis: Fortress Press, 1996); *Jesus and the Reign of God: The Cross in the Lotus World, Volume II* (Minneapolis: Fortress Press, 1993); and *Jesus in the Power of the Spirit: The Cross in the Lotus World, Volume III* (Minneapolis: Fortress Press, 1994). My discussion will be concerned primarily with Volume I, inasmuch as it sets forth the whole of Song's *Christology of solidarity*. Volume II specifies that the reign of God was the vehicle by which the solidarity was made known, while Volume III traces Jesus' ongoing presence in Christians through the Spirit.

73 Song, *Third Eye Theology*, p. 119.

and illiterate people in Asia than in the rest of the world put together. This impoverished Asia is 'betrayed' by the affluence of Hong Kong, Singapore, Japan and the 'pseudo-democracies'.[74] In the same way, the 'gold-crowned' Jesus found in many Christian churches betrays the 'real' Jesus, for this gold-crowned Jesus is not interested in the plight of the poor, while the real Jesus is found where the poor live. Thus, the search for the Saviour must begin from troubled humanity.[75] This is Song's presupposition and the hermeneutical key for his Christology.

For Song, Jesus is the story of God, whom he called '*Abba*'.[76] God united with Jesus at his baptism through the Spirit, which 'empowered him to become completely free for God and for all sorts of people'.[77] The cross stifled this radical freedom and so was truly the scandal that the apostle Paul labelled it, for it was a scandal that this 'compassionate man' was hung on a cross. God did not intend the crucifixion, for 'the God of Jesus is not a murderous God,' nor did Jesus seek martyrdom.[78] Song disputes traditional atonement theories as unnecessary in an Asian context, noting that they were devised by those for whom it was a scandal that a divine saviour suffer on a cross. For the suffering poor of Asia, however, it makes perfect sense that a saviour would suffer; this kind of saviour is relatable, for he has become one of the people he came to save.[79]

Song asserts that there are many Christologies ('biographies of Jesus') because there are many 'biographies' of God:[80] for example, God is a speaking God, a listening God, a remembering God and, in the crucifixion, a mute God.[81] The cross was the turning point in the biography of God, for Jesus on the cross was confronted by silence from his *Abba*.[82] This silence of God is the key to Song's Christology, which is actually a type of theodicy: suffering Asians know salvation through Jesus' cross because that was when God became silent; this was not the silence of apathy or unconcern, but rather the silence of grief, pity and compassion. God was shocked into silence. Asian Christians thus find compassion for themselves at the cross of Jesus; and this is what makes

---

74 Song, *Jesus, the Crucified People*, pp. 3, 8.
75 Song, *Jesus, the Crucified People*, pp. 3, 10–11.
76 Song, *Jesus, the Crucified People*, p. 14.
77 Song, *Jesus, the Crucified People*, p. 83.
78 Song, *Jesus, the Crucified People*, pp. 82–4.
79 Song, *Jesus, the Crucified People*, p. 94.
80 Song, *Jesus, the Crucified People*, p. 103.
81 Song, *Jesus, the Crucified People*, pp. 108–11.
82 Song, *Jesus, the Crucified People*, pp. 111, 114.

him Christ, for he is able to interpret God's shocked silence in the face of human suffering.[83]

The historical Jesus is important for Asian Christology, as he is for the other liberation Christologies, because the suffering poor need to know that their Lord was a flesh-and-blood person who suffered as they do and is in solidarity with them because they, like him, possess God's Spirit.[84] Jesus is a 'mirror of the people': that is, to know God, we must know Jesus; but to know Jesus, we must know people, for '[t]he history of Jesus becomes historical in the histories of people.'[85] But the Christness of Jesus is what transcends his historicity and makes solidarity possible. As Christ, Jesus does not remain a Jew or an Anglo-Saxon, but can be Indian, Indonesian, Chinese, Filipino or Thai.[86]

From the foregoing discussion, one can see what links the Christologies of Asians, Africans and African-Americans: each of these peoples images Christ as one of them, through whom they are able to relate to God so that God becomes tangible for them. Each of these peoples has suffered and continues to suffer the scourges of racism and colonization. But the Christ, who transcends race and culture even as he participates in it, delivers them through his ability to be one with them in their circumstances – 'a Savior just like me'.

---

83 Song, *Jesus, the Crucified People*, pp. 114–15, 118–19, 120, 122.
84 Song, *Jesus, the Crucified People*, p. 125.
85 Song, *Jesus, the Crucified People*, pp. 216–18.
86 Song, *Jesus, the Crucified People*, p. 223.

5

A Crucified God for a Crucified People: Latin American Liberation Christology

In the last third of the twentieth century, Latin America – that part of the Americas that includes Mexico, Central America and South America – gave birth to a particular type of theology known as 'the theology of liberation', or, simply, 'liberation theology'.[1] This theology developed among Roman Catholic theologians and clergy, but has influenced the Protestant churches in Latin America as well. It seeks to view all of theology and Church practice through a contextual lens – that is, through 'the eyes of the poor' in Latin America;[2] thus, it is a theology which is at once both critical and reality-based. Because the theology of liberation is a Christian theology, it is thoroughly Christological; nevertheless, a specific liberation Christology has developed alongside and out of the more general work of the liberation theologians. Before examining this Christology, however, it is important to review the origins of the theology of liberation in some detail.

Origins of a New Theology

Unlike more traditional theologies, which are primarily academic in nature, liberation theology has origins that are political and ecclesial as well as academic. Its political origins may be traced to the revolutionary movements of rural guerillas which, inspired by the Cuban revolution, arose in countries such as Venezuela, Guatemala, Brazil and Peru during the 1950s and early 1960s. These revolutionary movements were formed in response to efforts on the part of the sitting governments to

---

1 It is believed that this term was first used by Peruvian priest and theologian Gustavo Gutiérrez in a talk given at Chimbote, Peru, in July 1968. Phillip Berryman, *Liberation Theology: The Essential Facts About the Revolutionary Movement in Latin America and Beyond* (Oak Park, IL: Meyer Stone Books, 1987), p. 24.

2 Berryman, *Liberation Theology*, p. 4.

undo their countries' economic deprivation through 'developmental-ism', which was seen by the peasants as a 'technocratic' means of help-ing Latin Americans to become more economically prosperous through alliances with so-called 'developed' nations such as the United States, but which in fact benefited only those at the 'top' of society.[3] Leagues of dissatisfied peasants were joined by a radicalized middle class, including university students, who brought with them the concepts of Marxism and a new method for education known as *concientizacion* ('conscious-ness-raising').[4]

What started as a political movement began to affect the Church when many rural parish priests, witnessing the abject poverty and physi-cal suffering of the majority of their parishioners, began to see in this situation their Church's complicity with an unjust social order and thus became converted to radical action on behalf of the peasants and against the Church.

The major catalyst for ecclesial involvement, however, took place thousands of miles away from Latin America at the Second Vatican Council, a worldwide ecumenical gathering of Catholic leaders con-vened in Rome by Pope John XXIII in 1962 to stimulate Church reform. Latin American clergy, theologians, and especially bishops, in an atmos-phere of excitement, began to implement these changes, adopting one of Vatican II's key phrases, 'signs of the times', as an important and oft-used slogan for Latin American liberation theologians, who base their critiques of Church doctrine on the 'signs of the times' they see reflected in the lives of the Latin American poor.

Thus, in August 1968, Latin America bishops met at Medellín, Colombia, to correlate for perhaps the first time the Church's mission with the situation of the poor, calling for all Christians to be involved in the transformation of society through 'consciousness-raising evange-

---

3 Berryman, *Liberation Theology*, pp. 13–14; Gustavo Gutiérrez, *A Theology of Liberation: History, Politics and Salvation*, trans. and ed. Sister Caridad Inda and John Eagleson (Maryknoll, NY: Orbis Books, 1973), pp. 82–8.

4 Spanish translation of the Portuguese *conscientizaçao*, a term coined by Brazilian educational theorist Paulo Freire; see, for example, Freire, *Pedagogy of the Oppressed* (New York: Herder and Herder, 1970). Freire's methodology seeks to educate the oppressed out of the their own experience rather than in a conde-scending, 'top-down' fashion; for example, instead of utilizing reading materials on the order of the 'Dick–Jane–Spot' paradigm, according to Freire's method, agricultural workers should be taught to read through the use of concepts from their daily life of farming. This use of daily experience would have ramifications for liberation theology. For a more detailed discussion of Freire's work, see Gutiérrez, *Theology of Liberation*, pp. 91–2 and Chapter 11.

lization' and a commitment to sharing the condition of the poor out of solidarity.[5] A subsequent meeting of the bishops in 1979 at Puebla, Mexico, reaffirmed their commitment to the plight of the poor, especially in light of the coming to power of conservative and repressive governments in many Latin American countries (for example, Bolivia, Uruguay, Chile, Argentina, Peru and Ecuador) during the 1970s.

The Context of Liberation Theology

As a result of these unprecedented gatherings, the Latin American bishops demanded that the Church be converted to a 'preferential option for the poor', and these words became the phrase most associated with the theology of liberation articulated in Latin America. As adopted by theologians, it expressed their central premise: that solidarity with the poor is not only God's primary option but also God's will for the Church. One of the most important innovations of the theology of liberation is its realization that theology can be born at the grass-roots level and that ordinary people themselves are theologians.[6] The bishops went further, asserting that no longer must the Latin American Church be dependent upon Europe for its theological expression.

Subsequently, Latin American academics began to articulate a formal liberation theology. The difference between these theologians and their colleagues in Europe and North America, however, is that their exclusive environment is not academia; they are also committed to working among their people. Many of them divide their time between university or seminary teaching and direct work with the poor on the parish level and in the base communities, so that the questions they raise and address in their theology are those that arise out of this 'hands-on' work among the poor and oppressed of Latin America, for whom they seek to make a difference through the articulation of a theology of liberation.[7]

5 Berryman, *Liberation Theology*, pp. 23–4. One of the tangible ways mentioned by the bishops to demonstrate this solidarity was the support of the new *communidades de base* ('base communities'), small, lay-led groups of Christians which had recently begun springing up throughout Latin America and, as a result of the bishops' statement, would become widespread in later years.

6 Roberto Oliveros, 'History of the Theology of Liberation', trans. Robert R. Barr, in *Mysterium Liberationis: Fundamental Concepts of Liberation Theology*, ed. Ignacio Ellacuria and Jon Sobrino (Maryknoll, NY: Orbis Books, 1993), pp. 3, 13.

7 Berryman, *Liberation Theology*, p. 4. For example, Brazilian theologian and Servite priest Clodovis Boff for many years divided his time between teaching half the year in Rio de Janeiro and spending the other half of the year working with

Perhaps the greatest difference between the Latin American theologians and their First World counterparts, however, is the way in which they approach their task as theologians: They recognize that their method is determined by their context and their social location among the suffering poor and those who are marginalized by the dominant society. Thus, they critique traditional theology as not being 'normative' or 'universal' as commonly supposed, but rather the product of a North Atlantic consciousness resulting from the European Enlightenment.[8]

The Core of Liberation Theology

The 'primary text' of Latin American liberation theology is Gustavo Gutiérrez's A Theology of Liberation, for it recapitulated in scholarly form the theological efforts resulting from the Medellín conference, for which Gutiérrez served as an advisor. Much of the resulting work in liberation theology is an elaboration of the basic themes discussed in this book. In order to understand liberation Christology, therefore, it will be helpful to look at three of the most important themes of liberation theology.

Preferential Option for the Poor

Gutiérrez's theological starting point is more properly described as anthropological: human action must be the point of departure for all reflection; to support this statement, Gutiérrez cites Marxist thought with its emphasis upon 'praxis' as a way of transforming the world, thereby introducing one of the most important terms in the theology of liberation. It is *praxis* by which the Christian Church – and each individual Christian – is to be judged; 'orthopraxis' (right action) is to be valued over 'orthodoxy' (right belief), since, in Gutiérrez's estimation, the traditional Christian emphasis upon orthodoxy, 'often obsessive, [is] often nothing more than fidelity to an obsolete tradition or a debatable interpretation'.[9]

In the situation of Latin America, this praxis cannot be one's undirected action in the abstract but must be one's specific and concrete

---

poor rubber gatherers on the Bolivian border; as a result of this work, Boff developed what he calls *teologia pe-no-chao* ('feet-on-the-ground theology'); Berryman, *Liberation Theology*, pp. 80–1.

8 Berryman, *Liberation Theology*, p. 25.

9 Gutiérrez, *Theology of Liberation*, pp. 7–11.

action toward the poor, whose omnipresence in today's world Gutiérrez characterizes as an 'irruption', the reality of which must be read in the light of Christian revelation;[10] that is, the daily experience of unjust poverty leads to the reception of a Word from the God of Moses and Jesus – that this is not the will of God, that poverty comes from a social system, not from God.[11] In order to prove this, Gutiérrez looks at 'salvation history' in the Hebrew and Christian Scriptures as an organic whole overseen by Yahweh, the God of history, who 'reveals himself as a force in our future and not as an ahistorical being'.[12] He particularly focuses on the Old Testament prophets as programmatic of the Judaeo-Christian praxis which comes to fruition in Jesus.

According to Gutiérrez, all historical liberation takes place because of the incarnation of God in Jesus Christ; for, just as God dwelt in Jesus, the Spirit sent by God and Jesus dwells in each person, with the result that s/he is 'a temple of God', not in an abstract way, however, but, on the contrary, in that person's historical circumstances. This dwelling of God in every human indicates God's preference for humanity's situation. Moreover, because God is present in everyone, we find God in the plight of our neighbour; when we are 'converted' to our neighbour, we are 'converted' to God. Thus, we meet God in our praxis.[13] Moreover, establishment of justice for the poor and oppressed is God's plan for salvation history by means of the poor's own involvement in their liberation through *concientizacion*.[14]

The Political Situation as 'Sin'

Liberation theology's belief that God does not will poverty or oppression for any human person because of humanity's participation in the divine nature (and God's consequential preference for those who are in this situation) results in its second major premise: that whatever keeps humanity in a state of poverty or oppression is contrary to God's will and is therefore sin. This is where liberation theology becomes political theology, for it characterizes the people, structures and governments that relegate the majority of Latin Americans to poverty as sinful, that

10 Gustavo Gutiérrez, 'Option for the Poor', trans. Robert R. Barr, in *Systematic Theology: Perspectives from Liberation Theology*, ed. Jon Sobrino and Ignacio Ellacuria (Maryknoll, NY: Orbis Books, 1996), pp. 22, 26.

11 Oliveros, 'History of the Theology of Liberation', pp. 4–5.

12 Gutiérrez, *Theology of Liberation*, p. 165.

13 Gutiérrez, *Theology of Liberation*, pp. 192–4.

14 Gutiérrez, *Theology of Liberation*, pp. 195, 208.

is, as systemic evil which is contrary to God's intention for God's creation. Gutiérrez shows through careful exegesis that the greatest sins in the Old Testament are unfaithfulness and idolatry; God had provided a mechanism for the elimination of poverty – the sabbatical year (Exodus 23.11) and the jubilee year (Leviticus 25.2–7) – but, due to their arrogance, greed and egotism, sinful elements of the Hebrew nation had ignored Yahweh's instructions, with the result that the poor remained poor and the land became exhausted and unable to produce enough for everyone.[15]

In bold and prophetic rhetoric, Gutiérrez locates this sin in the contemporary world as the 'domination exercised by the great capitalist countries, and especially by the most powerful, the United States of America', noting that the only liberation from this situation will be through social revolution and the formation of a new society.[16]

Centrality of the Reign of God

The third major theme in liberation theology is its insistence on the centrality of the reign (kingdom) of God for any theological reflection or praxis in Latin America. Gutiérrez describes the establishment of the reign as God's ultimate fulfilment and establishment of God's will on earth and locates it in both the Hebrew and Christian Scriptures.[17]

Jon Sobrino has developed this notion in some detail, likening the reign of God to what is 'ultimate in Christian faith', concluding that, for the theology of liberation, '[t]hat to which this theology assigns the primacy is indicated in its very name, liberation, which is understood essentially as the liberation of the poor'.[18] The ramifications which Sobrino sees in this equating of the reign of God with the ultimate goal of liberation theology is that all liberation theology must be (1) *historical*, that is, grounded in actual human circumstances; (2) *praxic*, that is, committed to 'transforming reality'; and (3) *popular*, that is, rooted in the people's experience as both subject (the doers) and object (the recipients) of this theology.[19]

One of the most important aspects of Sobrino's articulation of the reign of God is his description of its opposite – the 'Anti-Reign, the

---

15 Gutiérrez, *Theology of Liberation*, pp. 291–4.
16 Gutiérrez, *Theology of Liberation*, pp. 88–9, 110.
17 Gutiérrez, *Theology of Liberation*, pp. 167–8, 176–7.
18 Jon Sobrino, 'Central Position of the Reign of God in Liberation Theology', trans. Robert R. Barr, in *Systematic Theology*, ed. Sobrino and Ellacuria, pp. 38–9.
19 Sobrino, 'Central Position of the Reign of God', pp. 40–1.

world of sin'[20] whose presence is revealed in the announcement of and quest for the reign. The anti-reign is all that stands against the establishment of God's reign of liberation and justice in this world, that is, the systemic evils of oppression, political repression, torture and 'institutionalized violence'.[21]

Moreover, Sobrino sees the reign of God as 'the Reign of the poor'; that is, 'the basic premise [implied by God's reign] is the primacy of the reality of the poor. In modern language, we should say that the basic premise is the option for the poor.'[22] To put it still another way, one might say that, in Latin America, the reign of God is *incarnated* in the poor and oppressed – a statement which, as we shall see, is programmatic for Latin American liberation Christology. Thus, the centrality of the reign of God in liberation theology also serves to recapitulate and summarize the other two primary themes of the theology – the preferential option for the poor as the content of the reign, and the notion of sin as the content of the anti-reign.

A Christology of Liberation

When one approaches the Christology that has been articulated by the Latin American liberation theologians,[23] one is immediately impressed by two things: first of all, the ecclesial setting of this Christology (in the Church) and its praxis (among the people) differentiate it from recent Christologies that are more theoretical, such as feminist Christology.[24]

---

20 Sobrino, 'Central Position of the Reign of God', p. 43.

21 Ignacio Ellacuria, *Freedom Made Flesh: The Mission of Christ and His Church*, trans. John Drury (Maryknoll, NY: Orbis Books, 1976), p. 168. Ellacuria, in his Marxist-influenced liberation ecclesiology, sees the Church, the recipient of the reign of God through the preaching of Jesus, as the locus of salvation, which must therefore confront sin as manifested in the class structure, the ownership of private property and the resulting class struggle (p. 146).

22 Sobrino, 'Central Position of the Reign of God', pp. 61–2.

23 Unfortunately, there is a dearth of Latin American Christology in English translation; thus, if one is unacquainted with Spanish, one must rely upon the major works that have been translated into English, as I shall do in the following discussion. I believe that these major works make use of the most important of the texts that are not available in English, so the discussion should not be invalidated by their absence.

24 See Chapter 6. It is my impression that the works of feminists of colour are more praxis-oriented than those of white feminists, probably due to the influence of black and Latin American liberation theologians; see Chapter 7.

In this regard, it is much more like the African-American and Asian Christologies that have developed in the past 30 years.[25] Second, and this is no doubt due to its praxic nature, Latin American liberation Christology employs the same information about Jesus as classical Christology, but interprets it differently; that is, rather than giving this information a spiritual focus to formulate theological notions about the Christ in Jesus, this Christology gives the 'facts' about Jesus a material interpretation in order to arrive at ways of seeing the Christ and his salvific power not only in the human Jesus but in every human person. These two characteristics are mandated by Latin American liberation theology's focus on the suffering poor as the contextual lens through which all of theology must be viewed.

Thus, Jon Sobrino is very clear about his method in articulating a Christology for Latin America. His work with populist and university groups has made him aware of the feeling in Latin America that traditional Christologies are 'not good enough'; as a result, his work (along with others') is rooted in the historical Jesus and in the people's pain, because the decision to follow Jesus must give rise to praxis.[26] Moreover, Latin Americans are suspicious of Christology as mediated by the Church's magisterium, because they compare it to what they see as the 'ignoring' of Christ's values by Christians.[27] Traditional Christology's failure for Latin America comes from the ways in which the tradition has described Christ: (1) as abstraction, (2) as universal reconciliation, and (3) as absolute rather than dialectical. An abstract Christ cannot give meaning to the lives of the suffering poor; universality is meaningless without a sense of particularity; and, most importantly, emphasis on the absoluteness of Christ leads to the maintaining of the absoluteness of the status quo, resulting in a deepening of the hopelessness that is already felt by most of the Latin American people.[28]

Thus, it is essential that any Latin American Christology begin with the historical Jesus, for it is from this Jesus that the first Christologies in

---

25 See, for example, James H. Cone, *A Black Theology of Liberation* (1970; Maryknoll: Orbis Books, revised edition 1990); Kelly Brown Douglas, *The Black Christ* (Maryknoll, NY: Orbis Books, 1994); Chung Hyun Kyung, *Struggle to Be the Sun Again: Introducing Asian Women's Theology* (Maryknoll: Orbis Books, 1990); and C. S. Song, *Jesus, the Crucified People: The Cross in the Lotus World* (Minneapolis: Fortress Press, 1996); as well as Chapter 4 of the present work.

26 Jon Sobrino, *Christology at the Crossroads: A Latin American Approach*, trans. John Drury (Maryknoll, NY: Orbis Books, 1978), pp. xi–xiii.

27 Sobrino, *Christology at the Crossroads*, p. xv.

28 Sobrino, *Christology at the Crossroads*, pp. xv–xix.

the New Testament developed. There can be no Christology apart from Jesus of Nazareth.[29] From a Latin American context, to articulate Christ without Jesus is to lift up an idol. This idolatrous Christ is what is preached in fundamentalist and mainline churches in an effort to propagate a 'feel-good Jesus'; but among the poor, a call to feel good is not a call to follow Jesus but to escape a reality from which there is no escape except through liberative praxis.[30]

Nevertheless, the historical Jesus employed by Latin American Christology is not the Jesus whom the so-called 'quests' for the historical Jesus sought to recover in European biblical studies of the nineteenth and twentieth centuries; nor is it the Jesus who has been reconstructed in the United States in recent years by the controversial Jesus Seminar. Unlike these other enquiries, which seek 'the real Jesus' and thus result in a type of 'Jesusology',[31] Latin American liberation theologians study and claim for the poor the Jesus Christ of the New Testament. Consequently, rather than examining only the Synoptic Gospels for the *ipsissima verba et acta* of Jesus, Latin American Christology employs the entire New Testament, not only the Synoptics but the Johannine and Pauline literature as well, recognizing that every New Testament document, including the Synoptics, was written with Christological intent that cannot be divorced from the text.[32] The Christology of the New Testament resulted from Jesus Christ's impact on *the people* around him; therefore, in a Christology of liberation which is being written for *the people*, all of the early reflections upon Jesus as Christ are important, whether or not individual sayings or deeds can be proved to go back to the historical Jesus himself.[33]

Having sketched in broad terms the major aims and characteristics of Latin American liberation Christology, I shall discuss in the following pages the specific Christologies of four of the leading Latin American liberation theologians. Each of these authors has his own area of

---

29 Sobrino, *Christology at the Crossroads*, p. xx.

30 Virgilio Elizondo, 'Foreword', in Justo L. Gonzalez, *Manana: Christian Theology from a Hispanic Perspective* (Nashville: Abingdon Press, 1990), p. 11.

31 Leonardo Boff, *Jesus Christ Liberator: A Critical Christology for Our Time* (Maryknoll, NY: Orbis Books, 1978), pp. 12–14.

32 Sobrino, *Christology at the Crossroads*, p. 13.

33 Thus, it has been noted that whereas the European quest of the historical Jesus sees Jesus as an 'object of investigation', the Latin American quest sees Jesus as the 'criterion of discipleship'. Julio Lois, 'Christology in the Theology of Liberation', trans. Robert R. Barr, in *Mysterium Liberationis*, ed. Ellacuria and Sobrino, p. 174.

concern and view of Jesus Christ, which becomes very clear when they are reviewed in this fashion.

Leonardo Boff, a Franciscan priest from Brazil, was the first of the liberation theologians to discuss Christology at length. Therefore, his book *Jesus Christ Liberator* goes into great detail summarizing European methods and Christological theories prior to describing his own. Boff, in developing his view of Jesus, notes that every theologian writes from his [*sic*] own social standpoint; thus, Boff's Christology comes from a particular moment in history resulting from his social location of solidarity with the oppressed.[34] He has no apology for this contextual approach, for this has been true from the very beginning of Christological reflection.[35] According to Boff, every New Testament author shapes the Jesus story for his [*sic*] community; so it should be no less acceptable for contemporary observers of Jesus to do so: Christology is the 'clarification done by the community afterwards'.[36]

The central element of Boff's Christology is his insistence that Jesus did not come to start a new religion or to preach about himself; rather, he came preaching the kingdom of God.[37] In this Boff is a forerunner of the contemporary Jesus scholars in the United States; however, Boff's dissimilarity to these Jesus scholars – and what makes his work Christology – is his emphasis on the eschatological and utopian nature of Jesus' message of the kingdom.

All Latin American theological reflection is done for the sake of the individual human person, whom it seeks to 'help, raise up, and humanize'. The 'determining element' in the Latin American person is not the past but the future, for the past is one of European colonization and subsequent oppression by those in power, while the future is one of potential and hope. Faith in God through Jesus Christ's announcement of the kingdom promises a 'utopia that consists in a world totally reconciled, a world that is the fulfillment of what we are creating here on earth with feeling and love'.[38] In this way, Boff uses the historical Jesus to make a faith claim based upon the needs of the Latin American people, whose plight he recognizes in the first audience of Jesus. This is why Latin Americans can call Jesus Christ 'Liberator' – because through his earthly proclamation and deeds he offers the possibility of liberation in the here and now.

34 Lois, 'Christology', p. 169. See also Boff, *Jesus Christ Liberator*, pp. 265–6.
35 Boff, *Jesus Christ Liberator*, pp. 5–6.
36 Boff, *Jesus Christ Liberator*, p. 13.
37 Boff, *Jesus Christ Liberator*, pp. 51–2.
38 Boff, *Jesus Christ Liberator*, pp. 44–5.

However, the preaching of the kingdom by Jesus is not something to be interpreted as merely spiritual or utopian; its power comes from its ability to stimulate faith that gives rise to praxis. Use of the word 'kingdom' had a political connotation when used in the context of Roman occupation. 'Messiah', whether or not Jesus understood himself in this way, was a term which ever since the Jewish return from exile carried political overtones and was applied to Jesus by his followers. The Jews had been waiting for a Messiah, who would 'install the kingdom of God'.[39] Nevertheless, Jesus' articulation of the kingdom went beyond the political, and for Boff this is what inspired and continues to inspire faith in Jesus as Christ and is the explanation of the incarnation itself: 'He came to heal all reality in all its dimensions, cosmic, human, social. . . . He really participated in our human condition and took on our deepest longings.'[40] Moreover, Jesus provoked a 'crisis' in his listeners in the original sense of that word: He forced his audience – whether Pharisee or publican – to make a *decision* as to what kind of life they wished to lead and who was in charge of their life (for example, God or mammon).[41]

Jesus' common-sense sayings and deeds of power pointed his followers toward God, and because of their experience of God in Jesus they began to see him as God: 'Only a God could be so human!'[42] Jesus provoked astonishment, both from his followers and from his detractors; this astonishment, for Boff, inspired and continues to inspire Christological reflection.[43]

Boff's view of Jesus as a source of freedom and empowerment logically leads the reader to wonder how he integrates the death of Jesus into his Christology.[44] For Boff, the meaning of Jesus' death must be seen as a continuation of the meaning of his life as a whole: He lived with God as the centre of his existence and proclaimed God's rule to all. Although the

---

39 Boff, *Jesus Christ Liberator*, pp. 57–8.

40 Boff, *Jesus Christ Liberator*, pp. 60–1.

41 Boff, *Jesus Christ Liberator*, p. 103. Boff calls this a 'change of life', his translation of Greek *metanoia*, rendered in most English translations as 'repentance'.

42 Boff, *Jesus Christ Liberator*, p. 178.

43 Boff, *Jesus Christ Liberator*, pp. 142, 233.

44 Boff's analysis of the death of Jesus is, in my opinion, the weakest point of his presentation; this is perhaps due to his reticence before a repressive government. He notes in the preface to the English translation of *Jesus Christ Liberator* (p. xii) that, when the book was originally published in 1972, use of the word 'liberation' in all communication media was forbidden by the government in power; as a result, a 'more open and straightforward type of socio-analytical thought' had to be omitted and subsequently surfaced in the English translation as an epilogue.

end of his life was a 'total disaster and debacle', Jesus was nevertheless confident of God's existence and acceptance to the very end.[45] The total disaster of Jesus' death, which his opponents and disciples alike saw as an abandonment by God and a disavowal of his mission, was overcome and 'revolutionalized' by the resurrection: everyone – including today's poor – can now see that God never abandons.[46] Resurrection is the realization of human utopia:[47] 'The resurrection tells us that the murderer shall not triumph over his [sic] victim.'[48] Thus, according to Boff's Christology, in Jesus' life, death and resurrection, we learn more about God, and, therefore, the possibility of human existence.[49]

Juan Luis Segundo, a theologian who before his recent death also served as chaplain to base communities in his native Uruguay, states emphatically that he would rather write an 'anti-Christology' than a Christology, for Christology is something that is taught, whereas he wishes to preach a gospel that is good news and an open door for the oppressed into the life of Jesus; Christology can never replace the ongoing task of remaking the gospel message.[50] Moreover, 'Christology' implies the study of just one Christ who is inseparable from Jesus of Nazareth; Segundo sees his work as 'anti-Christology' because it seeks to relate Jesus to others and point away from this one Christ who is historically ambiguous.[51] Thus, at once one finds a freshness and an immediacy in Segundo's examination of Jesus.

His purpose in doing (anti) Christology is fully articulated as praxic and contrary to the aims of the European academy: it does not matter from the standpoint of inspiration whether sayings or actions came from Jesus himself or from the evangelist, for the evangelists were writing Gospels, which by their very nature cannot be pinned down. The deposit of Scripture and revelation cannot be closed, according to Segundo. Thus, we can still write gospels; our world-view is different from that of the canonical Gospels, however, so our gospels will appear different. Nevertheless, our modern-day gospels can still capture Jesus if they proclaim the way of Jesus, his life, struggles and courage, along

---

45 Boff, *Jesus Christ Liberator*, pp. 118–19.

46 Boff, *Jesus Christ Liberator*, p.129.

47 Boff, *Jesus Christ Liberator*, pp. 119, 121.

48 Boff, *Jesus Christ Liberator*, p. 291.

49 Boff, *Jesus Christ Liberator*, pp. 243, 251.

50 Juan Luis Segundo, *The Historical Jesus of the Synoptics*, trans. John Drury (Maryknoll, NY: Orbis Books, 1985), pp. 8, 12, 17.

51 Segundo, *Historical Jesus*, pp. 15–16.

with his message that God is not indifferent but is in solidarity with humanity then and now.[52]

Part of Segundo's methodology is his belief that it is the fatal misunderstanding of Christology to assume that we know all we need to know about Jesus' life. The Gospels give us information, but the evangelists themselves were aware that they were writing Christologies not histories. They injected into the texts their own understanding based on his life, death and resurrection *after the fact*. Therefore, our faith in who Jesus can be for us must not come from any mere biography because we cannot fit Jesus into any one scheme.[53]

Christology is using faith in Jesus to interpret some aspect of our present situation. Nevertheless, for Segundo the faith *of* Jesus is more important and illuminating than faith *in* Jesus: what he believed in, for example, his openness, his view of God, his concept of the kingdom, is more dispositive than simple reflection upon his person.[54] The only valid approach to Jesus is through the New Testament with its many meanings, not through the dogmas of the Church. Thus, Christology must start 'from below' and multiply its meanings; to settle for only one meaning of Jesus Christ is idolatry, and to think that we can ever locate an uninterpreted Jesus is 'sheer illusion'.[55]

The central insight of Segundo's own (anti) Christology is his realization that if we strip away our preconceived, doctrinal notions of Jesus Christ, we will find a Jesus who was involved in conflict.[56] Segundo sees Jesus as a political agitator with roots in Old Testament prophetism. Jesus reveals God and judges humanity in order to lead people to meaningfulness in their lives; but in order to do this, Jesus had to attack the political structure of his day.[57] The kingdom of God is important because it is the key to Jesus' message and identity. 'Good news' and

---

52 Segundo, *Historical Jesus*, pp. 5–12. Segundo begins a later book with this quote from Jose Ramon Guerrero: 'Every human being and every generation has to experience, discover, and put together its own gospel about Jesus'; Juan Luis Segundo, *An Evolutionary Approach to Jesus of Nazareth*, ed. and trans. John Drury (Maryknoll, NY: Orbis Books, 1988), p. 1.

53 Segundo, *Evolutionary Approach*, pp. 2, 6.

54 Segundo, *Evolutionary Approach*, pp. 10–11.

55 Segundo, *Historical Jesus*, pp. 39–40.

56 Segundo, *Historical Jesus*, pp. 71–72. Segundo notes that Paul's Jesus is not conflictive because Paul's *Sitz im Leben* did not call for Jesus to be so; this seems to me a very cavalier way of dealing with a potential argument against Segundo's presentation of Jesus.

57 Segundo, *Historical Jesus*, pp. 72, 80, 85.

God's 'will on earth' carry political connotations, for good news to the poor means bad news for those outside the poor; a proposed upheaval in the social structure of society is a political demand.[58]

Moreover, Jesus reveals a compassionate God, one who will welcome more and more groups into the eschatological kingdom. This is a hard message for humanity to hear, however; Segundo states that the truly radical meaning of Jesus' presentation of the kingdom can only be arrived at through the lens of liberation. It requires a 'change of outlook' (his translation of *metanoia*); this is what the parables sought to reveal. Jesus' parables of liberation require a shift from a notion of privilege to a notion of responsibility; the key texts which demonstrate this shift are the Lost Sheep and the Prodigal (Luke 15), the Good Samaritan (Luke 10), and the Sheep and the Goats (Matthew 25), for each of these parables shows Jesus' 'systematic dismantling of oppressive ideologies'.[59]

One of Segundo's most striking suggestions in his portrayal of Jesus is that Jesus' intent was different depending upon whom he was addressing. Traditional Christology assumes that the message of Jesus was either one of judgement *or* of love. Segundo prefers to view the matter dialectically by suggesting that Jesus' preaching called for conversion by those opposed to the kingdom of God (that is, those in power), but called for prophetism and conscientization on the part of those already regarded as sinners (that is, those without power). He buttresses his claim on the fact that each of the Synoptic evangelists constitutes the mission of Jesus differently; three different Christologies give rise to three different ecclesiologies, leading Segundo to wonder whether this difference in mission might go back to the historical Jesus himself.[60]

In approaching the death of Jesus, Segundo notes that Jesus was mistaken regarding the end; he had taught with eschatological urgency and believed in an irruption of the kingdom of God during his lifetime. However, Segundo urges that in assessing the end of Jesus' life, contemporary interpreters must apply the 'political key', that is, recognize that Jesus, himself influenced by political events, became a victim of politics. Nevertheless, his community reaped the benefits of his struggle, for in the resurrection the kingdom was accomplished.[61] This so-called political key forces us to confront the very core of Christology: if one asserts,

---

58 Segundo, *Historical Jesus*, pp. 88, 91.
59 Segundo, *Historical Jesus*, pp. 118–20, 128, 131.
60 Segundo, *Historical Jesus*, pp. 134–5.
61 Segundo, *Historical Jesus*, pp. 164–5.

'Jesus is God,' one must ask, 'then why didn't he do something about the plight of the poor and oppressed?' But if one states, 'Jesus is human,' one is able to answer that question by asserting, 'He did – he demonstrated and brought to fruition the Kingdom of God.'[62]

Ignacio Ellacuria, a Spanish Jesuit priest who spent his professional life in El Salvador, displays his passion for liberative praxis by joining Christology with ecclesiology. He insists that Jesus, embodied in and incorporated into human history, is the historical body of God, the full actualization of God in humanity. The Church, carrying on what Jesus began, is the historical body of Jesus, as Jesus was of God; in this way, the Church functions as a 'sacrament of liberation', revealing Jesus Christ and his God.[63]

In exploring this new Christological dimension of the Church's role, Ellacuria is critical of previous Christologies, believing that Greek philosophical thought has 'deformed Christian praxis'. Only secularized faith and theology can have meaning for a secularized world; thus, the purpose of education and theology must be service to the community; for Ellacuria, this is what differentiates Latin American liberation theology from what has gone before. In serving the community, every Christian must be aware of the historicity of salvation; if this theme is not dealt with, other themes of theology will not acquire their full import. Thus, Ellacuria's most important theme in his mix of Christology and ecclesiology is the contrast between 'salvation history' (which has assumed a supernatural focus as a term of art) and 'salvation in history' (which comes from 'real life situation and necessity').[64]

The result of salvation becoming historical in Jesus is twofold: first, it differs according to time and place; and, second, it comes about in the historical reality of human persons. Jesus is 'the Lord *of History*', necessitating that Christianity take seriously the ramification of the Word becoming flesh *in human history*; to realize this, Ellacuria asserts, is to do political theology. By our praxis, Christians must continue to 'prepare the way of the Lord', for contemporary history lies in the interval between the first and second comings of Christ.[65] Nevertheless, the political nature of the first coming has been obscured by Christologies

---

62 Segundo, *Evolutionary Approach*, pp. 65–6.

63 Ignacio Ellacuria, 'The Church of the Poor, Historical Sacrament of Liberation', trans. Margaret D. Wilde, in *Mysterium Liberationis*, ed. Ellacuria and Sobrino, p. 546.

64 Ellacuria, *Freedom Made Flesh*, pp. 3–9.

65 Ellacuria, *Freedom Made Flesh*, pp. 13–18.

which Ellacuria characterizes as 'ahistorical', 'ignorant' of exegetical method, and infected with a 'mere desire to continue what has been said before'.[66] The political character of the New Testament gives rise to distinct Christologies as the same events were synthesized and systematized in different ways, dictated by the needs of the community; for example, Paul's treatment of Jesus differs from that of the Synoptics not because he was unacquainted with the historical Jesus but because the situations he addressed differed.[67]

In approaching the figure of Jesus, Ellacuria believes that what is most important about him is his prophetic nature. Like an Old Testament prophet, Jesus stood over against the 'hierarchical apparatus' of Judaism and rejected the 'moribund, ritualized' aspects of the religion in order to introduce a shift from a strictly religious emphasis to operative faith. The significance for Christology is that Ellacuria believes the realization of his prophetic status by the people led eventually to a realization of his 'divine Sonship' (citing John 6.14). As a result, the religious hierarchy regarded Jesus as a dangerous enemy, for they saw his preaching as presenting a radical judgement which led the common people, then as now, to make a conscious decision to follow the way of Jesus. This following of Jesus cannot be strictly personal but must involve a public, sociological conversion resulting in the transformation of a public situation.[68] Jesus places his lot with the poor and oppressed and demands that whoever would follow him do the same; praxis is the proof of one's devotion to Christ.[69]

That one cannot escape the political situation through spirituality and religion is demonstrated by the fact that Jesus' entire life was spent in a period of 'maximum politicization'.[70] Nevertheless, Ellacuria believes that Jesus was – and insisted upon being recognized as – more than a mere political figure. His own awareness of his Messiahship was slow and hesitant and was confirmed at his baptism; his self-presentation was grounded in messianic consciousness, as seen in the political nature of much of his preaching. However, what differentiated him from the Zealots and other messianic pretenders was his notion of the interiority

---

66 Ellacuria, *Freedom Made Flesh*, pp. 23–4.

67 Ellacuria, *Freedom Made Flesh*, pp. 25–6. One should note that his use of Paul and John distances Ellacuria's study of Jesus from other works on the historical Jesus; but this is due to his view of Christology as interpretation of the same events through the lens of one's individual historical situation.

68 Ellacuria, *Freedom Made Flesh*, pp. 27–33.

69 Ellacuria, *Freedom Made Flesh*, pp. 36–40.

70 Ellacuria, *Freedom Made Flesh*, pp. 41–50.

of the kingdom. It is *inward* conversion to God's reign that results in *outward* behaviour. Thus, Ellacuria notes that Jesus repeatedly rejected the temptations of 'false Messianism': in the desert with Satan (his disavowal of an earthly dominion), at Caesarea Philippi upon Peter's confession ('get behind me, Satan'), and at the Mount of Olives (his rejection of armed resistance).[71]

Ellacuria's greatest contribution to Latin American liberation Christology is his treatment of the crucifixion of Jesus and the cross of Christ. Citing the Medellín documents, he likens the situation of Latin America to that of Palestine at the time of Jesus: misery, frustration, poverty and the desire for revolution amid the egotistical and selfish interests of organized wealth in a class system. In a situation such as this, the people react to 'institutionalized violence' with struggle and aggression; but popular struggle and aggression are not the same as violence, which is derived from injustice and inequity, for the former are spontaneous while the latter is deliberate. Abuse of power, then as now, results in (1) legislation that tries to perpetuate an unjust situation, (2) political torture, and (3) falsehood propagated to mislead. 'Faced with such a situation, the Christian cannot remain inactive.'[72]

Thus, for Ellacuria, the crucifixion was a direct consequence of these social circumstances. Jesus did not come (was not sent) to be crucified but to convert; the crucifixion was a violent response from a violent and ungodly hierarchy. But if the crucifixion is understood in this way, as a political punishment rather than as a theological necessity, then the cross of Christ may be used to combat future violence by saying 'no' to repressive tactics on the part of oppressive governments.[73] Thus, rather than sentimentalizing the cross, Christians must recover the scandal of Jesus' passion if we do not wish to lose its relevance. When seen in this way, as a scandal rather than as a soteriological intention on the part of God, the lens of the cross allows us to recognize the poor and oppressed of this world as saved and liberated beings who can become saviours and liberators in their own right.[74]

---

71 Ellacuria, *Freedom Made Flesh*, pp. 53–63.

72 Ellacuria, *Freedom Made Flesh*, pp. 168–75, 198, 203. A key text for Ellacuria at this point is the Epistle of James, which equates love with praxis. For an excellent exegetical treatment of this text from a Latin American perspective, see Elsa Tamez, *The Scandalous Message of James: Faith Without Works Is Dead*, trans. John Eagleson (New York: Crossroad, 1992).

73 Ellacuria, *Freedom Made Flesh*, pp. 216, 227.

74 Ellacuria, 'The Crucified People', p. 582.

Ellacuria's view of the crucifixion as essential to a liberation Christology does not mean that he downplays the resurrection, however; but rather than seeing the resurrection as a great *deus ex machina* that saves the day after Jesus has failed (as Boff does), Ellacuria sees it as pointing back to the crucifixion: The crucifixion was an example of the reign of sin (the anti-reign) which the resurrection overcomes by showing the triumph of the reign of God as announced by Jesus in his life and person. 'Since his life was taken away for proclaiming the Reign, he receives new life as a fulfillment of the Reign of God.' One cannot transfer the meaning of the reign of God on to the resurrection alone, because this betrays Jesus' life and death. Rather, the resurrection points toward the passion and crucifixion, which in turn point back to the life of Jesus and his proclamation of God's reign. This carries an important theological message to the persecuted Christians of the early Church, as well as the persecuted masses in Latin America: that they must not give up on the realization of the reign of God.[75]

Jon Sobrino, also a Jesuit of Spanish descent living and working in El Salvador, has written several major works on Christology. For Sobrino, the frame of reference for a Latin American Christology must be the theology of liberation with its analysis of underdevelopment and oppression in the Third World.[76] The locus of Christology is 'where faith and life meet'; for liberation Christology, that is the 'congruence' between the historical Jesus' situation and the situation in Latin America – the utopian longing for liberation.[77] Sobrino's early Christology is 'dialectical' in nature: its centre is the reign[78] of God but one must realize that our notion of that reign is formulated in terms of Jesus, while Jesus' life is presented in the New Testament in terms of the reign. Thus, according to Sobrino, we can only know Jesus through the Reign, and we can only know the reign through Jesus; although the Jews already had a notion of God's reign, it was nevertheless 'radicalized' in Jesus' praxis.[79] Jesus expresses the very content of God's reign in his pardon of those considered as sinners by society and religion – those who had fallen through the

---

75 Ellacuria, 'The Crucified People', pp. 584–6.

76 Sobrino, *Christology at the Crossroads*, p. 33 (citing Gutiérrez).

77 Sobrino, *Christology at the Crossroads*, pp. 12, 34–5.

78 It is noteworthy that as early as 1978 Sobrino and his translator had begun using the more inclusive term 'reign' rather than 'kingdom' as a translation for Greek *basileia* and Hebrew *malkuth*. Sobrino explains in the text that it is a better translation because it conveys dynamism rather than staticity; *Christology at the Crossroads*, p. 43.

79 Sobrino, *Christology at the Crossroads*, pp. 37, 41–2.

cracks; true sin for Jesus is not one's status vis-à-vis religion but rather a saying 'no' to the reign of God.[80]

This saying no to God's reign was a denial of God's power and was manifested by an improper use of power and the creation of oppressors and oppressed – religious intolerance, ignorance and poverty emanated from the systemic sin of not sharing power. Power which is not dedicated to service is sin; conversion is making a choice (*metanoia*) to use one's power in service to others. Through his teaching of the reign of God and his revelation of appropriate power in his own person, Jesus demonstrated the true nature of God. Thus, according to Sobrino, the divinity of Jesus flows from his essential humanity: God is revealed in Jesus' understanding of God's reign, and salvation comes from a person's stance toward Jesus.[81] Jesus' fidelity to his mission (announcing God's reign) is true faith, and through this faith Jesus becomes the Son of God. Sobrino therefore believes that Jesus reveals to humanity more properly the Son rather than the Father (in contrast to the Gospel of John and later Church doctrine).[82]

In his later work, Sobrino refines his theory of Jesus' life by demonstrating systematically that the historical Jesus reveals two things through his life: the reign of God and the nature of God. The Gospels can supplement what we think we know of the reign from the Old Testament by what they present in Jesus' actions and in the recipients of his message; the reign is manifested in Jesus' acts of compassion, but, additionally, the reign's basic character is shown by the character of those to whom it was addressed: it is a kingdom of nobodies – the oppressed, those cast away by society, those on the margins. This is the essential good news of the kingdom – that God has come near to those heretofore considered expendable, and this is good news for today's Latin American people as well.[83]

Even more important is what Jesus' life tells us about the Divine through the ways in which Jesus himself related to God – as his Father. This Father God for Jesus was the positive force which gave his life meaning and to which he turned throughout his life during times of need and indecision.[84] Jesus' ultimate relation to this Father God was one of

---

80 Sobrino, *Christology at the Crossroads*, pp. 46–51.
81 Sobrino, *Christology at the Crossroads*, pp. 53–69.
82 Sobrino, *Christology at the Crossroads*, pp. 90, 105.
83 Sobrino, *Jesus the Liberator*, pp. 70–104. See also Lois, 'Christology', pp. 176–78; and Sobrino, 'Central Position of the Reign of God', pp. 46–58.
84 Sobrino, *Jesus the Liberator*, pp. 135–143.

trust, so that, even after the crisis in his ministry in Galilee, he was still able to journey to Jerusalem to reveal the inbreaking of this God's reign.[85] There, he confronts the 'anti-reign' and is put to death by the forces of that anti-reign – the very idols Jesus had sought to expose as opposers of his Father God.[86]

In approaching the death of Jesus, Sobrino differentiates between the historical issue of why Jesus was killed and the theological issue of why Jesus died.[87] This is an important component of his later Christological work, and it is clear that he is continuing the work of his late friend and colleague Ignacio Ellacuria. In his earlier work, Sobrino did not make this formal distinction, but instead discussed Jesus' death in terms of the suffering of God revealed through the suffering of God's Servant, Jesus.[88] He thus criticized other Christologies for concentrating on the 'what' of the cross rather than the 'why', maintaining that a cutting edge of the cross's scandal was lost in its interpretation as a soteriological tool in the hands of God. From a liberation perspective, the possibility of God's own suffering gives meaning to the cross; we must renounce Christological doctrine from Greek thought that portrayed God as impassable and immutable, for the inability of God to suffer contradicts the notion that God is love. (Compassion means 'fellow feeling'.) For Latin American people, 'only a God who suffers can save us'.[89]

Twenty years later, informed by his own experience, Sobrino begins his discussion of Jesus' death by stating that 'the cross of Jesus points us to the crosses that exist today . . . The crucified peoples of the Third World are today the great theological setting . . . in which to understand the cross of Jesus.'[90] Sobrino still believes in the suffering of God, but supplements his earlier interpretation with sober reflection on the historical reason for Jesus' death:

[I]n the simple words of Archbishop Romero, 'Those who get in the way get killed.' Jesus, surrounded by conflict, got in the way, in the

85 Sobrino, *Jesus the Liberator*, pp. 146, 152.

86 Sobrino, *Jesus the Liberator*, pp. 160–79. For a fuller treatment of this, see Sobrino's 'Excursus 2 – The Question of God: God of Life and Idols of Death', in *Jesus the Liberator*, pp. 180–92.

87 Sobrino, *Jesus the Liberator*, p. 195.

88 Sobrino, *Christology at the Crossroads*, p. 184. Sobrino believes that the Suffering Servant of Yahweh from Second Isaiah was lost as an important Christological image when the early Church chose to concentrate on more triumphalist images for Jesus such as Messiah, Lord, Son, and finally God.

89 Sobrino, *Christology at the Crossroads*, pp. 185–97.

90 Sobrino, *Jesus the Liberator*, pp. 195–6.

last resort because he got in the way of the other gods and got in their way in the name of God.[91]

Thus, in Sobrino's estimation, as long as people 'get in the way' of sinful ideologies and the anti-reign, there will continue to be crucifixions (for example, Archbishop Romero, the seven martyrs at Central American University, and all the poor who continue to die a slow death at the hands of oppression). This is why Jesus was killed. Consequently, we must not sentimentalize the cross of Christ, for, if we do, we risk trivializing his entire life and message. Instead, Sobrino urges his readers to see that by not sparing Jesus God showed greater solidarity with all those who suffer – that God entered into Jesus' suffering (and enters into today's suffering) in a more personal way.[92]

Ultimately, however, the 'why' of Jesus' death confronts every Christology with the issue of theodicy, a mystery which has been debated theologically and philosophically for thousands of years. Nevertheless, Sobrino boldly suggests that God, as Jesus' Father, through solidarity with 'His Son' becomes 'the Crucified God'.[93]

The solidarity of God with humanity and the trusting interpenetrating relationship between God and Jesus lead to the cross. It is in this cross that the revelation of God's nature is complete: God becomes a victim.[94] This is the central message that the cross conveys to the Latin American people today, and it is a message that inspires hope in the utopia of the reign of God. Nevertheless, Sobrino sees the resurrection as the definitive event that reveals God.[95] The resurrection indicates that in Jesus God was definitively revealed – God could be crucified but would rise again. Therefore Jesus became through this act of resurrection first the exalted Lord and then very God. Consequently, Sobrino asserts, the incarnation is not the starting point of Christology but rather the culmination.[96] The incarnation is the gradual becoming of Jesus into Christ through his life, his temptations, controversies and trials, his passion, his crucifixion and finally his resurrection. No part of this process is insignificant. This is what the mixture of humanity and divinity in Jesus reveals, and it is revelatory of not only God but of human potential.

---

91 Sobrino, *Christology at the Crossroads*, p. 196.
92 Sobrino, *Christology at the Crossroads*, p. 231.
93 Sobrino, *Christology at the Crossroads*, pp. 248–9.
94 Sobrino, *Christology at the Crossroads*, p. 251.
95 Sobrino, *Christology at the Crossroads*, p. 240.
96 Sobrino, *Christology at the Crossroads*, pp. 265–8.

Conclusion

It is clear from the foregoing discussion that Latin American liberation theology articulates a Christology different from what has gone before. By way of conclusion, let us summarize its major points.

First of all, Latin American liberation Christology sees Jesus not as the eternal Christ who condescended to become human in order to save the human race. Rather, it sees Jesus as a human person who, through his daily life experiences and his special connection with God, *gradually* became Christ and was subsequently recognized as 'God' by his followers. The praxic ramifications of this stance are obvious: if this happened to Jesus, it can happen to today's poor and oppressed; by persistence in their daily lives and by emulating Jesus in their struggle for liberation from the worldly structures of sin and evil, they can triumph and become 'Christ-ed'.

Second, Jesus reveals God in his person, through his practice, and through those to whom he addresses his message. He brings good news to the marginalized of every time and place through his inclusion of others, his openness to the human situation, and his special relationship with the Father God who is compassionate and all-loving. His healings, exorcisms and miraculous feedings are signs of this God and the fact that God's reign is coming near. This witnesses to contemporary Latin America that its present plight is not the will of God, and that God in Christ seeks to do something about it in the here and now.

Third, to assist God in this work, humans must become converted to the way of Jesus – praxis. This means undergoing conscientization, fighting for justice and liberation, and struggling against the 'Anti-Reign,' which manifests itself in unjust structures, systems and governments. It means boldly denouncing the status quo when it does not meet the needs of 'the least of these' and unmasking those who claim to speak in God's name but instead serve other gods.

Finally, this Christology recognizes that the God seen in Jesus is also the crucified God – the God who is a victim, who suffers and is humiliated, who will eventually triumph, but for now is consigned to the cross. This cross is God's sign of solidarity with those who suffer daily humiliation, oppression and death. Resurrection and the consummation of the reign of God are held out to all people as a utopia to be hoped for, but in the present the most important Word from God is the human Jesus who embraces all and suffers for all and, in this way, becomes God for all.

6

God's Representative as a Guide to Wholeness: Feminist Christology

Just as black theology and Latin American liberation theology grew out of the political awakening of blacks and poor people and their ensuing quest for liberation and social justice, feminist theology developed out of women's recognition of their inferior status in society and culture. Beginning in the 1970s, women joined together politically to assert their equality to men and to demand and pass equal rights legislation, a movement which is popularly known as the women's liberation movement or the second wave of feminism.[1] This new consciousness carried over into every area of daily life, including religion; thus, many women took what they were learning and experiencing in the political realm and put it into practice in communal expression in churches and synagogues, resulting in a thoroughgoing critique of traditional faith systems.[2] A central focus of this critique was Christology, specifically the relevance of the male person Jesus for the salvation of women. Before discussing the feminist Christologies that have developed over the past 30 years, however, it is necessary to review the origins of feminist theology in general, so that feminist Christology may be understood in the overall context of feminist religious consciousness.

Origins of Feminist Theology

At its core, the incipient feminist theology of the 1960s and 1970s was all about liberation. As women became more intent on becoming full

---

1 Yasmine Ergas, 'Feminisms of the 1970s', in *A History of Women in the West, Volume V: Toward a Cultural Identity in the Twentieth Century*, ed. Françoise Thébaud (Cambridge and London: The Belknap Press of Harvard University Press, 1994), p. 528.

2 Rita M. Gross, *Feminism and Religion: An Introduction* (Boston: Beacon Press, 1996), p. 39.

participants in Church and society, they began to formulate a new 'feminist' theology, which involves a 'profound criticism of every aspect of theology' in 'excruciating tension with the institutional church' for it brings to light what has been overlooked or deliberately silenced.[3] The ultimate goal of Christian feminists is the elimination of all dualisms (man vs woman, body vs spirit, rich vs poor, etc.) through the delegitimizing of hierarchy. Since women's oppression is structural in the Christian Church, many feminists believe that only when *male* reality is *de*constructed can it be *re*constructed in more *human* terms.[4] These new theological articulations of women's consciousness developed in universities and seminaries alongside direct activism within many Christian denominations around such issues as contraception, abortion and women's ordination.[5] At the same time, Catholic feminists were encouraged by indications of potential change resulting from the Second Vatican Council.[6]

It is customary, in discussing feminist religious scholars, to differentiate between 'reformists' and 'revolutionaries':[7] reformists are those who seek to remain in the Church while challenging structures and theologies which are unfriendly to women,[8] while revolutionaries are those

---

3 Sandra M. Schneiders, *Beyond Patching: Faith and Feminism in the Catholic Church* (New York/Mahwah: Paulist Press, 1991), pp. 1–3.

4 Schneiders, *Beyond Patching*, pp. 27, 33, 36. The primary problem, according to Schneiders, is that men have always been defined by their humanity, whereas women have been defined by their gender (i.e. their reproductive capacity), leading her to conclude that what are regarded as 'human rights' are, in actuality, 'male rights' (pp. 10–11).

5 Although not exclusively a feminist issue, the controversy over homosexuality should also be understood as stemming from the same new consciousness that arose from the questioning of gender roles. See Kathy Rudy, *Sex and the Church: Gender, Homosexuality, and the Transformation of Christian Ethics* (Boston: Beacon Press, 1997), especially Chapters 2 and 5, as well as my own discussion in Chapter 8 of the present work.

6 In remembering Vatican II, Mary Daly writes: 'It seemed to everyone . . . that the greatest breakthrough of nearly two thousand years was happening. . . . There was an ebullient sense of hope. Most of us thought then that this meant there was hope for the church. . . . [I]t appeared that a door had been opened *within* patriarchy which could admit an endless variety of human possibilities.' Mary Daly, *The Church and the Second Sex, with the Feminist PostChristian Introduction and New Archaic Afterwords by the Author* (1968; Boston: Beacon Press, 1985), p. 9.

7 See, for example, Gross, *Feminism and Religion*, p. 107.

8 Such 'reformists' would include, among others: in Catholicism, Anne E. Carr, Elizabeth A. Johnson, Rosemary Radford Ruether, Sandra M. Schneiders, Elisabeth Schüssler Fiorenza and Mary Jo Weaver; in Protestantism, Rita

who find the Church irredeemably sexist and thus advocate an exodus by women from the Church.[9] However, in the early days of religious feminism, even those who eventually left the Church were still hoping to reform it from within by offering a critique of its structures, systems and doctrine.[10]

The stage had been set for the rise of women's religious consciousness as early as 1960, when Valerie Saiving published a landmark and iconoclastic essay entitled 'The Human Situation: A Feminine View',[11] in which she suggested that women's differing life experience results in different religious sensibilities concerning such doctrinal issues as sin, grace, and the nature of the human person. Specifically, Saiving noted that male theologians described our estrangement from God ('sin') as a result of pride, whereas women's experience of sin is quite different. For women, struggling to develop self-esteem and self-actualization in a patriarchal and androcentric world, pride is *not* a sin; on the contrary, *lack* of pride is the sin.[12] In this way, Saiving deconstructs the notion that there is a 'common' humanity irrespective of our own social location, a belief that is essential to liberation theology, especially when discussing the issues of sin and salvation.

Saiving spoke theoretically and in generalities; nevertheless, her essay was the catalyst that stimulated women in seminaries and the academy to begin doing specific theological thinking from a women's perspective.[13] Nearly a decade later, Mary Daly, both the earliest and most

Nakashima Brock, Beverly Wildung Harrison, Carter Heyward and Susan Brooks Thistlethwaite; and in Judaism, Judith Plaskow.

9 Such 'revolutionaries' would include, among others, Carol Christ, Mary Daly, Naomi Goldenberg and Daphne Hampson.

10 For example, Carol Christ, after receiving her PhD from Yale Divinity School, taught Christian theology for several years before leaving to pursue Goddess spirituality; and Mary Daly, an associate professor at Jesuit-run Boston College, had the clear intention in her early writings of offering constructive criticism to the Church, but then began to believe that this effort was fruitless due to the patriarchal nature of every aspect of the Church.

11 Valerie Saiving, 'The Human Situation: A Feminine View' (*The Journal of Religion*, April 1960), reprinted in *Womanspirit Rising: A Feminist Reader in Religion*, ed. Carol P. Christ and Judith Plaskow (New York: Harper & Row, 1979), pp. 25–42.

12 Saiving, 'The Human Situation', p. 37.

13 For example, Carol Christ and Judith Plaskow, while graduate students at Yale Divinity School in the 1960s, began questioning how their curriculum interacted with their gender and what the ensuing relationship was (if any) to Church and society. See their comments in the Preface to their anthology, *Womanspirit Rising*, pp. ix–xi.

controversial of the feminist theologians, revisited Saiving's concerns in a more specific fashion. Desiring to obtain advanced degrees in sacred theology and philosophy – a path not open to women in the United States in the 1960s – Daly attended the University of Fribourg, Switzerland, and, due to her proximity, was able to attend Vatican II. In the immediate aftermath of the Council, Daly was inspired to begin critiquing the status of women vis-à-vis the Roman Catholic Church (with the intent of changing it), and the result was her landmark book *The Church and the Second Sex*, which after more than 30 years is still used as a basic text for religious feminism. Daly's primary contribution to the field of feminist theology was in articulating its major problem: that women cannot feel a part of a religion or Church that has 'restricted or mutilated [their] existence'.[14]

Using her training as theologian and philosopher, Daly examined Church history and traditional theology from a woman's vantage point,[15] and concluded that all of the Church's systems and structures were tainted with sexism and with a misguided view of 'the eternal feminine'[16] which is buttressed by Church teachings, doctrines and directives.[17] Daly took issue with the relegation of women in Church and society to a symbol, noting that 'women in fact are not symbols; they are people, and each person is a unique subject. To consider a person – a subject – as a symbol is to treat him or her as an object.'[18] She boldly asserted that such objectifying as symbol is at the heart of Catholic devotion to Mary the mother of Jesus, thereby enunciating a theme that has been developed by later feminist theology: that the image of Mary as virgin and mother is an impossible role for women to imitate, yet they are told by the Church that this should be their highest aspiration.[19] She

---

14 Daly, *The Church and the Second Sex*, p. 53.

15 Daly, *The Church and the Second Sex*, Chapter 2.

16 Daly, *The Church and the Second Sex*, Chapter 4.

17 Daly, *The Church and the Second Sex*, Chapter 3. This view of the 'eternal feminine', also called the 'cult of domesticity' or the 'cult of true womanhood', has been documented by feminist historians of religion; see, e.g., Rudy, *Sex and the Church*, Chapter 2, and Barbara J. MacHaffie, *Her Story: Women in Christian Tradition* (Philadelphia: Fortress Press, 1986), Chapter 6. Most recently, in post-colonial feminist discourse, this view has been termed the 'myth of the White Lady'. See Kwok Pui-lan, 'The Image of the "White Lady": Gender and Race in Christian Mission,' in *The Power of Naming: A Concilium Reader in Feminist Liberation Theology*, ed. Elisabeth Schüssler Fiorenza (London: SCM Press; Maryknoll, NY: Orbis Books, 1996), pp. 250–8.

18 Daly, *The Church and the Second Sex*, p. 161.

19 Daly, *The Church and the Second Sex*, 159–61. For a feminist discussion of

called for the Church to perform an 'exorcism' of all the images of women (such as the Eternal Woman, the Madonna and the Pin-up Girl) that do not promote wholeness,[20] insisting that 'radical surgery is required' in the Church's theology, particularly regarding the maleness of God.[21]

By the time Daly published *Beyond God the Father*[22] in 1973, however, she had abandoned any attempt to reform the Christian Church and, in a well-publicized event, staged her own 'exodus' from Christianity and its oppressive theology.[23] Perhaps because she had freed herself from the constraints of a traditional Christian identity, Daly was able to go much further in *Beyond God the Father* than she had in *The Church and the Second Sex*. For in this work she refused to be a slave to 'methodolatry',[24] preferring to quote women's oral tradition, rather than be limited by the usual academic means of citing previously published work. In a thorough examination of theological categories, Daly called for the 'castration' of God – indeed the 'death' of God the Father

---

Mary, see Elizabeth A. Johnson, CSJ, 'The Marian Tradition and the Reality of Women', in *Horizons on Catholic Feminist Theology*, ed. Joann Wolski Conn and Walter E. Conn (Washington, DC: Georgetown University Press, 1992), pp. 85–108; Rosemary Radford Ruether, *New Woman, New Earth: Sexist Ideologies and Human Liberation* (New York: The Seabury Press, 1975), Chapter 2; and Ruether, *Sexism and God-Talk: Toward a Feminist Theology* (Boston: Beacon Press, 1983), Chapter 6.

20 Daly, *The Church and the Second Sex*, pp. 170, 176.

21 Daly, *The Church and the Second Sex*, pp. 179–80.

22 Mary Daly, *Beyond God the Father: Toward a Philosophy of Women's Liberation, with an Original Reintroduction by the Author* (1973; Boston: Beacon Press, 1985).

23 On 14 November 1971, Daly was invited as the first woman to preach the Sunday morning sermon at Harvard Memorial Church. She used this opportunity to cut her ties with organized religion, calling for other women to join her in removing themselves from an institution that did not want them, stating that 'sisterhood is an *exodus community* that goes away from the land of our fathers . . . It is a positive refusal to be co-opted anymore . . . Let us affirm our faith in ourselves and our will to transcendence by rising and walking out together.' Mary Daly, 'The Women's Movement: An Exodus Community', reprinted in *Women and Religion: A Feminist Sourcebook of Christian Thought*, ed. Elizabeth Clark and Herbert Richardson (New York: Harper & Row, 1977), pp. 270–1.

24 Daly, *Beyond God the Father*, p. 11. This book sees Daly's creation of a new feminist language: ' [W]omen have had the power of naming stolen from us. . . . The method of liberation, then, involves a *castrating* of language and images that reflect and perpetuate the structures of a sexist world. It castrates precisely in the sense of cutting away the phallocentric value system imposed by patriarchy' (pp. 8–9).

– if women are to survive, making her famous statement, 'if God is male, then the male is God'.[25] Any anthropomorphizing of God, whether as Father or as Mother, is not only unnecessary but downright dangerous; rather, she insisted that God must become a *verb* of dynamic energy so that our human becoming may continue.[26]

Development of Feminist Theology

I have discussed Mary Daly in some detail because her thought is foundational to most subsequent feminist theology. In the decades succeeding the exodus of Daly and other post-Christian feminists from Christianity, countless dissertations, articles, monographs and books have been written on feminist theology, exploring a variety of themes including, as we shall see, Christology. Before turning to a detailed description of feminist Christology, however, it will be useful to examine the work of two other scholars who have greatly influenced feminist religious studies – one in the area of historical theology and the other in the area of biblical studies – inasmuch as their contributions to feminist theological theory in general have made possible the development of a specifically feminist Christology.

The presentation of a feminist systematic theology which Mary Daly had begun in *Beyond God the Father* came to fruition in the work of Rosemary Radford Ruether, who has rightly been included among the most important theologians of the twentieth century (feminist or non-feminist).[27] Ruether's major contribution to feminist studies in religion has been her contextualizing in history of the problem of patriarchy articulated by Daly. Ruether was the first to compile an anthology about sexism in religion[28] and in her own work has demonstrated the basic androcentrism of the Judaeo-Christian tradition, the insidiousness of dualism, and the realization that patriarchy can be found as the source of any pattern of domination and subjugation.[29] Her many criticisms of

---

25 Daly, *Beyond God the Father*, p. 19.

26 Daly, *Beyond God the Father*, pp. 32–3.

27 Ed L. Miller and Stanley J. Grenz, 'Theology of Women's Experience: Rosemary Radford Ruether', in Miller and Grenz, *Fortress Introduction to Contemporary Theologies* (Minneapolis: Fortress Press, 1998), pp. 159–76.

28 Rosemary Radford Ruether, ed., *Religion and Sexism: Images of Women in the Jewish and Christian Traditions* (New York: Simon and Schuster, 1974).

29 Miller and Grenz, 'Rosemary Radford Ruether', pp. 165–9. See especially Rosemary Radford Ruether, 'Motherearth and the Megamachine: A Theology of

Christianity (which have earned her the everlasting enmity of conservative Christians[30]) include her insistence that there can be no such thing as universal objective theology, thus necessitating a listening to the experience of the oppressed and a bringing forth of voices previously silenced. Her theological method is a dialectical one consisting of three interrelated parts: (a) the critical engagement of history to reveal patriarchy; (b) the recovery of alternative traditions; and (c) the recasting of traditional categories.[31]

Ruether's criticisms of Christianity long pre-dated her feminism, however. Her first book, *The Church Against Itself*, encouraged the contemporary Church to strip away the mythology and self-delusion of triumphalist ecclesiology, noting that the Church must be engaged in the human situation as the place where human estrangement from God is accepted and overcome.[32] Ruether thus articulated early in her career a theology of radical social change: the Church as an eschatological community must be at war with the historical church as a *communio peccatorum* (community of sinners): 'To be itself the Church must constantly repent of itself.'[33] Ruether's work in the area of human oppression began with the publication in 1972 of *Liberation Theology: Human Hope Confronts Christian History and American Power*, in which she used her work in the peace and civil rights movements, as well as the burgeoning Latin American liberation theology and feminist movements, to critique contemporary society. In acknowledging that *this* world we see is not God's creation, she asserted that the solution is not *flight* from the world (as encouraged by traditional Christian theologies), but rather engagement of this world through *fright*. Liberation comes from grace in the midst of fear, which leads to self-judgement and ultimately repentance. This repentance can undo social oppressions, the oldest of which is the oppression of women.[34]

Liberation in a Feminine, Somatic and Ecological Perspective' (*Christianity and Crisis*, April 1972), reprinted in *Womanspirit Rising*, ed. Christ and Plaskow, pp. 43–52; and Ruether, *Sexism and God-Talk*, Chapter 3.

30 For example, Elizabeth Achtemeier, who has questioned Ruether's Christianity (Miller and Grenz, 'Rosemary Radford Ruether', p. 174).

31 Miller and Grenz, 'Rosemary Radford Ruether', pp. 163, 164, 168.

32 Rosemary Radford Ruether, *The Church Against Itself: An Inquiry into the Conditions of Historical Existence for the Eschatological Community* (New York: Herder and Herder, 1967), pp. 2, 12.

33 Ruether, *The Church Against Itself*, pp. 223, 237.

34 Rosemary Radford Ruether, *Liberation Theology: Human Hope Confronts Christian History and American Power* (New York/Mahwah: Paulist Press, 1972), passim but especially pp. 4, 6, 9, 17–18, 95.

In 1975, Ruether 'threw down the gauntlet', as it were, by publishing *New Woman, New Earth: Sexist Ideologies and Human Liberation*, in which she began to incorporate the new feminist consciousness into her critique of religion and society. She directly confronted the Catholic Church for its sexism, noting, among other things, that Mariology is not liberating to women, that Church roles mirror societal roles, and that the Church's understanding of ministry must change.[35] She followed this up eight years later with *Sexism and God-Talk: Toward a Feminist Theology*, a thoroughgoing systematic theology from a feminist perspective. Ruether here takes as her starting point the proposition that women's experience is foundational to a feminist theology, just as male experience served as the basis for all theology up to this point.[36] She thus advocates a reclaiming of women's history, including female images of the Divine (which she names 'God/ess' due to the irredeemably androcentric nature of the word 'God'), the reclaiming of the prophetic and wisdom traditions, and the incorporating of strands of Christian tradition heretofore deemed heretical, such as Gnosticism.[37] Her conclusion regarding sin and grace is that the '-isms' in our current world result from the basic sin of hierarchy, that is, the cyclical pattern of domination and subjugation (which in a patriarchal world is the sin of patriarchy). Salvation comes through the undoing of social categories of oppression.[38] Feminism can be revelatory for the Church as it pushes it toward reconciliation between peoples, a respect for the earth, and an insistence upon realized eschatology, that is, the recognition that we must make this world a better place now rather than postpone liberation to some end-times scenario.[39]

When one approaches the work of Elisabeth Schüssler Fiorenza, one finds a very different feminist perspective, inasmuch as her training is in biblical studies and early Christian origins. Nevertheless, she maintains that an artificial separation has been enforced between biblical studies and theology, and she seeks to bridge this gap by joining theological interpretation to the task of biblical exegesis. Her methodology requires constant and vigilant contextualizing, inasmuch as these related yet dis-

---

35 Rosemary Radford Ruether, *New Woman, New Earth: Sexist Ideologies and Human Liberation* (New York: The Seabury Press, 1975), pp. 58, 74, 80.

36 Ruether, *Sexism and God-Talk*, Chapter 1.

37 Ruether, *Sexism and God-Talk*, Chapter 2.

38 Ruether, *Sexism and God-Talk*, Chapters 3, 4, 7.

39 Ruether, *Sexism and God-Talk*, Chapters 8, 9, 10.

crete areas of religious studies have been corrupted by both scholarly sexism and a misguided need to maintain detached objectivity.[40]

Schüssler Fiorenza, in pursuing her hermeneutical theory with regard to the texts of the early Christian Church, believes that one must approach the text with a 'hermeneutics of suspicion', the acknowledgement at the start of the endeavour that one is not receiving the entire story due to the patriarchal elimination of significant voices from the composition, translation and subsequent interpretation of the text; she therefore engages in a process of 'reading the silence' to regain those silenced voices.[41] Thus, her approach to the topic of women in the Church is in contrast to Daly's: whereas Daly would say that women have been deliberately kept out of the Church's history and structures, Schüssler Fiorenza would say that they have not; on the contrary, women have always been a part of the Church from its earliest days, but their presence has been intentionally erased or downplayed by those in power.[42] This she calls the 'patriarchalization' of the Church, which

---

40 Elisabeth Schüssler Fiorenza, *Bread Not Stone: The Challenge of Feminist Biblical Interpretation* (Boston: Beacon Press, 1984), pp. 130–1 (citations omitted).

41 Schüssler Fiorenza, *Bread Not Stone*, pp. 15–22. Schüssler Fiorenza presents here a new feminist model of biblical interpretation which because of its radicality is worth quoting at length: 'Since all biblical texts are formulated in androcentric language and reflect patriarchal social structures, a feminist critical interpretation begins with a *hermeneutics of suspicion* rather than with a hermeneutics of consent or affirmation. It develops a *hermeneutics of proclamation* rather than a hermeneutics of historical factualness . . . [I]t develops a *hermeneutics of remembrance* that moves from biblical texts about women to the reconstruction of women's history. Finally, this model moves from a hermeneutics of disinterested distance to a *hermeneutics of creative actualization* that involves the church of women in the imaginative articulation of women's biblical story' (p. 15). For an example of 'reading the silence', see Elisabeth Schüssler Fiorenza, *But She Said: Feminist Practices of Biblical Interpretation* (Boston: Beacon Press, 1992), p. 70. This method has also been employed in the new queer biblical interpretation; see, for example, Robert Goss, *Jesus ACTED UP: A Gay and Lesbian Manifesto* (New York: HarperCollins, 1993), Chapter 4; and Robert E. Goss and Mona West, eds, *Take Back the Word: A Queer Reading of the Bible* (Cleveland: The Pilgrim Press, 2000).

42 Unlike Daly, Schüssler Fiorenza sees the purpose of feminist theology as twofold: '[F]eminist theology as a critical theology of liberation has developed over and against symbolic androcentrism and patriarchal domination within biblical religion, while at the same time seeking to recover the biblical heritage of women for the sake of empowering women in the struggle for liberation'; Elisabeth Schüssler Fiorenza, *In Memory of Her: A Feminist Theological Reconstruction of Christian Origins* (New York: Crossroad, 1985), p. xxii.

changed the Christian community from the egalitarian community of Jesus to the hierarchical Church of the later books of the New Testament in order to adapt the new Church to the patriarchal structures of the Roman Empire.[43]

Much of Schüssler Fiorenza's work, therefore, has been in re-reading early Christian sources to ascertain women's actual role in the earliest communities. This work has been tremendously useful for the women's ordination movement, for Schüssler Fiorenza has demonstrated that there are examples in the New Testament of women who worked as apostles alongside the traditional male apostles,[44] combating the Vatican's statement that, since Jesus recognized only male apostles, then priests, as their successors, must also be male.[45] (This focus on the women around Jesus is also a key argument in her feminist Christology, as we shall see below.)

Having examined these feminist theologians' work at length, I believe it is possible to ascertain three distinct positions regarding women and religion, which will impact our discussion of feminist views of Jesus Christ: (1) Mary Daly's position is, *We women were never wanted in the Church; let's leave.* (2) Rosemary Radford Ruether's position is, *We women were never wanted; but let's stay and change that reality by our activism.* (3) Elisabeth Schüssler Fiorenza's position is, *We women were always present in the Church and were wanted by Jesus; let's stay and return the Church to its earliest state.*

Major Issues in Feminist Christology

When one turns to a feminist discussion of Jesus Christ, what, then, are the major issues? How do feminist theologians view the person and work of Christ through the lens of ongoing gender discrimination and the feminist aim of deconstructing patriarchy and its dualisms? I believe that the major feminist Christological issues may be summarized as follows:

---

43 Schüssler Fiorenza, *In Memory of Her*, pp. 288–94.

44 Elisabeth Schüssler Fiorenza, 'Word, Spirit and Power: Women in Early Christian Communities', in *Women of Spirit: Female Leadership in the Jewish and Christian Traditions*, ed. Rosemary Radford Ruether and Eleanor McLaughlin (New York: Simon and Schuster, 1979), pp. 29–70.

45 Both Popes Paul VI and John Paul II have been adamant about this. See Rosemary Radford Ruether, 'Entering the Sanctuary II: The Roman Catholic Story', in *Women of Spirit*, ed. Ruether and McLaughlin, pp. 373–83.

1 Who is Jesus for women?
2 What is the theological impact of the maleness of Jesus?
3 What does the patriarchal teaching about the relationship of God and Christ mean for women's existence?
4 How does the traditional view of the work of Christ (salvation and atonement) empower or oppress women?

We will learn the answer to these questions by examining some specific feminist Christologies that have developed in the past 20 years. For the sake of clarity, I organize the discussion around particular feminist authors rather than concepts; in this way one may see the uniqueness of individual feminist perspectives that tends to become obscured when grouping their thought by topic.

Specific Feminist Christologies

I begin with the Christology of so-called 'revolutionary' feminists, which is actually no Christology at all, for they totally dismiss the significance of Christ's person or work for women's human becoming, which is their central concern. Mary Daly, for example, describes Christology as 'Christolatry' that perpetuates the overall 'distortion' of reality perpetuated by Christian theology. A male saviour only serves to legitimize male superiority, which she sees as Christianity's 'original sin' against women. Instead, Daly proposes that 'Christianity itself should be castrated by cutting away the products of supermale arrogance.'[46]

Daly rejects attempts to 'reclaim' Jesus for women by portraying him as a feminist because of his interactions with women, stating, 'Fine. Wonderful. But even if he wasn't, *I am*.'[47] She does not believe that women's affirmation can be found in the past and its symbols, but only in the future through women's own becoming, concluding that 'women have the option of giving priority to what we find valid in our own experience without needing to look to the past for justification'.[48] Women's experience negates a Christ figure who is a scapegoat, for this image

---

46 Daly, *Beyond God the Father*, pp. 69, 71.

47 Daly, *Beyond God the Father*, p. 73, responding to the important and ground-breaking essay by Leonard Swidler entitled 'Jesus Was a Feminist', *The Catholic World* (January 1971), pp. 177–183. Daly asserts that Swidler's suggestion is another example of male naming, thus introducing the feminist argument that men can neither be feminists nor describe or define feminism.

48 Daly, *Beyond God the Father*, p. 74.

reaffirms the goodness and usefulness of victim status, a position that is deadly for women's self-actualization, inasmuch as they have been the victims of male dominance throughout history.[49] Daly concludes her Christological discussion by suggesting that perhaps the Antichrist feared by the Church patriarchs is really the coming of Woman to full personhood, a 'Second Coming' that is not a return of Christ but an 'arrival of female presence'.[50]

Concurring with Daly, other revolutionary feminists have turned to worship of the Goddess, believing that Jesus Christ cannot symbolize the liberation of women.[51] For these post-Christians, it is impossible to articulate a feminist Christology because Christ is the central symbol of the Christian faith: Christ's maleness is inextricable from both his person and the theology that has developed around him; moreover, Christ is Christianity's central symbol precisely because of the Christian belief that Christ is God, which reinscribes worship of a male deity. Thus, British feminist philosopher Daphne Hampson sees feminist efforts to concentrate on the 'Christ-Spirit' or 'Sophia' or the humanness of Jesus or his ethical teaching (theories to be discussed below) as the reducing of Christianity to mere humanism: 'Christianity is also a belief – if the salt is to retain its savour – in Christ.'[52] She is critical of the work of Rosemary Radford Ruether and Elisabeth Schüssler Fiorenza, charging that historical reconstruction of early Christianity is a fruitless endeavour since, in her estimation, the problem with Christianity is precisely its roots as a historical religion:[53] 'I deny that there could be a particular revelation of God in any one age which thenceforth becomes normative for all others.'[54] Christology is therefore incompatible with feminism's purpose of female empowerment, because the maleness of Christ 'cannot be evaded'. And, since there can be no Christianity without a Christology, true feminists cannot be proper Christians.[55]

---

49 Daly, *Beyond God the Father*, pp. 76–7.

50 Daly, *Beyond God the Father*, p. 96.

51 Naomi R. Goldenberg, *Changing of the Gods: Feminism and the End of Traditional Religions* (Boston: Beacon Press, 1979), pp. 22, 63. Some Goddess feminists have adopted the term 'thealogian', believing that the word 'theologian' refers to articulation of a male deity. See, for example, Carol P. Christ, 'Why Women Need the Goddess: Phenomenological, Psychological, and Political Reflections', in *Womanspirit Rising*, ed. Christ and Plaskow, pp. 273–87.

52 Daphne Hampson, *Theology and Feminism* (Oxford: Basil Blackwell, 1990), p. 4.

53 Hampson, *Theology and Feminism*, pp. 28, 34.

54 Hampson, *Theology and Feminism*, pp. 7–9.

55 Hampson, *Theology and Feminism*, pp. 50, 75.

One of the difficulties of Hampson's position is that she assumes that all Christology is high Christology, that is, belief in the absolute divinity of Christ, whereas many contemporary Christologies affirm a low Christology that de-emphasizes the divinity of Christ in favour of the humanness of Jesus.[56] She dismisses any feminist discussion of the usefulness of Jesus' message or his special relationship with God by flatly stating that admiration for Jesus' teachings or God-consciousness does not make one a Christian; Hampson has thus defined Christian identity quite narrowly as the belief that Jesus Christ was God Himself, was the representation of God, and, because male, confirmed the maleness of God that is oppressive to women.[57]

When one turns to the so-called 'revisionist' feminist theologians, Rosemary Radford Ruether would agree with Hampson that Christianity is a historical religion, but rather than using this as an excuse to abandon it, Ruether sees Christianity's historicity as the reason for embracing it and learning from its historical context in order to inform our own. Consequently, in her earliest Christological work, Ruether insisted that we must engage the 'hermeneutical circle' between one's own contemporary question or situation and the interpretation of Jesus as the Christ. The historical context of Jesus' message was 'political opposition both to Roman imperial domination and to the oppression of the Palestinian poor by the local ruling classes'.[58] It is precisely this historical setting that can elucidate contemporary struggles for liberation. Just as Latin American liberation Christology concentrates on the historical Jesus and his message of the reign of God, Ruether's early work seeks to show that Jesus' message was one of 'radical social iconoclasm' that looked to the fundamental roots of oppression and suggested a new concept of leadership based on service.[59] Ruether locates the problem of traditional Christology in the misunderstanding of the non-occurrence of the *parousia* (or Second Coming of Christ); she notes that when Jesus did not return as the disciples thought he would, his outwardly directed message was shifted onto his person (the messenger

---

56 Thus, British feminist theologian Julie Hopkins notes, in criticism of Hampson, that Christology cannot be monolithic and that it is possible to be a Christian and not profess the divinity of Christ; Julie Hopkins, *Towards a Feminist Christology: Jesus of Nazareth, European Women and the Christological Crisis* (London: SPCK, 1995), p. 76.

57 Hopkins, *Towards a Feminist Christology*, pp. 51–3.

58 Rosemary Radford Ruether, *To Change the World: Christology and Cultural Criticism* (New York: Crossroad, 1981), pp. 3, 7.

59 Ruether, *To Change the World*, pp. 15–17.

became the message[60]), thus relegating his immediate historical and social context to a position of less importance than his role as the Christ.[61] She notes that once this shift of emphasis to his person took place, Christological doctrine became both anti-female and anti-Jewish, as women and Jews began to be seen as 'the other', in relation to Jesus Christ, leading her to conclude that anti-Judaism developed as the 'left hand' of Christology.[62] This realization led Ruether to locate women's second-class status in the Church in the assumption that only a male could properly image and represent Christ because of his historical maleness,[63] which in turn led her to formulate the often-quoted question that has guided all of her subsequent Christological reflections: 'Can a male savior save women?'[64]

Ruether's initial answer to this question was to deflect the issue from the salvific ramifications of Jesus' divinity to a reclaiming of the biblical roots of the concept of 'Christ' – the Anointed One who would be the righteous ruler that the Israelite kings had not been. She thus concentrated in her early work upon Jesus' teaching and his message of an egalitarian reign of God, concluding that we must reformulate our views of Messiah as 'proleptic and anticipatory rather than final and fulfilled'.[65] Her view of Christ's work is consequently one of looking ahead to the creation of a better world, rather than the 'one-time occurrence' that a Christology of divine personhood and traditional atonement seeks to elaborate.

---

60 See Thomas Sheehan, *The First Coming: How the Kingdom of God Became Christianity* (New York: Vintage Books, 1986).

61 Ruether, *To Change the World*, p. 32.

62 Ruether, *To Change the World*, pp. 31, 45.

63 Ruether, *To Change the World*, p. 46. See also Ruether, 'Entering the Sanctuary II: The Roman Catholic Story', for a critique of the women's ordination debate in Roman Catholicism.

64 Ruether, *To Change the World*, p. 47: '[T]he question of whether a male saviour can save women is not merely a provocative theoretical question. It is one on which many thousands of women have already voted with their feet by leaving the church and seeking alternative feminist communities.' This is analogous to gay and lesbian persons' relationship to organized religion, to be discussed in Chapter 8 of the present work.

65 Ruether, *To Change the World*, pp. 11–12, 42. In an earlier work, Ruether had noted that this proleptic way of seeing the Christ Event as still continuing (with an 'already/not yet' dimension) also serves to delegitimize Christian anti-Judaism, for this looking ahead need not be supercessionist nor anti-Semitic. See Ruether, *Faith and Fratricide: The Theological Roots of Anti-Semitism* (New York: The Seabury Press, 1974), p. 250.

In *Sexism and God Talk*, describing what a systematic feminist theology might look like, Ruether elaborated this Christology by highlighting Jesus' placement in a long line of Hebrew prophets who battled the status quo in order to usher in a more just society for the poor and oppressed.[66] Thus, for Ruether, an essential part of contemporary Christology is articulating a new world order; this means first critiquing the existing order, which Ruether does by explaining the dualisms upon which the traditional doctrines of human personhood, sin and grace, and salvation are founded.[67] In Ruether's opinion, these dualisms stem from patriarchy as the ultimate sin that has created wrong relationship in the world; salvation occurs through the undoing of this wrong relation by the forging of right relation in the empowerment of all people as God's children created in God's image.[68] It is within this view of the present world as the locus of salvation that Ruether situates her later Christology, which sees Jesus not as an otherworldly king but as God's servant, who is sent to liberate but ultimately suffers.[69]

In applying this servant Christology to the status of women, Ruether points out that the women surrounding Jesus were the 'oppressed of the oppressed' and his ministering to them was an honouring of those who had no honour in the patriarchal system. She insists that in this view of Christ, the maleness of Jesus 'has no ultimate significance', for Jesus as servant of all – especially women – stands for the 'kenosis [emptying] of patriarchy, the announcement of the new humanity'.[70] In this new humanity, the notion of 'Christ' is not limited to one person but becomes the province of every person who seeks to follow Christ.[71]

Thus, Ruether's ultimate answer to her question, in contrast to Daly and Hampson, is that, yes, a male saviour *can* save women – not through his maleness, however, but because of his overthrowing of

---

66 Ruether, *Sexism and God-Talk*, pp. 33, 120.

67 Ruether, *Sexism and God-Talk*, Chapter 3.

68 Ruether, *Sexism and God-Talk*, p. 113: 'Women want to tear down the walls that separate the self and society into "male" and "female" spheres. This demands not just a new integrated self but a new integrated social order. Thus the recovery of holistic psychic capacities and egalitarian access to social roles point us toward that lost full human potential that we may call "redeemed humanity."'

69 Ruether, *Sexism and God-Talk*, pp. 120–1 (emphasis added).

70 Ruether, *Sexism and God-Talk*, pp. 136–7.

71 Ruether, *Sexism and God-Talk*, p. 138. Compare the statement of German medieval mystic Meister Eckhart (who was condemned as a heretic) that we are 'called to be other Christs'. See Matthew Fox, *Original Blessing: A Primer in Creation Spirituality* (Santa Fe, NM: Bear and Company, 1983).

patriarchal privilege and his empowerment of the personhood of the most oppressed of his day.[72] His context informs our context: because Jesus was a revelation to those of his day, he can provide ongoing revelation in our day.

Episcopal priest and feminist theologian Carter Heyward agrees with Ruether that redemption in Christ is not about Christ doing it for us, but about empowering us to human wholeness, which Heyward defines as mutuality.[73] Heyward is not interested in developing a systematic Christology for women, however; rather, she is more interested in how the person of Jesus intersects with Christian feminists' quest for mutuality and full personhood. The importance of Heyward's work for feminist and queer Christology is that, as an open lesbian, she seeks to link sexuality with notions of gender and redemption. The love that humans share with one another is the love of God, which is 'erotic power' to join us together sexually and otherwise in an ongoing interpenetration of mutual relation that is God.[74] Thus, for women and homosexuals, two groups that have traditionally been defined negatively by their sexuality, Heyward seeks to reclaim the connection between sexuality and spirituality.[75]

Theology for Heyward is all about relation; the incarnation of Jesus is about God 'relating' to humankind in a special way. But the incarnation of God did not begin and end in Jesus: it occurs in every person when we emulate Jesus and the image of God that he personified – not the male image, but rather the image of wholeness and right relation with all creation.[76] However, Heyward rejects the notion that Jesus was divine, asserting that 'Jesus matters only if he was fully, and only, human,' pre-

---

72 Rosemary Radford Ruether, *Women and Redemption: A Theological History* (Minneapolis: Fortress Press, 1998), pp. 277–8: 'What distinguishes Jesus as normative is not his maleness but the quality of his humanness . . . One imitates Christ by living in a like manner, not by possessing male genitalia.'

73 Isabel Carter Heyward, *The Redemption of God: A Theology of Mutual Relation* (Lanham, MD: University Press of America, 1982), p. 2: 'Simply because we are human, we are able to be co-creative agents of redemption. . . . The redemption of the world . . . is dependent upon our willingness to make love/justice in the world. In so doing, we co-operate with each other and with God in a process of mutual redemption.'

74 Carter Heyward, *Touching Our Strength: The Erotic as Power and the Love of God* (New York: Harper & Row, 1989), pp. 94–5.

75 See, for example, Carter Heyward, *Speaking of Christ: A Lesbian Feminist Voice*, ed. Ellen C. Davis (New York: The Pilgrim Press, 1989); and *Touching Our Strength*, Chapters 4 and 6.

76 Heyward, *Redemption of God*, pp. 9–11.

ferring to base her Christology not on who he was ontologically (as the Council of Chalcedon did), but rather on what he did, his fostering of love and justice in this world.[77] Heyward's relational Christology depends more upon others' reaction to Jesus than the actual sayings and deeds of Jesus, which may be seen in her interpretation of the resurrection:

> The resurrection may have been a reflection of Jesus' friends' unwillingness to admit his death. . . . But Christian faith does not rest on the fact of Jesus' physical resurrection. . . . Christian faith does not encourage us to deny the finality of death in the course of a lifetime. To the contrary, it seems to me most faithful – empowering – to acknowledge the death of Jesus as the final act of contempt against this lover of God and humanity; and to acknowledge the resurrection as an event not in Jesus' life but rather in the lives of his friends.[78]

Heyward's traditionalism may be seen in her unwillingness to dispense with Jesus, as Mary Daly has encouraged. She eschews the type of feminist separatism that has become Daly's battle cry, stating that she is 'hooked on Jesus' and regards him as a 'beloved brother'.[79] Yet she does recognize that Jesus' maleness has been deeply problematic for women; however, she locates the problem not with Jesus himself but with the patristic theologians who needed to reimage him as an eternal and triumphalist Christ.[80] The solution for a feminist Christology, according to Heyward, is a counter-reimaging through which we become one in our humanness with the humanness of Jesus that pointed toward God.[81]

The intersection of the human and the divine in the person of Jesus is the special focus of the Christology of Roman Catholic feminist theologian Elizabeth Johnson, who articulates what I would term a 'non-traditional traditional Christology', for, unlike Heyward, she does not

---

77 Heyward, *Redemption of God*, pp. 31–2.
78 Heyward, *Redemption of God*, p. 58.
79 Heyward, *Redemption of God*, pp. 196, 199.
80 Heyward, *Redemption of God*, p. 167.
81 Heyward, *Redemption of God*, p. 199: 'Jesus is to be remembered, not revered. Remembering Jesus does not warrant Jesusolatry or Christolatry, the idolatry of a male God. Remembering Jesus does not warrant the worshipping of Jesus, but rather compels us to be open to the God of Jesus.' Heyward's most recent Christological reflections are contained in *Saving Jesus from Those Who Are Right: Rethinking What It Means to Be Christian* (Minneapolis: Fortress Press, 1999).

see Jesus as only human; on the contrary, accepting the traditional Chalcedonian doctrine, she explores Scripture and tradition to ascertain what it meant for Jesus to be both human and divine. Nevertheless, Johnson cautions Christian women regarding the way Christ has been interpreted by a patriarchal Church, 'with the result that the good news of the gospel for all has been twisted into the bad news of masculine privilege'.[82] She thus concurs with Schüssler Fiorenza that the original Jesus movement was an egalitarian one that later 'distorted' the Christ figure. Unlike Daly and Hampson, Johnson believes that the maleness of Jesus is one historical detail among many that has no theological or Christological importance; rather, the difficulty is in how the Church has interpreted that maleness: (1) to reinforce a male image of God by portraying Jesus Christ as the only Son of the Father, bearing 'His' image to humanity; (2) to give the male gender superiority by virtue of the fact that God 'condescended' to become incarnate in a male body; and (3) to jeopardize women's salvation by obscuring whether God in Christ became 'human' (inclusive of women) or 'man' (exclusive of women).[83] Johnson rehearses the subtle ways in which Church teaching has used the historical Jesus' gender to create the eternal Christ as a weapon against women's empowerment, and concludes that the Church needs to become clearer about whether Jesus became 'human' or 'man'. If it is the latter, then this is obviously problematic for women's becoming, but Johnson believes unequivocally that it is the former: Jesus became human, thus allowing for the possibility of all types of human becoming.[84]

In insisting that the Word became human flesh and not necessarily male flesh, Johnson points out that the Word was associated with the Greek philosophical concept of *Logos*, a masculine hypostasis. In order to show that female flesh was included in the incarnation, she retrieves the older feminine hypostasis of Wisdom (*Sophia*) from the Judaeo-Christian tradition as a Christological image for women's empowerment and inclusion. She then uses Wisdom as the hermeneutical key for exploring the ministry of Jesus[85] and points out that when Jesus rose and

---

82 Elizabeth A. Johnson, 'Redeeming the Name of Christ', in *Freeing Theology: The Essentials of Theology in Feminist Perspective*, ed. Catherine Mowry LaCugna (New York: HarperCollins, 1993), p. 118.

83 Johnson, 'Redeeming the Name of Christ', p. 119.

84 Johnson, 'Redeeming the Name of Christ', pp. 119–20 (emphasis added).

85 Johnson, 'Redeeming the Name of Christ', pp. 120–4. See also Elizabeth A. Johnson, 'Wisdom Was Made Flesh and Pitched Her Tent Among Us', in *Reconstructing the Christ Symbol: Essays in Feminist Christology*, ed. MaryAnne

ascended, he sent the Spirit, another feminine hypostasis, to inspire the Christian community.[86]

Metaphorical theologian Sallie McFague has also explored alternative images for the Godhead in an effort to create more inclusive 'models of God'. She suggests an alternative trinity of God the Mother, God the Lover and God the Friend, in which the second person of her triad (God the Lover) can be represented by Jesus or, more importantly, by each of us modelling the passion that Jesus showed.

> Passion means suffering, and it also means deep feeling . . . The bond between the two meanings of passion emerges in the story of Jesus of Nazareth, whose deep feeling for those who believed themselves to be without value brought on his suffering with and for them. Disciples who model themselves on God the lover will inevitably find the same connection to obtain.[87]

The notion of human passion and erotic power explored by Heyward and McFague is examined in much more detail by Asian-American feminist theologian Rita Nakashima Brock, whose work is, in my opinion, the most important and best articulated feminist Christology to date. Brock stakes out a middle ground for herself somewhere between the outright rejection of Jesus Christ (Daly and Hampson) and the honouring of Jesus Christ as salvific because of his example (Ruether and Heyward). Hers is a radical Christology that seeks to make sense of the life and death of Jesus in the context of the trivialization and abuse of the weakest members of society. Brock's presupposition is that the Church has developed its traditional Christology and soteriology according to a

---

Stevens (New York/Mahwah: Paulist Press, 1993), pp. 95–117; Elizabeth A. Johnson, 'The Maleness of Christ', in *The Power of Naming: A Concilium Reader in Feminist Liberation Theology*, ed. Elisabeth Schüssler Fiorenza (London: SCM Press; Maryknoll, NY: Orbis Books, 1996), pp. 307–15; as well as Schüssler Fiorenza's work on Jesus as Wisdom, discussed below.

86 Johnson, 'Redeeming the Name of Christ', p. 131. See also Elizabeth A. Johnson, *She Who Is: The Mystery of God in Feminist Theological Discourse* (New York: Crossroad, 1992), Chapters 7 ('Spirit-Sophia') and 8 ('Jesus-Sophia').

87 Sallie McFague, *Models of God: Theology for an Ecological, Nuclear Age* (Minneapolis: Fortress Press, 1987), p. 129. However, McFague has been criticized for seeing the created order as manifesting Christ and relegating Jesus Christ to a mere example and not the Incarnate One, thus undermining Christian doctrine. See David A. Scott, 'Creation as Christ: A Problematic Theme in Some Feminist Theology', in *Speaking the Christian God: The Holy Trinity and the Challenge of Feminism*, ed. Alvin F. Kimel, Jr (Grand Rapids, MI: William B. Eerdmans Publishing Company, 1992), pp. 237–57.

militaristic and triumphalist mindset motivated by power.[88] The use of unhealthy power is what keeps the poor and oppressed poor and oppressed. Victimization of the powerless – especially women and children – is idealized and kept in place by the worship of a Jesus Christ who is the ultimate victim. Thus, Brock is especially critical of notions of atonement that see Jesus' suffering and death as willed by God, maintaining that such a belief not only empowers but renders as doctrine what she calls 'cosmic child abuse', which in turn sanctions contemporary child abuse at the hands of human parents.[89] Equally problematic for her is any Christology that sees Jesus as simply an obedient and innocent pawn in the hands of his Father, which obviates the human empowerment that a true Christology should image. Brock is adamant that humanity cannot find salvation in the grotesque and brutal death of Jesus, but must look instead to the community that gathered around him to become a resurrection community that survived and thrived despite (or because of?) the brutal execution of their leader at the hands of 'the political, patriarchal powers of his day'.[90]

This idea of community as salvific is explored by Brock in her award-winning book, *Journeys by Heart: A Christology of Erotic Power*, in which she defines the importance of Jesus as one who showed 'heart' to a brokenhearted world.[91] Brock defines sin as 'brokenheartedness' that confirms the defeated status of the powerless. Jesus' life and ministry mended the hearts of the oppressed of his day and stimulated a community of strong-hearted women and men who were the embodiment of resurrrection.

Brock's hermeneutical key for interpreting Jesus for post-patriarchal women and men is the notion of the erotic as power, first formulated by African-American lesbian feminist Audre Lorde and elaborated by Carter Heyward.[92] *Eros* as love has been downplayed in the Christian

---

88 Rita Nakashima Brock, 'Losing Your Innocence but Not Your Hope', in *Reconstructing the Christ Symbol*, ed. Stevens, p. 31.

89 Brock, 'Losing Your Innocence but Not Your Hope', pp. 37–9.

90 Brock, 'Losing Your Innocence but Not Your Hope', pp. 49–50.

91 Rita Nakashima Brock, *Journeys by Heart: A Christology of Erotic Power* (New York: Crossroad, 1991), pp. xi, xiv.

92 Audre Lorde, 'Uses of the Erotic: The Erotic as Power', in Lorde, *Sister Outsider: Essays and Speeches* (Trumansburg, NY: The Crossing Press, 1984), pp. 53–9; and Heyward, *Touching Our Strength*, Chapter 6. See also Brock's earliest work on this subject, 'The Feminist Redemption of Christ', in *Christian Feminism: Visions of a Just Humanity*, ed. Judith L. Weidman (New York: Harper & Row, 1984), pp. 55–74.

tradition because of its association with sex; unconditional and uncon-
cerned *agape* as love has instead been championed as the best kind of
love, with *philia* or friendship love as the next best kind. According to
Lorde, Heyward and Brock, when humans are allowed to reclaim their
capacity for erotic love as a good and essential part of their nature, they
are able to come into their power as self-determining individuals. This is
especially important for oppressed people who have been conditioned
to believe that it is acceptable for them to be controlled by others.

In examining brokenheartedness as the root problem of human existence, Brock sees erotic power as the solution for overcoming such
brokenheartedness.[93] It was this erotic power that Jesus modelled in his
person and his ministry (especially his healings and exorcisms) and this
erotic power is what made him Christ.[94] But Jesus is not the only Christ:
The resurrection community (which Brock calls *Christa/Community*)
has christic power when it, like Jesus, is in touch with its erotic power –
the capacity for overcoming brokenheartedness.[95] Her Christology is
thus one of personal embodiment and individual incarnation.[96]

Patricia Wilson-Kastner has formulated a feminist Christology that is
much more traditional than those discussed thus far. Although she
would classify herself as a liberal Protestant, Wilson-Kastner's Christology is rather conservative. She begins her work with the 'fundamental
conviction' that Christianity and feminism are 'compatible' and 'non-
contradictory'.[97] Wilson-Kastner names the quest for human wholeness
as the aim of feminism, and her feminist Christology describes Jesus
Christ as 'the agent of wholeness and reconciler of fragmentation in the
world'.[98] Using the language of process theology, she portrays Christ as
the archetype of healthy humanity (similar to the New Testament's 'new
Adam' Christology) who leads humans toward wholeness and away
from brokenness.[99] She does not seem to take seriously, however, the
feminist concern with the maleness of Jesus, but dispenses with the issue

---

93 Brock, *Journeys by Heart*, pp. 39–41.

94 Brock, *Journeys by Heart*, pp. 72–6.

95 Brock, *Journeys by Heart*, p. 88.

96 This view has been criticized by opponents of feminist theology for denying
the particularity of Jesus Christ that is essential for Christian salvation. See, for
example, Ray S. Anderson, 'The Incarnation of God in Feminist Christology: A
Theological Critique', in *Speaking the Christian God*, ed. Kimel, pp. 288–312.

97 Patricia Wilson-Kastner, *Faith, Feminism, and the Christ* (Philadelphia:
Fortress Press, 1983), pp. 5–6.

98 Wilson-Kastner, *Faith, Feminism, and the Christ*, p. 52.

99 Wilson-Kastner, *Faith, Feminism, and the Christ*, pp. 91–2.

rather summarily, as though, because it has not been troublesome to *her*, Jesus' gender should be a non-issue for feminists.[100] Instead, she shows how there have been feminine views of Jesus in the Christian spiritual tradition (such as Julian of Norwich's portrayal of Jesus as Mother[101]), as though this obviates the necessity of a feminist hermeneutics of suspicion. Moreover, she succumbs to the temptation to equate Jesus' relationship to women with his 'feminism',[102] a position that, as Elisabeth Schüssler Fiorenza has noted, can be dangerously anti-Jewish and anti-woman, inasmuch as it leaves in place the view of woman as helpless 'other', while perpetuating a view of Judaism as a corrupt, evil and misogynistic religion that Jesus was sent to correct.[103]

Perhaps the harshest criticism of Wilson-Kastner's position has come from Susan Brooks Thistlethwaite, who, as a white theologian bringing a racist critique to Euro/American feminist methodology, cautions against Wilson-Kastner's validation of a universal human wholeness coming out of a universal human experience. For Thistlethwaite, Wilson-Kastner's desire to build a uniform Christology out of a common feminist experience of wholeness ignores the fact that women of colour and poor women do not have the same experiences or concerns as privileged white feminists in the academy.[104]

As the foregoing discussion indicates, there is no one essential femi-

---

100 Wilson-Kastner, *Faith, Feminism, and the Christ*, p. 104. See the criticism of Wilson-Kastner's failure to address the problem of patriarchy in Ellen K. Wondra, *Humanity Has Been a Holy Thing: Toward a Contemporary Feminist Christology* (Lanham, MD: University Press of America, 1994), p. 217.

101 Wilson-Kastner, *Faith, Feminism, and the Christ*, pp. 89, 96, 101–04.

102 Wilson-Kastner, *Faith, Feminism, and the Christ*, pp. 72–3.

103 Elisabeth Schüssler Fiorenza, *Jesus and the Politics of Interpretation* (New York and London: Continuum, 2000), pp. 115–44, esp. pp. 116–18. See also Judith Plaskow, 'Anti-Judaism in Feminist Christian Interpretation', in *Searching the Scriptures, Volume One: A Feminist Introduction*, ed. Elisabeth Schüssler Fiorenza (New York: Crossroad, 1993), pp. 117–29; and Amy-Jill Levine, 'Discharging Responsibility: Matthean Jesus, Biblical Law, and Hemorrhaging Woman', in *A Feminist Companion to Matthew*, ed. Amy-Jill Levine with Marianne Blickenstaff (Sheffield: Sheffield Academic Press, 2001), pp. 70–87. For a summary of the view that Jesus, in his championing of women, was a total departure from Judaism, see René Laurentin, 'Jesus and Women: An Underestimated Revolution', trans. Lawrence Ginn, in *Women in a Men's Church*, ed. Virgil Elizondo and Norbert Greimacher (Edinburgh: T. & T. Clark; New York: The Seabury Press, 1980).

104 Susan Brooks Thistlethwaite, *Sex, Race, and God: Christian Feminism in Black and White* (New York: Crossroad, 1991), pp. 97–9. On the differing perspectives of feminists of colour, see Chapter 7 of the present work.

nist stance. Consequently, more recent feminist Christologies have been careful to articulate the particularity of every Christological reflection and the impossibility of creating a universal feminist Christology.[105] Nowhere is this concern for particularity and preciseness of Christological expression more apparent than in the Christology of Elisabeth Schüssler Fiorenza, who delimits her own work through concern for classism, racism, heterosexism and anti-Judaism, among other issues.

From the inception of her career, Schüssler Fiorenza has sought to find connections between women's experience and the earliest Christian message. Christologically, she believes that it is more important to focus on the witness of the earliest community gathered around Jesus, who perpetuated his message, rather than on Jesus himself.[106] Therefore, unlike Mary Daly, who would contend that Jesus has no relevance for women, or Rosemary Radford Ruether, who would ask whether Jesus in his maleness can help or save women, Schüssler Fiorenza looks to the women around Jesus themselves as indicators of his relevance. Like Elizabeth Johnson, Schüssler Fiorenza employs the concept of Wisdom as a hermeneutical clue for discovering who Jesus was and can be for women.[107] However, in contrast to Johnson, Schüssler Fiorenza does not see Jesus as Wisdom personified, but as Wisdom's messenger. This is a very subtle but important distinction; Johnson sees the incarnation in traditional terms, but substitutes Sophia for Logos as the divine hypostasis being incarnated in Jesus, whereas Schüssler Fiorenza sees Sophia/ Wisdom as God, who sends Jesus as her representative and not as an incarnation of Sophia/Wisdom herself.[108] Schüssler Fiorenza, by examining the Q sayings source in form critical reconstruction, demonstrates that the earliest stage of Q portrays Jesus as Sophia's emissary, while later redactions of Q have shifted to seeing Jesus as Sophia herself.[109]

---

105 Thus, Carter Heyward notes that one must always ask, 'Who am I leaving out?' See Heyward, *Touching Our Strength*, p. 96.

106 Schüssler Fiorenza , *In Memory of Her*, pp. 121–2.

107 Elisabeth Schüssler Fiorenza, *Jesus, Miriam's Child, Sophia's Prophet: Critical Issues in Feminist Christology* (New York: Continuum, 1994), p. 90: '[T]he emerging Galilean Jesus movement probably understood itself as a prophetic movement of Sophia-Wisdom. That it named itself after Jesus the Christ was probably due to the conviction that had emerged after Jesus' execution that he was the Vindicated or Resurrected One . . . [which] had its base in the tradition of the "empty tomb" attributed to women.'

108 Schüssler Fiorenza, *Jesus, Miriam's Child, Sophia's Prophet*, p. 157.

109 Elisabeth Schüssler Fiorenza, 'Wisdom Mythology in the Christological Hymns of the New Testament', in *Aspects of Wisdom in Judaism and Early*

Schüssler Fiorenza thus agrees with Brock that what is of primary Christological importance is not Jesus the individual but the community whom he inspires throughout history.[110] Consequently, her most recent Christological writing has been sharply critical of the contemporary quest for the historical Jesus as a politically inspired liberal response to biblical fundamentalism, noting that both groups seek to preserve their own patriarchal prerogatives.[111] To concentrate exclusively on the figure of Jesus once again marginalizes those whom his proclamation of the kingdom of God sought to set free; moreover, to portray Jesus as a non-political harbinger of the end-times (as Jesus scholars E. P. Sanders, Burton Mack and Dale Allison have done) points away from Jesus' very real concern with the suffering of his day and spiritualizes his message, a political ploy that has been used for millennia to justify oppressive conditions in the here-and-now.[112]

Conclusion

What conclusions, if any, might be drawn from this survey of the feminist Christological discussion? Since the experiences of women are remarkably varied according to their individual social locations, I realize that one cannot isolate one feminist view of Jesus as the Christ; nevertheless, I believe that it is possible to recognize some commonality among the leading feminist Christologies.

Christianity, ed. Robert L. Wilken (Notre Dame, IN: University of Notre Dame Press, 1975), p. 17. Schüssler Fiorenza compares the Jesus–Sophia relationship to the Osiris–Isis myth that had a wide adherence at the time Christianity was developing (p. 35). See also Gail Paterson Corrington, *Her Image of Salvation: Female Saviors and Formative Christianity* (Louisville: Westminster/John Knox Press, 1992), pp. 107–08.

110 Australian Catholic feminist biblical scholar Elaine Wainwright concurs, noting that the 'reign of God movement' focuses on the proclamation rather than the person of Jesus; Elaine M. Wainwright, *Shall We Look for Another? A Feminist Rereading of the Matthean Jesus* (Maryknoll, NY: Orbis Books, 1998), p. 122 n.17.

111 Schüssler Fiorenza, *Jesus and the Politics of Interpretation*, p. 87: '[O]ne must ask how much social-scientific Jesus research would contribute to change and transformation or how much it seeks to maintain the status quo. In short, one must ask by whom, why, and in whose interests social-scientific Historical-Jesus knowledge is produced.'

112 Schüssler Fiorenza, *Jesus and the Politics of Interpretation*, pp. 112–13. See also Sharon H. Ringe, *Jesus, Liberation, and the Biblical Jubilee: Images for Ethics and Christology* (Philadelphia: Fortress Press, 1985).

First, feminists are unwilling to see Christ as a vicarious saviour who bears salvation to humanity for them and without their participation, for this renders women powerless and is an impediment to their human becoming.

Second, feminists believe that Jesus was a model for how one may live in relationship with the Divine. They are reluctant, however, to see Jesus himself as divine, for this suggests the dangerous corollary that, because Jesus is male, God is male and that only men are created in God's image.

Third, feminists do not see the death of Jesus as salvific because of the implication that suffering is redemptive in and of itself, thus validating women's unjust suffering. They prefer to see Jesus' death as one more example of the systemic sin of the world that thwarts the efforts of good people and oppresses the innocent.

Feminist theologian Ellen Wondra, after examining the major feminist Christologies in her doctoral dissertation, draws an insightful conclusion, which can also summarize our discussion:

> [A] relatively adequate feminist Christology can be elaborated around the core affirmation that for Christians, Jesus is the Christ because he is the manifestation of the transformation of humanity in the struggle to resist dehumanization, *and* he is the definitive re-presentation of the only God who saves.[113]

---

113 Wondra, *Humanity Has Been a Holy Thing*, p. 326.

7

A Way Out of No Way: The
Christologies of Women of Colour

When I originally conceived the idea for this book, it was my impression that one chapter could adequately describe all women's Christology as 'feminist'; it was not until I researched the topic, however, that I discovered that women themselves do not see their theologizing in this way. The previous chapter, in outlining feminist Christology, noted that there are diverse Christologies among women. So true is this statement that women of colour have sought to differentiate their theological thinking from that of white, middle-class feminists. As the years have passed since the Civil Rights and women's movements of the 1960s and 1970s, disparate groups of women have begun raising their voices to say that their experience is often not included or even considered by the aims of feminism, which is seen as a product of the theorizing of white women in the academy.[1] Nowhere is this more apparent than in feminist theology and, particularly, feminist Christology. Moreover, Christian women from the Third World[2] (Africa, Asia and Latin America) have stepped forward to insist that their views of God and Christ must be distinguished not only from those of white women, but even their sisters of colour residing in the United States. Therefore, this chapter will discuss the Christologies that have developed among diverse groups of women of colour – specifically, women of African, Hispanic and Asian descent, both within the United States and in the Third World.

---

1 See, for example, bell hooks, *Ain't I a Woman: Black Women and Feminism* (Boston: South End Press, 1981).

2 In recent years, it has become politically correct to describe developing nations and unprivileged people as the 'Two-Thirds World' rather than the 'Third World', in order to acknowledge that the majority of the world falls within this designation. However, women of Africa, Asia and Latin America themselves prefer the term 'Third World' because it reflects their quality of life rather than numerical statistics, and so I shall use this designation for them, inasmuch as I believe it is important to refer to people using the words they themselves wish to

Black Women's Christology

Womanist Christology

African-American women were the first group to designate their experience as different from that of white feminists, preferring to call themselves 'womanists'.[3] The problem of racism in the feminist movement was first brought to light by black feminist[4] sociologists and theorists. Thus, bell hooks has asserted that 'the issue is not whether white women are more or less racist than white men, but that they are racist. . . . Every women's movement in America from its earliest origin to the present day has been built on a racist foundation.'[5]

The oppressive nature of white feminist theology in particular was first articulated by poet and theorist Audre Lorde in an 'open letter' to

---

be called. See Virginia Fabella and Mercy Amba Oduyoye, 'Introduction', in *With Passion and Compassion: Third World Women Doing Theology*, ed. Virginia Fabella and Mercy Amba Oduyoye (Maryknoll, NY: Orbis Books, 1988), p. ix.

3 This word is taken from the definition promulgated by Alice Walker, *In Search of Our Mothers' Gardens: Womanist Prose* (Orlando, FL: Harcourt, Brace, and Jovanovich, 1983), p. xi: 'Womanist: 1. From *womanish*. (Opp. of "girlish," i.e., frivolous, irresponsible, not serious). A black feminist or feminist of color. From the black folk expression of mothers to female children, "You acting womanish," i.e., like a woman. Usually referring to outrageous, audacious, courageous or *willful* behavior. Wanting to know more and in greater depth than is considered "good" for one. . . . 2. Also: A woman who loves other women, sexually and/or nonsexually. . . . 3. Loves herself. *Regardless*. 4. Womanist is to feminist as purple to lavender.' I believe it is important to quote Walker's definition at length, inasmuch as it has been essential for womanist theologians' self-definition. Nevertheless, even those black women theologians who call themselves 'womanists' do not agree on every aspect of this definition; for example, womanist ethicist Cheryl Sanders has pointed out that the embracing of the non-heterosexual elements of this definition threatens the African-American family, which is already besieged from many quarters. See Cheryl J. Sanders, 'Christian Ethics and Theology in Womanist Perspective', in *Black Theology: A Documentary History*, ed. James H. Cone and Gayraud S. Wilmore, 2 volumes (Maryknoll, NY: Orbis Books, 1993), Vol. 2, pp. 336–44. See also the discussion in Kelly Brown Douglas, *The Black Christ* (Maryknoll, NY: Orbis Books, 1994), pp. 100–01; and the lesbian womanist response in Renee L. Hill, 'Who Are We for Each Other? Sexism, Sexuality and Womanist Theology', in *Black Theology*, ed. Cone and Wilmore, Vol. 2, pp. 345–51.

4 Not all black women who are committed to the self-actualization of black women call themselves 'womanists'; some still prefer to call themselves 'black feminists'.

5 hooks, *Ain't I a Woman*, pp. 122, 124.

radical feminist theologian/philosopher Mary Daly, in which she pointed out that all women do not suffer simply from one form of oppression, since the patriarchy has 'many varied tools' which white women themselves take up unawares. Moreover, to place all women's oppression under the banner of 'sexism' ignores the fact that racism is a 'reality force' in the lives of women of colour that it will never be in white women's experience.[6]

Additionally and in similar fashion, black women have had to endure their second-class status within the black community in general and in the black churches in particular. In the struggle for black liberation, any concern with women's issues was seen as disloyalty to the black male and to the agenda of black power: 'Black men have been sexist throughout their history in America, but in contemporary times that sexism has taken the form of outright misogyny – undisguised woman-hating.'[7] Women in the black churches have occupied an ambivalent position both as pillars of the church (making up 70 per cent of black church membership) and as scapegoats; they have either been placed on pedestals or denounced as the root cause of the demise of the black community. If misogyny was challenged, the response was name-calling: 'manhater' (if the complainant was female) or 'wimp' (if male).[8]

Moreover, African-American women struggle not only with the racism of their white sisters and the sexism of their black fathers, brothers

---

6 Audre Lorde, 'An Open Letter to Mary Daly', in Lorde, *Sister Outsider: Essays and Speeches* (Trumansburg, NY: The Crossing Press, 1984), pp. 66–8, 70. Daly never responded to Lorde's overtures. A similar effort to dialogue across race was attempted more recently by Asian postcolonial feminist theologian Kwok Pui-lan, to no avail. See Kwok Pui-lan, 'Unbinding Our Feet: Saving Brown Women and Feminist Religious Discourse', in *Postcolonialism, Feminism, and Religious Discourse*, ed. Laura E. Donaldson and Kwok Pui-lan (New York and London: Routledge, 2002), pp. 62–81.

7 hooks, *Ain't I a Woman*, p. 102. For a discussion of how this sexism manifests itself specifically in the black church, see Kelly Brown Douglas, *Sexuality and the Black Church: A Womanist Perspective* (Maryknoll, NY: Orbis Books, 1999); and Theressa Hoover, 'Black Women and the Churches: Triple Jeopardy,' in *Black Theology*, ed. Cone and Wilmore, Vol. 1, pp. 293–303.

8 Frances E. Wood, '"Take My Yoke Upon You": The Role of the Church in the Oppression of African American Women', in *A Troubling in My Soul: Womanist Perspectives on Evil and Suffering*, ed. Emilie M. Townes (Maryknoll, NY: Orbis Books, 1993), p. 41. Wood sarcastically notes that this name-calling was the punishment for transgressing the eleventh commandment, 'Thou shalt not criticize male behavior.' Note the homophobic overtones of such name-calling; see Suzanne Pharr, *Homophobia: A Weapon of Sexism* (Little Rock, AR: Chardon Press, 1988).

and husbands, but also with the classism of American society, which relegates black women and children to its lowest economic level.[9] Thus, most womanist theological discourse bases its discussion upon the threefold nature of African-American women's oppression through an analysis of gender, race and class.[10]

A specifically womanist theology developed among a group of doctoral students at Union Theological Seminary in the 1980s.[11] Stimulated by the black liberation theology of James Cone and the feminist theology of Beverly Wildung Harrison and Dorothée Sölle, each of whom were their professors at Union, these women began to ask themselves how theology, biblical studies and ethics might be challenged through a black woman's analysis. Because these scholars were Christian, this womanist analysis naturally extended to Christology; before discussing womanist Christology, however, it will be helpful to examine some general womanist theological positions.

Most importantly, womanist theologians seek to critique not only traditional theology but also the more recent liberation theologies, by subjecting both black theology and feminist theology to a careful examination. They contend that the triple oppression of African-American women puts them in a unique position from which to 'do' theology.[12]

The crux of the issue is one of personhood: black women, as 'the oppressed of the oppressed' have been conditioned to believe that they must deny elements of their person in order to attain salvation. Thus, an important element of womanist theology is restoring to black women an appreciation of their status as the *imago dei* ('image of God'). Black theology is unable to do this fully because of its concentration on male personhood as normative, while feminist theology also misses the mark because of its assumption that there is a 'universal' female experience (which usually turns out to be the experience of white women).[13]

---

9 Marcia Y. Riggs, *Awake, Arise, and Act: A Womanist Call for Black Liberation* (Cleveland: The Pilgrim Press, 1994), Chapter 2. See also Angela Y. Davis, *Women, Race, and Class* (New York: Vintage Books, 1983).

10 Jacquelyn Grant, 'Black Theology and the Black Woman', in *Black Theology*, ed. Cone and Wilmore, Vol. 1, p. 323.

11 This group included, among others, Katie Geneva Cannon, Jacquelyn Grant, Kelly Delaine Brown [Douglas] and Delores S. Williams, who have gone on to successfully represent the womanist theological endeavour in Church and academy.

12 Delores S. Williams, 'Womanist Theology: Black Women's Voices', in *Black Theology*, ed. Cone and Wilmore, Vol. 2, pp. 270–1.

13 Diana L. Hayes, 'Feminist Theology, Womanist Theology: A Black Catholic Perspective', in *Black Theology*, ed. Cone and Wilmore, Vol. 2, pp. 326–8. As

Moreover, womanist scholars, as they articulate the *imago dei* of black women, must also contend with the poverty of the majority of their constituents; otherwise, womanist theology remains meaningless for the majority of black women and is 'no different from any other bourgeois theology'. Instead, womanists use the daily experiences of poor black women as 'the gauge for the verification of the claims of womanist theology'.[14]

Womanist theologian Delores Williams, in examining the person-hood of black women, has termed their plight in American society a 'wilderness' experience. Employing a womanist biblical interpretation of Genesis 16, Williams retells the story of Abraham and Sarah's election from the perspective of Sarah's maid, Hagar, a woman of African descent, who, at Sarah's insistence, becomes a surrogate mother for the childless couple. Likening Hagar's abuse at her mistress's hands to the abuse endured by black slavewomen in the South, Williams character-izes Hagar's flight into the wilderness as a journey to self-actualization that reaches its culmination when God meets Hagar in the wilderness and Hagar names God ('the One who really sees,' Genesis 16.13).[15] Williams thus compares Hagar's encountering of God in the wilderness to black women's ability to find God in their experiences of marginal-ization, alienation and oppression and to rise above these experiences through survival: 'God gives personal direction to the believer and thereby helps her make a way out of what she thought was no way.'[16] In this way, Williams urges black women to reclaim those characters of Scripture who have been made invisible according to the dominant reading, just as black women in contemporary society have been 'invisi-bilized' through their triple oppression, while at the same time challeng-ing mainstream biblical scholars to become aware of how their work propagates such 'invisibilization'.[17]

Womanist sociologist of religion Marcia Riggs sees black women's

---

described in Part III of the present work, the recovery of the *imago dei* is also a pri-mary goal of queer theology.

14 Jacquelyn Grant, 'Womanist Theology: Black Women's Experience as a Source for Doing Theology, with Special Reference to Christology', in *Black Theology*, ed. Cone and Wilmore, Vol. 2, pp. 278–9. This concentration on poor women's experience is also a characteristic of Asian women's theology; see further below.

15 Delores S. Williams, *Sisters in the Wilderness: The Challenge of Womanist God-Talk* (Maryknoll, NY: Orbis Books, 1993), pp. 15–33.

16 Williams, *Sisters in the Wilderness*, pp. 108–09.

17 Williams, *Sisters in the Wilderness*, p. 149.

ability to serve as social critics throughout history as the key to black liberation and womanist religious consciousness. Riggs thus engages the rhetoric of former slavewomen Sojourner Truth and Anna Julia Cooper in order to show that the race/gender/class agenda of black women is not something recent, and she quotes Jarena Lee, a woman denied ordination in the African Methodist Episcopal Church:

> For as unseemly as it may appear now-a-days for a woman to preach, it should be remembered that nothing is impossible with God. And why should it be thought impossible, heterodox, or improper for a woman to preach? Seeing the Savior died for the woman as well as for the man. . . . Is He not a whole Savior instead of a half one?[18]

Lee's Christological insight provides a fitting transition into womanist Christology, for her comment about the nature of saviourhood highlights the major differences between feminist and womanist Christology: (1) the person of Jesus and (2) what he did. First, whereas some feminist theologians, in order to escape possible theological conclusions regarding Jesus' maleness, are more concerned with de-emphasizing his humanity in favour of the 'Christ/Sophia' that resided in him, womanist theologians, like black and Latin American liberation theologians, emphasize the humanness of Jesus in order to demonstrate his solidarity with poor, oppressed, black women; his maleness is not of major concern. Second, whereas most feminist theologians downplay the salvific work of Christ in favour of a Christology of personal empowerment to wholeness through Jesus' example, some womanist theologians prefer to see the work of Christ and the cross in more traditional terms. Moreover, womanist theologians, rather than seeing the incarnation as limiting their personhood, see it instead as the empowering of African-American women, for God sent God's own Son to 'make a way out of no way'. Let us examine these positions in more detail.

Jacquelyn Grant has contributed greatly toward the construction of a specifically womanist Christology. Her doctoral dissertation at Union Theological Seminary was an examination of the deficiencies of feminist Christology when examined through an emerging womanist Christology.[19] She centres her work on answering Rosemary Radford

---

18 Riggs, *Awake, Arise, and Act*, pp. 55–8, quoting from Jarena Lee, *Religious Experience and Journal of Mrs. Jarena Lee, Giving an Account of Her Call to Preach the Gospel* (1849).

19 Jacquelyn Grant, *White Women's Christ and Black Women's Jesus: Feminist Christology and Womanist Response* (Atlanta: Scholars Press, 1989).

Ruether's question whether a male saviour can save women; she does so through the lens of black women's experience and concludes that, inasmuch as soteriology (the study of what Jesus did) emerges from Christology (the study of who Jesus was), one must examine how the (male) Jesus acted then and interacts with human lives now.[20]

However, Grant notes that 'liberation feminists' such as Rosemary Radford Ruether and Letty Russell do not properly understand the 'particularity of non-white women's experience'.[21] In this sense, black theologians such as James Cone seem more attuned to black women's reality; yet, for Grant, they do not go far enough, for they see Jesus' identity as the black Christ in terms of his particularity, whereas the significance of the black Christ for black women lies in his ability to become universalized. Just as black women share racist suffering with black men, sexist suffering with non-black women, and economic travail with people of every colour and gender, in the same way Jesus of Nazareth is able to share each of these burdens because of his ability to empathize across borders: 'Likewise, with Jesus, there was an implied universality which made him identify with others.'[22]

Thus, Grant urges womanists to seek an inclusive view of Jesus Christ, in which he is not only the black Christ but the black *female* Christ: '[F]or me, it means today, this Christ, found in the experiences of Black women, is a Black woman.'[23] However, this does not mean denying the maleness of the historical Jesus, but seeing it as a historical reality that did not limit Jesus but allowed him, in his privilege as a man, to reach across the boundaries to those who were marginalized in his day.

Grant points out that historically African-American women have based their faith in God and in Jesus on the Bible; therefore, a womanist Christology must be biblically based.[24] It must also be guided by the tradition of early womanists such as Sojourner Truth and Jarena Lee, whose vision of Jesus was guided by their belief that he was God incarnate, for, if their suffering brother Jesus was God, this meant that white people were not God.[25]

---

20 Grant, *White Women's Christ and Black Women's Jesus*, pp. 82–3.

21 Grant, *White Women's Christ and Black Women's Jesus*, p. 145.

22 Grant, *White Women's Christ and Black Women's Jesus*, pp. 216–17.

23 Grant, *White Women's Christ and Black Women's Jesus*, p. 220.

24 Grant, 'Womanist Theology', pp. 279–81.

25 Grant, 'Womanist Theology', pp. 281–2. Grant quotes Sojourner Truth's affirmation: 'When I preaches, I has jest one text to preach from, an' I always preaches from this one. My text is, "When I found Jesus!"' (p. 283)

Grant cautions black women, however, from identifying too much with the victim status of Jesus as 'the suffering servant', for historically black women have been the servants of all – white men, white women and black men. If one glorifies servanthood in the figure of Jesus, this confirms black women's subservient status. Instead, Grant insists that Christians should reconsider servant language and distinguish Jesus' servanthood, which was voluntary, from that of black women, which is enforced.[26] She also cautions against the use of the terms 'Lord' and 'Master' to refer to Jesus, particularly in black/white dialogue; in exclusively black settings, these words could be used if one is saying that Jesus is the *only* Lord and the *only* Master, rather than a representative of the white masters and mistresses.[27] One is thus able to see how complicated and at times problematic the multilayered relationship of black women to Jesus can be.

Black women's relationship with Jesus affects how they view sin and salvation. Delores Williams has pointed out that, for oppressed people, sin often takes the form of personal unworthiness and unknowing collusion with their oppressors by internalizing their message of hatred. This personal unworthiness and self-hatred is overcome by an encounter with Jesus that leads to 'somebodiness'. According to this view, sin is not only systemic but also individual, when the oppressed person participates in her devaluing through silence, invisibility and submission to stereotypes.[28] Williams notes that in both the Old and New Testaments 'defilement' is the greatest sin. The encounter with Jesus that leads to 'somebodiness' helps black women avoid participation in the defilement that is inflicted upon them by white society and black men.[29]

---

26 Jacquelyn Grant, 'The Sin of Servanthood and the Deliverance of Discipleship', in *Troubling in My Soul*, ed. Townes, pp. 199–201. See also Wood, '"Take My Yoke Upon You"', p. 37, who suggests that Jesus' encouragement to 'take his yoke' encourages acceptance of suffering and victimization, while the Christian Church's traditional definition of sin has served to 'function to maintain a lethal sociological and ecclesiastical status quo'.

27 Grant, 'The Sin of Servanthood', pp. 212–13. She likens black women calling Jesus their only Lord and Master to the early Christians' confession that Jesus was Lord (*kyrios*) instead of Caesar.

28 Delores S. Williams, 'A Womanist Perspective on Sin', in *Troubling in My Soul*, ed. Townes, pp. 140, 146.

29 Williams, 'A Womanist Perspective on Sin', pp. 144–5. For example, Dinah's raped body was defiled in Genesis 34; and Jesus, in discussing food laws, asserted that defilement comes not from food but from the human heart. Williams sees these biblical illustrations as empowering for black women – God made Dinah 'somebody' after her rape; Jesus named defilement as having an organic

Unlike Grant, Williams sees the cross as problematic for a womanist Christology. Continuing her use of the Hagar story as paradigmatic for black women's experience of servanthood and surrogacy,[30] Williams cautions that traditional views of the atonement may confirm the black woman's position of enforced surrogacy (maid, mammy, wet-nurse, sex toy) that has damaged her personhood by lifting up this surrogate role as good, healthy and salvific, when in reality it is not.[31] Instead, Williams urges black women to base their Christology in the notion that 'their salvation is assured by Jesus' life of resistance and by the survival strategies he used to help people survive the death of identity', thus 'free[ing] redemption from the cross'.[32] Because black women have been dismissed by white oppressors as carnal and sex-focused, Williams also encourages womanist Christologians to reclaim the figure of Mary as one who incarnated God in her own body, indicating that the Christ Event commenced before even the life of Jesus, let alone his death.[33]

The contrasting positions of Grant and Williams are examined and synthesized in the womanist Christology of JoAnne Marie Terrell, who notes that black people's fascination with the cross is linked to their fascination with (and puzzlement over) theodicy.[34] Black women's lived experience illustrates an ambivalence toward the cross; like Jesus, they have been betrayed – by black men and white women – and have endured 'crosses of racism and sexism they still bear in the society, the church and the academy'.[35] Through historical analysis of the African-American slavery experience, Terrell notes that the cross has in the past given blacks the power to survive and has affirmed their innocence – 'Jesus went there before you.'[36] However, in a postmodern world in which atonement theories and a 'hermeneutics of sacrifice' are employed to serve the status quo and keep blacks 'in their place', she questions the

---

(human) source, rather than being something that one acquires through an outside (non-human) source, thus combating the view that black oppression is 'deserved' or is something beyond anyone's control.

30 Williams, *Sisters in the Wilderness*, pp. 60–83.

31 Williams, *Sisters in the Wilderness*, p. 162.

32 Williams, *Sisters in the Wilderness*, p. 164.

33 Williams, *Sisters in the Wilderness*, p. 168. See also Hayes, 'Feminist Theology, Womanist Theology', pp. 332–3, on how Mary can be a womanist role model since she was a '"womanish" woman'.

34 JoAnne Marie Terrell, *Power in the Blood? The Cross in the African-American Experience* (Maryknoll, NY: Orbis Books, 1998), p. 4.

35 Terrell, *Power in the Blood?*, p. 5.

36 Terrell, *Power in the Blood?*, p. 34.

necessity of retaining the cross in its heretofore cherished place in black theology. Terrell warns that postmodern blood-related realities such as AIDS and inner-city bloodletting within the black community 'place the onus for ethical deliberation on the significance of Christ's blood/blood-loss squarely on the African-American community'.[37] Instead, she encourages womanists to move toward a Christology that recognizes the 'once-and-for-all' character of Christ's death, so that today's crucifixions are not seen as salvific or God-willed.[38]

Episcopal priest and womanist theologian Kelly Brown Douglas agrees that black theology's view of Christ's sacrificial death has not always been helpful for the contemporary African-American community. She notes that the black Christ portrayed by James Cone, J. Deotis Roberts and Albert Cleage[39] 'explicitly disavows' white oppression but 'do[es] not confront the reality of oppression *within* the Black community'.[40] According to Douglas's analysis, the one-dimensional nature of black liberation Christology that focuses only on white racism does nothing to dismantle the sexism, classism and heterosexism that are destroying the black community from within: black men oppress black women; well-to-do blacks look down upon those who have not 'made it'; homophobic blacks of both genders relegate black gays and lesbians to the status of 'other' within the black community.[41] She argues that womanist Christology therefore must contribute a wholistic notion of Christ that addresses all of these contemporary issues. The womanist Christ must be a prophet who not only challenges the black community to become more Christ-like and attuned to human wholeness, but also challenges womanist theologians themselves to break the silence regarding such issues as economic justice and heterosexism.[42]

African Women's Christology

When one turns to the Christology of women living on the continent of Africa, one finds a vastly different situation. The majority of black Africans, except for those who reside in South Africa, do not have to cope with racism, as their African-American sisters and brothers do.

---

37 Terrell, *Power in the Blood?*, p. 121.
38 Terrell, *Power in the Blood?*, p. 124.
39 For a discussion of the black Christ in black liberation theology, see Chapter 4 of the present work.
40 Douglas, *The Black Christ*, p. 85.
41 Douglas, *The Black Christ*, pp. 85–7.
42 Douglas, *The Black Christ*, pp. 101, 107, 109.

Some African women insist that sexism is a problem that merits attention;[43] however, African women must deal with poverty on a scale unknown in the United States, and thus it is primarily the struggle for economic well-being that informs their Christology.

This economic situation is a product of colonialism, which not only dictated that Africans should have an economy based on European capitalism but also insisted that they become Christian if they were to become 'civilized' and 'acculturated'. As a result, Africa is (nominally) 46 per cent Christian. Nevertheless, this Christianity was imported to Africa by white Western Europeans and North Americans; consequently, the encounter of Africans with Jesus Christ went hand-in-hand with the process of colonization. Thus, as Africans struggle to become 'postcolonial', many also struggle to become post-Christian or differently Christian.[44] As a result, the Church has had to realize that it must be more accepting of African traditions, especially the role of women in traditional African spirituality and ritual: for example, in tribal religion women preside at the important rites of passage (birth, puberty, marriage, birthing, death and mourning), and women seek to bring this same presence to Christian ritual.[45]

This twofold focus on economic concerns and the honouring of tradition guides African women's Christology. Jesus Christ is the true Human who makes possible fulfilment for all and reveals God, empowering the possibility that 'the laws of history can be overcome by means of crucified love'.[46] However, African women insist that they are disciples of Christ, not of the first disciples;[47] they thus subscribe to the view

---

43 Mercy Amba Oduyoye, 'Reflections from a Third World Woman's Perspective: Women's Experience and Liberation Theologies', in *Feminist Theology from the Third World: A Reader*, ed. Ursula King (London: SPCK; Maryknoll, NY: Orbis Books, 1994), pp. 32–4.

44 Bernadette Mbuy-Beya, 'African Spirituality: A Cry for Life', trans. David Patrick Mahoney, in *Spirituality of the Third World: A Cry for Life*, ed. K. C. Abraham and Bernadette Mbuy-Beya (Maryknoll, NY: Orbis Books, 1994), pp. 64–6.

45 See Mercy Amba Oduyoye, 'Women and Ritual in Africa', in *The Will to Arise: Women, Tradition, and the Church in Africa*, ed. Mercy Amba Oduyoye and Musimbi R. A. Kanyoro (Maryknoll, NY: Orbis Books, 1992), pp. 9–24.

46 Thérèse Souza, 'The Christ-Event from the Viewpoint of African Women, I: A Catholic Perspective', trans. Phillip Berryman, in *With Passion and Compassion*, ed. Fabella and Oduyoye, pp. 22, 28.

47 Louise Tappa, 'The Christ Event from the Viewpoint of African Women, II: A Protestant Perspective', trans. Phillip Berryman, in *With Passion and Compassion*, ed. Fabella and Oduyoye, p. 30.

of Elisabeth Schüssler Fiorenza that the message of Jesus was an egalitarian one that included women.[48]

Alongside this recognition that the earliest Christian mission was a diverse, egalitarian endeavour is the realization that in the religiously pluralistic Africa of today there needs to be room for many Christs. The images of 'Christ the King' and 'the Coming One' preached by African male Christology do not suit women's needs as they struggle for basic humanity, for this Christ was brought by the conquerors. Rather, African women worship the victorious Christ who overcomes adversity, the Christ who is a refugee from Europe and America and craves hospitality as a guest of Africa.[49] Thus, African women image Christ as their personal saviour and personal friend, one who embodies the Spirit and the power of God rather than the colonial overlords; this Jesus is an iconoclastic prophet who restores to women their sense of self amid the changing landscape of Africa.[50] As women theologians from Ghana note, 'One thing is certain: whatever the age or place, the most articulate Christology is that silently performed in the drama of everyday living.'[51]

Hispanic Women's Christology

Just as women of African descent have different contexts for Christology depending upon whether they reside in the United States or Africa, in the same way, women of Hispanic descent bring different issues and backgrounds to their vision of the Christ. Thus, women living in Latin America (South America, Central America and the Caribbean) articulate their theology differently – and in different languages, such as Spanish and Portuguese – than their Hispanic sisters who reside in the United States and write in English. For that reason, this discussion will have a twofold focus – the Christology of Latin American women and the Christology of North American women of Hispanic descent, who sometimes call themselves *mujeristas*.[52]

---

48 See Chapter 6.

49 Elizabeth Amoah and Mercy Amba Oduyoye, 'The Christ for African Women', in *With Passion and Compassion*, ed. Fabella and Oduyoye, pp. 35–46.

50 Teresa M. Hinga, 'Jesus and the Liberation of Women in Africa', in *With Passion and Compassion*, ed. Fabella and Oduyoye, pp. 190–1.

51 Amoah and Oduyoye, 'The Christ for African Women', p. 45.

52 To my knowledge, this term was first used by Ada María Isasi-Díaz; see her definition below.

Latin American Women's Christology

Argentinian theologian Nelly Ritchie has called Latin America the 'continent that is bleeding to death',[53] inasmuch as the masses of people there suffer from disease, poverty, starvation and the threat of death squads from repressive governments. As noted in Chapter 5, Latin American liberation theology from its inception has taken the side of the struggling poor, affirming that God has a 'preferential option' for the poor and oppressed of this world. Nevertheless, Latin American women theologians have noted that the theology of liberation as constructed by Gustavo Gutiérrez and others is the product of an androcentric Latin American society;[54] although this theology utilizes a political and economic critique of prevailing theologies, it still does not take a feminist critique into account.

For that reason, Latin American women have begun speaking out in order to supplement the theology of liberation so that it might represent more adequately the majority of people. For example, Mexican theologian María Pilar Aquino in her feminist theological analysis employs both a feminist and a materialist critique of both patriarchy and capitalism, and reaches the conclusion that God is a god of life who will not tolerate the current condition of Latin American women and their dependent children.[55]

Uruguayan theologian Ana María Bidegain notes that it was not only Spanish and Portuguese colonists who determined Latin American women's plight, but that, perhaps even more, missionaries from Great Britain and the United States condemned Latinas to a life of degradation. She points out that the Anglo-American colonists brought with them a Puritan dogmatism that, combined with Stoicism and Neoplatonism, affirmed sex negativity and the mindset that women were more carnal than men and thus the originators and bearers of sin.[56] The resulting denigration of the body lends itself naturally to the exploitation of female bodies by the capitalism of multinational corporations.

---

53 Nelly Ritchie, 'Women and Christology', trans. Jeltje Aukema, in *Through Her Eyes: Women's Theology from Latin America*, ed. Elsa Tamez (Maryknoll, NY: Orbis Books, 1989), p. 83.

54 Ana María Bidegain, 'Women and the Theology of Liberation', trans. Robert R. Barr, in *Through Her Eyes*, ed. Tamez, p. 28.

55 María Pilar Aquino, *Our Cry for Life: Feminist Theology from Latin America*, trans. Dinah Livingstone (Maryknoll, NY: Orbis Books, 1993), pp. 1, 64, 132.

56 Bidegain, 'Women and the Theology of Liberation', pp. 16, 19.

Moreover, this imported sex negativity – which is alien to native culture – champions the belief that sin is individual rather than systemic, leading to the maintenance of the status quo.[57] Therefore, Latina scholars' contribution to liberation theology must be their critiques of puritanical sexual views, patriarchal ideologies and the 'feminization' of poverty.[58]

Methodologically, Latin American women have employed both traditional and non-traditional approaches to Christology. Thus, Nicaraguan theologian Luz Beatriz Arellano asserts that women of Central America, in the midst of their own struggle, discover new images of Jesus that go beyond the traditional: Jesus becomes both a *hermano/a* (brother *and* sister) and a *compañero/a* (colleague, fellow revolutionary); Jesus can be man or woman, for Jesus' importance is not his/her gender but rather his/her solidarity in the midst of (and sensitivity to) human suffering; this is the truer meaning of the incarnation than what has been imposed by the Church hierarchy from above.[59]

Therefore, Latin American women's Christology is communal rather than individual. Jesus functions as the ambassador of God's grace of pardon, but not one who came to do it for them once and for all; they must be involved *with* Jesus in the struggle. The resurrection is a paradigm of what it means to be totally transformed through solidarity, and women were the first witnesses of this transformation.[60] Moreover, not only Jesus himself but his entire movement was inclusive of women, unlike the gender-segregated society of Qumran.[61] Consequently, details in the Gospels often dismissed as unimportant gain a new significance for Latinas: Jesus' presiding at a meal reaches out to women's experience and sacramentalizes it;[62] and Martha of Bethany, rather than her sister Mary, becomes a role model as a strong, working woman who takes the initiative, speaks her mind, and is rewarded in the Fourth Gospel with the Christological confession that the Synoptics give to Simon Peter.[63]

---

57 Bidegain, 'Women and the Theology of Liberation', pp. 19–20.

58 Bidegain, 'Women and the Theology of Liberation', p. 29.

59 Luz Beatriz Arellano, 'Women's Experience of God in Emerging Spirituality', in *Feminist Theology from the Third World*, ed. King, pp. 321–2.

60 Ritchie, 'Women and Christology', pp. 83, 86, 88.

61 María Clara Bingemer, 'Reflections on the Trinity', trans. Jeltje Aukema, in *Through Her Eyes*, ed. Tamez, p. 71. See also Ivone Gebara, 'A Cry for Life from Latin America', in *Spirituality of the Third World*, ed. Abraham and Mbuy-Beya, p. 117.

62 Aquino, *Our Cry for Life*, p. 144.

63 Ana María Tepedino, 'Feminist Theology as the Fruit of Passion and

Perhaps the most significant and unique Latina Christological insight is that of Brazilian theologian and Catholic sister Ivone Gebara, who insists that 'the centrality of Jesus [for Christian faith] opens us to *the centrality of persons*, especially the outcast'.[64] Gebara, explicating an ecofeminist Latin American Christology, describes the outcast not only in human terms but also includes as outcasts the oppressed environment and non-human life forms of the earth. She focuses on the Christ power of the believer rather than of Jesus Christ himself, inasmuch as it is *human* Christic power and responsibility that will make a difference for oppressed ecosystems, animals and people. She notes pointedly that Latin Americans have historically had to rely on other people and other countries to 'do us a favor so that we can live with dignity'. A patriarchal and paternalistic reading of the Gospels and Jesus' activities in them focuses attention on power outside of persons 'from above' rather than the power of self-initiative and self-determination that the believer receives by virtue of God's grace as revealed in Jesus Christ. For Gebara, a more wholistic and realistic salvation comes from recognizing the agency of the unnamed people in the Gospels who took what they saw and heard in Jesus and made a difference in their own lives. 'Why not shine spotlights on the insignificant actors and appreciate their daily struggle to survive and maintain their dignity?' she asks, for to do so allows us to 'move away from an excessive emphasis on the savior, the hero, the martyr, the king, the saint – as well as the victorious warrior, the only Son of God'.[65] As a result of her Christology, Gebara, with others, encourages a paradigmatic shift for all Latin Americans in their thinking about Jesus, a shift that has already started among communities of Latin American Christian women.[66]

Mujerista Christology

In the same way that African-American feminists have chosen to call themselves 'womanists', some Hispanic-American feminists have selected the name *mujeristas* to designate themselves and their particular the-

---

Compassion', trans. Phillip Berryman, in *With Passion and Compassion*, ed. Fabella and Oduyoye, pp. 168–70.

64 Ivone Gebara, *Longing for Running Water: Ecofeminism and Liberation*, trans. David Molineaux (Minneapolis: Fortress Press, 1999), p. 180 (emphasis added).

65 Gebara, *Longing for Running Water*, pp. 179–80.

66 Gebara, *Longing for Running Water*, p. 192.

ology.[67] *Mujerista* theologians are adamant that their theology must come from the individual voices of women; their theology is therefore accountable only to Hispanic women and to no one else. The social location of these *mujeristas* is quite diverse, and thus their theology must be flexible and open-ended: some reside in the United States by choice; some were born there; some, especially Cuban women, are there 'in exile' through no choice of their own. They suffer multilayered oppression in the United States because of their gender, their ethnicity, their economic status, their citizenship or lack thereof, their (in)ability to speak English, and, often, their status as mixed-race individuals who are either *mestizaje* (Hispanic and Native American) or *mulatta* (Hispanic and African).[68] Despite their diverse social locations, *mujeristas* have the common purpose of relocating the sacred 'in the midst of the marginalized'.[69] They struggle against oppression, poverty and the 'American myth' that the United States is the best place to live; some believe they have no options, no choice, and no vision of the future (*proyecto histórico*).[70]

Ada María Isasi-Díaz, the primary architect of *mujerista* theology, believes that Hispanic women have a special, intimate relationship with God that places God in the same position as a beloved relative; their view of 'God' is often syncretistic, an amalgamation of God the Father, the historical Jesus, the saints, manifestations of the Virgin as an indigenous Mother Goddess, dead ancestors, and Amerindian and African deities.[71] She denies, however, that *mujeristas* are concerned with

---

67 'In our search for a name of our own, we have turned to our music, an intrinsic part of the soul of our culture. In our songs, love songs as well as protest songs, we are simply called *mujer*. And so, those of us who make a preferential option for *mujeres* are *mujeristas*'; Ada María Isasi-Díaz, 'The Task of Hispanic Women's Liberation Theology – *Mujeristas*: Who We Are and What We Are About', in *Feminist Theology from the Third World*, ed. King, pp. 97–8.

68 Ada María Isasi-Díaz and Yolanda Tarango, *Hispanic Women: Prophetic Voice in the Church – Toward a Hispanic Woman's Liberation Theology* (New York: Harper & Row, 1988), pp. ix, x–xii. For the *cubana* feeling of 'exile', see Isasi-Díaz, 'The Task of Hispanic Women's Liberation Theology,' p. 88.

69 Ada María Isasi-Díaz, *Mujerista Theology: A Theology for the Twenty-First Century* (Maryknoll, NY: Orbis Books, 1996), p. 197.

70 Ada María Isasi-Díaz, *En La Lucha = In the Struggle: A Hispanic Women's Liberation Theology* (Minneapolis: Fortress Press, 1993), pp. 38–9.

71 Isasi-Díaz, *En La Lucha*, p. 39; see especially note 17. In *Hispanic Women*, p. 68, Isasi-Díaz and Yolanda Tarango point out that such syncretism must be acceptable because it comes from Hispanic women's experience, noting that official Church doctrine was syncretism that was judged 'acceptable' syncretism.

Christology, noting that 'Jesus is not one of the main figures of popular religiosity.'[72] Instead, they are more concerned with Jesus' proclamation of the 'kin-dom'[73] of God and its ramifications for the poor people and women of his time.

Nevertheless, in her first book, co-authored with Yolanda Tarango, Isasi-Díaz goes to great lengths to reveal Hispanic women's thoughts about Jesus in published interviews with ordinary *mujeres*: 'Look, I see Jesus as a perfect example of *lucha* [struggle] . . . He is a person I admire and contemplate.' 'Jesus was a man who gave everything for us.' Jesus is 'God's pilot project'. 'I see [Jesus] as my equal because he came here and was among us.' 'I always think of God and Jesus together.'[74] Moreover, in a more recent book, Isasi-Díaz quotes a young woman named Olivia, who states, 'I have to believe in Jesus in order to know God. I know that God sent His Son.'[75] Consequently, I find Isasi-Díaz's contradictory views of *mujerista* Christology (or lack thereof) mystifying. It is my impression from reading most of her published work that Isasi-Díaz is attempting to construct her *mujerista* theology single-handedly; her work is fuelled by much anger and resentment toward patriarchy, Catholicism and the United States, which is not, in itself, a bad thing; however, her theology should be evaluated and critiqued as any scholarship would be, whether feminist or non-feminist, traditional or non-traditional. It is my hope that other Hispanic-American women will develop her thought and go deeper into who Christ is for *mujeres*, so that inquisitive non-Hispanics may obtain a view that is not just one

---

72 Ada María Isasi-Díaz, 'The Bible and *Mujerista* Theology', in *Lift Every Voice: Constructing Christian Theologies from the Underside*, revised and expanded edition, ed. Susan Brooks Thistlethwaite and Mary Potter Engel (Maryknoll, NY: Orbis Books, 1998), p. 269. I have a problem with Isasi-Díaz's frequent sweeping generalizations, especially with regard to Christology, since 'popular religiosity' that exalts Jesus may be seen in the frequent use of *Jésus* as a first name in Hispanic-American culture. See Luis G. Pedraja, *Jesus Is My Uncle: Christology from a Hispanic Perspective* (Nashville: Abingdon Press, 1999).

73 Isasi-Díaz has coined this term to translate Greek *basileia*. She notes, 'There are two reasons for not using the regular word "kingdom," employed by English Bibles. First, it is obviously a sexist word that presumes that God is male. Second, the concept of kingdom in our world today is both hierarchical and elitist – as is the word "reign." The word "kin-dom" makes it clear that when the fullness of God becomes a day-to-day reality in the world at large, we will all be sisters and brothers – kin to each other; we will indeed be the family of God.' Isasi-Díaz, 'The Bible and *Mujerista* Theology', p. 306 n.8.

74 Isasi-Díaz and Tarango, *Hispanic Women*, pp. 16, 22, 31, 36, 41.

75 Isasi-Díaz, *En La Lucha*, p. 120.

person's. Until such time, the Christology of Latin American women such as Ivone Gebara will be much more provocative and instructional for the student of Christology.

Asian Women's Christology

When one turns to the theology and Christology of Asian women, one finds a vastly different situation. Christianity is the dominant religion in Latin America and the majority religion in Africa. For the most part (with some exceptions), Christianity in Africa and Latin America has remained relatively untouched by indigenous spirituality, which, as noted above, is one of the specific complaints of African women; in Latin America, Christian missionaries and colonial overlords have almost completely obliterated indigenous religion.[76] The religious landscape is quite different in Asia, where the prevailing atmosphere is one of diversity, with Christianity viewed as one religion among many. Asians make up 58 per cent of the world population; yet Christians in Asia are in the minority and must coexist with Muslims, Hindus, Buddhists and followers of ancestral spiritualities such as Shintoism, Taoism and Confucianism.[77] Nevertheless, even though Western Christian religious practice has not prevailed in Asia, as a result of colonialism, Western (Christian) values and customs have greatly influenced Asian culture and self-determination. Asian women's theology[78] thus lives amid the tensions of religious pluralism and Western imperialism.

---

76 An exception would be the African Yoruba spirituality that has melded with Christianity in the form of *voudon* in the Caribbean. See, for example, Tom F. Driver, *The Magic of Ritual, Our Need for Liberating Rites that Transform Our Lives and Our Communities* (New York: HarperCollins, 1991), pp. 69–75.

77 Virginia Fabella, 'A Common Methodology for Diverse Christologies?' in *With Passion and Compassion*, ed. Fabella and Oduyoye, p. 108.

78 Like African-American and Hispanic-American women, many Asian women are suspicious of the term 'feminism' as a description of the concerns of white women of the leisure classes; they view Western feminism as radical and separatist and therefore seek to distance themselves from it. Thus, many female theologians in Asia prefer to call their work 'Asian women's theology'. (There is no separate term such as 'womanist' or *mujerista* due to the absence of a common language.) Kwok Pui-lan of Hong Kong, however, prefers to use the term 'Asian feminist theology' for her work, because when 'feminism' is translated into Chinese it carries a political connotation that she believes it is important to preserve. Kwok Pui-lan, *Introducing Asian Feminist Theology* (Cleveland: The Pilgrim Press, 2000), pp. 9–10.

Chapter 4 examined the Christology of Asian male theologians such as C. S. Song. However, much of what is called Asian theology has been written for a Western audience in order to broaden Western consciousness. In contrast, Asian women do their theology and publish their work not for Westerners but for Asian women themselves. Korean theologian Chung Hyun Kyung, who received her doctorate from Union Theological Seminary, notes that her Western education is meaningless if she cannot articulate theology that her mother can understand and find meaningful in her life as an impoverished, oppressed woman.[79]

What, then, in the situation of Asian women? Asian women make up one quarter of the world's population; moreover, the majority of the world's poor reside in Asia, and the majority of these poor people are women and children. Their customs are diverse: they are multilingual, multireligious and multiracial. Theology for these women must therefore be 'pluralistic and multivocal, woven out of many separate strands'.[80] Moreover, in doing theology from Asian women's perspective, one must constantly be aware that Asian women, in addition to undergoing the patriarchal, racial and economic oppression suffered by other women of colour, are also the primary victims of the 'sex tourism' industry that has become in recent years the most insidious and unaddressed of Asia's postcolonial problems.[81]

---

79 Chung Hyun Kyung, *Struggle to Be the Sun Again: Introducing Asian Women's Theology* (Maryknoll, NY: Orbis Books, 1990), pp. 1–5. Kwok Pui-lan, in her survey of Asian women theologians, quotes Chung as saying that 'we are the text,' whereas the Bible and tradition are context (Kwok, *Introducing Asian Feminist Theology*, p. 38). Kwok also notes, 'In the past, Asian Christians, let alone Christian women, have seldom been invited to help set the theological agenda. We are seen more as "missiological objects" of Christian mission, rather than as "theological subjects."' Kwok Pui-lan, 'The Future of Feminist Theology: An Asian Perspective' in *Feminist Theology from the Third World*, ed. King, p. 64.

80 Kwok, *Introducing Asian Feminist Theology*, p. 10.

81 See Rita Nakashima Brock and Susan Brooks Thistlethwaite, *Casting Stones: Prostitution and Liberation in Asia and the United States* (Minneapolis: Fortress Press, 1996). See also Mary John Mananzan and Sun Ai Park, 'Emerging Spirituality of Asian Women', in *With Passion and Compassion*, ed. Fabella and Oduyoye, pp. 78–9, who note that 'the concretization of [specific Asian women's] oppression varies'. For example: Malaysian women suffer from a resurgence of religious fundamentalism and worsening communal relations; Korean women suffer from the imposed division of their country into North and South Koreas and oppression from Confucian family law; Indian women suffer from caste structure and the dowry system; Muslim women throughout Asia suffer from the effects of genital mutilation (so-called female circumcision); Sri Lankan women undergo constant ethnic struggles on their multi-ethnic island; and Japanese

Because of these economic, cultural and political realities, Asian women bring a unique voice to theology and have created what I consider some of the most meaningful theological language to be found in all of the various liberation theologies. Using an 'epistemology of the broken body', Asian Christian women seek to understand the nature of God, the nature of humanity and, ultimately, the nature of the Christ; their brokenness, pain and suffering cannot be extracted from their theological pursuits because it is such an integral part of their social location, 'the major element of their life experiences'.[82] God is defined by their experiences: God is to be found in community, in nature and in history; God is a life-giving Spirit, 'an all-inclusive reality in everything', who returns Asian women to their personal power. 'This God is a God who talks to Asian women, listens to their story, and weeps with them.'[83] Because indigenous Asian spiritualities and Hinduism image the Divine as both male and female, inclusive language for God is not the most important item on Asian women's agenda; rather, there must be a change of the mind and heart in addition to language. 'What one practices in life is more important than what one believes.' They look instead for diverse experiences of the Divine that can address important life situations – sex tourism, neocolonialism, militarism and poverty. Moreover, Asian women caution against triumphalism that assumes Christian superiority and reinforces the conquered status of Asian peoples.[84]

Like womanist and queer theologians, Asian women theologians seek to restore to their people an appreciation of their creation as the *imago dei*. Using cosmological imagery, Hiratsuka Raicho of Japan has expressed this in a poem:

Originally, woman was the Sun.
She was an authentic person.
But now woman is the moon.
She lives by depending on another
and shines by reflecting
another's light.

women, although Japan enjoys a First World economy, still suffer Third World oppression in the form of the emperor system, colonization, and the ongoing effects of nuclear bombing in World War II (p. 79).

82 Chung, *Struggle to Be the Sun Again*, p. 39.
83 Chung, *Struggle to Be the Sun Again*, pp. 47–51.
84 Kwok, *Introducing Asian Feminist Theology*, pp. 67–73.

Her face has a sickly pallor.
We must now regain our hidden sun.
'Reveal our hidden sun!
Rediscover our natural gifts!'
This is the ceaseless cry
Which forces itself into our hearts . . .[85]

Thus, Chung Hyun Kyung concludes:

> In Asian women's perspective, knowledge of self leads to a knowledge of God. In their suffering, Asian women meet God, who in turn discloses that they were created in the divine image, full and equal participants in the community with men.[86]

What role does Jesus Christ play in this theology of personal empowerment? As one might expect, Asian women's view of the Christ is unique and multifaceted. Asian diversity makes a common Christology impossible;[87] however, one can see some commonalities. The understanding of Jesus' suffering and how it relates to their own suffering is of primary importance to Asian women. Rather than seeing Jesus as a passive victim who encourages women to endure their suffering quietly, Asian women categorize Jesus' suffering as an inevitable product of oppression, and they see Jesus' suffering as an act of solidarity with all who suffer: 'Like Jesus' suffering, women's active suffering has salvific value, for . . . every suffering . . . falls within the ambit of salvation history.'[88]

Kwok Pui-lan sees traditional Christology as supporting the agenda of oppressors. In articulating a postcolonial feminist theology, Kwok distinguishes between truly salvific images of Christ and those characteristics – silent endurance as a model to be followed, submission, obedience and Jesus as 'Lord' of all – that were 'proclaimed during colonial times [to justify] the domination of the oppressors'.[89] Instead, she notes that some Korean and Japanese feminists interpret Jesus' endurance

---

85 Hiratsuka Raicho, 'The Hidden Sun', quoted in Chung, *Struggle to Be the Sun Again*, pp. 51–2.
86 Chung, *Struggle to Be the Sun Again*, p. 52.
87 Fabella, 'A Common Methodology for Diverse Christologies?' p. 108.
88 Fabella, 'A Common Methodology for Diverse Christologies?' pp. 110–11.
89 Kwok, *Introducing Asian Feminist Theology*, p. 80. See Kwok's detailed analysis in her magisterial work *Postcolonial Imagination and Feminist Theology* (Louisville and London: Westminster/John Knox Press), 2005, esp. Chapters 2 and 5.

through the hermeneutical lens of the Buddhist principle of the inevitability of suffering, while Filipina theologians in their political struggles reclaim the subversive aspects of the Passion story and focus especially on the anger of Jesus and his refusal to be labelled by Pilate.[90] Chinese feminists find meaning in non-human metaphors for Jesus such as vine and branches, bread and water, due to their ecological and cosmological concerns; additionally, Jesus as Divine Wisdom is congruent with aspects of Confucianism.[91] Indian women image Jesus as the feminine principle embodied in a man; he incarnated *shakti*, the harmonious principle uniting dualisms.[92]

One of the most important Asian Christological images comes from Korean spirituality and culture. Koreans seek to do theology from the perspective of the *minjung* (Korean, 'the suffering masses'), whom they associate with Jesus' ministry to the *ochlos* (Greek, 'the crowds' of oppressed in the Synoptic Gospels, to be distinguished from *laos*, 'the people').[93] The *minjung* are in the grip of *han*, the negative energy in the universe from which comes all oppression, unhappiness and evil. Korean women see Jesus as a priest or shaman whose task is to undo *han* and restore humanity to peace and order; in this context, the exorcisms in the Gospels assume a central role as the manifestation of the 'exorcizing' of *han*. In Korean culture, these shamans of *han* have traditionally been women; therefore, the image of Jesus Christ as a priest of *han* is a female Christological image.[94]

Chung Hyun Kyung notes, however, that the prevailing image of Jesus among the majority of Korean and other Asian women is still that of suffering servant. Their response to this image is ambivalent, however, and these woman have begun asking some hard questions:

> Where was Jesus when Asian women's bodies were battered, raped, and burned? What has he done to protect them from suffering? Who is Jesus for Asian women? Is he like his own father, who allowed his son to be killed by Roman colonial power and religious hierarchies even though he cried out for help? . . . Is Jesus like one of those

---

90 Kwok, *Introducing Asian Feminist Theology*, pp. 81, 84.

91 Kwok, *Introducing Asian Feminist Theology*, pp. 90–2.

92 Kwok, *Introducing Asian Feminist Theology*, pp. 94–5.

93 Kwok Pui-lan, 'Discovering the Bible in the Non-Biblical World', in *Lift Every Voice*, ed. Thistlethwaite and Engel, p. 283, summarizing the work of Ahn Byung Mu.

94 Kwok, *Introducing Asian Feminist Theology*, pp. 86–8; Fabella, 'A Common Methodology for Diverse Christologies?', pp. 111–12.

irresponsible, frustrated Asian men who promise their lover and wife love and 'the good life' but then, after stealing the woman's heart and body say, 'I will come back soon with money and gifts. While I am away, take care of *my* children and old parents. Be loyal to me.' . . . Are Asian women stuck in the battered women's vicious cycle of passive dependency? In Jesus are they again choosing a male whom they again try to love in spite of his neglect and abandonment . . . ?[95]

Chung concludes that Asian women answer a resounding 'no' to this last question and say they love Jesus '*because of* and not *in spite of* who he is'. Their incorporation of the suffering servant into their Christology is because through all his suffering his self-respect remained intact, and this leads Asian women toward a recognition and a reclaiming of their self-respect: 'Through Jesus Christ, Asian women see new meaning in their suffering and service.'[96] Japanese biblical scholar Hisako Kinukawa even suggests that it was the women in Jesus' life who helped him to understand and embrace his role as suffering servant and thereby to become Christ.[97]

Korean North American feminist theologian Grace Ji-Sun Kim has adopted and adapted Chung's Korean Christology for her Canadian milieu, inasmuch as inculturation requires those Koreans who have immigrated to North America to somehow rework their faith or lose it altogether. Unfortunately, when non-European-American people attempt to interweave their cultures with Christianity, they are pejoratively accused of 'syncretism'. Nevertheless, Kim asserts, rightly, that 'pure Christianity does not exist, has never existed, and never can exist'.[98] In Korea, Christianity was informed by indigenous shamanism, Buddhism and Confucianism; however, those Korean Christians who emigrated to the United States and Canada often took the most conservative, patriarchal elements of religion and culture with them.[99] Kim believes that Korean North American women can fight against their particular oppression (racism, ethnocentrism, sexism and classism) by empowering wisdom Christology. Her particular brand of wisdom Christology, however, differs from its embrace by white feminists, for it is deliber-

---

95 Chung, *Struggle to Be the Sun Again*, p. 55.

96 Chung, *Struggle to Be the Sun Again*, pp. 56–7.

97 Hisako Kinukawa, *Women and Jesus in Mark: A Japanese Feminist Perspective* (Maryknoll, NY: Orbis Books, 1994), p. 141.

98 Grace Ji-Sun Kim, *The Grace of Sophia: A Korean North American Women's Christology* (Cleveland: The Pilgrim Press, 2002), p. 34.

99 Kim, *The Grace of Sophia*, p. 71.

ately and unapologetically syncretistic: she not only imbues the traditional Christ figure with characteristics of Hebrew *hokmah* and Greek *sophia* but also with the Buddhist notion of *prajna*, 'the absolute knowledge through which enlightenment is attained'.[100] In this way, Asian emigrant women are able to seek empowerment not only through the message and ministry of Jesus Christ but through Asian female wisdom/saviour figures such as Kuan-yin (Chinese) and Kannon (Japanese).[101]

I pointed out in an earlier part of this chapter that womanist Delores Williams locates the Christ Event as beginning even before the life of Jesus, in the life of Mary, his mother. Asian women, most likely because of the missionary and colonial efforts of Roman Catholicism, also see Mary in Christological terms. However, like white Western feminists, they reject the Church's traditional view of Mary as the model of true womanhood because, as a virgin, her motherhood is impossible to emulate.[102] Nevertheless, they do not totally abandon Mary as some Western feminists do, but instead reincorporate Mary into their Christology as a co-redemptrix with Christ. As such, Mary, along with her son, is a Liberator, a woman who, through her choice to be a virgin mother (however that occurred), defined herself in her own terms and empowers Asian women to do the same: 'Virgin is "the symbol for the autonomy of women."'[103] The Magnificat in Luke's Gospel is Mary's 'song of revolution',[104] and her status as co-Christ with her son Jesus is perfectly natural because woman's wisdom knows that every son needs his mother.[105]

Conclusion

As we have seen, women of colour throughout the world envision the Divine and its manifestation in Christ in diverse ways that are important for a complete presentation of liberation Christology. Women of

---

100 Kim, *The Grace of Sophia*, p. 83.

101 Kim, *The Grace of Sophia*, pp. 90–6.

102 Chung, *Struggle to Be the Sun Again*, pp. 75–6: 'When Mary is placed as a norm for "ideal womanhood" outside of Asian women's everyday, concrete, bodily experiences, she becomes a source of disempowerment for Asian women.'

103 Chung, *Struggle to Be the Sun Again*, p. 77, quoting Indonesian theologian Marianne Katoppo.

104 Chung, *Struggle to Be the Sun Again*, p. 81.

105 Chung, *Struggle to Be the Sun Again*, p. 83, citing Filipina theologian Loretto-Eugenia Mapa.

African, Hispanic and Asian descent counsel all of us not to settle for easy answers when it comes to describing the Christ Event. This is of paramount importance for the development of a queer Christology, the subject of Part III, for those who self-define as 'queer' must, of necessity, see theology, anthropology and Christology in a different way from the majority of the world, which is heterosexual.

Part III

Queering Christ

Part I reviewed the development of traditional Christology in the Christian tradition, by examining the New Testament beginnings, the establishment of Christological doctrine in the Nicene Creed, subsequent theological discussions and, finally, the contemporary quest for the historical Jesus.

Part II presented the developing Christologies of groups marginalized by the mainstream tradition. Thus, we explored how women and those of African, Asian and Hispanic descent, both male and female, view the Christ figure from their social locations of varying types of oppression. These systemic societal oppressions include racism, sexism, classism and imperialism. For the most part, however, these liberation Christologies do not address one of the most widespread oppressions in contemporary Church and society – heterosexism, as manifested in compulsory heterosexuality, the assumption that heterosexuality is normative and superior to other expressions of sexuality, and homophobia, the fear or hatred of, and resulting violence against, those whose affections are for those of the same gender.

Therefore, Part III will address this void in contemporary Christology by suggesting a Christology from the social location of sexual orientation. One of the first questions that I anticipate in doing such Christological work is whether it is necessary. I believe that it is vitally necessary, not only for those who are practising Christians but especially for those who have 'given up' on the Christ message because Jesus Christ has been portrayed as a 'holy terror' who hates them and judges them for their sexual activity. It is precisely this equating of homophobia with Christ that necessitates a queer Christology.

With this in mind, Chapter 8 traces the rise of homophobia among Christians and what I call 'Christophobia' (fear of Christ) among the homosexual community. I deliberately use the word 'Christophobia' rather than 'ecclesiophobia' (fear of the Church) because homosexual persons' aversion is not only toward the churches that have oppressed them, but toward Christ, in whose name they have been rejected. Next, Chapter 9 addresses the question of whether sexual orientation is a legitimate social location, exploring the new 'queer' consciousness, as well as recent queer theology and biblical interpretation, which has made progress in reclaiming Christianity for queer people but has stopped short of articulating a queer view of Jesus Christ. Finally, having established its validity and necessity, in Chapters 10 and 11, I discuss elements of a specifically 'queer' Christology. Chapter 10 lays out my initial musings on the topic and then explores some queer Christological thinking which has influenced my own, while Chapter 11 introduces my own examination of the life of Jesus and how his life revealed his 'Christness' so that we might discover our own. In this task I remain aware that my work is speculative and travels into uncharted territory. Moreover, I am quite cognizant that this is only one person's idea of what a queering of Christ might mean. My own social location as a middle-aged, middle-class, educated, gay, white, male clergyman from a Roman Catholic background informs my work; however, I am also aware that the extensive research and reflection of Parts I and II empower me to realize my context and constantly examine who is being left out of my Christological imaginings.

8

Homophobia among Christians, Christophobia among Homosexuals

Introduction

Sociologists and historians have demonstrated that oppressions are interlocking. For example, historian Gerda Lerner, in her study of the development of patriarchy, has concluded that slavery has its roots in the domestic treatment of women by men; male leaders of society saw their enslavement of women as a 'test case' and precedent for their enslavement of men and women of other races and ethnic origins.[1] Historian John Boswell, studying the origins of Christian intolerance of gay people, has shown how the same tactics that had successfully marginalized the Jews in Europe were used against gay people once they were judged to be 'the other'.[2] Women's Studies scholar Suzanne Pharr has demonstrated that homophobia has its roots in sexism; misogyny, the hatred of women, underlies the hatred of gay men for 'acting like women' and lesbians for not 'knowing their place' and striving to 'be like men'.[3] More recently, law professor Didi Herman has described the identical tactics and rhetoric that the Christian Right in the United States has used in its demonization of groups such as Catholics, Jews, Communists, feminists and homosexuals.[4]

This interconnectedness of various types of oppression must be kept in mind throughout the following discussion of homophobia in

---

1 Gerda Lerner, *The Creation of Patriarchy* (New York: Oxford University Press, 1986).

2 John Boswell, *Christianity, Social Tolerance, and Homosexuality: Gay People in Western Europe from the Beginning of the Christian Era to the Fourteenth Century* (Chicago and London: University of Chicago Press, 1980).

3 Suzanne Pharr, *Homophobia: A Weapon of Sexism* (Little Rock, AR: Chardon Press, 1988).

4 Didi Herman, *The Antigay Agenda: Orthodox Vision and the Christian Right* (Chicago and London: University of Chicago Press, 1997).

Christianity and my subsequent articulation of a queer Christology, for I believe that any liberation theology must take into account other oppressed groups and not focus exclusively upon its own context. Thus, in noting how Christian Scripture and tradition have been used against gay and lesbian persons, one must also bear in mind the ways in which interpretation of Scripture and tradition have marginalized other groups and even sought to turn various oppressed groups against one another.

In a recent study of the phenomenon of homophobia in history, gay and lesbian studies pioneer Byrne Fone states:

> Over time people have found sufficient cause to distrust, despise, assault, and sometimes slaughter their neighbors because of differences in religion, nationality, and color. Indeed, few social groups have been frcc from the effects of prejudice, but most warring factions – men and women, Jews, Muslims, and Christians, blacks and whites – have been united in one central hatred: detestation of a particular group whose presence is universal. Religious precepts condemn this group; the laws of most Western nations have punished them. Few people care to admit to their presence among them. This group is, of course, those we call homosexuals. Antipathy to them – and condemnation, loathing, fear, and proscription of homosexual behavior – is what we call homophobia. . . . Indeed, in modern Western society, where racism is disapproved, anti-Semitism is condemned, and misogyny has lost its legitimacy, homophobia remains perhaps the last acceptable prejudice.[5]

Fone makes the integral connection between the Judaeo-Christian underpinnings of European and American society and society's enduring heterosexism – the belief that heterosexuality not only is a superior sexual orientation but should be compulsory for everyone, whether that means denying one's sexuality, remaining celibate or becoming an 'ex-gay'.[6] Because Western political systems were founded upon Judaeo-Christian principles (even when, in the case of the United States, there is supposedly a separation between Church and State), the heterosexist

---

5 Byrne Fone, *Homophobia: A History* (New York: Metropolitan Books/ Henry Holt and Company, 2000), p. 3.

6 Fone, *Homophobia*, Chapters 7 and 8. See also Mark D. Jordan, *The Invention of Sodomy in Christian Theology* (Chicago and London: University of Chicago Press, 1997); and Boswell, *Christianity, Social Tolerance, and Homosexuality*.

bias of many legal statutes stems directly from the Judaeo-Christian Bible and Christian Church tradition.[7]

Sexologist Vern Bullough has stated that '[hu]mankind has encompassed a wide variety of attitudes towards sex in general and towards homosexuality in particular', noting that '[c]ertain peoples ... tended to set the mold for the others'.[8] Some cultures are more sex-negative than others; certain cultures attach a sacredness to sexuality which allows them to blur the lines between ritual and daily life, while other cultures have erected strong boundaries to keep sexuality and spirituality separate.[9] Further complicating the landscape is what Bullough, writing in 1976, articulated as a major problem in modern sexology: what precisely constitutes 'homosexual behavior', for new categories such as transvestism and transsexualism used to be subsumed under the general category of homosexuality.[10] A quarter of a century later, observers of sexuality and gender are presented with even newer categories such as bisexuality, transgenderism and the differently sexual.[11]

---

7 For example, in a concurring opinion in the 1986 US Supreme Court decision upholding the constitutionality of anti-sodomy laws (*Bowers v. Hardwick*), Chief Justice Warren Burger, cited Judaeo-Christian biblical teachings as authority for the majority decision, asserting that 'homosexual conduct [has] been subject to state intervention throughout the history of Western Civilization' and that to protect homosexual acts 'would be to cast aside millennia of moral teaching'. Richard D. Mohr, *Gays/Justice: A Study of Ethics, Society, and Law* (New York: Columbia University Press, 1988), p. 78. Mohr notes that Burger relied solely upon a 1955 work on biblical injunctions against homosexuality (Derrick Sherwin Bailey's *Homosexuality in the Western Christian Tradition*), but totally ignored the more recent pioneering scholarship of Yale historian John Boswell (*Christianity, Social Tolerance, and Homosexuality*), which demonstrated shifting attitudes towards homosexuality throughout the first thirteen centuries of the Common Era. See also Fone, *Homophobia*, pp. 414–15.

8 Vern L. Bullough, *Sex, Society, and History* (New York: Science History Publications, 1976), pp. 18–19.

9 Further complicating the issue is the tendency of Victorian-era scholars to equate any sort of sex involved in religion with the notion of 'fertility cults' and 'sacred prostitution'. As more recent scholarship has attempted to put aside Western Judaeo-Christian notions of appropriateness, it has become clear that the relation between sexuality and spirituality in other cultures is more complex. Martti Nissinen, *Homoeroticism in the Biblical World: A Historical Perspective*, trans. Kirsi Stjerna (Minneapolis: Fortress Press, 1998), p. 39.

10 Vern L. Bullough, *Sexual Variance in Society and History* (Chicago and London: University of Chicago Press, 1976), p. 23.

11 See, for example, Carol Queen and Lawrence Schimel, eds, *PoMoSexuals: Challenging Assumptions About Gender and Sexuality* (San Francisco: Cleis Press, 1997).

One must begin by acknowledging that the term *homosexuality* has only been in use for a little over 100 years,[12] while *sexual orientation* is even more recent. Further, homosexuality as a category usually reflects a Judaeo-Christian cosmology[13] in which persons are divided into *homosexuals* (male/male and female/female affiliation) and *heterosexuals* (male/female affiliation); this is not necessarily so in other cultures. Throughout history there have been varieties of homosexual behaviour:

1 *transgenerational* homosexuality, in which the elder mentors the younger in various ways, including sexually;
2 *transgenderal* homosexuality, in which someone takes on the characteristics and lifestyle of the opposite gender;
3 *class-structured* homosexuality, which involves prostitution or slavery;
4 *egalitarian* homosexuality, in which the parties to the activity are similar in age and social standing.[14]

Each of these types of homosexuality has been condemned and accepted at various times and in various places, and acceptance of one form does not guarantee acceptance of another form.[15]

Moreover, by condemning or accepting such behaviour, religion has attached *value* to it. Power is bestowed upon what is *different*: when this difference is viewed negatively, that power manifests itself in classification as *taboo* or *sin*, as demonstrated in Judaeo-Christian religion and society. If, on the other hand, the difference is regarded positively, that power results in *sanctification* of the individuals involved, as in many indigenous cultures.[16] Thus, in addition to being shunned and punished, those categorized by the modern appellation of 'homosexual' have also played an important role throughout the world when it comes to religious ritual and celebration.[17] This discussion, however, will focus

---

12 David F. Greenberg, *The Construction of Homosexuality* (Chicago and London: University of Chicago Press, 1988), p. 3.

13 Gilbert Herdt, 'Homosexuality', in *The Encyclopedia of Religion*, ed. Mircea Eliade, volume 6 (New York: Macmillan Publishing Company, 1987), pp. 445–7.

14 Greenberg, *Construction of Homosexuality*, Chapters 2–3.

15 Greenberg, *Construction of Homosexuality*, p. 73.

16 Walter L. Williams, *The Spirit and the Flesh: Sexual Diversity in American Indian Culture* (Boston: Beacon Press, 1986), p. 3.

17 'Throughout history, and across many cultures, queer people often have

upon the Judaeo-Christian tradition, since it is within this tradition that a queer Christology is situated.

The Biblical Texts

The Judaeo-Christian tradition comprises two of the three faith systems that trace their lineage to the patriarch Abraham.[18] In approaching the Scriptures recognized by Jews and Christians (the Hebrew, 'Old' or 'First' Testament and the Christian, 'Second' or 'New' Testament), one might assume that there would not be much to say, inasmuch as the prevailing view is that the Bible condemns homosexuality outright; however, this is an unfortunate oversimplification which retards meaningful study and dialogue. Both Judaism and Christianity have grappled with the clash between their revelatory texts, generations of tradition and interpretation, and the lived experience of their adherents.

The Jewish Prohibitions

Bullough noted that, compared to Christianity, Judaism is a sex-positive religion.[19] This might be true from a heterosexual perspective: ancient Hebrew tradition placed great emphasis upon the family, as might be expected in a society that valued its place in the world and, due to deaths from illness and warfare, needed to be constantly vigilant regarding the

---

assumed roles of spiritual leadership, and have been honored, respected, and revered for doing so. . . . [H]omoerotically inclined and gender-variant individuals have directly fulfilled spiritual functions, assuming the role of shamans, healers, seers, diviners, spiritual teachers, priests, priestesses, and sacred prostitutes'; Christian de la Huerta, *Coming Out Spiritually: The Next Step* (New York: Jeremy P. Tarcher/Putnam, 1999), p. 31. As early as 1914, Edward Carpenter noted an 'original connection of some kind between homosexuality and divination'; Edward Carpenter, *Intermediate Types Among Primitive Folk*, excerpted in 'Edward Carpenter: Selected Insights', in *Gay Spirit: Myth and Meaning*, ed. Mark Thompson (New York: St. Martin's Press, 1987), p. 158.

18 The third is Islam. Jews and Christians believe that they are descended from Isaac, the son of Abraham and Sarah, while Muslims claim descent from Ishmael, the son of Abraham and Hagar. The story of Abraham and his progeny is told in Genesis 16—18.

19 Bullough, *Sexual Variance*, p. 75; but Bullough adds: 'Toleration of sexuality did not, however, include the deposit of semen anywhere else than in the female vagina.' (p. 78)

propagation of the race.[20] However, the ancients were also very clear that any sexual act which did not result in the man's semen being placed in the woman's vagina was proscribed, and, in a religiously focused society, this prohibition was called a 'sin'.[21] Moreover, there was ignorance regarding biology and anatomy that allowed the ancients to believe that the woman contributed nothing genetically to a child other than her body as a virtual incubator and that the entire person was included in the man's semen.[22] Thus, activities such as masturbation, *coitus interruptus*, anal intercourse and oral gratification were regarded as not only sinful but murderous since they involved the 'wasting' of the seed that contained the new life.[23] With this heavy emphasis upon progeny, barren women were denigrated (Genesis 30.2), and those men who did not procreate, such as eunuchs, were barred from participation in Hebrew ritual (Deuteronomy 23.1).

In Israel's patriarchal society, tremendous importance was placed upon gender roles, and many of the biblical injunctions against homosexual acts and other gender-related issues such as cross-dressing (Deuteronomy 22.5) originate in the belief that men should be men and women should be women.[24] The God-given distinctions between the sexes must not be blurred,[25] and, since men were believed to be the very image of God, acts seen as dishonouring another's manhood were believed to dishonour God 'himself'.[26] Further, as in many of the world's religions, the reasoning behind the prohibition was integrally

20 Tom Horner, *Jonathan Loved David: Homosexuality in Biblical Times* (Philadelphia: The Westminster Press, 1978), pp. 23–4.

21 Vern L. Bullough, *Homosexuality: A History* (New York: New American Library, 1979), p. 17.

22 Monica Sjöo and Barbara Mor, *The Great Cosmic Mother: Rediscovering the Religion of the Earth* (New York: Harper & Row, 1987), p. 278.

23 Immanuel Jakobovits, 'Homosexuality', in *Encyclopaedia Judaica*, volume 8 (New York: The Macmillan Company, 1971), p. 961. Further, the 'mixing' of semens which might accompany homosexual relations was seen as an unacceptable breach of a man's responsibility to use his semen to birth a child. Saul M. Olyan, '"And with a Male You Shall Not Lie the Lying Down of a Woman": On the Meaning and Significance of Leviticus 18.22 and 20.13', in *Que(e)rying Religion: A Critical Anthology*, ed. Gary David Comstock and Susan E. Henking (New York: Continuum, 1997), pp. 411–12.

24 Judith Romney Wegner, 'Leviticus', in *The Women's Bible Commentary*, ed. Carol A. Newsom and Sharon H. Ringe (Louisville: Westminster/John Knox Press, 1992), pp. 38–9.

25 Olyan, 'And with a Male', p. 409.

26 *Sefer ha-Chinnukh* 209 calls homosexual activity 'unnatural perversion, debasing the dignity of man'.

connected to patriarchal abhorrence of anal penetration.[27] Thus, the Holiness Code of the Torah states in Leviticus 18.22, 'You shall not lie with a male as with a woman; it is an abomination.'[28] This is the biblical injunction upon which the Judaeo-Christian prohibition of homosexuality is based; its companion verse, Leviticus 20.13, establishes the death penalty for its commission.

Throughout the centuries, however, this Levitical prohibition has been subject to expansion and commentary by interpreters both ancient and modern; for example, Talmudic law extends the punishment to lesbian acts (*Sifra* 9:8), which are not addressed anywhere in the Hebrew Bible. Nevertheless, the prevailing (albeit naïve) Jewish view up to the present time has been that Jews do not engage in homosexual acts, that this is activity engaged in by non-Jews.[29] The prohibition is in the Torah to remind the Hebrew nation that they are to be 'separate' (the root meaning of 'holy,' *qdsh*) and not commit various acts that are indulged in by their Canaanite and Egyptian neighbours; the story of the destruction of Sodom (Genesis 19) is used by the sages as an example of non-Israelites whose general wickedness was manifested in their antisocial behaviour toward divine visitors. Genesis 19.5 states that the men of Sodom wanted Abraham's nephew Lot to bring out his angelic guests so that they could 'know' (*yadha*) them. Intrabiblical commentary on the Sodom story (for example, Ezekiel 16.49–50; Sirach 16.8; Wisdom of Solomon 10.6–8 and 19.13–14) indicates that originally this story was

---

27 In discussing Arab and Hispanic cultures, Christian de la Huerta states, 'A closer inspection of cultural mores reveals that homosexuality is socially objectionable only if a male is the recipient of penetration. Active insertion is not considered homosexuality. Its rejection is therefore associated to the perceived loss of masculine status in a highly misogynistic society.' *Coming Out Spiritually*, pp. 180–1.

28 Unless stated otherwise, Hebrew Testament quotations are from the New Revised Standard Version of the Bible (1989), published by the Division of Christian Education of the National Council of Churches of Christ in the USA, and Greek Testament quotations are the author's own translations.

29 Conservative Jewish scholar David Novak, in noting that the rabbinical commentary *Leviticus Rabbah* 23.9 states that the generation of the flood was blotted out because of same-sex unions, hastens to add his own comment that 'they are a burlesque of family life'; due to the impossibility of procreation, homosexuals cannot cleave to one another and become one flesh (Genesis 2.24) through anal intercourse. David Novak, 'Some Aspects of the Relationship of Sex, Society, and God in Judaism', in *Contemporary Ethical Issues in the Jewish and Christian Traditions*, ed. Frederick E. Greenspahn (Hoboken, NJ: Ktav Publishing House, 1986), p. 148.

seen as describing the gentile sin of inhospitality, which, according to Leviticus 19.33–34, Hebrews must not commit.[30] Thus, the sages felt there was really no need for a safeguard against homosexuality (*Kiddush* 82a) because it was a 'gentile thing';[31] nevertheless, the prohibition of same-sex intercourse was still a universal one included in the seven commandments given to the sons of Noah (*Sanhedrin* 57b–58a).

In the modern era, Jewish legal and religious arguments have consistently rejected arguments that homosexuality is a disease or morally neutral, insisting that it is within the person's ability to choose whether to engage in behaviour that is sinful and biblically prohibited. Further, David Novak, a member of the controversial Ramsey Colloquium,[32] has classified homosexuality as not only 'counterfamilial' and 'counterprocreative', but also 'purely sensual' in its intentionality. He sees homosexuality as a 'regression' in that, unlike heterosexuality, which involves a human person seeking 'the other side' of her/his nature, it 'does not seek that "other side"' but remains with its own kind.[33]

In recent years, however, there has been a lessening of this attitude among some segments of Judaism. While the Orthodox and Conservative movements still seem fixed in their condemnation of homosexuality, the Reformed and Reconstructionist movements have sought to read the biblical and rabbinical injunctions in their societal context, noting that gay and lesbian lifestyles and orientation were not present in ancient societies.[34] Additionally, it has been suggested that, when the emphasis

30 The Sodom story has had much more significance for Christianity than for Judaism. See Horner, *Jonathan Loved David*, pp. 50–52; and John J. McNeill, *The Church and the Homosexual* (Kansas City, MO: Sheed, Andrews, and McMeel, 1976), p. 46.

31 Likewise, Moses Maimonides states that 'Jews are not suspect to practice homosexuality' (*Yad, Issurei Bi'ah* 22.2), and Rabbi Joseph Caro's medieval compendium of Jewish law omits it. As recently as 1971, Immanuel Jakobovitz, in the *Encyclopaedia Judaica*, p. 961, says that this omission 'reflects the virtual absence of homosexuality among Jews'!

32 The Ramsey Colloquium is a gathering of conservative religious scholars who in 1994 published an article entitled 'The Homosexual Movement, a Response by the Ramsey Colloquium', *First Things* 41 (March 1994), pp. 15–20, which affirmed traditional conservative prohibitions of homosexuality and criticized tolerance of gays and lesbians as mere political correctness.

33 Novak, 'Sex, Society, and God in Judaism', p. 147. One is reminded of Freud's stance that homosexuals were immature or 'stuck' in their 'natural' sexual development.

34 Lewis John Eron, 'Homosexuality and Judaism', in *Homosexuality and World Religions*, ed. Arlene Swidler (Valley Forge, PA: Trinity Press International, 1993), pp. 124–5.

on compulsory procreation is eased in a modern context, perhaps the condemnation of homosexuality is unnecessary.[35] This new attitude is seen most vividly in the establishment of gay and lesbian Jewish syna-gogues and the decision by the Central Conference of American Rabbis to allow their members to officiate at same-sex unions.[36]

The Christian Prohibitions

When one turns to Christianity, the prohibition of homosexual acts is the same, but the scriptural emphasis is different; additionally, within Christianity Roman Catholicism and Protestantism have addressed the issue of homosexuality in different ways and with varying emphases.[37] Christian tradition sees the story of the destruction of Sodom as the *ur-text* for the prohibition of homosexual activity. Even though, as stated above, the Bible itself interprets the Sodom story as an indictment of godless wickedness and inhospitality, nevertheless, beginning sometime in the intertestamental period, interpretations of this story began to change, continuing into the early centuries of Christianity.[38] 'Sodomy' became a synonym for homosexual activity, while 'sodomite' became the term for those who indulged in such activity.[39]

This condemnatory attitude was buttressed by two passages in the New Testament in which the apostle Paul condemns relations between members of the same sex; it is believed that Jesus never addressed the subject.[40] Modern interpreters of the Pauline passages have focused on

---

35 Timothy E. Connell, 'Sexuality and the Procreative Norm', in *Ethical Issues in the Jewish and Christian Traditions*, ed. Greenspahn, p. 104. This modern cultural view of homosexuality in Judaism is reflected in the legalization in 1988 by the Israeli Parliament (the Knesset) of sexual relations between adult males. Eron, 'Homosexuality and Judaism', p. 103.

36 Gustav Niebuhr, 'Pioneer Among Rabbis Helps Extend Blessing of Unions', *New York Times* (1 April 2000).

37 I omit discussion of Eastern Orthodoxy due to the lack of source material. Homosexuality is condemned by the Eastern churches; nevertheless, unlike their Western counterparts, they have been largely silent on the issue. Official Orthodox teaching is that 'homosexuality is the result of humanity's rebellion against God'; de la Huerta, *Coming Out Spiritually*, p. 186.

38 Horner, *Jonathan Loved David*, pp. 52–4; Nissinen, *Homoeroticism*, pp. 47–8.

39 This may be seen in the fact that many translations of the Bible use the word 'sodomite' anachronistically to refer to those who commit same-sex acts, when in biblical times a 'sodomite' would have merely referred to an inhabitant of Sodom.

40 Nevertheless, queer biblical interpreters point out that certain stories in the

their social and historical context – Paul's writing to Christians in the cosmopolitan cities of Rome and Corinth who would have been exposed to practices that Paul believed would lead them away from their commitment to God in Christ. Thus, in Romans 1.26, 27, Paul writes:

> Therefore, God gave them up to degrading passions. Their women exchanged natural intercourse for unnatural, and in the same way also the men, giving up natural intercourse with women, were consumed with passion for one another. Men committed shameless acts with men and received in their own persons the due penalty for their error.

The first verse is said by some to be the only place in the Bible where lesbianism is addressed; however, this is not a unanimous opinion.[41] Historian John Boswell has suggested that Paul was describing those who were innately heterosexual but were going against their nature (*para phusin*) to engage in homosexual activity; thus, Boswell does not see Paul's words as a blanket condemnation of homosexuality.[42] Other scholars have responded vehemently, pointing out that Boswell's assumption that there have been those of a homosexual 'orientation' in every age is unfounded.[43] I must agree; one cannot take modern categories and make ancient Scriptures or society 'fit' them. It is clear that

---

life of Jesus might indicate Jesus' tacit approval of homosexuality: for example, the story of the centurion and 'his boy' in Matthew 8.5–13 might be a reference to a pederastic relationship, while the statement on eunuchs who have been so from birth in Matthew 19.10–12 might be referring to those born gay or lesbian. See my discussion in 'Matthew', in *The Queer Bible Commentary*, ed. Deryn Guest, Robert E. Goss, Mona West and Thomas Bohache (London: SCM Press, 2006), pp. 507–11, and the sources cited there. See also Nissinen, *Homoeroticism*, pp. 118–22, regarding Jesus' overall silence on sexuality in general.

41 Nissinen points out that lesbianism is assumed here by analogy to what follows regarding men's relations with one another, but states that this 'assumption is conceivable, but not conclusive'. Among the early Church Fathers, Augustine believed that this referred to a distorted version of heterosexual activity. Modern interpretations allow for the possibility that women's unnatural acts involved heterosexual anal intercourse and oral sex. Nissinen, *Homoeroticism*, pp. 108, 176 n.29.

42 Boswell, *Christianity, Social Tolerance, and Homosexuality*, p. 109.

43 '[T]he categories of sexual orientation play no role here. . . . The distinction between sexual orientations is clearly an anachronism that does not help to understand Paul's line of argumentation.' Nissinen, *Homoeroticism*, p. 109. See also Richard B. Hays, 'Relations Natural and Unnatural: A Response to John Boswell's Exegesis of Romans 1', *Journal of Religious Ethics* 14 (1986), pp. 199–202.

Paul was condemning homosexual acts between males (and possibly between females). 'Unnatural' relations in Paul's patriarchal world most likely involved the aversion to penetration of one man by another and to women and men overturning the sexual roles allotted to them by 'nature'.[44]

The other Pauline text used to condemn homosexuality for Christians is 1 Corinthians 6.9, where, in discussing the various types of people who will not merit entry into the kingdom of God, Paul states:

> Do you not know that wrongdoers will not inherit the kingdom of God? Do not be deceived! Fornicators, idolaters, adulterers, male prostitutes [Greek *malakoi*], sodomites [Greek *arsenokoitai*], thieves, the greedy, drunkards, revilers, robbers – none of these will inherit the kingdom of God.

The difficulty with this passage is the two words *malakoi* and *arseno-koitai*, which the New Revised Standard Version renders 'male prostitutes' and 'sodomites',[45] while other translations conflate the two words into one term such as 'sexual perverts' (Revised Standard Version) or 'homosexual offenders' (New International Version).

In the original Greek, they are two separate words of uncertain meaning. *Malakoi* (which simply means 'soft' and must therefore be interpreted by the reader), as pointed out by Boswell, could refer to those who were weak-willed or lacking in self control; it is a term that has been used by both Catholic and Protestant writers to refer to those who masturbate.[46] It is possible that it referred to men who were 'soft' in the sense of being 'effeminate' (and thus in a patriarchal society looked down upon for not acting like 'real men'), suggesting to some scholars that Paul is referring to the passive partner in a pederastic relationship.[47]

Arsenokoitai (which comes from the words for 'male' and 'bed') is a compound which first appears in Greek in Paul; it is a word Paul

---

44 Bernadette J. Brooten, *Love Between Women: Early Christian Responses to Female Homoeroticism* (Chicago and London: University of Chicago Press, 1996), pp. 216, 240–1. ('"Natural" intercourse means penetration of a subordinate person by a dominant one', p. 241.)

45 Clearly a mistranslation, since, as noted above, 'sodomite' is an anachronism. Perhaps the most reliable translation in this instance is the usually imprecise King James Version, which renders the two words 'effeminate' and 'abusers of themselves with mankind'.

46 Boswell, *Christianity, Social Tolerance, and Homosexuality*, pp. 106–07.

47 Derrick Sherwin Bailey, *Homosexuality and the Western Christian Tradition* (London: Longmans-Green, 1955), p. 38.

apparently created to stand for a particular group in Corinth. Who this group is has been a matter of conjecture. One view is that if *malakoi* refers to the passive partner in a pederastic relationship, then *arsenokoitai* must refer to the active partner.[48] Another position holds that Paul is discussing so-called cultic 'prostitutes' in service at the pagan temples in Corinth, thus associating this term with a phenomenon of worship that involved sexual acts between the worshipper and the temple attendants, both male and female.[49] The latter theory, as developed by Boswell, seeks to remove entirely the homosexual nuances of *arsenokoitai*, since it is unclear whether these 'temple prostitutes' would have had relations with women or men.[50] This is quite problematic, however, for explanation of *arsenokoitai* in this way fails to account of its relation to *malakoi*. Moreover, it seems irresponsible to pin this argument on a phenomenon as disputed and misunderstood as that of temple prostitution; if there were indeed sexual acts performed in the context of pagan worship, to call them acts of prostitution displays a Western sex-negativity and an intolerance of other forms of worship.[51]

Having examined Christianity's scriptural prohibitions of homosexuality, it is important to note that these Scriptures were not extensively discussed or subjected to historical critical interpretation until the mid 1950s; since then there has been a significant amount of study devoted to this topic. However, for the majority of the Christian era, the texts were read literally, especially in Protestantism, as definitive condemna-

---

48 Bailey, *Homosexuality and the Western Christian Tradition*, p. 38. Robin Scroggs, *The New Testament and Homosexuality: Contextual Background for Contemporary Debate* (Philadelphia: Fortress Press, 1983), pp. 107–08, believes that *arsenokoitai* is a direct translation of Leviticus 18.22's prohibition of 'a man lying with a man'.

49 Horner, *Jonathan Loved David*, pp. 59–70.

50 Boswell, *Christianity, Social Tolerance, and Homosexuality*, pp. 107, 341–2.

51 Tikva Frymer-Kensky, 'Deuteronomy', in *The Women's Bible Commentary*, ed. Newsom and Ringe, p. 59, believes that the terms translated 'temple prostitute' in some modern Bibles simply refer to Canaanite priests of both genders. Nevertheless, the context of idolatry is tempting, for that might have led Paul to create a term such as *arsenokoitai* to condemn various forms of idolatry, whereas a simple condemnation of homosexual conduct would not, since Greek had plenty of other existing words to describe these types of acts. I agree with L. William Countryman, who has written that '[t]he evidence is too meager to allow for much more than an educated guess'; *Dirt, Greed, and Sex: Sexual Ethics in the New Testament and Their Implications for Today* (Philadelphia: Fortress Press, 1988), p. 119.

tion of homosexual acts. Roman Catholicism fortified its prohibition of same-sex affinity with a theology of natural law as enunciated by Thomas Aquinas, whereby acts not found 'in nature' and which did not lead to procreation were consequently not of God.[52]

In the past 30 years, however, many Christians have begun to question the correctness of the Churches' prohibition of homosexuality.[53] Caucuses have been formed in most of the major denominations to address the issue and to provide ministry for gay and lesbian persons.[54] Some denominations such as the Unitarian Universalist Association and the predominately gay/lesbian Metropolitan Community Churches are welcoming of homosexuals, while others such as the Episcopal, Methodist and Presbyterian Churches have engaged in heated debate that has often resulted in the official exclusion of gays and lesbians from the clergy, marriage and even sometimes the Church itself.[55] The Vatican has continued to insist that active homosexuality is incompatible with Catholic salvation while at the same time urging an attitude of compassion for gay and lesbian persons.[56]

---

52 Denise Carmody and John Carmody, 'Homosexuality and Roman Catholicism', in Homosexuality and World Religions, ed. Swidler, p. 142; Lisa Sowle Cahill, 'Moral Methodology: A Case Study', in A Challenge to Love: Gay and Lesbian Catholics in the Church, ed. Robert Nugent (New York: Crossroad, 1983), p. 79. Moral theology delineates a spectrum of attitudes: homosexuality is (a) intrinsically evil, (b) essentially imperfect, (c) to be evaluated in terms of relational significance, or (d) natural and good. Edward Batchelor, Jr, ed., Homo sexuality and Ethics (New York: The Pilgrim Press, 1980).

53 The issue of homosexuality has been called 'a fishbone' caught in the Churches' throat which they can neither eject nor swallow. Robert Nugent and Jeannine Gramick, 'Homosexuality: Protestant, Catholic, and Jewish Issues – A Fishbone Tale', in Homosexuality and Religion, ed. Richard Hasbany (New York and London: Harrington Park Press, 1989), p. 8. In 2000, Nugent and Gramick were ordered to stop their ministry to gay and lesbian Catholics (New Ways Ministry in Baltimore, MD).

54 Marvin Ellison, 'Homosexuality and Protestantism', in Homosexuality and World Religions, ed. Swidler, p. 152.

55 Ellison, 'Homosexuality and Protestantism', pp. 152–4. See also de la Huerta, Coming Out Spiritually, pp. 182–97; and Troy D. Perry, with Thomas L. P. Swicegood, Don't Be Afraid Anymore: The Story of Reverend Troy Perry and the Metropolitan Community Churches (New York: St. Martin's Press, 1990).

56 Joseph Cardinal Ratzinger (now Pope Benedict XVI), 'Letter to the Bishops of the Catholic Church on the Pastoral Care of Homosexual Persons' (Rome: Sacred Congregation for the Doctrine of the Faith, 1 October 1986). See the responses to this letter in Jeannine Gramick and Pat Furey, eds, The Vatican and Homosexuality (New York: Crossroad, 1988).

I have gone into detail regarding the biblical texts that support hetero-sexism because I do not believe that the biblical prohibitions of homo-sexuality should be understated. They are at the heart of all subsequent homophobia in the Christian Church and in countries whose laws are founded upon Judaeo-Christian principles. The continuing importance of these biblical passages can be seen in the ongoing proliferation of books on the topic. A number of works by reputable scholars have situ-ated the anti-homosexual scriptural passages in their historical and social context;[57] nevertheless, a more recent book has sought to reclaim a 'traditional' view of the Bible and homosexuality. Robert Gagnon, a professor of New Testament at Pittsburgh Theological Seminary, gives the following reasons for publishing this book:

> First, there is clear, strong, and credible evidence that the Bible unequivocally defines same-sex intercourse as sin. Second, there exist no valid hermeneutical arguments, derived from either general princi-ples of biblical interpretation or contemporary scientific knowledge and experience, for overriding the Bible's authority on this matter. In sum, the Bible presents the anatomical, sexual, and procreative com-plementarity of male and female as clear and convincing proof of God's will for sexual unions. Even those who do not accept the reve-latory authority of Scripture should be able to perceive the divine will through the visible testimony of the structure of creation. Thus same-sex intercourse constitutes an inexcusable rebellion against the intentional design of the created order.[58]

Homophobia among Christians

Gagnon's book provides a fitting transition from discussion of the biblical texts to what I perceive as homophobia among Christians, for he is not engaging in scholarly biblical exegesis or interpretation but in

---

57 See, for example, the works by John Boswell, Bernadette Brooten, Daniel Helminiak, Tom Horner, Martti Nissinen, and Robin Scroggs, cited in the Bibliography.

58 Robert A. J. Gagnon, *The Bible and Homosexual Practice: Texts and Hermeneutics* (Nashville: Abingdon Press, 2001), p. 37. For a 'pro-gay' view of Scripture, see esp. Robert Goss and Mona West, eds, *Take Back the Word: A Queer Reading of the Bible* (Cleveland: The Pilgrim Press, 2000); Ken Stone, ed., *Queer Commentary and the Hebrew Bible* (Cleveland: The Pilgrim Press, 2001); and *The Queer Bible Commentary*, ed. Guest, et al.

anti-homosexual polemic. Of course, this is his right in a society founded on freedom of expression; however, if someone were to publish a thoroughly racist theory with outmoded views of the inferiority of African Americans, they would not be taken seriously in the academy. Gagnon, on the contrary, has been lauded by such reputable biblical scholars as Martti Nissinen, author of *Homoeroticism in the Biblical World*, and John Barton of Oxford University.[59] Clearly, this is an example of Byrne Fone's statement that homophobia is the last acceptable prejudice. Nor is this type of homophobia even seen as prejudice by its adherents. Gagnon, in enumerating the 'risks' he has taken in publishing his book, asserts:

> Opposing intolerance of the sexual practices of others functions as a badge of intellectual open-mindedness and membership among the avant-garde of cultured society – part of a cherished perception of being on the 'cutting edge.' There is an undeniable, built-in bias among many of the intellectual elite against advocates of traditional sexual values. . . . In the politics of personal destruction, the first risk [in writing such a book] is to be labeled *homophobic* . . . This label is employed as part of an overall strategy of intimidation to forestall genuine debate and belittle vocal dissenters. . . . A second risk is that of being labeled *intolerant* . . . Finally, some will charge that a book such as this *promotes violence against homosexuals*, even though readers of this book receive not the slightest encouragement to be anything less than loving in personal dealings with homosexuals. While antihomosexual violence deserves to be vigorously denounced, it does nobody any good to ignore the dangerous way in which *isolated and relatively rare incidents of violence against homosexuals have been exploited* to stifle freedom of speech and coerce societal endorsement of homosexual practice.[60]

Perhaps Gagnon can rest comfortably in his belief that he has not encouraged his readers to be 'anything less than loving'; nevertheless, I believe that his rhetoric feeds homophobic hatred, whether implicit or explicit, by reaffirming its biblical origins. Moreover, his assertion that violence against homosexuals is 'isolated and relatively rare' insults those who have been the victims of anti-gay hate crimes; even one incident of hatred is too many, whether or not the perpetrator takes

---

59 See their quotes on the cover of his book.
60 Gagnon, *The Bible and Homosexual Practice*, pp. 26–9 (emphasis added).

comfort in the fact that s/he is acting in compliance with the Bible.[61] Finally, his claim that these incidents are exploited in order to stifle freedom of speech is clearly wrong-headed and has no basis in reality. One only has to look at the funeral of Matthew Shepard to see that the free expression of homophobes is alive and well.[62]

Even those politically liberal individuals who believe that homosexuals should have civil rights nevertheless frequently believe that homosexuality is sinful or against God. The majority of Americans, however, even if they 'tolerate' gay and lesbian people, still believe that they are somehow of a different status from heterosexuals and undeserving of the same rights, which they persist in calling 'special rights'.[63] The issue of homosexuals in the military resulting in the 'solution' known as the 'don't ask, don't tell' policy and the subsequent passage of the Defense of Marriage Act (DOMA) by the US Congress highlight the fact that, however many strides have been made by the gay and lesbian community since the beginning of the contemporary gay rights movement, they are still in many respects second-class citizens.[64]

John Boswell has portrayed the earliest Christian Church as a place of equality where the mandate of Galatians 3.28 was a reality – no male or female, no slave or free, no Jew or Greek, and – he would add – no straight or gay.[65] As noted above, Boswell's work has been criticized by subsequent scholarship for its essentialist thinking and for anachronistically suggesting that one can take a modern category like 'gay' and retro-

---

61 Moreover, as in the case of rape and domestic violence, one cannot be sure how widespread the violence is against gay and lesbian persons, due to the unwillingness of the victims to come forward. For some statistics on violence against gays and lesbians, see Urvashi Vaid, *Virtual Equality: The Mainstreaming of Gay and Lesbian Liberation* (New York: Anchor Books/Doubleday, 1995), p. 12.

62 Matthew Shepard was a 21-year-old gay college student who was brutally murdered by two heterosexual men in Laramie, Wyoming, in October 1998, allegedly because he had 'come on' to them in a bar. His funeral was a media event at which 'the Reverend' Fred Phelps and his congregants demonstrated with signs assuring the mourners that Matthew was burning in hell, as affirmed in their website 'GodHatesFags.com.' See Beth Loffreda, *Losing Matt Shepard: Life and Politics in the Aftermath of Anti-Gay Murder* (New York: Columbia University Press, 2000); and Edward J. Ingebretsen, *At Stake: Monsters and the Rhetoric of Fear in Public Culture* (Chicago and London: University of Chicago Press, 2001), Chapter 7.

63 Fone, *Homophobia*, p. 421; see also the rhetoric of the Ramsey Colloquium in 'The Homosexual Movement'.

64 Fone, *Homophobia*, p. 415.

65 Boswell, *Christianity, Social Tolerance, and Homosexuality*, pp. 333–4.

ject it into ancient society. Nevertheless, Boswell's research is still valid when one examines his evidence for the persecution of those who engaged in acts labelled 'sodomy'. There seems to have been a certain time in the Church's history when same-sex relations began to be seen as a threat against the social order, and those engaging in such acts began to be ostracized as sinners and even of diabolical character.[66] Along with countless women, gay men were burned in the European witch-hunts (hence the derogatory epithet 'faggot'), while strong, independent women who practised folk medicine were accused not only of witchcraft but of lesbianism.[67]

It was not until the 1970s, however, that overt homophobia became a familiar part of the Christian landscape. Until then, most homosexuals either took their places quietly and invisibly in the churches or fell by the wayside, embracing the agnosticism of the times.[68] However, when the gay liberation movement was born in the late 1960s,[69] gay men and lesbians began to assert their right to exist openly. This movement, in addition to manifesting itself in secular society and politics, began to infiltrate religion as gays and lesbians, fuelled by a burgeoning self-

---

66 Fone, *Homophobia*, Chapters 7 and 8.

67 Fone, *Homophobia*, pp. 201–04, documenting the Spanish Inquisition.

68 Of course, there are many examples of gays and lesbians who were 'thrown out' of their churches; my point here is that, until the dawn of the gay liberation movement, these displaced homosexuals did not fight back or attempt to establish a place in their home churches or in new churches of their own devising, but instead accepted the fact that this exclusion was their divinely ordained 'lot' in life. See Reverend Troy Perry with Charles L. Lucas, *The Lord Is My Shepherd and He Knows I'm Gay* (Los Angeles: Nash Publishing, 1972); and Dann Hazel, *Witness: Gay and Lesbian Clergy Report from the Front* (Louisville: Westminster/John Knox Press, 2000).

69 The two events seen as precipitating the gay liberation movement are the establishment of the Metropolitan Community Church (MCC) in October 1968 and the Stonewall Rebellion in June 1969. The Reverend Troy Perry, a former Pentecostal minister, hosted a meeting in his home for gay and lesbian Christians to 'come home' and worship God 'in spirit and in truth'; the result was the Universal Fellowship of Metropolitan Community Churches, a denomination that is now represented in almost all 50 states and in 18 countries around the world. (This author has been clergy in MCC since 1988.) See Perry, *The Lord Is My Shepherd* and *Don't Be Afraid Anymore*. The Stonewall Rebellion took place at the Stonewall Inn on Christopher Street in Greenwich Village, New York, when, perhaps for the first time, gays and lesbians fought back against police harassment; this event is commemorated each year with Gay Pride parades throughout the United States. See Fone, *Homophobia*, p. 407; and Martin Duberman, *Stonewall* (New York: E. P. Dutton, 1993).

esteem, sought to practise their Christianity openly and authentically. This in turn created a backlash in the Christian churches, as congregations, synods, councils and denominations grappled with the new visibility of gays and lesbians in their midst.[70] Moreover, the 'Christian Right,' as conservative and fundamentalist Christians have begun to call themselves, took on homosexuality as a cause that threatened not just traditional American values but the very fibre of Christianity itself.[71]

The homophobic rhetoric of the Christian Right (or 'Christian Wrong', as I prefer to call them) manifests itself in the blatant misuse of Scripture, the ignoring of the latest biblical scholarship and scientific discoveries regarding the causes of homosexuality, and the fuelling of fear and distrust of gays and lesbians among the general population through pointed propaganda that constantly depicts homosexuals as paedophiles who are exclusively into so-called 'kinky' sex, public displays of nudity and sexual acts, cross-dressing, and the deliberate defiance of societal norms in order to destroy the American family.[72] Didi Herman has pointed out that, far from being a grass-roots campaign to 'save' the morals of America, the Christian Right's assault upon the gay and lesbian community is, rather, an intentional, well-thought-out and carefully funded manipulation of the public's sensibilities that has been going on for over four decades. Homosexuals are only the latest target in the Christian Right's millennialist paranoia, and gays and lesbians, as the newest examples of the demonized 'other', have been deliberately and opportunistically chosen as the ultimate scapegoats.[73]

As lethal as it is, the Christian Right's agenda is fairly straightforward and easy to understand, if, in my opinion, misguided. Much more problematic and subtle, however, is the homophobia that manifests itself

---

70 See de la Huerta, *Coming Out Spiritually*, pp. 182–97, for a survey of attitudes toward homosexuality in the various Christian denominations.

71 Herman, *The Antigay Agenda*, Chapter 2.

72 The most prominent example of this is a videotape entitled 'The Gay Agenda', which has been successfully marketed by televangelists to middle America as 'the truth' about homosexuality. See Herman, *The Antigay Agenda*, pp. 80–2. My characterization of the gay community's depiction here is in no way meant to criticize or judge those segments of the community who do cross-dress or are differently sexual (e.g. the S/M and bear subcultures) or utilize transgressive tactics to make a political statement (e.g. organizations such as QueerNation and ACTUP); my concern is that the Christian Right portrays *all* gay and lesbian people as the same and labels us sick and perverted, while at the same time ignoring the fact that the majority of paedophiles are of heterosexual orientation.

73 Herman, *The Antigay Agenda*, Chapters 2 and 3.

in statements and decisions from the so-called 'mainline' Protestant denominations, who would, in most matters theological and political, seek to distance themselves from the Christian Right. For example:

- In October 2001, the United Methodist Church affirmed the non-appointment of a lesbian clergywoman as pastor of a church in Seattle on the grounds that she had 'admitted' in a letter to her bishop that she was 'a self-avowed practicing homosexual', which is forbidden by the denomination's Book of Discipline.[74] This decision, by punishing the clergy in question for being honest, encourages gay and lesbian clergy to live inauthentic lives of secrecy and shame and to deny their life partners if they wish to pursue their calling.
- In August, 2001, the Evangelical Lutheran Church in America affirmed its ban on the ordination of non-celibate gay clergy, while both pro-gay groups and the Revd Fred Phelps picketed outside the meeting.[75]
- In August, 2001, the members of Central Presbyterian Church of Owensboro, Kentucky, voted to remove their pastor after he began to welcome gays and lesbians and multiracial families.[76]
- In June 2001, a forum sponsored by the Presbyterian Church in the USA for pastors and lay leaders who are seeking to minister to those who are 'confused about their sexuality' included a presentation by the Executive Director of the National Association for the Research and Therapy of Homosexuality, who stated, 'We are all hetero-sexuals. Homosexuality is a description of a condition. It is not a description of the intrinsic nature of the person,' adding that this 'dis-order . . . can be corrected through "reparative therapy".'[77]
- In October 1999, the Adventist Church issued a statement that 'Adventists are opposed to homosexual practices and relationships.

---

74 Joretta Purdue, 'Judicial Council Rules on Declaration of Homosexuality', *Worldwide Faith News Archives* (29 October 2001). I am indebted to Wayne Juneau for furnishing the information cited in notes 74 to 79. I am pleased to report that, after this chapter was written, but before the book went to print, both the Evangelical Lutheran Church in America and the Presbyterian Church in the USA have reversed their policies regarding ordination of gay/lesbian persons.

75 Kevin Eckstrom, 'Lutherans Retain Ban on Gay Clergy', *Worldwide Faith News Archives* (14 August 2001).

76 Evan Silverstein, 'Kentucky Congregation Ousts Pastor After He Opened Church to Gays', *Worldwide Faith News Archives* (17 August 2001).

77 Evan Silverstein, 'Homosexuality Starts as a Developmental Disorder That Can End with Therapy', *Worldwide Faith News Archives* (27 June 2000). This forum did not include 'equal time' for the prevailing psychiatric view that homosexuality is not a disorder that can be cured.

. . . [T]he marital relationship of a man and a woman . . . was the design established by God at creation.'[78]

* In August 1998, the Lambeth Conference once again affirmed the Anglican Communion's stance against homosexual relationships, same-sex unions, and gay and lesbian clergy as 'incompatible with scripture'.[79] This occurred despite the fact that some components of the Anglican Communion, such as the Episcopal Church in the United States and the Church of England, have blessed same-sex unions and have ordained openly gay and lesbian clergy.

Perhaps the most homophobic and contradictory messages regarding homosexuality, however, continue to emanate from the Roman Catholic Church. Even before he ascended to the papacy as Benedict XVI, Joseph Cardinal Ratzinger seemed to have a vendetta against homosexual persons and sought to undo any progress that was made on the issue as part of the new spirit of the Second Vatican Council.[80] While affirming that homosexuals are deserving of pastoral care, Ratzinger nevertheless insists that homosexual persons are 'disordered' and must remain celibate. Theologians such as John McNeill and Matthew Fox have been expelled from the priesthood for their affirmation of same-sex affection and sexual expression, while New Ways Ministry was forced to cease its ministry to the gay and lesbian community. Dignity, a group for gay and lesbian Catholics who seek to remain in the Church, has been forbidden by order of the Vatican to meet on property owned by the Roman Catholic Church.[81] A significant indicator of the Catholic hierarchy's deep-seated prejudice is the refusal of the Vatican to ever use the words 'gay' or 'lesbian' in its papers, directives or press releases, preferring the terms 'homosexual' or 'same-sex', which emphasize the Vatican's insistence upon genital sexual activity rather than affectional orientation.[82]

---

78 John Beckett, 'Adventist Church Statement Affirms Biblical View on Homosexuality', *Worldwide Faith News Archives* (5 October 1999).

79 David Skidmore, 'Lambeth Struggles Over Homosexuality in Emotional Plenary', *Worldwide Faith News Archives* (7 August 1998).

80 See note 56, above.

81 Chester Gillis, *Roman Catholicism in America* (New York: Columbia University Press, 1999), pp. 36–7.

82 One of the first lessons one learns in any sort of consciousness-raising or diversity training is that, if one seeks to understand another, one must call him or her what s/he wishes to be called. In similar fashion, the Church of England in its official documents employs the term 'homophile'. (I am indebted to Natalie Watson for pointing this out to me.)

In 2000, during millennial celebrations that included same-sex revelry, Alfonso Cardinal López Trujillo, President of the Pontifical Council for the Family, responded to the Resolution of the European Parliament that sought to make 'de facto unions, including same sex unions, equal to the family' by posing the question, 'Doesn't making . . . homosexual unions equivalent to marriage . . . represent a refusal to recognize the deep aspirations of peoples in their innermost identity?'[83] This statement, in addition to sending mixed messages about personal identity, contradicts itself by refusing to recognize that gay and lesbians people have 'deep aspirations in their innermost identity'. Once again, the gay or lesbian person is reduced to the category of 'other' through heteropatriarchal privilege and the assumption of compulsory heterosexuality.

A few months later, in July 2000, the late Pope John Paul II himself addressed the contemporary situation of homosexuals, precipitated by demonstrations in Rome that gay and lesbian protesters launched against the Church's Jubilee Year celebration in July, 2000.

> In the name of the Church of Rome I can only express my deep sadness at the affront to the Great Jubilee of the Year 2000 and the offence to the Christian values of a city that is so dear to the hearts of Catholics throughout the world. The Church cannot remain silent about the truth, because she would fail in her fidelity to God the Creator and would not help to distinguish good from evil. . . . In this regard, I wish merely to read what is said in the Catechism of the Catholic Church . . . : 'The number of men and women who have deep-seated homosexual tendencies is not negligible. *This inclination, which is objectively disordered, constitutes for most of them a trial.* . . . These persons are called to fulfil God's will in their lives and, if they are Christians, to unite to the sacrifice of the Lord's Cross the difficulties they may encounter from their condition.'[84]

---

83 Alfonso Cardinal López Trujillo, 'Declaration of the Pontifical Council for the Family Regarding the Resolution of the European Parliament Dated March 16, 2000', www.vatican.va (17 March 2000).

84 John Paul II, 'Angelus: Jubilee in Prisons', www.vatican.va (9 July 2000), quoting the *Catechism of the Catholic Church*, n. 2358 (emphasis added). It is ironic to me that the occasion of this Angelus was the Holy Father's visit to the Regina Caeli Prison; he fails to see the connection between his remarks and the entrapment of gay and lesbian persons in prisons of heterosexism and self-hatred motivated by ongoing homophobia.

The italicized phrase demonstrates the Vatican's continuous disavowal of contemporary psychological and medical findings regarding gender and sexuality.[85] To ignore scientific evidence in this manner is not only less than truthful; I believe it is a sin, for it perpetuates the systemic oppression of individuals who seek to share their authentic selves and embrace their God-given prerogative of sexual expression 'in Spirit and in truth' (John 4.23). Moreover, John Paul II was in effect telling gay and lesbian persons 'encountering difficulties' to 'offer it up' with 'the sacrifice of the Lord's Cross', a statement that, in my opinion, distorts the Christological importance of Christ's cross and the very doctrine of the atonement as articulated by the Church Fathers. As a queer Christology recognizes, gay men and lesbians are crucified day by day with Jesus, but the good news that comes out of those crucifixions is that in Christ we may be resurrected, leaving behind in the empty tomb the grave clothes of homophobia, compulsory heterosexuality, and verbal and physical gay bashing, whether at the hands of a fundamentalist hatemonger like Fred Phelps or the beloved head of the Roman Catholic Church.[86]

Christophobia among Homosexuals

Our discussion thus far has revealed one reason why a queer Christology might be needed: the ongoing marginalization of gay and lesbian persons from full participation in Christianity due to the homophobia that is manifested by individual Christians and by Church structures and systems. There is, however, another, more pressing reason why there must be a queer Christology: the deep-seated feeling among many gays and lesbians that Jesus Christ is not an option for them, that he, as the embodied representative of God, hates them, and that they have no place in either Christ's Church or the kingdom of God he announced during his earthly ministry. This is a mindset that I call 'Christophobia'. It is as factually bankrupt as homophobia and just as pernicious, for it

---

85 For a discussion of the difficulties of the Vatican's position, see Gillis, *Roman Catholicism*, pp. 176–8.

86 The Vatican's view has remained unchanged despite (or perhaps because of) a change in popes. Benedict XVI, though willing to apologize for the Church's stance vis-à-vis Adolf Hitler and the behaviour of paedophile priests, remains adamant in his refusal to reconsider his earlier words on homosexuality as 'objectively disordered'. See the *New York Times* coverage for his April 2006 visit to the United States.

separates many spiritually focused and religiously gifted individuals from a path that could bring them the fulfilment that they have sought and been unable to find elsewhere. Let me be clear at the outset that I am in no way suggesting that Christ is 'the only way' for everyone, especially for all gays and lesbians. My point is that there are many in the queer community who yearn to be followers of Christ but believe that this is impossible. Many have successfully found meaning in twelve step spirituality, New Age theosophy and Eastern religions, and they have a spiritual home.[87] Others, like myself, spent years 'in the wilderness' flitting from one spiritual fad to another before an experience of the *true* Christ made us realize the pointlessness of our Christophobia. This work is for those who are still in the wilderness, seeking the Christ who meets them in their wandering and welcomes them home.

How do I know there is Christophobia among homosexuals? Why, it's there, wherever one looks, if one has an eye to see it. It's in the self-deprecating humour found in gay novels and plays. It's in the 'I'm going to hell anyway, so I'm going to have a good time doing it' attitude among many of the young people with whom I come in contact through my ministry in the Metropolitan Community Church. It's in the relief and tears I see when someone really 'gets it' that Christ can be their friend, their teacher and their saviour, if they will let him. It's in the joy they radiate when they receive Holy Communion for the first time with that new mindset of what womanist theologian Delores Williams calls 'somebodiness'.[88] And it's in the sadness and despair that I see when Church and society's homophobia has done its job so well and the insidious spectre of Christopobia has gained such a strong foothold in the queer psyche, that the gay or lesbian person just walks away, further down the path of loneliness, despair and degradation and into the arms of addiction, casual sex or – worst case scenario – suicide.

A recent coming-of-age novel points out that many queer youth live

---

87 'Perhaps the most compelling evidence of gay people's shifting away from their religions backgrounds is the consistency with which various studies have reported their current religious affiliations. Differing noticeably from their religious backgrounds, the current religious affiliations of gay people in various geographical areas at various times over twenty years have remained consistently low with regard to Protestantism and Catholicism, high with regard to Judaism, and very high with regard to "other" and "no" affiliation.' Gary David Comstock, *Unrepentant, Self-Affirming, Practicing: Lesbian/Bisexual/Gay People within Organized Religion* (New York: Continuum, 1996), p. 58.

88 Delores S. Williams, 'A Womanist Perspective on Sin', in *A Troubling in My Soul*, ed. Emilie M. Townes (Maryknoll, NY: Orbis Books, 1993), p. 140.

in this tension between their nascent feelings and their religious upbringing.

'Of course, things are on the up and up now that we've got one of *us* in the Vatican.' A delighted smile takes hold of her; Nana has treated the recent appointment of the first Polish pope as a kind of modern-day miracle.

Robin bites into his sandwich and stops listening. He likes everything about his grandmother but her unwavering belief. . . . Flashes of going to mass: people mumbling lengthy, memorized prayers, standing, sitting, kneeling like robots, the priest trying to convince everyone (even himself?) about the lessons in the Bible. Lessons thousands of years old! What did the Bible have to say about guys like Larry, who bullied and hurt people and got away with it? What did it have to say about high school? Or wet dreams, or Todd Spicer, or thinking about boys the way you're supposed to think about girls?

He shakes his head to clear his thoughts, hating the fact that one piece of confusion inevitably leads to another: that thought he just had about boys – about liking boys instead of girls – that was a thought he'd never quite made into a sentence before, with a beginning, a middle and an end, even in his head. He concentrates on chewing his sandwich, on the way the slippery meat with the smooth flecks of green olives and pimentos sliced into it wads up into the bread between his teeth. Salt and sweet on his tongue. A lump going down his throat into his belly. A beginning, a middle, and an end. Communion never had any taste at all.[89]

Gay playwright Christopher Durang, himself a refugee from Catholicism, in his hilarious and bittersweet play *Sister Mary Ignatius Explains It All to You*, has the protagonist, Sister Mary, rail against her pupils that homosexuality is 'the sin that makes Jesus throw up!' and the play concludes with Sister Mary, in a homophobic frenzy, shooting dead a former student whom she has learned is gay but has just gone to confession, so that his soul might still go to heaven.[90] In this way, by caricaturing one nun's homophobia, Durang also reveals his own deep-seated Christopobia.

---

89 K. M. Soehnlein, *The World of Normal Boys* (New York: Kensington Books, 2000), pp. 52–3.

90 Christopher Durang, 'Sister Mary Ignatius Explains It All to You' (*c.*1986), in Durang, *Christopher Durang Explains It All to You: Six Plays* (New York: Grove Press, 1990), pp. 167–214.

Gay culture critic Bruce Bawer relates a personal anecdote in which he tries to defend his religious views to Christophobic gay friends:

'Jesus loves you,' the evangelist says, still beaming, and moves along.

As he does, my Baptist friends and I look down at our tracts. Each consists of four three-by-five inch pages. 'THOUSANDS OF DEGREES HOT!' scream out bright red uppercase letters on the first page. 'AND NOT A DROP OF WATER.' . . .

The inside pages are all text: 'Jesus Christ believed in a BURNING HELL, that is why He left the Father's bosom and came to the world of sorrow. . . . One day in HELL, you will not have to be bothered by some Christian trying to give you a gospel tract. . . . You will be crying, and begging for one drop of water to cool your scorching tongue. But it will be too late.' . . .

After the evangelist's repeated declarations of Jesus' love, my Baptist friends and I are a bit jolted by the tract's hellfire message. . . . I shake my head. . . . 'To embrace Jesus because you fear God's wrath is to misunderstand God entirely. In fact it's to embrace something, or someone, that isn't Jesus at all.'[91]

Gay journalist Dann Hazel documents his own Christophobia:

[H]omosexuality grew into a controversy of faith – *my* controversy of faith. I became a 'marginalized Christian.' . . . For many years, I thought of Jesus as a maverick, a revolutionary, an innovator. He was the pattern for my life. He was a savior personal enough that I could speak to him in prayer and tap into the strength I gleaned from our conversation to move forward – always forward – in life. Now, because I am part of 'the controversy,' I often feel betrayed by the same religion that once gave my life meaning. But most of all, I experience sadness and anger – the way a surgery patient might feel after he discovers he's gone under the knife unnecessarily. . . . How could I find it in my heart to pledge myself to this faith, the way I had once pledged? How could any of us – gay and lesbian Christians, and straight allies in the fight with us – take that leap? We had become what [Bishop John Shelby] Spong calls 'believers in exile.'[92]

---

91 Bruce Bawer, *Stealing Jesus: How Fundamentalism Betrays Christianity* (New York: Crown Publishers, 1997), pp. 31–2.

92 Hazel, *Witness*, pp. 136–7, citing John Shelby Spong, *Why Christianity Must Change or Die: A Bishop Speaks to Believers in Exile* (New York: Harper-Collins, 1998).

Gay/lesbian church founder Troy Perry relates that the single most challenging thing he encountered when attempting to found a Christian church for homosexual persons was the belief among gays and lesbians themselves that they could not be gay and Christian, that Jesus Christ was no longer an option for them, as long as they were 'practising' homosexuals.[93]

Some examples of real-life Christophobia will document that it is a fact of queer life that a queer Christology might ameloriate:

> The attempt of gay men to merge their Catholicism with homosexuality has always seemed to me touching but doomed. . . . There can be no commerce, no conflation of, these two things. Fellatio has nothing to do with Holy Communion. Better to frankly admit that you have changed gods, and are now worshipping Priapus, not Christ.[94]

> I cannot be queer in church, though I've tried . . . I long for a kind of spiritual intensity, a passion . . . I don't know what I want in a church, finally; I think the truth is that I don't want a church.[95]

> A Jewish lesbian friend told me that she can't fathom how anyone of conscience would live in the South. Along the backroads of the state in which I live, one finds enormous crosses erected in threes. She told me, half-jokingly, that she's afraid that if her car breaks down while she's driving through the South, she'll be nailed to one of those crosses.[96]

> I'm at a place in my life where I'm clarifying and answering questions. I wish I knew of a religion that will fill in all the blanks for me . . . At ten years old I was confirmed, and I learned a lot about how to follow Jesus. But basically I believed it to please Mama. . . . Yet a couple years later I accepted Christ. . . . I have a feeling that something touched me. Somebody, something, I felt the power; I knew there was something out there that had picked me to love. . . . Anyway, when I

---

93 Perry, *The Lord Is My Shepherd*, pp. 77, 103–05; and Perry, in a 1981 sermon memorialized in the documentary film *God, Gays, and the Gospel: This Is Our Story* (1983).

94 Andrew Holleran, 'The Sense of Sin', in *Wrestling with the Angel: Faith and Religion in the Lives of Gay Men*, ed. Brian Bouldrey (New York: Riverhead Books, 1995), p. 83.

95 Mark Doty, 'Sweet Chariot', in *Wrestling with the Angel*, ed. Bouldrey, p. 6.

96 D. G. Miller, 'Trying Grace', in *Wrestling with the Angel*, ed. Bouldrey, p. 136.

went to the performing arts high school, I started falling away . . .
Little things made me believe that 'I'm such a sinner; I can't handle it,'
and I started getting into that deep valley . . . [and, after attending a
non-Christian church] my early beliefs that Jesus was God's only son
kept creeping in, so I felt blasphemous . . . My mother and my sister
follow the Bible, point-blank, and if it's [lesbianism] a sin, then I'm
wrong; they keep saying, 'All you have to do is turn back and ask God
for forgiveness, and we'll never mention this again.'[97]

[I]f I honestly state who I am – a gay woman, a gay Christian – then I
apparently am part of a movement which you find 'outrageous' and
'unacceptable.'[98]

Fortunately, many gay and lesbian people are able to separate the
message of Jesus Christ from the message of a homophobic Christian
Church and have been able to remain within traditional Christianity.
However, many others – perhaps even the majority of gays and lesbians
– find themselves separated not only from Christianity but also from
Christ, because the origin of Christian homophobia has been wrongly
attributed to Christ.[99] So integrated has the message of homophobia
become with the Christ message that it has given birth to a very real
inward consciousness that I have termed 'Christophobia'. Many other
examples and personal testimonies could be cited here, but I believe the
above discussion will suffice to show that a new, queer Christology is
required if gays and lesbians are to overcome contemporary Christian
homophobia and their own Christophobia.

Conclusion

Are there general principles that might explain the Judaeo-Christian
tradition's condemnation or acceptance of homosexuality? I believe
there are. First, there seems to be a strong prohibition of same-sex
affinity in patriarchal cultures. When patriarchy delineates particular
sex roles and behaviours as appropriate and expected for the genders,

---

97 'Denise: Moving Beyond the "Fashion Show,"' in David Shellenberger,
Reclaiming the Spirit: Gay Men and Lesbians Come to Terms with Religion (New
Brunswick, NJ, and London: Rutgers University Press, 1998), pp. 56–9, 61, 64.
98 Comstock, *Unrepentant, Self-Affirming, Practicing*, p. 69, quoting a
woman named Tracy Archibald on her exit from the Presbyterian Church.
99 See the statistics in Comstock, *Unrepentant, Self-Affirming, Practicing*.

there is an intolerance of those who assume roles seen as belonging to the other gender or engage in acts that blur the genders. Thus, we see the Holiness Code in the Hebrew Testament of the Bible forbidding a man to lie with another man 'as with a woman' and the apostle Paul in the Christian Testament indicting those who give up what is 'natural' to pursue what is 'unnatural'. One of the hallmarks of a patriarchal society is an underlying misogyny and sexism that seeks to keep women 'in their place' (figuratively and literally under the man). This misogyny affects views of what it means to 'be a man'. Especially abhorrent in patriarchal societies is for one man to submit to another as the passive participant in anal intercourse. Passivity and penetration remove one's 'maleness' and make one akin to the female who is thought of as inferior and in some respects less than human. Patriarchy fosters this 'sex panic', which manifests itself in a double standard ('don't ask, don't tell'), obsessive fear of and violence against those who are different, and the encouragement of inauthenticity and shame on the part of those who are relegated to the status of 'other'.

Second, there is a connection between gender mutuality and the image of God promulgated by Judaeo-Christian Scripture and tradition. As noted in Chapter 6, God has been imaged as a male for most of Christian history, and, as Mary Daly says, 'If God is male, then the male is God.'[100] A male God created and controlled by the patriarchy keeps sexist and heterosexist views of sexuality in place, while a God freed from the constraints of heteropatriarchal interpretation – whether imaged as male, female or neither – would broaden the concepts of what it means to be 'masculine', 'feminine', 'straight' or 'gay', because no one image or characteristic would be sanctified (or codified) as reflecting the Divine. An interesting question implicitly posed by gay scholar Randy Conner is whether there is a connection between the establishment of gender roles and the disestablishment of gender-variant individuals as conduits for the Divine.[101] I believe there is. When only one gender is honoured as reflective of the 'image and likeness of God', there is a resulting dishonouring of the other gender and those persons who are seen as somehow blurring or bridging the genders through their mannerisms, behaviour or sexual acts. Thus, one sees in indigenous cultures

---

100 Mary Daly, *Beyond God the Father: Toward a Philosophy of Women's Liberation, with an Original Reintroduction by the Author* (1973; Boston: Beacon Press, 1985), p. 19.

101 Randy P. Conner, *Blossom of Bone: Reclaiming the Connections Between Homoeroticism and the Sacred* (New York: HarperCollins, 1993).

not only an honouring of individuals whose sexuality is non-heterosexual but an honouring of the Divine Feminine both as deity and as embodied in the human person. I believe, with feminist scholars of religion, that if patriarchy can be 'disestablished' as the prevailing pattern for our interpersonal relations and the maintenance of society, there would be not only a more inclusive view of the Divine but a paradigm shift in how women and men see themselves and others. A direct benefit of such a change would be the tolerance – no, the complete acceptance – of those whose lives do not move in the heterosexual mainstream.

And what of the homosexual community's feelings about Christianity and its central figure, Jesus Christ? The testimonies and anecdotes included in this chapter suggest that, for many gays and lesbians, Jesus Christ is a 'holy terror' who is used as a bludgeon against queer identity and existence. Thankfully, at the turn of the century, a new queer theology and biblical hermeneutics began springing forth from a new crop of gay and lesbian scholars and grass-roots religious organizations. The next chapter will analyse this movement, which has not yet articulated a specifically queer Christology, the topic of Chapter 11. This new self-affirmation among self-identified 'queers' differentiates it from the early 'gay and lesbian' strides for liberation and inclusion in religion. It has a stridency and 'in-your-face' tone that is summed up in the use of the word 'queer', the pros and cons of which will also be discussed in the next chapter. This intentional, proactive stance – and its risks – are summarized well by gay theologian and sociologist Gary David Comstock:

As gay people contemplate the future, we should know that if mainstream religion becomes more humane, charitable, and welcoming of all people, such changes will depend significantly on us. If we choose to take responsibility to advocate for and participate in those changes, we should also know that our lives will be marked with some moments of exhilarating freedom and hope as well as unrelenting if not crushing defeats and humiliation.[102]

Homophobia and Christophobia as delineated in this chapter intersect in a powerful and poignant way in a gay short film entitled 'The Confession', one of four films gathered together under the title *Boys to Men*.[103] In the film, Caesar and Joseph are a gay couple who have been

---

102 Comstock, *Unrepentant, Self-Affirming, Practicing*, p. 235.
103 Carl Pfirman, director, 'The Confession', UCLA School of Film, Theatre, and Television, in *Boys to Men* (Jour de Fête Films, Strand Releasing, 2000).

together for 35 years. Joseph is dying of undisclosed causes and, after much soul-searching, has asked Caesar to have a priest come to their home to hear his last confession. Father Marcus, a young priest from the local Catholic Church, arrives and is ushered upstairs to the sickroom. After realizing that Caesar and Joseph are in a homosexual relationship, Father Marcus reminds Joseph that homosexual acts are a sin and that absolution cannot be granted if there is the intention of engaging in the acts again. Joseph, torn between his feelings for his partner and his desire to reconcile with God, sends the priest away; however, his fear of impending death and the spectre of eternal damnation cause him to call the priest back and make his confession. The film's final scene shows Caesar and Joseph in bed; Joseph cannot breathe or speak very well, but he asks Caesar why he doesn't move closer to him. Caesar replies that if he does so, they might commit a sin, and sadly remarks that their entire 35 years have been one big sin. The film ends with the unasked – and certainly unanswered – question hanging in the air: should Joseph have had to deny his love for Caesar to be acceptable to God in Christ? I believe that this film, in its bittersweet simplicity and its stark realism, illustrates the homophobia of the Christian Church and its adherents and also the Christophobia among gay people: Father Marcus cannot hide his disgust and disapproval, even though he can be no more than 28 years old; Caesar reveals his disdain for Father Marcus and all he stands for; and Joseph is trapped, caught between (at least) 35 years of Christophobia and the internalized homophobia that tells him his life and love have been a sin. Because Christophobia has done its work so well, it is homophobia that wins out in the end.

9

'Queer' as Social Location: Legitimate Category or just Propaganda?

Introduction

The preceding chapter began by examining the negative treatment of homosexual persons – what some refer to as 'homophobia' – by Christians throughout history and concluded by suggesting a parallel stance among homosexuals vis-à-vis the One whom Christians revere as Christ – what I have termed 'Christophobia'. The discussion demonstrated that homophobia and Christophobia continue to coexist in exquisite tension in today's Church and society. I contend that a new vision of Christ from the perspective of sexual orientation will contribute to the alleviation of this tension and to a greater wholeness among gays and lesbians who wish to join their spiritual journey to the Christ.

Before I can proceed to describe what a Christology of sexual orientation might look like, however, I must address an issue that I am sure will be raised (if it has not been already): whether 'sexual orientation' is a legitimate 'social location' from which to do theology. Additionally, there is debate within the homosexual community regarding how we should characterize ourselves: Are we 'gay, lesbian, bisexual and transgendered' or are we 'queer'? What nuances does the word 'queer' bring to the discussion that other terms lack? Can heterosexuals be 'queer'?

Thus, this chapter will begin by staking a claim for sexual orientation as a social location alongside race, gender and class. It will then examine the meanings of the word 'queer' in today's world. Finally, in preparation for the explicitly queer Christology of Chapters 10 and 11, I will conclude with a brief look at what type of theology and biblical interpretation have been done through the lens of sexual orientation.

Sexual Orientation as Social Location

'Sexual orientation' has become the accepted term for one's affectional/sexual inclinations, while 'sexual preference' has fallen into disfavour, due to its suggestion that one's sexuality can be chosen. Sexologists, feminist theorists, and queer theorists have differentiated between 'sex', 'gender', and 'sexuality', while asking whether one's gender and sexual orientation are universal and innate or created and conditioned by culture.[1] This is a vast and complex topic; I do not propose to rehearse all of the theories and points of view that have been expressed regarding gender and sexuality over the past three decades, for to do so would lead me away from my topic. Nevertheless, I believe that I must touch briefly upon the idea of sexual orientation, in order to dispel the notion promulgated by conservative Christians that all of this talk of sexual orientation is just politically correct nonsense that is actually propaganda masquerading as social scientific data.

The aforementioned view was expressed most vividly by the Ramsey Colloquium in a 1994 manifesto entitled, 'The Homosexual Movement, a Response by the Ramsey Colloquium'. The Colloquium is a group of biblical scholars, theologians and ethicists who 'meet periodically to consider questions of morality, religion, and public life'.[2] The Colloquium's presupposition of condemnation and disdain may be seen in their repeated use of quotation marks to highlight certain ideas that they perceive the gay and lesbian 'movement' using as propaganda to push its views of society and sexuality upon an unsuspecting populace. For example, throughout this article, the Colloquium so designates the following words or phrases: 'Stonewall Riot', 'orientation', 'lifestyle', 'sexual identity', 'in the closet', 'coming out of the closet', 'domestic partnerships', 'straights', and 'homophobia'. Additionally, the Colloquium insists upon using the words 'gay' and 'lesbian' to refer only to the 'movement', while repeatedly referring to individual persons as 'homosexuals', in order to bolster their claim that homosexuality is a matter of genital sexual activity rather than cultural symbiosis and sexual orientation.[3] I do not wish to give the Colloquium too much importance in this discussion; nevertheless, I believe that its perspective is representative of many in our society who base their discrimination of gays and lesbians

---

1 See, for example, Judith Butler, *Gender Trouble: Feminism and the Subversion of Identity* (New York and London: Routledge, 1990).

2 The Ramsey Colloquium, 'The Homosexual Movement, a Response by the Ramsey Colloquium', *First Things* 41 (March 1994), p. 15.

3 Ramsey Colloquium, 'The Homosexual Movement', passim.

upon outmoded notions of society, sexuality and partnership, and so I
quote from this document at some length. For example, the Colloquium
states:

> The gay and lesbian movement, and the dramatic changes in sexual
> attitudes and behaviors of which that movement is part, have
> unloosed a great moral agitation in our culture. . . . To endure (toler-
> ance), to pity (compassion), to embrace (affirmation): that is the
> sequence of change in attitude and judgment that has been advanced
> by the gay and lesbian movement with notable success. *We expect
> that this success will encounter certain limits and that what is truly
> natural will reassert itself,* but this may not happen before more
> damage is done to innumerable individuals and to our common life.[4]

The Colloquium paints a picture of a 'gay and lesbian movement' that is
helmed by radical malcontents who seek social revolution, while portraying the majority of 'homosexuals' as socially 'normal' individuals
who want to stay 'in the closet' and live their lives quietly and privately.
This is a familiar tactic that the Christian Right has employed in
portraying feminists as evil revolutionaries who do not represent the
majority of women but only a radical fringe of lesbian man-haters.[5]

The Colloquium denies that sexual orientation is a legitimate social
category from which to do human rights work.

> Gay and lesbian advocates sometimes claim that they are asking for no
> more than an end to discrimination, drawing an earlier analogy with
> the earlier civil rights movement that sought justice for black
> Americans. The analogy is unconvincing and misleading. Differences
> in race are in accord with – not contrary to – our nature, and such
> differences do not provide justification for behavior otherwise un-
> acceptable. It is sometimes claimed that homosexuals want only a
> recognition of their status, not necessarily of their behavior. But in this
> case the distinction between status and behavior does not hold. The
> public declaration of status ('coming out of the closet') is a declaration

---

4 Ramsey Colloquium, 'The Homosexual Movement', pp. 19–20 (emphasis
added).

5 See Didi Herman, *The Antigay Agenda: Orthodox Vision and the Christian
Right* (Chicago and London: University of Chicago Press, 1997), Chapter 4; and
Suzanne Pharr, *Homophobia: A Weapon of Sexism* (Little Rock, AR: Chardon
Press, 1988), pp. 36–40.

of intended behavior. Certain discriminations are necessary within society; it is not too much to say that civilization itself depends on the making of such distinctions (between, finally, right and wrong).[6]

This refusal to see anti-homosexual discrimination as analogous to other types of discrimination goes hand in hand with the Colloquium's insistence upon a narrow construction of homosexuality as exclusively sexual in nature.

> Our statement is directed chiefly to debates over public policy and what should be socially normative. We share the uneasiness of most Americans with the proposals advanced by the gay and lesbian movement . . . To depict marriage as simply one of several alternative 'lifestyles' is seriously to undermine the normative vision required for social well-being. . . . We believe that any understanding of sexuality, including heterosexuality, that makes it chiefly an arena for the satisfaction of personal desire is harmful to individuals and society. . . . Perhaps the key supposition of the [sexual] revolution is that human health and flourishing require that sexual desire, understood as 'need', be acted upon and satisfied. Any discipline of denial or restraint has been popularly depicted as unhealthy and dehumanizing. We insist, however, that it is dehumanizing to define ourselves, or our personhood as male and female, by our desires alone. Nor does it seem plausible to suggest that what millennia of human experience have taught us to regard as self-command should now be dismissed as mere repression. . . . Not all marriages and families 'work', but it is unwise to let pathology and failure, rather than a vision of what is normative and ideal, guide us in the development of social policy.[7]

Nor was the Ramsey Colloquium concerned with being perceived as homophobic, a stance that not only set the precedent for Robert Gagnon's recent disclaimer, noted in the preceding chapter,[8] but also confirms Byrne Fone's observation that homophobia is indeed the 'last acceptable prejudice'.[9]

---

6 Ramsey Colloquium, 'The Homosexual Movement', p. 19.

7 Ramsey Colloquium, 'The Homosexual Movement', pp. 16–18.

8 Robert A. J. Gagnon, *The Bible and Homosexual Practice: Texts and Hermeneutics* (Nashville: Abingdon Press, 2001), pp. 26–9. See the discussion of Gagnon's perspective in Chapter 8.

9 Byrne Fone, *Homophobia: A History* (New York: Metropolitan Books/ Henry Holt and Company, 2000), p. 3.

We are well aware that this declaration will be dismissed by some as a display of 'homophobia,' but such dismissals have become unpersuasive and have ceased to intimidate. Indeed, we do not think it a bad thing that people should experience a reflexive recoil from what is wrong.[10]

However, what should guide one's classification of discrimination and what constitutes a legitimate social location is not what society considers 'right and wrong', for history reminds us that blacks were quite recently seen as subhuman and savage (as reflected in miscegenation statutes), while women were regarded as the devil's plaything (as reflected in heteropatriarchal efforts to control women's bodies and sexuality). What one must use instead is the lived experience of the group claiming discrimination and seeking redress. Thus, few in today's world would even attempt an academic argument that disputes the humanity and rights of African Americans or the demands of women for full personhood. Therefore, we must turn to the testimonies of those gay and lesbian persons who have articulated the need for liberation and equality in a heteropatriarchal world.

In this regard, culture critic Russell Ferguson has asserted:

When we say marginal, we must always ask, marginal to what? But this question is difficult to answer. The place from which power is exercised is often a hidden place. When we try to pin it down, the center always seems to be somewhere else. Yet we know that this phantom center, elusive as it is, exerts a real, undeniable power over the whole social framework of our culture, and over the ways we think about it. [African-American lesbian poet and theorist] Audre Lorde calls this center the mythical norm, defined as 'white, thin, male, young, heterosexual, Christian, and financially secure.' Although each of these characteristics carries a somewhat different weight, their combination describes a status with which we are all familiar. It

---

10 Ramsey Colloquium, 'The Homosexual Movement', p. 19. This refusal to recognize their perspective as homophobic was belied by the aftermath of the publication of the Ramsey document. I was a student at the University of Virginia at the time, and the Chair of the Department of Religious Studies, of whose faculty two of the Ramsey Colloquium signatories (Robert L. Wilken and David Novak) were members, issued a statement to all students that the remarks of the Ramsey Colloquium should in no way be seen as representing the views of the University or the rest of the Religious Studies faculty. (The University of Virginia has in place a non-discrimination policy that includes sexual orientation.)

defines the tacit standards from which specific others can then be declared to deviate, and while that myth is perpetuated by those whose interests it serves, it can also be internalized by those who are oppressed by it.[11]

African-American religious and cultural scholar Cornel West notes that the struggle for rights must be a collective and cross-cultural effort among diverse groups of people, privileged and unprivileged alike.[12] A heterosexual man, West has nevertheless been quite vocal about hetero-sexism in religion, the academy and the African-American community.[13] Womanist theologian, church historian and Episcopal priest Kelly Brown Douglas concurs, advocating a 'sexual discourse of resistance' to efforts by the dominant society to turn oppressed groups against one another.[14] Thus, two heterosexual scholars who are themselves members of a recognized social location support the affirmation of sexual orientation as a social location when confronting interlocking oppressions in Church and society.

Lesbian activist Urvashi Vaid notes that internalized homophobia often leads gays and lesbians themselves to downplay their inclusion among recognized minorities and seek instead to be 'mainstreamed' into heteropatriarchal culture. She encourages gays and lesbians to work toward more than just 'virtual equality – a state of conditional equality based more on the appearance of acceptance by straight America than on genuine civic parity'.[15] She laments the fact that initially the gay and lesbian movement was about liberation, whereas recently many gays and lesbians have settled for mere toleration or legitimation.[16] Vaid points out that mainstream culture is still unwilling to believe that gays and lesbians are discriminated against and that the myth of gay and lesbian wealth is promulgated as a 'smoke screen' by keepers of the

---

11 Russell Ferguson, 'Introduction: Invisible Center', in *Out There: Marginalization and Contemporary Cultures*, ed. Russell Ferguson, Martha Gever, Trinh T. Minh-ha and Cornel West (Cambridge, MA, and London: The MIT Press, 1990), p. 9.

12 Cornel West, 'The New Cultural Politics of Difference', in *Out There*, ed. Ferguson et al., pp. 19–20.

13 See, for example, Cornel West, 'Christian Love and Heterosexism,' in *The Cornel West Reader* (New York: Basic Civitas Books, 1999), pp. 401–14.

14 Kelly Brown Douglas, *Sexuality and the Black Church: A Womanist Perspective* (Maryknoll, NY: Orbis Books, 1999), pp. 106–07.

15 Urvashi Vaid, *Virtual Equality: The Mainstreaming of Gay and Lesbian Liberation* (New York: Anchor Books/Doubleday, 1995), p. xvi.

16 Vaid, *Virtual Equality*, pp. 3, 37.

status quo in order to create suspicion in the minds of middle America that any talk of gay/lesbian equality has to do with 'special rights'.[17]

French feminist theorist Monique Wittig calls this overarching attitude 'the straight mind', which she equates with the universalizing tendency of a compulsory heterosexuality that tyrannizes people into believing that one truth should hold for 'all societies, all epochs, all individuals'. According to Wittig, the end result of this straight mind is the constant reminder to those of marginal sexuality that 'you-will-be-straight-or-you-will-not-be'.[18]

Lesbian religious scholar L. J. Tessier concurs, noting that society's encouragement of gay and lesbian invisibility leads to an erosion of identity due to continuous denial of self ('"seeming" is denial in action').[19] She asserts that true transformation both societally and spiritually will only come when all women and gays and lesbians are allowed to access their authentic selves both in public and in private.[20] This will not occur for gays and lesbians, however, unless and until sexual orientation is recognized as a legitimate social location from which to critique society and culture, including religion and theology.

In this sense, I believe that the situation of gays and lesbians is analogous to that of colonized peoples, who seek to differentiate notions of what is inherent from what is cultural. As long as Western, Christian characteristics were seen as universal, the ancestral customs of people from the colonized Third World were seen as 'other' and were suppressed; in the same way, as long as the perspective of heterosexuals is seen as normative and heterosexuality as compulsory and 'natural', gay and lesbian experience will be similarly marginalized and suppressed, a situation I call 'heterocolonialism'.[21]

---

17 Vaid, *Virtual Equality*, pp. 9, 247–9. See also Herman, *The Antigay Agenda*, pp. 116–20.

18 Monique Wittig, 'The Straight Mind', trans. Mary Jo Lakeland and Susan Ellis Wolf, in *Out There*, ed. Ferguson et al., p. 54.

19 L. J. Tessier, *Dancing After the Whirlwind: Feminist Reflections on Sex, Denial, and Spiritual Transformation* (Boston: Beacon Press, 1997), p. 94, but see the entirety of Chapter 3 for her discussion of the effects of denial upon identity.

20 Tessier, *Dancing After the Whirlwind*, p. 159.

21 Thomas Bohache, 'Heterocolonialism Queered: Eros Comes to Church' (unpublished doctoral dissertation, Episcopal Divinity School, 2007). See also Laura E. Donaldson and Kwok Pui-lan, eds, *Postcolonialism, Feminism, and Religious Discourse* (New York and London: Routledge, 2002); Fernando F. Segovia, *Decolonizing Biblical Studies: A View from the Margins* (Maryknoll, NY: Orbis Books, 2000); and Homi K. Bhabha, 'The Other Question: Difference, Discrimination, and the Discourse of Colonialism', in *Out There*, ed. Ferguson, et al., pp. 71–87.

What's in a Name?

Sodomite. Pederast. One who engages in the love that dare not speak its name. Uranian. Homosexual. Invert. Gay. Lesbian. Queer. These are just some of the words used during the Christian era to describe those whose affinity is toward one of the same sex.[22] In recent years, other terms have arisen for those whose sexual nature does not move in the heteropatriarchal mainstream: *Bisexual. Transgendered. Differently sexual. Pan-Sexual. Omni-Sexual. Seeking/Questioning. Lavender Tribe. Rainbow Nation.*[23]

The changing nomenclature within the gay/lesbian/queer community parallels the debate that has been raging for some time regarding the aetiology of gender and sexuality – whether these are universal, inborn categories or cultural constructs ('essentialism' vs 'constructionism'). As journalist Martha Gever points out, '[T]here is far too much disagreement among those of us who are affected to pretend that the task is so simple. Better yet, more voices should be introduced into the discussion.'[24] She cites as illustrations articles regarding the portrayal of lesbians and gays in film that assert, on the one hand, that 'homosexuality is not a sexual preference . . . that homosexuals are born homosexual and that homosexuality is not a chosen activity but a state of being',[25] and, on the other, that '[t]he [gay] New Wave abandons the myth of an innate gay identity, focussing instead on the particularities of sexuality in a given culture'.[26] Gever also details the reluctance that contemporary gay and lesbian theorists feel in discussing universality, for,

22 For a discussion of the various names by which homosexuals have been called, see Fone, *Homophobia*; John Boswell, *Christianity, Social Tolerance, and Homosexuality: Gay People in Western Europe from the Beginning of the Christian Era to the Fourteenth Century* (Chicago and London: University of Chicago Press, 1980); and David Halperin, *One Hundred Years of Homosexuality* (New York and London: Routledge, 1990).

23 For use of these terms, see Carol Queen and Lawrence Schimel, eds, *PoMo-Sexuals: Challenging Assumptions About Gender and Sexuality* (San Francisco: Cleis Press, 1997); Virginia Ramey Mollenkott, *Omnigender: A Trans-Religious Approach* (Cleveland: The Pilgrim Press, 2001); and Robert E. Goss and Amy Adams Squire Strongheart, eds, *Our Families, Our Values: Snapshots of Queer Kinship* (New York and London: The Haworth Press, 1997).

24 Martha Gever, 'The Names We Give Ourselves', in *Out There*, ed. Ferguson, et al., p. 192.

25 Gever, 'The Names We Give Ourselves', p. 192, citing film historian Vito Russo.

26 Gever, 'The Names We Give Ourselves', p. 192, citing film critic Richard Goldstein.

just as when one discusses feminism, there can be no one gay/lesbian 'identity' that fits every person's experience: homosexuality and homophobia are expressed and experienced differently in non-white cultures; moreover, 'the politics of gender . . . saturate every aspect' of any attempt to link the male and female homosexual communities.[27] She concludes that at the turn of the century there can be no definitive, across-the-board definition or description of gay, lesbian, bisexual or transgendered identity and experience. Labelling oneself as 'gay' or 'lesbian' was important in the early days of the homosexual liberation movement, for to 'come out' as gay or lesbian was a political, transgressive act.[28] Now that diversity has been recognized throughout society, and particularly in the realm of sexuality, it is much more transgressive and political in today's world to refuse to be labelled and to champion the fluidity of gender and sexuality.[29]

For this very reason, in the past ten years or so, the word 'queer' has been reclaimed by those who are not 'traditionally' heterosexual. Use of the terms 'gay and lesbian' or even 'gay, lesbian, bisexual and transgendered (GLBT)' has been seen as an attempt to impose a unity upon the parts of this subculture that is not there, whereas the word 'queer' is seen as empowering diversity because of its imprecise and hard-to-pin-down meaning. Moreover, 'queer' has both an adjectival (descriptive) and verbal (active) meaning: When something or someone is 'queer', they are uncommon, out of the ordinary, unusual and non-conforming to the dominant culture; 'to queer' something is to spoil it, disrupt it or thoroughly confound it.[30] Queer theorists and activists like the double meaning of this term because they are indeed out of the ordinary in not conforming to gender expectations, and – perhaps more importantly – they are seeking to spoil, disrupt and thoroughly confound traditional heteropatriarchal categories.[31] Where many 'gays and lesbians' in the

27 Gever, 'The Names We Give Ourselves', p. 194.

28 Gever, 'The Names We Give Ourselves', pp. 194–5.

29 The best example of this new reluctance to be labeled or classified is demonstrated by the essays in the anthology *PoMoSexuals* (see note 23). One even sees something of a 'generation gap' around this issue; one can guess another's age by whether they say 'gay' or 'gay and lesbian,' 'lesbians' or 'gay women,' or 'queer'.

30 I am indebted to queer theologian and activist Robert Goss for this insight (personal correspondence, 1995–present).

31 It is noteworthy that the pre-eminent queer theorist is a heterosexual woman, Eve Kosofsky Sedgwick of Duke University, whose *Epistemology of the Closet* is a basic text for queer studies (Berkeley: University of California Press, 1990). This supports my claim that in a heteropatriarchal society, heterosexual persons who actively support homosexuals and our causes (rather than merely

1970s and 1980s sought to be assimilated into the dominant culture, 'queers' today do not want mere assimilation but rather total accept-ance, freedom and self-determination.[32] Thus, Urvashi Vaid suggests that 'gays' have sold out, while 'queers' are more 'in your face'.[33] On the other hand, a conservative gay writer such as former *New Republic* editor Andrew Sullivan uses the term 'homosexual' almost exclusively, perhaps in order to ingratiate himself with the heteropatriarchal elite.[34]

Thus, Byrne Fone concludes:

> The terminology of sexuality has come under scrutiny. . . . Some con-temporary theory urges that we abandon any notion of a fixed gay and lesbian 'sexual identity' – an idea ascendant since Stonewall – in favor of a politics of 'difference' in which 'gay' and 'lesbian' identity is constantly renegotiated by race, class, and gender, and may at times be better defined by 'queer' or 'transgendered.'[35]

Lesbian theologian Virginia Mollenkott puts a theological spin on the notion of queerness:

> I have noticed that th[e] One Source likes variety and has chosen to be incarnated in millions of diverse ways. I therefore assume that the *ultimate* reason for 'queerness' does not lie in concepts constructed by society, or some eternal essence like 'male' and 'female' or 'bi-gendered,' but rather the fact that God has chosen to embody Himself/Herself/Itself in just this person's particularities at just this time and place. . . . I am therefore in full agreement . . . that 'We need

---

'tolerating' or 'accepting') are, themselves, queer. See the humorous discussion of Sedgwick's self-designation as 'queer' and the ensuing puzzlement of a journalist in Lisa Duggan, 'Queering the State', in *Social Perspectives in Lesbian and Gay Studies: A Reader*, ed. Peter M. Nardi and Beth E. Schneider (New York and London: Routledge, 1998), pp. 565–6. Duggan concludes, 'I tell this story . . . to illustrate the difficulty of communication across the gap between the predomi-nantly constructionist language of queer studies and the essentialist presumptions of public discourse.' (p. 566)

32 Vaid, *Virtual Equality*, pp. 202–09.

33 Vaid, *Virtual Equality*, Chapter 8.

34 See Andrew Sullivan, *Virtually Normal: An Argument About Homo-sexuality* (New York: Alfred A. Knopf, 1995); and the subsequent response of Michael Warner, *The Trouble with Normal: Sex, Politics, and the Ethics of Queer Life* (New York: The Free Press/Simon & Schuster, 1999).

35 Fone, *Homophobia*, p. 410.

to move beyond the facile dichotomy of "essentialism" and "constructionism" to embrace other theoretical paradigms.'[36]

Queer theorist Judith Butler concurs, noting that 'there is no reason to assume that genders ought also to remain as two'.[37] Journalist Joshua Gamson has suggested that it is 'socially produced' binaries such as man/woman and gay/straight that are the basis of oppression itself; thus, an embrace of a 'queer' sensibility deconstructs both gender and identity politics.[38]

It is even possible for non-homosexuals to be 'queer', according to some queer theorists. Thus, in explaining what it means to do 'queer commentary' of the Bible, Hebrew Bible scholar, Ken Stone, observes that 'in certain contexts' heterosexuals can be considered queer to the extent that they are willing to challenge sexual normativity.[39] Lesbian feminist theologian and Episcopal priest Carter Heyward concurs, asserting that she uses the term 'queer' to refer to anyone, regardless of their personal sexual orientation, who 'struggle[s] enthusiastically without apology against heterosexism'.[40]

Not everyone is happy with the selection of the word 'queer' as a new description of non-heterosexual orientation, however, due to its use as a derogatory epithet for so many decades. Older gays and lesbians especially have problems with this term, and it is my belief that part of this is because of the ingrained need of those over 40 to label themselves as 'gay' members of society in contradistinction to 'straight', whereas younger queers are more willing (indeed, eager) to retain 'outlaw'

---

36 Mollenkott, *Omnigender*, p. 16, quoting Chicana lesbian theorist Gloria Anzaldúa.

37 Butler, *Gender Trouble*, p. 10, concluding: 'The presumption of a binary gender system implicitly retains the belief in a mimetic relationship of gender to sex whereby gender mirrors sex or is otherwise restricted by it. When the constructed status of gender is theorized as radically independent of sex, gender itself becomes a free-floating artifice.'

38 Joshua Gamson, 'Must Identity Movements Self-Destruct? A Queer Dilemma', in *Social Perspectives in Lesbian and Gay Studies*, ed. Nardi and Schneider, pp. 589–92, citing queer theorist Steven Seidman.

39 Ken Stone, 'Queer Commentary and Biblical Interpretation: An Introduction', in *Queer Commentary and the Hebrew Bible*, ed. Ken Stone (Cleveland: The Pilgrim Press, 2001), p. 28.

40 Carter Heyward, *Saving Jesus from Those Who Are Right: Rethinking What It Means to Be Christian* (Minneapolis: Fortress Press, 1999), p. 224 n.3.

status.[41] Queer activist Michael Warner explains use of the word 'queer' as a gesture by those who do not wish to be considered 'normal' in order to avoid what he calls 'social suicide' (the non-being of assimilation).[42]

Nevertheless, outside the realm of the theoretical, the debate becomes quite heated regarding use of the word 'queer' as a catch-all term. Some people do not want to be made invisible within this designation, while others (such as some supportive heterosexuals) do not want to be co-opted by the wideness of its definition. Gamson describes some 75 letters to the editor of the *San Francisco Bay Times* that were received after the newspaper carried the story that the 1993 Freedom Day Parade would be called 'The Year of the Queer'. These passionate letters included the following rhetoric:

> How did you ever miss out on [selecting as a new term] 'Faggot' or 'Cocksucker'?

> All those dumb closeted people who don't like the Q-word can go fuck themselves and go to somebody else's parade.

> This new generation assumes we were too busy in the '70s lining up at Macy's to purchase sweaters to find time for the revolution – as if their piercings and tattoos were any cheaper.

> I am sure [another letter writer] isn't old enough to have experienced that feeling of cringing when the word 'queer' was said.

> They want to work from within and I just want to crash in from the outside and say, 'Hey! Hello, I'm queer. I can make out with my girl-friend. Ha ha. Live with it. Deal with it.'[43]

Warner points out that the words 'gay, lesbian, bisexual, and trans-gendered' call to mind what people do sexually, whereas 'queer' has political connotations.[44] It is his contention that use of this word can help queer people get over the sexual shame to which society has rele-gated them.[45] Additionally, Fone reminds us that 'queer' was originally a word employed by homosexuals themselves before it became a slur

---

41 For a discussion of the 'queer rage' that this sometimes entails, see Frank Browning, *The Culture of Desire: Paradox and Perversity in Gay Lives Today* (New York: Crown Publishers, 1993), pp. 26–54.

42 Warner, *The Trouble with Normal*, p. 59.

43 Gamson, 'Must Identity Movements Self-Destruct?', pp. 589, 592–3.

44 Warner, *The Trouble with Normal*, p. 39.

45 Warner, *The Trouble with Normal*, pp. 1–3.

used by homophobes, resulting in its virtual disappearance from gay parlance.[46]

Like it or not, it seems that 'queer' is here to stay: it has entered the vocabulary of sexuality as well as the curricula of some of the country's most venerable universities. In addition, queer theologians and biblical scholars have recently begun 'queering' Church doctrines and biblical texts, staking out a radical place in progressive academia where the more tentative 'gay theology' of 20 years ago did not dare to go. It is within this new queer sensibility that my own queer Christology will be situated, for I believe that, like Jesus' earthly ministry, a queer Christology must 'stir up' and 'spoil' what has been assumed for so long in religious circles about Christ. But before describing this queer Christology, I conclude this chapter with a brief examination of what has been done in gay/lesbian/queer theology and the new queer biblical scholarship.

Beginnings of Gay and Lesbian Theology

Lesbian feminists have been articulating their theology since the advent of feminist theology during the Women's Movement of the 1970s and 1980s, the topic of Chapter 6; the work of most lesbian theologians during this time was devoted to gender equality, however, rather than issues of sexual orientation. A 'Lesbian-Feminist Issues in Religion' section had been started in the American Academy of Religion in the early 1980s and precipitated the founding of a 'Gay Men's Issues in Religion' section in the late 1980s.[47] Until the late 1980s, however, gay and lesbian religious discourse consisted, for the most part, of apologetics to the biblical injunctions against homosexuality, discussions of natural law and whether 'gay is good' in the sight of God, and ethical issues.[48] A genuine gay/lesbian 'theology' did not really appear until the late 1980s and early

---

46 Fone, *Homophobia*, pp. 410–11.

47 Michael L. Stemmeler, 'Introduction', in *Homophobia and the Judaeo-Christian Tradition*, ed. Michael L. Stemmeler and J. Michael Clark (Dallas: Monument Press, 1990), pp. 1–2.

48 See, for example, George Edwards, *Gay/Lesbian Liberation: A Biblical Perspective* (New York: The Pilgrim Press, 1984); Tom Horner, *Jonathan Loved David: Homosexuality in Biblical Times* (Philadelphia: The Westminster Press, 1978); John J. McNeill, *The Church and the Homosexual* (Kansas City, MO: Sheed, Andrews, and McMeel, 1976); and Richard Woods, *Another Kind of Love: Homosexuality and Spirituality* (Chicago: Thomas More Publishing, 1977).

1990s. Additionally, many of the books and articles written on gay/lesbian spirituality focused upon non-Christian religions,[49] for, like many women,[50] some gays and lesbians believed that they had no choice but to exit Christianity because of its homophobia (and what I have called their own Christophobia). The following discussion will briefly describe some of the earliest theology that was done from the social location of sexual orientation; it is noteworthy that most of this early gay/lesbian theology steered clear of articulating any sort of Christology.

The earliest attempt to construct a gay liberation theology was J. Michael Clark's 1989 book, *A Place to Start: Toward an Unapologetic Gay Liberation Theology*.[51] Clark's doctorate was in literature and theology, and he therefore has approached his theology through the lens of literary and cultural criticism and the budding gay studies movement of the 1980s. Clark employs feminist methodology and critiques patriarchy as the source of the homophobia that was manifesting itself during his research and writing as AIDS-phobia.[52] His theology is experience-based, and therefore seeks to ground a gay/lesbian wholeness of identity in a new view of God as one who empowers all beings toward wholeness.[53] His view of God does not necessarily include Christ; Clark feels that for Jesus to have meaning for gay people, he must be 'dechristologized'.[54] Clark is very concerned in this earliest work with staking out a place for gays and lesbians in the realm of spirituality (not necessarily religion or church); he views 'coming out' as a gay or lesbian person as a process of spiritual transformation that can bring us closer to God.[55] Because the gay and lesbian community was undergoing fragmentation in the first decade of the AIDS crisis, Clark suggested a theology of community, whereby gays and lesbians can access God's power and wholeness through strengthening the gay and lesbian community.[56] Because of his social location as a gay man in Atlanta at the commence-

---

49 One can see this from perusing the bibliography in J. Michael Clark, *A Place to Start: Toward an Unapologetic Gay Liberation Theology* (Dallas: Monument Press, 1989), the earliest contribution to gay theology.

50 See Carol P. Christ and Judith Plaskow, eds, *Womanspirit Rising: A Feminist Reader in Religion* (New York: Harper & Row, 1979).

51 See note 49.

52 Clark, *A Place to Start*, Chapter 3.

53 Clark, *A Place to Start*, Chapter 4.

54 Clark, *A Place to Start*, Chapter 6; see my discussion of his 'dechristologizing' in Chapter 10.

55 Clark, *A Place to Start*, Chapter 7.

56 Clark, *A Place to Start*, Chapter 8.

ment of the AIDS pandemic and his subsequent HIV-positive status, Clark's later work has concentrated almost completely upon theodicy and ecology – how we are to make sense of this world and how we are to leave it for those who survive us.[57]

The next major contribution to gay theology was Gary David Comstock's 1993 book, *Gay Theology Without Apology*,[58] in which Comstock, a theologian-sociologist, concentrated almost completely upon the Hebrew Bible as a paradigm for the spiritual journey of gay people, especially the Exodus experiences as analogous to gay/lesbian 'coming out'.[59] Comstock's immediate context for doing theology was his involvement in AIDS work with the Gay Men's Health Crisis during his doctoral studies at Union Theological Seminary in New York City. His 'unapologetic' stance comes from his intention not to fit gays and lesbians into organized religion but rather to examine theological concepts, the Bible and Christianity with a view toward 'fitting them into and changing them according to the particular experiences of lesbian/ bisexual/gay people'.[60] Comstock's early work is really a hybrid of biblical interpretation and theology, for he examines the biblical condemnations of homosexuality but also looks for characters in Scripture (like Vashti and Jonathan) who have been 'silenced', as gay/lesbian people have been silenced.[61] Like Clark, he includes what I call an 'anti-Christology' in which he encourages his audience to leave Jesus because he has left them.

> As regards Jesus, we remember him as a friend, as a friend who has departed, and who in his own terms said, I am dead, you are alive. Jesus gives us not a model to follow, not a how-to for running our lives, but a nudge to get on without him.[62]

57 For example, J. Michael Clark, *Beyond Our Ghettos: Gay Theology in Ecological Perspective* (Cleveland: The Pilgrim Press, 1993); *Defying the Darkness: Gay Theology in the Shadows* (Cleveland: The Pilgrim Press, 1997); and 'Prophecy, Subjectivity, and Theodicy in Gay Theology: Developing a Constructive Methodology', in *Constructing Gay Theology*, ed. Michael L. Stemmeler and J. Michael Clark (Las Colinas, TX: Monument Press, 1991), p. 34.

58 Gary David Comstock, *Gay Theology Without Apology* (Cleveland: The Pilgrim Press, 1993).

59 Comstock, *Gay Theology Without Apology*, Chapter 1.

60 Comstock, *Gay Theology Without Apology*, p. 4.

61 Comstock, *Gay Theology Without Apology*, Chapters 3–5.

62 Comstock, *Gay Theology Without Apology*, p. 102; see my further discussion of his views in Chapter 10.

Comstock's subsequent work has been almost exclusively in the area of gay and lesbian sociology of religion, rather than theology.[63]

Gay religious scholar Chris Glaser has written several books that have articulated a gay and lesbian spirituality for non-scholarly readers. In sharing his own story and the struggles he has encountered in attempting to remain within mainline Christianity, Glaser has created a popular gay theology based upon the Bible and gay/lesbian daily life. He encourages embodiment, the development of a gay sexual ethics, the building of esteem through 'coming out' to God and self, and the healing of the brokenness of homophobia and AIDS.[64]

A more recent gay male liberation theology is that of Richard Cleaver in *Know My Name*. Cleaver's methodology is to reclaim biblical texts as warrant for gay wholeness. He is particularly at pains to show that gays have been created in the image and likeness of God (*imago dei*) and that God makes no distinctions among persons.[65] I was personally disappointed in Cleaver's approach to gay theology, for, writing in the mid 1990s, he seems not to have progressed beyond the incipient gay theology of a decade before; he has totally ignored the implications of the new 'queer' theology that developed in the early 1990s, to be discussed below.

Between Gay/Lesbian and Queer

Subsequent to the 'gay' theology of Clark and Comstock but prior to the articulation of a 'queer' theology, Carter Heyward suggested a sexual theology that cannot be called specifically 'gay' or 'lesbian', but is geared instead toward the human becoming of all persons as they embrace the God-given gift of sexuality. As noted in Chapter 6, Heyward's lens for doing theology is 'mutuality', for her view of God is

63 For example, Gary David Comstock, *Unrepentant, Self-Affirming, Practicing: Lesbian/Bisexual/Gay People within Organized Religion* (New York: Continuum, 1996); and *A Whosoever Church: Welcoming Lesbians and Gay Men into African American Congregations* (Louisville: Westminster/John Knox Press, 2001).

64 See, for example, Chris Glaser, *Come Home! Reclaiming Spirituality and Community as Gays and Lesbians*, second edition (Gaithersburg, MD: Chi Rho Press, 1998; originally published in 1990 by HarperCollins).

65 Richard Cleaver, *Know My Name: A Gay Liberation Theology* (Louisville: Westminster/John Knox Press, 1995), Chapters 3 and 4.

'our power in mutual relation'.[66] God becomes 'immersed' in human flesh, blessing us so that we may bless others: 'Healed and forgiven, we take on the work of healing, liberation, and forgiveness.'[67] It is precisely the erotically motivated nature of gay and lesbian flesh that empowers those of non-normative sexual orientations to do the work of healing and liberation.[68]

Heyward's major contribution to a sexual theology is her 1989 book, *Touching Our Strength: The Erotic as Power and the Love of God*,[69] in which she elaborates upon the work of Audre Lorde[70] and anticipates the subsequent elaboration of her own work by Rita Nakashima Brock:[71]

> We fear this life force, our erotic power, because, if celebrated rather than denied, our YES would force us to evaluate all aspects of our existence honestly . . . Our lives would be transformed. Nothing would remain the same. . . . As we come to experience the erotic as sacred, we begin to know ourselves as holy and to imagine ourselves sharing in the creation of one another and of our common well-being. . . . We begin to realize that God moves among us, transcending our particularities. She is born and embodied in our midst. . . . [T]he erotic crosses over among us, moving us to change the ways we are living in relation. Touched by this sacred power, we are never the same again.[72]

The New Queer Theology

A specifically 'queer' theology emerged in 1993 with the publication of Robert Goss's *Jesus ACTED UP: A Gay and Lesbian Manifesto*.[73] A former Roman Catholic priest, Goss, upon his resignation from the

---

66 See, for example, Isabel Carter Heyward, *The Redemption of God: A Theology of Mutual Relation* (Lanham, MD: University Press of America, 1982).

67 Carter Heyward, *Staying Power: Reflections on Gender, Justice, and Compassion* (Cleveland: The Pilgrim Press, 1995), p. 36.

68 Heyward, *Staying Power*, p. 114.

69 Carter Heyward, *Touching Our Strength: The Erotic as Power and the Love of God* (New York: Harper & Row, 1989).

70 Audre Lorde, 'Uses of the Erotic: The Erotic as Power', in Lorde, *Sister Outsider: Essays and Speeches* (Trumansburg, NY: The Crossing Press, 1984), pp. 53–9.

71 Rita Nakashima Brock, *Journeys by Heart: A Christology of Erotic Power* (New York: Crossroad, 1991).

72 Heyward, *Touching Our Strength*, p. 102.

73 Robert Goss, *Jesus ACTED UP: A Gay and Lesbian Manifesto* (New York: HarperCollins, 1993).

Jesuits, became an activist-theologian involved in direct action political groups such as ACTUP and QueerNation, and brought this type of confrontational, 'in your face' direct action to the task of Christian theology, urging transgressive praxis on the part of the queer community because Jesus himself had 'acted up'. Goss comes the closest of any of the theologians examined thus far toward articulating a queer Christology; nevertheless, he stops short of a comprehensive queer view of Christ because his broader purpose has been to introduce queer notions into the field of political theology and political notions into gay/lesbian religious thought, using the hermeneutical key of Jesus' notion of the reign of God.[74]

Not content with simply unmasking the homophobia of Christianity, Goss also criticizes the gay and lesbian community itself. He recognizes that much of the gay and lesbian community's pain is self-induced and calls for an exodus from denial, 'oppression sickness', and 'horizontal hostility'. Where the incipient gay theology described above was more 'touchy-feely' and 'feel good' in assuring gays and lesbians that they too were God's children, Goss's later queer methodology attempts to heal the community by naming unpleasant aspects of its existence:

> We must look inward to surface destructive and oppressive patterns of social behavior. White, middle-class queers must be sensitive to exclusions of people of color. . . . Many gay men must examine their misogynistic attitudes while some lesbians must shed their radical separatism. . . . I think our own oppression sickness is the most dangerous force around.[75]

With Goss, one sees a change in the tenor of gay and lesbian theology. There is a stridency heretofore lacking as well as an emphasis upon direct action and transgressive politics to change structures and systems, rather than merely theologize in the academy. Moreover, this theology becomes truly 'queer' in the verbal sense of that word: it seeks to 'stir up' and to 'spoil' heteronormative and heteropatriarchal theology through imagination, outrageousness, questioning, playfulness, and the intersection of religious consciousness and the personal experience of homophobia and queer bashing. In this regard, British theologian Elizabeth Stuart advances a queer sensibility in her articulation of a theology of friendship as the best way for lesbians and gays to embody the love of

---

74 Goss, *Jesus ACTED UP*, pp. xiv–xv.
75 Goss, *Jesus ACTED UP*, pp. 156–7.

God: 'We can all have friends, and all friendships are embodied and expressions of our passion.'[76] With Lisa Isherwood, Stuart has described a 'body theology', in which women and men can reclaim their bodies as the social location of their connection with the Divine. This is of course inclusive of queer bodies as a social location for doing theology.[77] Isherwood and Stuart suggest that bodily passion and the need for transgression is what erupted at the Stonewall Riot that gave birth to the gay and lesbian liberation movement.[78] I concur and suspect that it is an underlying estrangement from their bodies that makes queer people of faith unable to accept the embodiment (incarnation) of God in Christ and embrace instead what I have termed 'Christophobia'.

This new queer body consciousness is also seen in the work of queer ethicist and church historian Kathy Rudy, who not only questions the construction of gender that has become reified in the Christian Church,[79] but also dares to defend the transgressive sexual activity of many gay men that society labels 'promiscuity'.[80]

It is evident that today's queer theology is quite different from the gay/lesbian theology that developed in the 1980s. Where that earlier theology was more apologetic in nature, seeking inclusion of gay and lesbian people within conventional society, queer theology advocates queer existence on its own terms rather than inclusion in anyone else's Church, theological paradigm or society.[81]

Queer Biblical Interpretation

One also sees this new queer consciousness revealed in the proliferation of queer biblical interpretation during the past several years. Formerly,

76 Elizabeth Stuart, *Just Good Friends: Towards a Lesbian and Gay Theology of Relationships* (London and New York: Mowbray, 1995), p. xv.

77 Lisa Isherwood and Elizabeth Stuart, *Introducing Body Theology* (Cleveland: The Pilgrim Press, 1998), p. 100.

78 Isherwood and Stuart, *Introducing Body Theology*, p. 103.

79 Kathy Rudy, *Sex and the Church: Gender, Homosexuality, and the Transformation of Christian Ethics* (Boston: Beacon Press, 1997), esp. Chapter 5.

80 Kathy Rudy, '"Where Two or More Are Gathered": Using Gay Communities as a Model for Christian Sexual Ethics', *Theology and Sexuality* 4 (1986), pp. 81–99 (p. 90).

81 Perhaps the 'queerest' queer theology is that of Marcella Althaus-Reid in *Indecent Theology: Theological Perversions in Sex, Gender and Politics* (London and New York: Routledge, 2000). See my discussion of her Christology and Mariology in Chapter 10.

gays and lesbians were concerned with 'explaining away' the biblical injunctions against homosexuality or else discarded the Bible entirely. Perhaps the first interpreter to take a proactive stance vis-à-vis the Bible was lesbian pastor Nancy Wilson, who now serves as the Presiding Elder of the Metropolitan Community Churches. In a non-scholarly, anecdotal style which emanates from her experience counselling gay and lesbian refugees from Christianity, Wilson encourages queers to look for themselves inside the Bible. She comes down firmly on the side of the essentialists (such as John Boswell) in affirming that queer folks have always been here, and therefore must be represented within the pages of the Bible.[82] Her hermeneutical key is the category of 'eunuch', those castrated men who are mentioned at several points in the Bible; she fancifully sees these eunuchs as the prototypes for gay men and includes a 'roll call' of eunuchs in the back of her book.[83] Although technically not a contribution to theology or biblical interpretation, *Our Tribe* is an important milestone in queer religious studies, for it directs queers to look within themselves for affirmation of their scriptural heritage and gives them warrant for remaining in the Christian Church despite the Christian homophobia and the queer Christophobia discussed in the last chapter.

A more scholarly and daring undertaking is the anthology entitled *Take Back the Word: A Queer Reading of the Bible*,[84] edited by Robert Goss and Mona West, a mixture of academic and popular 'queerings' of Scripture that had its 'grass-roots' origin in a workshop Goss and West co-facilitated at the Metropolitan Community Churches' General Conference in 1995.[85] In her contribution to this anthology, lesbian theologian Virginia Mollenkott suggests a particularly queer 'reading strategy':

---

82 Nancy L. Wilson, *Our Tribe: Queer Folks, God, Jesus, and the Bible* (New York: HarperCollins, 1995), Chapter 4.

83 Wilson, *Our Tribe*, pp. 281–5. In my opinion, eunuchs come closer to the modern category of transsexual than gay men.

84 Robert E. Goss and Mona West, eds, *Take Back the Word: A Queer Reading of the Bible* (Cleveland: The Pilgrim Press, 2000). For other recent examples of queer biblical commentary, see Stone, ed., *Queer Commentary and the Hebrew Bible*; and Goss and Strongheart, eds, *Our Families, Our Values*, Chapters 3, 4, and 11.

85 This volume gave rise to a full-scale commentary on every book of the Bible from a queer perspective, *The Queer Bible Commentary*, ed. Deryn Guest, Robert E. Goss, Mona West and Thomas Bohache (London: SCM Press, 2006).

I had to learn to read the scriptures from low and outside because I had been trained to identify with the white heterosexual male point of view . . . It seems to me vital that queer people learn to empower our-selves by reading the Bible from low and outside instead of identify-ing our agenda as we read with that of the heterosexual normative group.[86]

What makes this anthology 'queer' is the contributors' refusal to persist in the reactive stance of gay/lesbian biblical commentary of the 1970s and 1980s, when the only discussion of the Bible was a defensive revisiting of the 'texts of terror'[87] of Leviticus, Romans, 1 Corinthians and the Sodom story. Instead, these queer interpreters have selected texts that on the surface would seem to say nothing to gay, lesbian, bisexual or transgendered people; nevertheless, by reading texts with their bodies and from the social location of their varied sexual orienta-tions, these authors find queer overtones in the stories of such biblical characters as Ruth and Naomi, Jezebel, Jonah, Mary of Magdala, Lazarus and the Beloved Disciple.[88] The concluding selection of the anthology, my own, argues passionately for queer people to love their flesh and realize that – like the Galatian Christians whom Paul coun-selled *not* to change their body-selves through circumcision – we need do *nothing* to be acceptable to God.

To be pleasing to God, one must do nothing except believe. . . . What this means for queer Christians is this: We do not have to circumcise the foreskins of our sexual orientation in order to be acceptable to almighty God. Our status as children of God is not dependent upon outside forces or rules or lists of sins created by human beings. . . . We are assured in Genesis 1.26–27 that each one of us is created in 'the image and likeness' of God. . . . We must never destroy that divine image by ignoring or stifling that piece of our human 'god-ness' –

86 Virginia Ramey Mollenkott, 'Reading the Bible from Low and Outside: Lesbitransgay People as God's Tricksters', in *Take Back the Word*, ed. Goss and West, p. 18.

87 Robert Goss has appropriated this term to a queer context from the work of feminist Hebrew Bible scholar Phyllis Trible. See Goss, *Jesus ACTED UP*, p. 91.

88 *Take Back the Word*, Chapters 8, 9, 15, 17, 18, and 19. These contributors are: Celina M. Duncan, Victoria S. Kolakowski, Sharon Bezner, Thomas Hanks, Benjamin Perkins and Robert E. Goss.

sexuality – with which we have been gifted by a loving God of amazing diversity.[89]

Conclusion

My discussion of queer biblical interpretation makes a fitting transition to the next two chapters, which set forth my own views, for my queer Christology mixes, on the one hand, theologizing about Christ's meaning in the context of sexual orientation with, on the other hand, biblical interpretation that 'queers' the life of Jesus, much as he 'queered' the society and religion of his times. The present chapter has prepared the way for this endeavour by demonstrating that sexual orientation is indeed a legitimate social location from which to do theology and examine Scripture. Moreover, this chapter has differentiated a queer sensibility from earlier gay/lesbian religious discourse and therefore has situated the reader for a foray into queer imaginings about who Christ can be for us when we allow him to escape the confines of heteropatriarchal categories and expectations.

---

89 Thomas Bohache, '"To Cut or Not to Cut": Is Compulsory Heterosexuality a Prerequisite for Christianity?' in *Take Back the Word*, ed. Goss and West, pp. 235–6.

'Who do *you* say that I am?' I: *Towards* a Queer Christology[1]

Introduction

The Gospels record that Jesus of Nazareth asked his disciples what people were saying about him. They gave a varied response that summarized the opinions circulating throughout Palestine. However, Jesus was not satisfied with this response; he pushed the disciples, asking, 'But who do *you* say that I am?' Simon Peter answered him, 'You are the Christ.' (See Mark 8.27–33; Matthew 16.13–23; Luke 9.18–22.) Nevertheless, as we have seen throughout the preceding chapters, almost as soon as these words were recorded, followers of Jesus began to elaborate upon what it meant to say that Jesus was 'the Christ'. In Part I, I examined the New Testament and early Church images of the Christ figure that reached culmination in the Nicene Creed and were then further unpacked by two millennia of Christological discourse and the more recent search for the historical Jesus. In Part II, I examined the voices of marginalized people and revealed the individual ways in which women and people of other colours, ethnicities and economic statuses see Jesus as Christ.

We have thus encountered many answers to that timeless question, 'Who do people say that I am?' Yet, like the first followers of Jesus, I am now confronted with Jesus Christ's refusal to take these explanations as definitive. Jesus speaks down the centuries into my consciousness and asks, 'But what about *you*? Who do *you* say that I am?' I have therefore finally come to the end of my journey and have arrived back at the very question with which I began. For, when all is said and done, other people's views and theories and 'proofs' – the triangle of Scripture, tradition

---

1 Portions of Chapters 10 and 11 appeared in a slightly different form in my essay 'Embodiment as Incarnation: An Incipient Queer Christology', *Theology and Sexuality* 10:1 (September 2003), pp. 9–29.

and experience – cannot speak for me. I must, from my social location as a queer in an anti-queer world, articulate a Christology that speaks to my experience and social location, as well as those with whom I have dialogued over the past 20 years of ministry and education.

In this task I am guided by a double purpose: First, I need to be authentic to my own beliefs, that is, my view of God in Christ and how that impacts my sexuality. To some, it will appear that I have not gone far enough or been radical enough in my Christology; nevertheless, I can only describe the Christ whom I have met on my journey and no one else's. Other queer interpreters will sketch other Christs, and that is as it should be; there need be no one, definitive queering of Christ, but rather there should be a plethora, as mirrored in the diversity of God's creation. Second, I am writing with the intent of unmasking homophobic Christologies that limit human becoming and also with the goal of reclaiming the Christ figure for those whose Christophobia has been such a large part of their religious consciousness that they had not even imagined that there could be a queer Christology that would meet them in their circumstances. By and large, these are middle-of-the-road queer people – not academic, not feminist, not cutting-edge, and not politically activist. They are people who have wanted Christ to be a part of their lives but have been told that this is not an option; many of them have tried other religions and spiritual paths but have returned, feeling empty and unfulfilled, wanting a relationship with a Christ who will not bludgeon them but show them a new view of the Divine. Therefore, my Christology will seek to examine familiar biblical texts with a view toward 'reclaiming' them for twenty-first-century queers who have been disenfranchised and accorded refugee status by Christianity. Mine is a biblical Christology, rather than a political or sexual Christology. Of course, it will have both political and sexual elements, but, in the end, this Christology will seek to place the Jesus of the Christian Scriptures (canonical and non-canonical) within the ambit of queer consciousness. In this way, perhaps both the Bible and Jesus Christ will cease to be weapons in the arsenal of homophobic Christians and self-condemning queers.

What is a 'Queer' Christ?

Invariably, when the topic of a queer view of Christ or a queer Christology or a queering of Christ or the queer Christ comes up, it leads to the question, 'Are you saying that Jesus was gay?' I believe the answer to this question must be a combination statement and question: 'Not necessarily, but what if he were?' The fact is we have no evidence that the historical Jesus was even sexual, let alone homosexual or heterosexual. There is disagreement as to whether there were even such categories in ancient society; essentialists such as John Boswell and Nancy Wilson[2] will tell us that 'gays and lesbians' have existed in all times and must therefore have been present in Jesus' day and age, while constructionists such as Judith Butler and Virginia Mollenkott[3] will tell us that the categories of gender and sexuality cannot be universalized today, let alone retrojected into the past. There is evidence, however, that same-sex sexual activity was recognized in the ancient world and both embraced and castigated at different times and in different places.[4] Contrary to traditional Church teaching, there is no scriptural evidence that Jesus was celibate or that he engaged in sexual activity; there is no mention of whether he was married or unmarried; there is no evidence that he had ever experienced sexual passion or fathered children.[5] One can only 'read the silence' and speculate upon what the texts do and do not say.

All Christology is interpretation – the intersection of the Jesus figure with one's theological sensibilities and social location. This is what differentiates Christology from the quests for the historical Jesus. Christology goes beyond the mere retrieval of historical information in order to impose a 'meaning' on that data which transcends space and time and any historical or social categories. Thus, women have been able to develop a Christology that is broader than the fact of Jesus' physical maleness, while those of African, Asian, and Hispanic descent have been

---

2 John Boswell, *Christianity, Social Tolerance, and Homosexuality: Gay People in Western Europe from the Beginning of the Christian Era to the Fourteenth Century* (Chicago and London: University of Chicago Press, 1980); Nancy L. Wilson, *Our Tribe: Queer Folks, God, Jesus, and the Bible* (New York: HarperCollins, 1995).

3 Judith Butler, *Gender Trouble: Feminism and the Subversion of Identity* (New York and London: Routledge, 1990); Virginia Ramey Mollenkott, *Omnigender: A Trans-Religious Approach* (Cleveland: The Pilgrim Press, 2001).

4 See, for example, Tom Horner, *Jonathan Loved David: Homosexuality in Biblical Times* (Philadelphia: The Westminster Press, 1978); Bernadette J. Brooten, *Love Between Women: Early Christian Responses to Female Homoeroticism* (Chicago and London: University of Chicago Press, 1996); and Martti Nissinen, *Homoeroticism in the Biblical World: A Historical Perspective*, trans. Kirsi Stjerna (Minneapolis: Fortress Press, 1998).

5 William E. Phipps, *Was Jesus Married? The Distortion of Sexuality in the Christian Tradition* (New York: Harper & Row, 1970); and *The Sexuality of Jesus* (Cleveland: The Pilgrim Press, 1996).

able to develop a Christ figure that looks like them and endures their torment in a white world, despite the fact that the historical Jesus would not have belonged to their race or ethnicity. In this sense, perhaps queer Christologists have an easier time of it, for we do not prescind from a historical datum of Jesus' heteronormativity; the Gospels are silent regarding his sexuality or lack thereof. Thus, my answer, 'Not necessarily.' One cannot answer any question about Jesus' sexual orientation or sexual activity. Nevertheless, one can extrapolate from the fact that if one is fully human, as the Nicene Creed declares Jesus to be, then at least the possibility of a sexuality is implied in his personhood. Moreover, excessive concentration on whether or not Jesus was gay distorts the issue of how he can be a queer Christ, for it injects the spectre of homophobia into the discussion. There are many in our heteropatriarchal world who see deviation from the standard of compulsory heterosexuality and rigid gender roles as sinful and unnatural; even to suggest that Jesus could have so deviated becomes the ultimate blasphemy. Indeed, even among queer people who have not yet fully grappled with their internalized homophobia and what it means that they themselves are gay, lesbian, bisexual, transgendered, seeking, or supportively straight, there is a knee-jerk reaction when the words 'gay'/'queer' and 'Jesus' are mentioned in the same sentence. One must ask about the source of such a reaction; hence, my question, 'What if he were?'

Some gay/lesbian interpreters have stated that they believe that Jesus was gay and had homosexual relations with his disciples.[6] They place much emphasis upon the fact that Jesus travelled and lived with twelve other men and assume, using modern categories, that this evidences a gay sensibility. What they ignore, however, is that in ancient Palestine the genders were largely segregated; it would have been perfectly commonplace for a group of men to travel, work, eat and relax together; it also would not have been unheard of for them to engage in some sexual activity with one another.[7] The purpose of the Gospels was not to record social or sexual history, but to inspire belief in Jesus' Christ-ness. The evangelists evidently did not think that the issue of same-sex relations affected Jesus' ability to be Christ, or else I suspect that they would

6 Robert Williams, *Just As I Am: A Practical Guide to Being Out, Proud, and Christian* (New York: Crown Publishers, Inc., 1992), pp. 116–23.

7 Regarding gender issues, see the articles in Carol A. Newsom and Sharon H. Ringe, eds, *The Women's Bible Commentary* (Louisville: Westminster/John Knox Press, 1992), as well as the essays on individual books of the Bible. Regarding same-sex affinity in the ancient world, see Nissinen, *Homoeroticism in the Biblical World*.

have found a way to include a prohibition from the lips of Jesus.[8]

A queer Christology will not try to argue for or against the gayness of Jesus, but will seek rather to determine what his Christ-ness says to marginalized peoples of all generations, including today's queer community. As we saw in the last chapter, the new queer consciousness goes beyond notions of 'gay' or 'lesbian' and seeks to critique heteronormativity and heteropatriarchal patterns of domination. This is where a queer Christology intersects with biblical studies, for we can discern from Jesus' recorded words and deeds how he felt about power relations. I believe this is a much more interesting and productive area of discussion than wondering about Jesus' sex life, for, when it comes to Jesus' social and political philosophy, we know a great deal. Thus, if someone were to persist in asking me about Jesus' sexuality, I would facetiously answer, 'Well, I don't know if he was gay, but he certainly was queer!'

To be 'queer' means to stir things up and even perhaps spoil them, in order not to settle for the easy answers of the status quo. The queer Christ articulates a solidarity with the 'fags', 'bitches' and 'niggers' of his day and our day, in order to show that the God-consciousness of each person goes beyond the limitations of one's own physical existence. The incarnation of God in a human body (whether it is Jesus' alone or that of every human person) demonstrates that the Divine and the physical intersect in a powerful and mystical way, that the physical is important and can never be divorced from the spiritual, and that the Divine yearns to become one with the human over and over again, resulting in the eternal cycle of birth and rebirth, death and resurrection, creation and salvation.

Other Queer Christologies

In examining the Christology of other queer interpreters, I note several different styles of Christology: (1) an 'anti-Christology' that encourages queer people to just forget about Jesus Christ and get on with their lives

---

8 In fact, some would say that Matthew has included an implicit *approval* of same-sex relations by Jesus in his comments about 'eunuchs who have been so from birth' (Matthew 19.12). Wilson, *Our Tribe*, pp. 128–9. Wilson credits John McNeil, SJ, for originally applying this dominical remark about eunuchs to gay and lesbian people in *The Church and the Homosexual* (Kansas City, MO: Sheed, Andrews, and McMeel, 1976). See also Frederick J. Gaiser, 'A New Word on Homosexuality? Isaiah 56.1–8 as Case Study', *Word and World* 14:3 (Summer 1994), pp. 280–93. See also the discussion below.

and their spiritual journeys; (2) a Christology of queer embodiment; (3) a radical Christology focusing on deconstructing the human Jesus by a queer methodology; and (4) a mystical Christology of the Christ within all people. Let us examine each of these positions as preparation for my own Christological views.

Anti-Christology

'Anti-Christology' is how I categorize the discussion of Jesus by early gay theologians such as J. Michael Clark and Gary David Comstock. Both of these scholars have successfully created gay liberation theologies; nevertheless, each of them, in his own way, has shied away from reclaiming the Christ figure for gay people. I wonder if this is because of their own Christophobia and its reinforcement by the homophobia they encountered in Church and academy as they strove to be authentic and open about their sexuality in the early days of the gay/lesbian theological movement, coinciding with the AIDS crisis among the gay community?

J. Michael Clark is quite clear that any retrieval of Jesus for gay people must be 'dechristologized', that is, stripped of any theological or mystical trappings that have accrued in 2,000 years of Church history and Christology, because, in his estimation, 'One of the major problems with Christological development, with the divinization of Jesus as Christ for *any* liberation theology, is the way in which that process becomes oppressive. Displacing Jesus with Christ provided an image of male Lordship (the *Kyrios Christos*) which was no longer liberating.'[9]

Clark seems to labour under the misapprehension that there was an original 'golden era' of the Jesus movement which degenerated into a Church where Christ was worshipped and Jesus forgotten. This is an oversimplification, to say the least. Although Elisabeth Schüssler Fiorenza has convincingly demonstrated that, with regard to gender relations, an original egalitarian flavour gave way to the 'patriarchalization' of the Church,[10] that is not to say that the second and third Christian generations forgot about the human Jesus in favour of a new god they called 'Christ'. In fact, this view overlooks the historical fact of the development of a New Testament canon that was careful to include

---

9 J. Michael Clark, *A Place to Start: Toward an Unapologetic Gay Liberation Theology* (Dallas: Monument Press, 1989), pp. 99–102.

10 Elisabeth Schüssler Fiorenza, *In Memory of Her: A Feminist Theological Reconstruction of Christian Origins* (New York: Crossroad, 1983), pp. 288–94.

four different portraits of the human Jesus as a means of combating the Gnostic 'heresy' of a disembodied Christ Spirit.[11]

A more serious weakness in Clark's dechristologizing is his dismissal of the resurrection as a creation of post-Pauline Christianity that sought to exalt a divine Christ figure and forget the human Jesus who suffered and died on the cross.[12] However, Clark overlooks the fact that the successors of Paul, including the authors of the Deutero-Pauline Epistles, in developing Christian theology, were at pains to deal with the 'scandal' of the cross and to show how a crucified Messiah could be reigning in heaven with God. (See, for example, Colossians 1.15–20.) This is how Christ as the *imago dei* who is exemplar for our own condition of *imago dei* began. Resurrection was not and never has been a curative for the cross or a means of sanitizing the horror of crucifixion; on the contrary, it is a theological explanation for how such a brutal death could be salvific and how an executed criminal could be God's Anointed. It is true that certain atonement theologies and the soteriologies resulting from them have been a bit farfetched and misguided in their attempts to explain a theological phenomenon in literal terms. However, at no time has Christian theology ever downplayed the cross in favour of the resurrection; on the contrary, in looking at the Christology and ritual in some churches, one wonders if they are even conscious of Good Friday giving way to Easter Sunday.

Gary David Comstock articulates anti-Christology in a different way. Rather than seeing the risen Christ as a mythological symbol that must be overcome, as Clark does, Comstock instead believes that the historical Jesus is the one from whom we must distance ourselves because he has distanced himself from us. Comstock challenges those who would follow the human Jesus as an example for how to live their lives (as feminist and Latin American liberation Christologies do), charging that to do so is both 'opportunistic' ('we use him as we wish for our own ends') and inauthentic ('we do not mean it'), inasmuch as those who make such appeals to Jesus do so merely to use him as a 'rationale or support' for what they have already decided to do.[13] Such cynicism is surely a mischaracterization of the liberation Christologies that I have examined

---

11 See Harry Y. Gamble, Jr., *The New Testament Canon: Its Making and Meaning* (Philadelphia: Fortress Press, 1985); and Hans von Campenhausen, *The Formation of the Christian Bible*, trans. J. A. Baker (Philadelphia: Fortress Press, 1972).

12 Clark, *A Place to Start*, p. 105.

13 Gary David Comstock, *Gay Theology Without Apology* (Cleveland: The Pilgrim Press, 1993), pp. 92–3.

in this study. Comstock encourages his gay readership to believe that we are on our own and that Jesus Christ cannot help us. He is a dead and gone friend, much like those we have lost to AIDS who can do nothing to save us from the plague. It is almost as though Comstock is Peter Pan asking the audience if they believe in fairies (pun intended).[14] Comstock's theology, while very good for its time, is, in my opinion, not a Christian theology, for it removes Jesus Christ from a position of making any difference in the lives of gay and lesbian people. Salvation comes instead from God who, as in the Exodus, encourages gays and lesbians to come out of oppression into freedom.[15]

Embodiment Christology

The next type of Christology found among queer authors is what I call a Christology of queer embodiment, as represented in the work of Carter Heyward and Lisa Isherwood. This Christology seeks to locate in queer flesh the union of our humanity with Christ's divinity.

Heyward, for her entire scholarly career, has flirted with Christology without delineating a full-scale Christology, whether feminist or queer. As noted in previous chapters, Heyward's guiding principle in her theology is mutuality and relation. For her, Christ is what brings together the relation of God and humankind. This is a quality that can be found in Jesus 'our brother', but is also found in each one of us – the erotic groundedness that enables us to 'god'. For Heyward, this is Christic power that is not limited to Jesus but is possible for every human person who is in right relation with God and her/his sisters and brothers, leading her to conclude, 'Our vocation is to join Jesus and many others in giving God a voice, giving God an embodied life on earth.'[16] Thus, for Heyward, Jesus is not God in any sense other than the way in which each of us has the power to become divine.[17] Unlike Comstock,

---

14 Comstock, *Gay Theology Without Apology*, p. 99.

15 Comstock, *Gay Theology Without Apology*, p. 106. I am not opposed to a soteriology that is theocentric rather than Christocentric; however, I do believe that if a theology is labelled as 'Christian', it must somehow account for the importance of Jesus Christ, which Comstock's theology does not do.

16 Carter Heyward, *Speaking of Christ: A Lesbian Feminist Voice*, ed. Ellen C. Davis (New York: The Pilgrim Press, 1989), p. 51.

17 'I believe that this relational power is the same God that sparked the life and infuses the ongoing presence of our brother Jesus, just as it moves you and me into each new day'; Carter Heyward, *Saving Jesus from Those Who Are Right: Rethinking What It Means to Be Christian* (Minneapolis: Fortress Press, 1999), p. 5.

Heyward sees the human Jesus as an important example who is still with us, empowering us through his life and its possibilities to embodiment of all God would have us be. Perhaps her most important Christological insight is that 'Jesus was not the exception, he was the norm – the normal human being, what each of us is created to be.'[18] Hers is thus a mixture of 'high' and 'low' Christology that shows us how truly bankrupt those terms have become: it is 'high' in the sense that she believes there was really something of divinity within Jesus that made him Christ; it is 'low' in the sense that she feels that Jesus was simply a man who, in Schleiermacher's phrase, had a perfect God-consciousness. But that is the beauty of her Christology and what makes it queer, even though she does not describe it as such: she is unwilling to fit her notion of Jesus the Christ into reified categories; she uses her imagination and her enfleshed experience as a lesbian woman to reimagine the God of Jesus that pulls all of us into Christic relation. 'This is what Christians are called to do: to remember him and, in so doing, to re-member – heal and liberate – one another.'[19]

In remembering Jesus, Heyward places primary emphasis upon his 'passion', but broadens that term to include more than just his suffering and death, as the Christian Church has so defined it. Rather, she sees Jesus' entire life and being as examples of his 'passion', his feeling-with others ('com/passion'[20]) and his embodied sense of God; unfortunately, according to Heyward, the Christian Church that grew up in Jesus' name has discounted and deliberately demonized embodied needs and yearnings and thereby the sacred, erotic power through which we express our passion for God and for one another. Such erotophobia in her estimation misses the whole point of 'the Jesus story', for it ignores the extreme passion for life in all of its mystery and manifestation that was central to the teachings of Jesus.[21] Heyward's Christology is thus

---

18 Heyward, *Saving Jesus*, p. 8.

19 Heyward, *Saving Jesus*, p. 149.

20 Heyward, *Saving Jesus*, p. 141: '[C]ompassion is what distinguishes what passion truly is of God, and what is not.' In other words, passion that is inwardly focused on the self or the self's personal desires alone is not godly passion, whereas outwardly-directed passion is com/passion, the passion of God for her creation. For this notion of compassion as God's passion, see Phyllis Trible, *God and the Rhetoric of Sexuality* (Philadelphia: Fortress Press, 1978), p. 45, who notes that in Hebrew the words for 'womb' and 'compassion' are related, leading her to conclude that compassion is God's 'womb-love' and thus a female attribute of the Godhead.

21 Heyward, *Saving Jesus*, pp. 130, 138.

intimately connected with her notion of a sexual theology in which our passion and our erotic power are ways of accessing the Divine and importing it into the world to work for justice.[22] When we do so, we are 'in Christ'; we are 'Christ-ing' and 'Christ-ed'.

Lisa Isherwood, a British feminist theologian, in surveying the various liberation Christologies on the theological landscape, has included a chapter on 'queering Christ'. She primarily summarizes the work of other theologians, such as Robert Goss and Carter Heyward; however, if one reads her chapter carefully, I believe one is able to detect Isherwood's own contribution to the realm of a queer Christology of embodiment. She notes that a high Christology of otherwordly divine sonship of Jesus by God is not helpful in today's world, especially within the queer communities, for in its exaltation such Christology empowers exclusivity and as a result condemns and marginalizes ordinary human beings: 'I suggest that the extent to which we claim exclusive and remote divinity for Jesus is the extent to which we show our lack of faith and commit idolatry through turning Jesus into everything that he stood against, in other words, a false God.'[23] This is nowhere more evident than in the Christian Right's insistence that Jesus would have championed the traditional nuclear family (which homosexuals are supposedly out to destroy), when, in actuality, Jesus pointedly criticized the patriarchal family of his day.[24]

Isherwood believes that a queer Christology's primary contribution will be in the area of a Christology of embodied friendship. Many queers see Jesus as their friend and their lover; he is the model for what true relationship can be, freed of heteropatriarchal patterns of ownership, domination and subjugation.[25] Instead, queer Christology brings a freedom and contentment to the topic that is lacking in many Christologies, which she believes may be accounted for by queer emphasis upon the body. Rather than accepting condemnatory rhetoric about their bodies, many queer groups have instead deliberately celebrated

---

22 Carter Heyward, *Staying Power: Reflections on Gender, Justice, and Compassion* (Cleveland: The Pilgrim Press, 1995), pp. 114–15. See also Carter Heyward, *Touching Our Strength: The Erotic as Power and the Love of God* (New York: Harper & Row, 1989), Chapter 6.

23 Lisa Isherwood, *Liberating Christ: Exploring the Christologies of Contemporary Liberation Movements* (Cleveland: The Pilgrim Press, 1999), p. 99.

24 Isherwood, *Liberating Christ*, p. 107. See also Halvor Moxnes, *Putting Jesus in His Place: A Radical Vision of Household and Kingdom* (Louisville and London: Westminster/John Knox Press, 2003), esp. Chapter 2.

25 Isherwood, *Liberating Christ*, pp. 106–07.

what some cultures have vilified and annihilated. Moreover, in appreciating their bodies in all their diversity, queer people suggest that the embodied Christ is 'as varied as those who inhabit bodies'.[26]

Radical Christology

The third type of queer Christology is what I call a 'radical' queer Christology. By this I mean a Christology that advocates a total break with what has gone before in the realm of Christology, based upon the exclusion of queers from the dialogue and the decision-making process. This is Christology modelled on the new queer activism that began in the 1980s with direct-action groups such as ACTUP and QueerNation, who grew tired of discussing gay/lesbian rights through 'normal' channels and instead began advocating for radical change through demonstrations and civil disobedience. There is an irreverence and a disrespect present in this Christology that flaunts queer sexual activity in the face of preconceived notions of propriety and theological correctness.

It is my personal belief that there is a place for this Christology; it has opened dialogue by forcing Church and academy to examine the issue of sexual orientation and embodied spirituality by insisting, 'We're here, we're queer, and we're not going anywhere!'[27] Much of this Christology is shocking and distasteful, reminding one of the outrageousness among the queer community that is often portrayed on the evening news in connection with gay pride celebrations. Nevertheless, privileged queers who have 'made it' often forget that it was the drag queens who birthed the gay liberation movement through their civil disobedience at Stonewall.[28] When this type of expression makes us uncomfortable, we need to ask where that discomfort originates, and we must always ensure that there are other points of view – even what we ourselves might consider obscene or indecent – represented at the table of theological discourse.

By far the best and most compelling queer Christology to date is that of Robert Goss, whose 'gay and lesbian manifesto', *Jesus ACTED UP*,[29]

---

26 Isherwood, *Liberating Christ*, p. 109.

27 This is the rallying cry of the queer movement. See Joshua Gamson, 'Must Identity Movements Self-Destruct? A Queer Dilemma', in *Social Perspectives in Lesbian and Gay Studies: A Reader*, ed. Peter M. Nardi and Beth E. Schneider (New York and London: Routledge, 1998), p. 593.

28 See Martin Duberman, *Stonewall* (New York: E. P. Dutton, 1993).

29 Robert Goss, *Jesus ACTED UP: A Gay and Lesbian Manifesto* (New York: HarperCollins, 1993).

cracked open the theological world by staking a direct-action claim for inclusion of queer consciousness in theology, with special attention to Christology. As noted in the preceding chapter, it is Goss's work that really initiated the shift from 'gay/lesbian' to 'queer' theological consciousness. Goss's hermeneutical key for unlocking the importance of Jesus Christ for queers is the action of Jesus in the temple at Jerusalem, recorded in all four of the canonical Gospels. (See Matthew 21.12–17; Mark 11.15–19; Luke 19.45–48; John 2.13–25.) In the same way that ACTUP has engaged in 'Stop the Church' demonstrations, Goss believes that Jesus was engaging in a 'Stop the Temple' demonstration in order to point out that the way Jewish religious affairs were being conducted was not in compliance with the justice-love of God that Jesus represented in his person and ministry.[30] For Goss, like most liberation theologians, the essential image of Jesus' message and ministry was the *basileia* ('kingdom', 'realm', 'reign') of God that was inbreaking upon the world through Jesus' demonstration of radical love for the marginalized and his opposition to the status quo.[31] It is this *basileia* message that got Jesus killed, according to Goss, just as in the past and present many oppressed people (including queers) have been and are being killed for 'acting up'.[32]

Goss's queer Christology is done in the overall context of his intention to push queers into 'acting up' in Church and society for their rights; it is a political and sexual theology that seeks to instil in the queer community a sense of pride and esteem that has been stolen by a homophobic Church. Thus, it is not necessarily a comprehensive Christology that addresses the same Christological questions that I propose to discuss in my own contribution, below. Perhaps Goss's most important – and radical – proposal is what he says about Jesus' crucifixion and resurrection and how he reinterprets the idea of atonement. Because his rhetoric is essential in understanding the new queer Christology, I quote it at some length.

> Early in Christian history, Jesus' crucifixion was stripped of its political reality, transformed and spiritualized . . . A queer reclamation of Jesus retrieves the socially embedded Jesus and the political dimensions of his crucifixion. It was a brutal political death at the hands of a repressive political infrastructure.

---

30 Goss, *Jesus ACTED UP*, pp. 147–9.
31 Goss, *Jesus ACTED UP*, pp. 72–5.
32 Goss, *Jesus ACTED UP*, pp. 82–5.

It was not God's will that Jesus die. . . . Jesus was radical in his practice of solidarity with oppressed men and women. His was a commitment aware of the political risks. Jesus' death is a tragic death at the
hands of an oppressive political structure in first-century Palestine.
The cross is God's invasive identification with the oppressed. . . .
*God's revelation on Easter aims to bring an end to crucifixions, not
perpetuate them* in the deployment of oppressive power relations.

The gay and lesbian reclamation of Jesus and his *basileia* practice
becomes the generative matrix for reinterpreting Jesus' death and
the Christ event in a nonhomophobic, nonheterosexist, and non-
oppressive context. . . . The cross now belongs to us. We have been
crucified. We have been martyred. We have been nailed to that cross
by most of the Christian churches. . . . Jesus died in solidarity with gay
men and lesbians. . . . *For gay and lesbian Christians, Easter becomes
the event at which God says no to homophobic violence and sexual
oppression.* . . .

On Easter, God made Jesus queer in his solidarity with us. In other
words, Jesus 'came out of the closet' and became the 'queer' Christ.[33]

For Goss, the queer Christ is a Christ who is *for* queers and *is* queer
himself, by virtue of representing all of the oppressed throughout history
who have been brutalized, killed or simply rendered invisible. This is
true atonement, standing in for all of the hurts and slights that have
afflicted God's queer sons and daughters for millennia.[34] But Goss does
not stop there; instead he issues a challenge to homophobic Christians
who would dismiss his claim that Christ is queer:

If Jesus the Christ is not queer, then his *basileia* message of solidarity
and justice is irrelevant. If the Christ is not queer, then the gospel message is no longer good news but oppressive news . . . If the Christ is
not queer, then the incarnation has no meaning.[35]

---

33 Goss, *Jesus ACTED UP*, pp. 81–4 (emphasis added).

34 Goss, *Jesus ACTED UP*, p. 85: 'Jesus the Christ is "queer-bashed." . . . The
queer Christ is politically identified with all queers – people who have suffered the
murders, assaults, hate crime activities, campus violence, police abuse, ecclesial
exclusion, denial of ordination and the blessing of same-sex unions, harassment,
discrimination, HIV-related violence, defamation, and denial of civil rights and
protections. Jesus the queer Christ is crucified repeatedly by homophobic violence.'

35 Goss, *Jesus ACTED UP*, p. 85.

A more radical and, in my opinion, troubling contribution to queer Christology has been made by Marcella Althaus-Reid, who self-identifies as a queer, Argentinian, feminist, liberation theologian and seeks to queer theology by introducing the notion of obscenity, perversion and indecency into the theological discussion. In this she is appropriating Goss's notion of queer as a stirring up or a spoiling, but she goes far beyond Goss's suggestions, for whereas Goss constructively addresses homophobia and suggests a queer paradigm for its dismantling, Althaus-Reid shocks and tears down without necessarily suggesting any constructive alternatives. In her first book, *Indecent Theology*,[36] she attempts to render indecent traditional theological concepts in order to provide liberation for those who have been marginalized by the Christian (especially Roman Catholic) Church. Among her topics for indecenting are the Virgin Mary and Jesus Christ, although she does not articulate a full-scale Mariology or Christology, but uses her comments as mere illustrations of her broader purpose. Like other Hispanic women (see Chapter 7 above), she sees Mary as a partner of Christ in the work of salvation, so that their stories and the theologies accruing from them cannot be separated; however, Althaus-Reid's view of Mary is a controversial one. Rather than seeing Mary as a poor, marginalized woman as many feminists do (see Chapters 6 and 7 above), she sees Mary as the exalted and privileged (white European?) Madonna, the construct of the Church who is 'the icon of a no-body', 'a myth of a woman without a vagina', with the result that Mary has been rendered a '"thing" called the Virgin Mary':

> For me, if the Virgin Mary had paws instead of hands and her vagina was in her ear, thus making it easier for the Word of God, the Logos, to 'say its Word' and penetrate her, it would not make any theological difference.[37]

Rather than seeing what theological meaning could be gleaned from deconstructing traditional incarnation, Althaus-Reid chooses to view Christian tradition as a sort of burlesque, ridiculing the concepts without really saying why or suggesting something better. While her work is provocative and fun to read (almost like sneaking a peak at pornography during adolescence), I do not think that Althaus-Reid has con-

---

36 Marcella Althaus-Reid, *Indecent Theology: Theological Perversions in Sex, Gender and Politics* (London and New York: Routledge, 2000).

37 Althaus-Reid, *Indecent Theology*, p. 39.

nected her indecenting of the Virgin to any theological ramifications vis-
à-vis the incarnation; for example, in calling Mary the 'Queer of Heaven
and Mother of Faggots',[38] she does not explain what she means by the
juxtaposition of these terms or how they claim Mary for a queer milieu.

When it comes to discussing who Jesus was in relation to God, she
attaches a literalness to the biblical texts and Church doctrines that truly
does render them obscene because it perverts them from their original
context as metaphors expressive of a deeper theological truth that she
does not take time to examine; in this she is not unlike those fundamentalist Christians who ignore biblical exegesis and insist that every
Scripture has a 'clear, plain meaning'. In perhaps her most shocking
statement among many, Althaus-Reid asserts:

> If we were to follow that dictum from the Reformation, that we know
> nothing about God except for what we know of Jesus, then we need
> to confront a Jesus/God whose theological identity has become a
> unique mess of being the one who fucked Mary and is yet her son at
> the same time . . . The point is that what cannot be made indecent in
> theology is not worth being called theology because it will mean that
> 'God,' 'Jesus' and 'Mary' only may have meaning in a determined
> heterosexual economic system.[39]

I suppose I must be missing the point of theology, for I do not see any
purpose in such indecenting unless something constructive results.
What is indecent is what is done with the symbols, not the symbols
themselves. Thus, in the aftermath of Althaus-Reid's treatment of the
Christ, I am left feeling as though I had eaten a wonderful meal that was
in all respects sumptuous, cutting-edge and inventive, yet in the end ultimately unsatisfying because I am still hungry for more.

In her actual discussion of the Christ figure, Althaus-Reid is rather
vague. She suggests a 'Bi/Christ' as one who is elliptical and hard to pin
down, just as bisexuality even among the queer community is often misunderstood or simply dismissed. A Bi/Christ will transgress borders and
open up the categories so that 'Jesus may have been a transvestite, a
butch lesbian, a gay or a heterosexual person.'[40] I am at a loss, however,
to understand what difference this makes. How we label Jesus or Christ
or into which category we place him is irrelevant if we do not also say

---

38 Althaus-Reid, *Indecent Theology*, p. 63.
39 Althaus-Reid, *Indecent Theology*, pp. 68–9.
40 Althaus-Reid, *Indecent Theology*, p. 114.

what that might mean for his praxis among people then and now. It does no good to suggest that Jesus 'fucked' men and/or women or cross-dressed or was androgynous or hermaphroditic, if one does not follow this claim with some interpretation for why that makes any difference to one's theological journey. This is precisely the criticism levelled by womanist theologian Kelly Brown Douglas against the notion of a black Christ.[41] It does no good to say Christ is black or female or gay or lesbian if one does not unpack what significance that has for members of those oppressed groups today. Nor does saying Christ is of one's own social location automatically render everything about that social location 'divine'. Just as Douglas suggests that not everything black is good, in the same way, not everything we could call queer or gay or lesbian is healthy or productive of wholeness. My discomfort with Althaus-Reid's work does not come from a position of prudery by any means; it is from the position of frustration that a brilliant possibility has been lost in her need to shock rather than to suggest preventive measures for the healing of brokenness. While I am disappointed in Althaus-Reid's early Christological comments, I am nevertheless enthusiastic about and supportive of the way she has called heterosexist theology to account for its colonizing of queer people.[42] I am further heartened by her more constructive comments about Jesus in *The Queer Bible Commentary*: 'Was the killing of Jesus an attempt to eliminate that difference which Jesus presented in the idea of God?'[43] This is a provocative question, one that needs to be answered; I hope to do so in what follows.

Another contribution to radical queer Christology comes from the realm of popular entertainment, the controversial off-Broadway play *Corpus Christi* by Terrence McNally.[44] In the play, 'Joshua' is a modern-day gay Christ figure in Texas, who is gay bashed, betrayed by his lover Judas, and killed. The staging is eclectic, and the action is a bit hard to follow. Yet what comes across loud and clear is McNally's desire to make the passion of Jesus live for us today in the context of homophobia, intolerance and gay-bashing. The Christology of this play is a very 'low'

41 See Kelly Brown Douglas, *The Black Christ* (Maryknoll, NY: Orbis Books, 1994), pp. 84–6, and my discussion in Chapter 4.

42 See, especially, Marcella Althaus-Reid, *The Queer God* (London and New York: Routledge, 2003), a brilliant exposition on how God can and should be allowed to 'come out of the closet'.

43 Marcella Althaus-Reid, 'Mark', in *The Queer Bible Commentary*, ed. Deryn Guest, Robert E. Goss, Mona West and Thomas Bohache (London: SCM Press, 2006), p. 523.

44 Terrence McNally, *Corpus Christi: A Play* (New York: Grove Press, 1998).

one: McNally's Joshua wants to be just a regular guy. He has no illusions or delusions of grandeur. He just wants to live his life and love someone completely, but outside forces will not let him. McNally has created a powerful modern-day parable that shows that if Jesus Christ was truly human, he had to have been one of us, one of the lowest and most despised of society. Unfortunately, the play ends with the crucifixion and does not explore the ramifications of resurrection nor the transcendence that might signal. Though thought-provoking and compelling, *Corpus Christi* is nevertheless a pessimistic view of homophobia's effects that subtly betrays McNally's own Christophobia.

My concern with the Christologies of Althaus-Reid and McNally is that they evidence the sort of Christophobia I described in Chapter 8. Althaus-Reid seems to have bought the notion that the Christ of the Christian Church is a 'holy terror' who must be 'brought down', debased, humiliated and turned into an obscene example of human excess, while McNally tells a sad story that lacks the possibility of redemption. This does nothing to instil wholeness or an appreciation of the Christ power in gay and lesbian people and others who self-identify as 'queer'. Instead, it encourages separatism from traditional religion that does not have to be there. Open and affirming churches have sought to reclaim Jesus Christ for the queer community, along with traditions and rituals that still have meaning for many queer Christians. Recent 'queerings' of sacred texts[45] have demonstrated that queers can reclaim the word of God that is Scripture in the same way that Robert Goss has encouraged us to reclaim the Word of God that was Christ. While I would be the last to advocate censoring of the more 'obscene' Christological imaginings that I have reviewed here, my final question is whether they are really necessary for developing a Christology of queer wholeness, embodiment and community solidarity.

Mystical Christology

The fourth type of queer Christology that I have discovered is what I will call a 'mystical' Christology. It is mystical because it does not seek to ground itself in the historical Jesus or any literal reading of the

---

45 For example, Robert F. Goss and Mona West, eds, *Take Back the Word: A Queer Reading of the Bible* (Cleveland: The Pilgrim Press, 2000); Deryn Guest, Robert E. Goss, Mona West and Thomas Bohache, eds, *The Queer Bible Commentary* (London: SCM Press, 2006); and Ken Stone, ed., *Queer Commentary and the Hebrew Bible* (Cleveland: The Pilgrim Press, 2001).

Gospels, but rather seeks to take clues for human development from the significant events of Jesus' life. A mystical Christology takes the historical framework and 'mythologizes' it so that it becomes paradigmatic or archetypal for the becoming of human, in this case queer, identity. This type of Christology is quite close to my own, for I believe that the stories of Jesus are there as signposts for us along our journey. If they are literalized, they lose their freshness to speak to every day and age. If they are interpreted only in their historical context, they are unable to motivate us to growth and change, which is what I believe any good theology, including Christology, must do.

The most important queer mystical Christology is that of gay mystic Andrew Harvey in his book *Son of Man: The Mystical Path to Christ*.[46] Harvey relates a personal experience he had of Jesus:

> Summoning up all my courage and praying for humility, I asked Jesus Christ directly to reveal to me the laws of his Christing and the stages by which he reached and became the One. And this is what, at my stage of understanding, I heard the Christ say within me:
>   Everything you need to become one with the life I am will be revealed to you if you meditate with all your heart and body and mind and soul on the life I led when I lived with you. I passed through all of the difficult thresholds and mysteries that you, too, must pass through to become one with the One. . . . [W]hat I am you are and what you are I am; I am in everything around you with my arms outstretched to help you. What I have done, you can do . . . I came as the first sign of a new creation, the first brother-sister of a whole new race of brothers and sisters. I came to birth the divine Child on earth, the Child of the Father-Mother whose essence is wisdom and compassion and whose every action blazes with the truth of love.[47]

One can therefore see from the outset that Harvey's is a very 'high' Christology. For him, Jesus was 'the One' sent from God to be the divine child who could serve as a model and guide for each of us in order that we might become divine children as well. Nevertheless, unlike the high Christologies of traditional Church doctrine, Harvey grounds his Christology in the story of the human Jesus. Seeing Jesus as a sort of 'avatar', Harvey delineates eight thresholds through which all human

---

46 Andrew Harvey, *Son of Man: The Mystical Path to Christ* ((New York: Jeremy P. Tarcher/Putnam, 1998).
47 Harvey, *Son of Man*, p. 92.

beings must progress if they wish to travel along the Christ way: baptism, temptation, transfiguration, agony in Gethsemane, crucifixion, resurrection, ascension and descent at Pentecost.[48]

Harvey then details each of these eight thresholds,[49] leading his reader on a journey through life that, like Eastern spirituality, honours every part of the journey, negative as well as positive, for what it can teach us about the destination. The beauty of Harvey's Christology is that it is wholistic and dialectic, for it seeks to make use of the work on the historical Jesus of recent years, while nevertheless going beyond the verifiable into the realm of the spiritual. Thus, his view of Christ is refreshingly unique in its quest to escape the 'either/or' thinking that has plagued biblical studies and theology since the Enlightenment.

One of Harvey's other contributions to Christology involves his dedication to Mariology. He sees the Virgin Mary as the embodiment of the Divine Feminine, a manifestation of the great Mother Goddess worshipped across the world for over six millennia.[50] He rejects the limitations placed upon Mary by Catholic doctrine and believes that just as Jesus' life can show us elements of our journey toward divinity, in the same way Mary's life can reveal to us the depths of human creativity through birth and regeneration. Moreover, because Jesus comes from Mary, he can be Christ the Mother, a favourite image among Christian mystics.[51] Christ the Mother gives birth through his passion, death and resurrection, constantly replenishing the Divine Feminine that he received from Mary and gives to each one of those who follow him along the mystical path.

Although not technically a 'queer' Christology since he has never publicly identified as 'gay' or 'queer', the creation Christology of Matthew Fox may be classified as a mystical Christology, for he too seeks to rise above the facts of Jesus' earthly life in order to birth God in us through the Christ Event. Fox, a former Roman Catholic priest, was first silenced by the Vatican and then ejected from the Dominican order for refusing to desist from, among other things, his ministry to the homosexual community. Now calling himself 'post-denominational', Fox in all of his

---

48 Harvey, *Son of Man*, p. 93.

49 Harvey, *Son of Man*, pp. 102–28.

50 Harvey, *Son of Man*, pp. 177–93. See also Andrew Harvey, *The Return of the Mother* (Berkeley, CA: Frog, 1995).

51 Harvey, *Son of Man*, pp. 162–6. For example, Julian of Norwich in her *Showings* imaged Jesus as Mother. See Caroline Walker Bynum, *Jesus As Mother: Studies in the Spirituality of the High Middle Ages* (Berkeley: University of California Press, 1982).

work espouses the principles of 'creation spirituality', seeking to distance himself from the fall/redemption paradigm of Christian soteriology and Christology. He urges his reader to travel along the 'fourfold path' elucidated by medieval mystical theologian Meister Eckhart:[52] (1) the *via positiva* is a path of embracing all that is good in creation; (2) the *via negativa* is a process of emptying oneself out and living with pain and emptiness, in order to embrace (3) the *via creativa*, a way of creativity and birthing out of nothingness, through which we enter (4) the *via transformativa*, a transcendent breakthrough into all of the possibilities of creation. Since this fourfold path is spiral, the fourth path leads back to the first; after we are transformed, we can then begin to appreciate the positive, release whatever negative has accrued, create anew, and be transformed once again, on an endless cycle.

Fox's Christology is quite eclectic. He utilizes the story of the historical Jesus in order to reach 'the cosmic Christ'. It is only through conversion to the cosmic Christ that humanity can hope to heal the global village. This is the Christ who was resurrected and ascended to rule over the universe. This Christ is a nurturing being who displays the characteristics of the gentle and loving earthly Jesus, but also exerts prophetic judgement against those who would harm the creation.[53] Fox believes that to embrace the cosmic Christ in addition to the historical Jesus requires a paradigm shift, since the two have been kept discreetly separate by traditional Christologies.[54] Like Harvey's mystical Christology, Fox's encourages the believer to transcend the earthly and enter into the realm of the spiritual. For Fox, this means letting go of the belief that Jesus is the only Son of God; instead, we must believe that all of us have the potential of becoming sons and daughters of God. He demonstrates that this idea is not 'new age', but is a teaching that has been around for nearly 1,000 years, inasmuch as Meister Eckhart celebrated the *Logos* or 'word' of God as 'applying to each and every creature'. Moreover, Meister Eckhart's Christology (which has influenced Fox's own) is founded upon the tradition of the *imago dei* ('image of God'): 'The seed of God is in us. . . . Now the seed of a pear tree grows into a pear tree, a hazel seed into a hazel tree, the seed of God into God.'[55] This gives rise

---

52 Matthew Fox, *Original Blessing: A Primer in Creation Spirituality* (Santa Fe, NM: Bear and Company, 1983).

53 Matthew Fox, *The Coming of the Cosmic Christ: The Healing of Mother Earth and the Birth of a Global Renaissance* (New York: Harper & Row, 1988).

54 Fox, *The Coming of the Cosmic Christ*, p. 79.

55 Fox, *The Coming of the Cosmic Christ*, p. 121.

to Fox's central Christological statement: he reiterates Eckhart's belief that 'we are called to be other Christs'.[56] This means that our lives as Christians are a process of becoming 'Christ-ed': as we learn the story of Jesus and apply it to our lives, through our faithfulness, we become Christ in the same way that Jesus, through his faithfulness, became Christ.

I have included Matthew Fox in my survey of other queer Christologies because, although he does not self-identify as queer, his theology has an ability to stir up and to spoil that makes it quintessentially queer. Moreover, he has been in constant solidarity with gay and lesbian people, describing them as today's *anawim* (Hebrew, 'little ones', 'poor', 'afflicted', 'oppressed').[57] Having surveyed other Christologies which in some way reflect a queer sensibility, I now propose, in the next and final chapter, to set forth my own.

---

56 Fox, *The Coming of the Cosmic Christ*, p. 121.

57 See, for example, Matthew Fox, 'The Spiritual Journey of the Homosexual . . . and Just About Everyone Else', in Fox, *Wrestling with the Prophets: Essays on Creation Spirituality and Everyday Life* (New York: HarperCollins, 1995), pp. 243–66.

'Who do *you* say that I am?' II:
A Queer Christology

I implied in the preceding chapters, and would like to make explicit here, that, for me, the idea of a 'queer' approach to theology, Christology or Scripture connotes imagination, playfulness, stirring up and, to some extent, spoiling what has gone before. The queer theologies and tentative moves toward queer Christology already discussed indicate that a queer methodology does not necessarily 'play by the rules'. In this, it is very much akin to feminist methodology, for we, like women, have had to search for ourselves not only in Scripture but throughout history and have often had to 'write ourselves in' to the story and force our inclusion in theological or ecclesiological discussion.

Thus, while it is helpful to study traditional Christology and the scholarly pursuit of the historical Jesus in order to be exposed to as many views as possible, nevertheless, in proposing a queer Christology, I do not feel obliged to adhere to what has gone before, either theologically or methodologically. I will elaborate by giving some examples. First, while most historical Jesus study limits itself to the Synoptic Gospels (Matthew, Mark and Luke) for reliable information about the life of Jesus and largely ignores the Gospel of John, I will take all of the canonical Gospels into account in developing my Christology. I believe that something does not have to be 'factual' to be 'true'; that is, I believe we can acquire truth from the memories of the Fourth Evangelist as well as the other three, for what is important for me is how Jesus inspired others to believe that he was the Christ. Their remembrances and their Christological interpretations are important sources for my Christology, whether or not it can be 'proved' that Jesus said or did a particular thing. In fact, many of the most Christologically meaningful passages in the New Testament would be placed in black letters by the Jesus Seminar.[1] Additionally, I propose to use other Christological memories

---

1 See Chapter 3. The Jesus Seminar's findings are published in Robert W.

of the early Church contained in the New Testament, even though they may not specifically discuss what Jesus himself said or did. My aim is to capture a feeling about the Christ, not to record a biography of Jesus. As we have seen in the discussion of other contextual Christologies in Part II, Christ has been imaginatively described by other marginalized groups.

Second, the scholarly community debates whether one should use non-canonical materials in doing research into the nature of Jesus Christ. For example, John Meier in his massive work *A Marginal Jew*,[2] dismisses the Gospel of Thomas from consideration as a valid source, whereas John Dominic Crossan places Thomas within the earliest stratum of historical Jesus material.[3] I use non-canonical materials without making any judgement about their historical reliability, for, again, I believe that the reminiscences of the early Christians reflect their diverse Christologies. Whether they were factual or later termed 'heretical' is irrelevant to my purposes. I am interested in the truth that the Christ inspired in the hearts of believers.

Third, Albert Schweitzer and others have sought to differentiate the 'Jesus of history' from the 'Christ of faith'.[4] I will not be doing that in my Christology, for I do not think it is possible to do so. Every writing about Jesus Christ, whether ancient, medieval, modern or postmodern, is, in its own way, an interpretation that comes from a place of belief or unbelief. Thus, the devout belief of Pope John Paul II inspires what he says about Christ, just as the indecent (un)belief of Marcella Althaus-Reid affects what she says.

Fourth, each evangelist began his/her account of Jesus and the Christology therein from a different temporal perspective. As noted in

---

Funk, Roy W. Hoover and the Jesus Seminar, *The Five Gospels: The Search for the Authentic Words of Jesus* (New York: Macmillan Publishing Company, 1993); and *The Acts of Jesus: The Search for the Authentic Deeds of Jesus* (New York: HarperCollins, 1998).

2 John P. Meier, *A Marginal Jew: Rethinking the Historical Jesus*, 3 volumes (New York: Doubleday, 1991–2001). His discussion of sources may be found in the first volume.

3 John Dominic Crossan, *The Historical Jesus: The Life of a Mediterranean Jewish Peasant* (New York: HarperCollins, 1991).

4 See, especially, Albert Schweitzer, *The Quest of the Historical Jesus: A Critical Study of Its Progress from Reimarus to Wrede*, trans. W. Montgomery (1906; New York: Collier/Macmillan, 1968); and Stephen J. Patterson, *The God of Jesus: The Historical Jesus and the Search for Meaning* (Harrisburg, PA: Trinity Press International, 1998).

Chapter 1, in Mark's view, Jesus' Christ-ness began at his baptism; for Matthew and Luke, it occurred at conception or birth; while for John, it always was, for Christ was the pre-existent Logos. Following in their footsteps, my Christology will begin in still another place: with Mary, for I believe that the incarnation of Christ began with his Blessed Mother, as will become much more evident as my Christology takes shape.

Some Autobiography

My concept of the Christ is most similar to the mystical views of Andrew Harvey and Matthew Fox discussed above. Indeed, Matthew Fox has been one of the most important influences upon the development of my queer spirituality and theology, for it was while reading his book *Original Blessing* that I first embraced the concept that we are all created good. In order for my reader to understand the importance of this for my theological becoming, it requires me to digress with a brief autobiographical sketch.

Growing up as a 'sissy-boy' in the Roman Catholic Church and parochial school in the period during and after Vatican II, but before its reforms had begun to filter down into local parishes,[5] I integrated into my very personhood the notion of original sin, that each person is created with the stain of sin on his or her soul and that baptism is necessary for its removal. Moreover, I believed that 'the devil' constantly seeks a way to make us fall from God's grace and that we must be ever-vigilant to fight off Satan's temptations. My third-grade teacher (a nun) told my classmates and me in vivid detail the reason Jesus was on that cross over the chalkboard: 'You did that, because you are such bad children!' The feelings for other boys and grown men that I began to experience at puberty confused me and turned me toward God for an answer that was not forthcoming. Instead, during my four years at a Jesuit-run high school, I learned that these feelings were 'not OK', that they should not be talked about, that what 'fags' did together was disgusting, and that God hated anyone who did not get married and have children. In the 1960s and early 1970s, gender roles were relatively fixed and were just beginning to be examined by the burgeoning feminist movement. I began to be labelled because of some mannerisms and interests that

---

5 For a discussion of Vatican II and its effects, see Chester Gillis, *Roman Catholicism in America* (New York: Columbia University Press, 1999).

today would not necessarily result in emotional queer bashing but did back then. Though I had never had any sexual experience and did not even know what two men or two women (or a man and woman, for that matter) could do together, I was branded a 'fag', a 'sissy', a 'cocksucker' and a 'queer', just by virtue of the fact that I was quiet, studious, did not like sports and played with girls. (How ironic that my favourite word for myself now is one that I initially heard in derision!)

After high school, I went on an odyssey of self-hatred. I had been brought up to revere the Catholic Church and priests and nuns as divine representatives to such an extent that, unlike many queers, I believed that they spoke for God and that God was saying, 'I hate you; get away from me.' There ensued a period of tremendous emptiness. During college, I found solace in academics; after college, I found solace in alcohol, drugs and anonymous sex. My philosophy in those years seems to have been, 'Well, if God hates me anyway, and if I am going to hell, then what's the difference? I might as well have a good time doing it!' But the problem was, I was not having a good time doing it. I was miserable, empty and self-hating. I never for a moment believed that I was afflicted with a sin; I knew I had always been the way that I was and had done nothing to cause it or provoke it. Nor did I believe that my inclinations could be taken away if I prayed hard enough or fasted or abstained or did novenas to Our Lady. I stopped going to church; my attitude toward God was that he (and in those days, God was definitely 'he') had abandoned me. Unlike some queers, I never felt guilty or ashamed, only puzzled, because I could not understand how God could hate something that was so natural, so beautiful and so fulfilling.

When I was 25, I met a man the same age as I was, who suggested that I come with him to church. I said, 'You've gotta be kidding me!' and began to ridicule him. He told me that his church was different, it was 'the gay church' (Metropolitan Community Church). I told him I had heard about it and was not interested in being part of a group of queers who were playing church; didn't they know that God hates them? Well, I may have been vehement in my reaction to the suggestion, but I did go to church because I wanted to see this fellow again. I will never forget my first visit. The pastor was a woman, which was shocking to me. I realize now that had the pastor been a man, I would not have integrated the message in the way that I did, because the priests had done their work well. Reverend Jane preached a message entitled 'Prosperity', and she said over and over again that God loves everyone – even gays and lesbians (we weren't 'queer' yet) – and that God wants the best for us and offers to us the gift of prosperity if we will accept it. She made it sound so simple. I chose to accept God's gift, and for me that meant accepting the gift of my sexuality and the realization that I was born good, that I was born queer, and that God looks upon me and says, 'This is my beloved son, in whom I am well pleased' (Matthew 3.17).[6]

I became quite involved in the church and am celebrating my twentieth anniversary as clergy in the Metropolitan Community Churches. It has been a rewarding journey that has been enriched by my natural bent toward academics. I began to want 'proof' for what I now knew in the depths of my being. Could one really be a follower of Christ and a 'practising' homosexual? I was assured spiritually that one could, but I wanted to find out for myself in a concrete way. Thus began my 20-year relationship with the Bible and theology, culminating in this queer Christology.

What is 'Christ'?

As noted above, it was Matthew Fox's notion of original blessing that first stimulated me to Christological reflection. When I stopped believing in original sin and embraced instead the notion that all creatures are born from the goodness of the One Source, God, that realization made me begin to ask about Christ. What was the purpose of the Christ? How did Jesus' life intermingle with the Christ figure? What was the meaning of Jesus' death? What happened in the resurrection? And what happens now? I received no one answer to these questions, nor did the answers come all at once. My Christological journey has been one of 'becoming', a bit at a time, as I meet new people and become exposed to new Scriptures, books, and theologies, take them in, process them with God, and begin to believe anew.

My initial understanding of the Christ comes from the Greek root, meaning 'anointed'. A 'Christ' is an anointed being. This anointed being has received its essence from God. For me, Christ is a part of God that has always existed (John 1.1) and that has become one with humanity. I believe that the Christ is the relational part of God, the part that is anointed to bring good news to humanity. This was how Jesus was Christ – he was anointed to bring good news, to set captives free and to announce God's favour (Luke 4.18–19). Unlike many Christians, how-

---

6 Throughout this chapter, unless otherwise noted, translations from the New Testament are my own.

ever, I do not believe that this Christ presence resided only in Jesus of Nazareth. I believe that this Christ presence dwells in all people, that it is innate to our being and our consciousness. Many people choose to embrace this Christ presence and allow it to animate their lives, to anoint them and make them prophets of good news who, like Jesus, proclaim God's favour. Others do not recognize the Christ within; consciously or unconsciously, they block their anointedness and do not share the good news of Christ. With Meister Eckhart, I believe that we are called 'to be other Christs'. We study the life of Jesus whom we call Christ because the fullness of his life, the tragedy of his death, and the mystery of his resurrection show us the possibilities of human becoming – how human persons may accept their Christ-ness and move into wholeness with God. I believe that human life is a journey to this wholeness, this Christic consciousness, this oneness with God within and without. Like Jesus, we have detours along the way, but I believe that God is always at the end of the journey, leading us on, welcoming us as the parent welcomed the prodigal (Luke 15.11–32).

The foundational Scriptures from the Bible that solidify this notion for me are found in Genesis and in John, and both involve what is referred to as God's Spirit or, in Christian parlance, 'the Holy Spirit'. The Hebrew word for 'spirit' also means 'breath' or 'wind'. This is the Spirit that soared over the primal waters before creation (Genesis 1.1) and is the same Spirit that was 'breathed' into the first human creature after God formed that human creature from the soil of the earth (Genesis 2.7). God created humanity in God's very own image: 'In God's image, God created them; male and female God created them', and challenged them to protect and take care of the earth (Genesis 1.27–28). This Scripture tells me that whatever God creates carries God's imprint; God's Spirit is contained in humankind, and after humankind was created, God noted that now the creation was '*very* good' (Genesis 1.31). We are very good creatures of a very good God. We are each created in God's own image, so everywhere we see humanity, we see God; every person we encounter can teach us something about God, for they carry the divine spirit/breath within. Think about the ramifications of this thought: that means that God is white, black, brown, yellow, red; God is male, female, intersexual, transgendered; God is gay, lesbian, straight, bisexual and non-sexual; God is strong and weak, old and young, able-bodied and physically challenged. And yet God is greater than all of this and more than all of this, for God has not stopped creating. There will come forth many more manifestations of God. Throughout the Hebrew Testament, 'anointed' people, kings and prophets, women and men, carried God's special commission to lead people. If we continue with the notion of anointedness meaning Christness, there were other Christs before Jesus and after Jesus. They have pointed people toward wholeness. But people do not always do what is best for them; human greed, pride and arrogance get in the way of us accepting our divine commission and our own anointedness (Genesis 3). Thus, Christ figures have continued to be born, continued to tell their truth, and – many times – continued to be ignored, killed, or both. But the creation goes on, and the Christing of human lives continues.

What makes me believe that we each carry this Christ-ness within us? The Gospel of John tells us the story of Jesus' disciples gathered in a room that was locked out of fear. But the risen Christ came through the walls and said, 'Peace be with you!' The risen Christ breathed on them and said, 'Receive the Holy Spirit.' This Holy Spirit is Christ's breath, communicated to us to inspire us to be Christs in our own time: 'As my Parent has sent me, so I send you.' (John 20.19–22) The disciples used that Christ-ness to found a movement that has persisted to the present day. The hope of the world lies in that Christ breath that we carry within, that anointedness that we have received.

This is a Christian view of the Christ. I am constantly aware of how this Christ is used as a weapon by Christians against Jews, Muslims, Buddhists, Hindus, Wiccans and people of other faiths, as well as those of any religion who are considered to be 'other', for example, feminist women, non-heterosexuals, the poor and the colonized. Therefore, one must be on guard, in developing a Christology, to be inclusive and address the reality of our pluralistic world. Theologian Chester Gillis reminds us, 'Only a Christianity that sees itself in the context of the world religions will make sense in the twenty-first century,'[7] that we must be vigilant to root out Christian imperialism and what I call 'Christofascism'.[8]

Therefore, I need to position my Christology with regard to the other religions of the world. I see the Christ figure as being a part of God – the Source, the Real, the Ultimate, whatever we choose to call it. I said

7 Chester Gillis, *Pluralism: A New Paradigm for Theology* (Louvain: Peeters Press, Grand Rapids: W. B. Eerdmans, 1998), p. 28.

8 I have encountered this term in the writings of Carter Heyward, who attributes it to German political theologian Dorothée Sölle. Sölle first uses the term in *Beyond Mere Obedience: Reflections on a Christian Ethic for the Future*, trans. Lawrence W. Denef (Minneapolis: Augsburg Publishing House, 1970). I am indebted to Lawrence Osborn for this citation.

above that I believe the Christ is the relatedness of God, but to use the very word 'Christ' is to capture that relatedness for a Christian milieu. Nevertheless, the concept of 'anointedness' can be meaningful in every culture and in every religion. The concept of relatedness and sharing good news is a part of every spiritual tradition. My thoughts of Christ are meant for a Christian audience, and a queer one at that. Nevertheless, because queers have been excluded in history and today, I believe we cannot be exclusive of others. Queer Christology must acknowledge other paths to the one Source and other forms of anointedness and relatedness that have no relation to our concept of Christ. In saying that the Christ Spirit is present in all people, I do not mean to co-opt anyone's tradition or thrust my Christ upon them. It is simply my limited, Christian vocabulary for saying that the divine relatedness and anointedness dwells in all people. We must allow others to express that divinity in the ways that bring them wholeness and lead them onward to their human becoming.[9]

Incarnation

My queer Christology begins with Mary of Nazareth, for if each of us carries the Christ within us, I believe that we can learn much about what it means to bear Christ from the few glimpses of Mary that we see in the New Testament. Most of the information we have about Mary comes from the first and second chapters of Luke, known by biblical scholars as the Infancy Narrative.[10] Those who do historical Jesus research dismiss the infancy narratives in Luke and in Matthew as containing nothing historically reliable about Jesus' conception or birth; they point out the inconsistencies, the mythological elements and the sheer unbelievability of a virginal conception.[11] I will leave aside questions of the virgin birth, for I suspect that much of the (Catholic) Church's insistence upon Mary's (perpetual) virginity comes from discomfort with sexuality, the

---

9 See Chapter 2 for a more complete discussion of the new pluralism in theology and Christology.

10 See, for example, Luke Timothy Johnson, *The Gospel of Luke* (Collegeville, MN: The Liturgical Press, 1991), pp. 36–44, 49–53; for a feminist reconstruction of the infancy narratives, see Jane Schaberg, *The Illegitimacy of Jesus: A Feminist Theological Interpretation of the Infancy Narratives* (New York: Harper & Row, 1987).

11 See, for example, John Shelby Spong, *Born of a Woman: A Bishop Rethinks the Birth of Jesus* (New York: HarperCollins, 1992).

origin of sin and the nature of the atonement; the early Church Fathers and others, in believing that Jesus came to ransom humanity from sin, believed that he himself had to be incapable of sin and that, therefore, his conception and birth had to be 'sinless' as well.[12] I have stated above that I believe that sexuality is a gift from God;[13] sexual intercourse does not transmit sin; thus, in my Christology there is no need of a virginal conception, although I would not discourage others from holding such a view if that were theologically and personally meaningful (provided it did not mask an unconscious sex negativity).

Luke 1.26–38 describes how Mary finds out that she is pregnant. The narrative tells us that an angel from God visits her and tells her that she will bear a child who will be called 'Son of the Most High'. Rather than dismissing this story as a fanciful creation of the early Church, I would read it with a queer hermeneutic of stirring up, possibly spoiling, and imagining what God has to say to queers through this story. Indeed, a queer hermeneutic and Christology will not only *queer* but it will *query*: it must be a questioning and a turning over of layers of heteropatriarchal tradition to reveal what lies beneath. I understand seven elements to this story:

1 Mary is greeted, 'God is with you!'
2 Mary is perplexed.
3 She is told, 'Don't be afraid!'
4 She is assured, 'You will do great things.'
5 Mary doubts, asking, 'How can this be?'
6 Mary is reminded, 'Nothing is impossible with God.'
7 Mary decides, 'Here I am, God's servant.'

I believe that Mary of Nazareth in this story can serve as the paradigm for queer empowerment. Most queer people have gone through periods of their lives when they have felt lost or alone or abandoned by God; but often, a stranger comes into our path, announcing to us, 'God is with you!' The queer person, based on past experience, is perplexed by a greeting such as this; doesn't God hate queers? Past hurts and internalized oppression bring up a wall of fear. At this point, often the queer person turns away and goes off on his or her own. But there are just as

12 See Elaine H. Pagels, *Adam, Eve, and the Serpent* (New York: Random House 1988).

13 See Phyllis Trible, *God and the Rhetoric of Sexuality* (Philadelphia: Fortress Press, 1978), Chapters 1–2, for the rhetorical-critical view that the interlocking word order of Genesis 1.26–28 indicates that sexuality can be understood as 'the image and likeness of God'.

many who face their fear and listen to the next message, 'Don't be afraid.' The messenger from God tells us, 'Walk out of your past. Do not give the past the satisfaction. There is a whole future awaiting you, if you will receive it.' The messenger assures us, 'You will do great things because God is with you.' Nevertheless, the queer person is still in doubt, because homophobia and Christophobia have done their work so well. We ask, 'How can this be? Who, me? What could God possibly have in store for me?' Once these doubts are expressed and spoken to the universe, however, if we are truly open to letting go of our doubt and insecurity, the messenger speaks on and reminds us that 'nothing is impossible with God'. 'I can love queer people if I want to', God says; 'no church or state can place a boundary upon my love. I created every person in my very own image. I am a queer kind of God; I stir up and spoil what humans create with their agendas of power and oppression. Turn to me; allow me to queer you.' And in the end, for many queer people, there comes the gift of acceptance of the situation. 'Here I am, God! Let it be for me according to what your messenger has promised.' The gift of acceptance from God is a powerful gift for those who have been refused acceptance, and it leads toward self-acceptance. This is the beginning of queer Christology: acceptance.

But acceptance of what? If we look at the seven elements I have delineated, a chiasm will become clear:

'God is with you!'	Divine presence
Perplexed	Doubt
'Don't be afraid!'	Confrontation of fear
'You will do great things.'	
'How can this be?'	Questioning
'Nothing is impossible with God.'	Resolution of doubt
'Here I am!'	Acceptance

In a chiasm, each of the elements balances another. Thus, here the announcement of the divine presence is balanced by the concluding acceptance of that presence; the doubt is balanced by the resolution of doubt; the confrontation of fear is balanced by further questioning prior to the resolution of doubt.

Literary critics acknowledge that the most important element in a chiasm is the centrepiece.[14] Here the idea in the centre of the chiasm is

---

14 On chiasms in biblical interpretation, see, for example, David E. Garland, *Reading Matthew: A Literary and Theological Commentary on the First Gospel* (New York: Crossroad, 1995), p. 164.

the messenger's statement, 'You will do great things,' highlighted in boldface. A queering/querying of the annunciation story will have as its central meaning the affirmation that God calls us to do great things. For Mary, that great thing is conceiving the Christ in her body. For queers, that great thing can consist of allowing Christ to take Christ's place within us: it means conceiving of our self-worth, our creativity and our birthright as children of God (sons and daughters of the Most High) who can give birth to the Christ. This is good news for every oppressed person, but especially for queers, who are often led to believe that we cannot and should not give birth to anything.

We would like to think that, once we accept God's love and agree to birth the Christ, that it will be a smooth journey, but again the story of Mary of Nazareth (Luke 1.39–56) tells us otherwise. Directly after Mary's acceptance in Luke 1.38, we are told that she set out 'with haste' (Greek *meta spoudés*) and went to visit her cousin, who was also pregnant. Feminist biblical scholar Jane Schaberg has pointed out that in Greek the expression *meta spoudés* is a phrase used in emergency situations:[15] Mary was running for her life! She was in a panic, and she fled. This was not a simple trip to visit a friend and pass the time of day. This was denial and escape from a terrifying situation. But her cousin Elizabeth was pregnant, too; her cousin Elizabeth had been given a gift from God also. They shared their experiences, and Mary again came to resolution and spoke one of the most beautiful and moving passages of Scripture, a manifesto for all oppressed people:

> My soul magnifies the Sovereign One, and my spirit rejoices in God my rescuer. For God has examined and approved the low in status. Surely from now on people of every time will call me fortunate, for the Mighty One has done great things for me, and God's name is holy. . . . God has brought down the powerful and has lifted up the oppressed. (Luke 1.47–49, 52)[16]

If the annunciation story may be seen as a story of queer self-acceptance and a 'coming out' into our creativity to birth the good news of Christ, then the story of the visitation follows the queer journey as

---

15 Schaberg, *Illegitimacy*, p. 89: 'But *meta spoudés* is a phrase that merits some pause and study. In the Greek translations of the Hebrew Bible it often has *overtones of terror, alarm, flight, and anxiety*.' (Emphasis added.)

16 Of course, most biblical scholars recognize that the Magnificat is an adaptation of Hannah's song in 1 Samuel 2.1–10. See Schaberg, *Illegitimacy*, pp. 93–4.

well, showing us that even after we accept who we are and our status as children of the Most High, we will still encounter panic that would tempt us to flee. Often we find someone else who has gone before us, someone who can share her or his experience with us that, indeed, God is in control; and then we, like Mary, can achieve final resolution, as we declare that our inner beings are a mirror of God's very being and that what has happened to us in finding the Divine will mean a reversal of fortune for our oppressors: they will topple from their positions of power and heteronormativity and those who have been oppressed will be lifted up and given a place in God's realm. This is the good news that Elizabeth teaches Mary and that older queers who have travelled the journey can teach the young.

We next see Mary when Jesus is born in Luke 2.1–20. It is a difficult birth: the journey is long and arduous; there is no room at the inn. But Mary gives birth anyway, because she has promised to do so; and God's messengers appear once again, this time proclaiming, 'Glory to God in the highest! And peace to all those whom God favours!' A queer appreciation of the Nativity is the realization that Christ *will* be born, no matter what the circumstances. No matter how hard it is, no matter how perilous the journey, no matter that folks might not receive us, once we have agreed to give birth to the Christ in self-empowerment and creativity, Christ *will* be born. Much of the world will have no knowledge that we have given birth to this Christ; most will continue to go about their business and their oppressing of others. Some, like King Herod in Matthew's version of the birth of Jesus (Matthew 1—2), will seek to destroy what we have birthed; they will seek to take our Christ presence from us. But those who witness the birth of queer self-worth and creativity will offer the assurance, 'Peace attaches to all those whom God favours,' through the gift of God's Christ Spirit.

Thus, in my queer Christology, incarnation is an acceptance that we bear Christ within us – the part of God that is instilled in us to bring forth from ourselves the offspring of Christ-ness: self-empowerment, creativity, awareness of creation, joy, love, peace and justice-making, to name but a few.[17] That's what a queer sense of incarnation means for me – that God becomes one with humanity through the assurance that God has always been present and that the realization of this presence will

---

17 Matthew Fox, in his book *Sins of the Spirit, Blessings of the Flesh: Lessons for Transforming Evil in Soul and Society* (New York: Three Rivers Press, 1999), seeks to have a Christian dialogue with Eastern religions by enumerating the gifts that can be birthed from within if we pay attention to our body chakras.

give birth to human infusion with divine anointedness as Christ. In relation to Jesus' incarnation, my view is that Jesus is a model for one who had, in Schleiermacher's words, a 'perfect God consciousness'. Jesus was so open to receiving God's anointing that his life and ministry can be paradigmatic for all of those who seek to walk the Christ Way, to become Christ themselves, and, like our mother Mary, to birth other Christs.

Life and Ministry

From the incarnation, this queer Christology moves on to the life and ministry of Jesus of Nazareth, through which we can glimpse the Christ's journey to carry out his mission of proclaiming the good news, liberating others from oppression, and proclaiming God's favour. Like the other liberation Christologies discussed in Part II, my queer Christology gives a central place to the concept of the reign of God (Greek *basileia tou theou*). It is widely agreed that Jesus' primary message was that God's rule/reign/realm/kingdom was coming near (Mark 1.15). I prefer the verbal, 'action' quality of the words 'reign' or 'rule' because they show that God's *basileia* is active and immediate among us, not a specific place where we go at some appointed time. For me, the word *basileia* carries both a temporal and spatial connotation: Jesus was telling the crowds, 'The place and time of God's power is here.' That was indeed good news for people who had been held in bondage by a series of foreign governments and the more oppressive strains of Judaism. Jesus' announcement of the reign of God was meant to let people know that no other ruler or government or religion or hierarchy could hold sway over their lives; only God could. To contemporary queer people, this proffering of the reign of God as a gift of the Christ through Jesus' preaching is good news, for it affirms for us that, although we may be second-class citizens in many countries, although we are unable to marry and may have our children taken from us, although in many jurisdictions it is a crime to express our love, nevertheless in the reign of God – the place where *God* rules – there is freedom and liberation for all people. A queer Christology of empowerment that sees all of us as anointed Christs requires that each one of us proclaim this good news to all we meet. By queering the status quo – stirring it up and spoiling it – we can help to make that reign of God a more present reality day by day.

Prior to announcing God's reign, however, Jesus was baptized, an event that each of the canonical Gospels records in its own way

(Matthew 3.13–17; Mark 1.9–11; Luke 3.21–22; John 1.32–34). The baptism is one of the first of the eight thresholds mentioned by Andrew Harvey in his mystical Christology; it is a threshold humans must cross, too, if they wish to follow Christ. In a queer context, I believe the baptism symbolizes the 'coming out' process, when gay and lesbian persons finally come to terms with who they are and seek to shed the homophobia that has accrued in their psyches during their formative years. The coming out process 'cleanses' the queer person so that they are able to preach good news without the impediment of past baggage.[18] Nor is it limited to gay/lesbian queers: I believe that every person who is 'queer' according to my definition has to 'come out' and be 'baptized' into non-heteronormativity; my own father is a wonderful example of a heterosexual man who 'came out' as the father of a gay son and is now a champion of homosexual rights in Church and society, but, like my own coming out, his was a process that did not happen overnight.

Once Jesus was baptized, he began his public ministry, which, according to the Gospel record, consisted of parables, sayings, sermons, healings, exorcisms and other miracles. In examining this public ministry, I would like to focus upon Matthew's Gospel; for I propose that, in the ways set forth below, Matthew, for whatever reason, is the 'queerest' Gospel. It contains stories and sayings that have special relevance to a queer consciousness, just as Luke's Gospel has been claimed by liberation theology as the Gospel of the poor: 'Jesus always communicates meaning to human existence by responding to the implied questions of those searching for a salvation or liberation.'[19] In the case of queer Christians seeking inclusion in the heterosexually dominated institutional Church, I believe that Matthew's Gospel is prophetic, for the author of Matthew (whoever he or she may have been) was writing to a community of Jewish Christians who were having trouble accepting the influx of gentiles into their midst.[20] The message of inclusion of those who are different is a theme that one can see throughout the Matthean account of Jesus' ministry, and this is good news for queers who seek

---

18 See L. J. Tessier, *Dancing After the Whirlwind: Feminist Reflections on Sex, Denial, and Spiritual Transformation* (Boston: Beacon Press, 1997), pp. 104–11.

19 Roger Haight, *Jesus Symbol of God* (Maryknoll, NY: Orbis Books, 1999), p. 78.

20 Matthean scholar J. P. Meier even goes so far as to say that Matthew's Gospel centres on 'one central *crisis*: a once strongly Jewish-Christian church is becoming increasingly Gentile in composition'; John P. Meier, *The Vision of Matthew: Christ, Church, and Morality in the First Gospel* (New York: Paulist Press, 1979), p. 28 (emphasis added).

both to be included themselves and to include others. Some examples will demonstrate my theory.[21]

'Raca'

Matthew's is the only Gospel to include an obscure reference to a derogatory epithet from the ancient world. In explaining how he would not abolish the Torah but fulfil it, Jesus broadens some of the Mosaic laws that were being taken legalistically among some sectors of Judaism. For example, he notes that adultery can be a sin of the heart and mind in addition to a sin of the body (Matthew 5.27–28); and he encourages his followers to 'turn the other cheek' rather than exact 'an eye for an eye' (Matthew 5.38–39). In the same way, Jesus expands the concept of harming another: instead of merely condemning the act of murder, Jesus points out that 'if you are angry with someone, you will be liable to judgement' and 'if you call someone *raca*, you will be liable to the council' (Matthew 5.21–22). The New Revised Standard Version translates this phrase 'insult a brother or sister' and adds in a footnote that the Greek text literally reads 'say *raca* to', noting that this is 'an obscure term of abuse'.[22] A number of years ago, biblical scholar Warren Johansson suggested that this might be an obscure reference to same-sex intercourse, similar to calling someone a 'fag' or 'dyke' today.[23] I am not certain I agree with Johansson's conclusion due to his lack of solid evidence; however, I do see in this 'fulfilment' of Mosaic law an encouragement on Jesus' part to be more tolerant of others. Surely this is good news for those who are marginalized in contemporary society – that, in Jesus' estimation, when one insults another or calls another names, one is in effect guilty of murder – literally, character assassination.

The Centurion and his Boy

The next example is more concrete. Matthew 8.5–13 tells the story of a Roman centurion who approaches Jesus to request healing for what most translations render as his 'servant'. However, the Greek calls the

---

21 For traditional commentary on these passages, see Daniel J. Harrington, *The Gospel of Matthew* (Collegeville, MN: The Liturgical Press, 1991).

22 The Society of Biblical Literature, *The HarperCollins Study Bible*, New Revised Standard Version (New York: HarperCollins, 1993), p. 1866.

23 Warren Johansson, 'Whoever Shall Say to His Brother, *Racha* (Matthew 5:22)', *Cabirion* 10 (1984), pp. 2–4.

one in need of healing the centurion's 'boy' (Greek *pais*). In the ancient world it was not uncommon for a master and a slave to be in a pederastic relationship.[24] (Even in today's world in some segments of the queer community, one can still hear references to a man and his 'boy'.[25]) Clearly, the centurion cares deeply for his 'boy'; though a gentile, he comes to a Jewish healer for relief, admitting that he is not 'worthy' for Jesus to come into his house. According to a queer hermeneutic, might this not be an example of possible shame on the part of the centurion for the type of relationship in which he was involved – one that ancient society frowned upon? Perhaps this story of the centurion requesting healing is more than just a master wanting to save a beloved servant, as traditional exegesis has held; it is in fact plausible that Jesus is tacitly approving a same-sex relationship. I realize that arguments from silence are problematic; nevertheless, in the same way that feminist biblical interpreters are able to 'read the silence',[26] I believe that queer interpreters can read between the lines of this story and see not only an example of same-sex devotion, but also an instance where Jesus could have condemned the practice of homosexuality but did not. Moreover, Jesus not only heals the centurion's boy but remarks that he has not found such faithfulness among his own Jewish people (Matthew 8.10). In this way, Matthew once again may be urging his Jewish Christian community to include those who are different, a theme of some concern to him. Further, that this status of master and 'boy' was of importance to Matthew is evidenced by the fact that Luke, in using a common source, refers to the centurion's 'slave' (Greek *doulos*).[27] (See Luke 7.1–10.)

---

24 '"Boy" in Greek connotes a catamite or youth in a homosexual/pederastic relationship in the Greco-Roman world. These relationships were socially acceptable and not uncommon in that culture. . . . When the Gospels were written the practice was very alive. . . . [R]eaders or hearers of the story in the first century would unquestionably conclude, given the language that is used, that the centurion was a pederast and his boy a catamite'; Raymond J. Lawrence, Jr, *The Poisoning of Eros: Sexual Values in Conflict* (New York: Augustine Moore Press, 1989), pp. 70–1. See also Nissinen, *Homoeroticism in the Ancient World*, p. 71: 'Young male slaves in Rome could serve as long-term beloved.'

25 See, for example, Carol Queen and Lawrence Schimel, eds, *PoMoSexuals: Challenging Assumptions About Gender and Sexuality* (San Francisco: Cleis Press, 1997).

26 For this reading strategy, see Elisabeth Schüssler Fiorenza, *Bread Not Stone: The Challenge of Feminist Biblical Interpretation* (Boston: Beacon Press, 1984).

27 This is one of many examples in the Gospels of Jesus praising the faith of a person whom society would dismiss as 'other'. For example, Luke 7.36–50, tells of the woman 'with a bad reputation' – whom exegetes persist in referring to as a

The Canaanite Woman

Matthew 15.21–28 relates a similar story in which another non-Jew, this time a Canaanite woman, is rewarded for her perseverance in her quest for healing for her daughter. Matthew's version of this story even has Jesus himself go so far as to utter a racial slur, comparing gentiles to 'dogs':

> Jesus replied [to her request], 'I was sent only to the lost sheep of the house of Israel.' But she came and prostrated herself before him, saying, 'Help me, Lord.' He answered, 'It's not fair to take food meant for children and throw it to dogs.' She replied, 'Indeed, Lord; yet even dogs eat crumbs from the master's table.' At this point Jesus answered her, 'Woman, great is your faith!' (Matthew 15.24–28a)

Once again, Jesus commends the faith of one who is a non-Jew. Moreover, Jesus seems reluctant at first to minister to the gentile in this story; the woman herself must be assertive in getting the treatment she deserves. I believe a queer interpretation of this story will notice that oftentimes the Christian Church, like Jesus in the story, is reluctant to give queer folks their just deserts; frequently queer activists must resort to extraordinary means to get a hearing, as in the demonstrations by ACTUP and QueerNation.[28] A queer Christology recognizes that the justice of God supersedes all human conventions, a message that Matthew was intent on sharing with his community as they struggled to cope with gentiles encroaching upon their territory.[29] Perhaps one might also suggest Christologically that in this situation the Christ Spirit over-ruled the man Jesus and his human prejudices. A queer Christology sees hope in this story that the Christ Spirit in our world and in all people will somehow overcome the predisposition of many toward intolerance and homophobia.

---

prostitute although it says this nowhere in the text – who had such great faith in Jesus that she crashed a dinner party and washed his feet with her tears.

28 See Goss, *Jesus ACTED UP*, Chapter 2.

29 See Warren Carter, *Matthew and the Margins: A Sociopolitical and Religious Reading* (Maryknoll, NY: Orbis Books, 2000).

Clean and Unclean

Immediately preceding the story of the Canaanite woman, Jesus addresses the difference between clean and unclean, when it is pointed out to him
that his disciples eat without washing their hands (Matthew 15.10–20).
Jesus differentiates between bodily cleanliness and cleanliness of the
heart, noting that 'what comes out' of a person's heart is what renders
that person unclean – 'evil intentions, murder, adultery, fornication,
theft, false witness, slander' (Matthew 15.19). While I am sure many
Christians would include homosexuality under the category of 'fornication' in Jesus' remark, nevertheless I believe that Jesus is pointedly telling
his followers that they should not judge others' behaviour but instead
examine the state of their own hearts. A queer Christology will always
keep this in mind; the state of the heart is that by which God judges the
state of one's life. Outsiders are not in a position to judge.

Miraculous Feedings

The theme of nourishment raised in the story of the Canaanite woman
is made explicit in the two instances of miraculous feedings that bracket
her story (Matthew 14.13–21 and 15.32–39). Most Jesus scholars have
dismissed the so-called 'nature' miracles as fanciful creations of the early
Church.[30] However, a queer Christology, in seeking a deeper truth
beyond what is factual, will see that whenever the Christ Spirit is at large
in the world, people's needs will be met. The hospitality of God is infec-
tious. The reign of God as envisioned by Jesus is a place and a state of
mind and heart where all people are welcome, where all people are min-
istered to, and where all people have enough. Thus, John Dominic
Crossan points out that Jesus' 'open commensality' is the determining
element of both his message and his danger to the status quo.[31] A queer
sensibility that seeks to stir up and spoil the status quo will be welcoming of everyone; we who have been kept from many tables, both literally
and figuratively, dare not keep others from the table. In this regard, I
must point out that one of the most disquieting and painful issues that I

---

30 See Chapter 3.

31 John Dominic Crossan, *The Historical Jesus: The Life of a Mediterranean
Jewish Peasant* (New York: HarperCollins, 1991), pp. 341–4. See also Marcus J.
Borg, *Conflict, Holiness, and Politics in the Teachings of Jesus* (Harrisburg, PA:
Trinity Press International, 1984; second edition 1998), pp. 93ff; and Schüssler
Fiorenza, *In Memory of Her*, p. 137.

see in the queer community is the intolerance and divisiveness that one sometimes finds among segments of the community; for example, rich, privileged 'A-gays' often discriminate against drag queens, transgendered folk, leather people and those whose sexuality is considered 'kinky' or 'bizarre'. I contend that, in our quest for a place at the table, we must never become the 'new Pharisees' in the lavender togas.

Eunuchs

Matthew is the only evangelist to include the dominical remarks about marriage concerning eunuchs. When the disciples suggest that because Jesus' policy on divorce is so stringent, perhaps it is better not to marry, Jesus replies:

> Not everyone can accept this teaching, but only those to whom it is given. For there are *eunuchs who have been so from birth*, and there are eunuchs who have been made so by others, and there are eunuchs who have made themselves so because of the realm of heaven. May anyone who is able receive this saying. (Matthew 19:11–12; emphasis added)

Nancy Wilson has pointed out that two of the three categories of eunuch enumerated by Jesus are fairly easy to figure out: those who have been made eunuchs by others are those men who have been castrated, perhaps because of slavery or conquest of war. Those who have made themselves eunuchs might be those who castrate themselves (such as the priests of the Mother Goddess known as the *galli*) or those who deliberately refrain from procreation. But what about those who are 'eunuchs from birth'? Essentialists such as Wilson would say that this refers to gay and lesbian people.[32] Though I am not a strict essentialist, I know that I did not intentionally choose my sexual orientation. Could Jesus not be referring to those who, from their birth, have not 'fit' into the predominant gender and sexuality categories?[33] I believe so, and if this hypothesis is tenable, it is yet another example of Matthew's desire to

---

32 Wilson, *Our Tribe*, pp. 128–9.

33 This lack of congruence with established categories of gender and sexuality would include not only those with same-sex affinity, but could also include women who act outside of gender expectations such as Lydia in Acts and heterosexual men who are sterile (although in patriarchal antiquity the man was never sterile; it was always the woman!).

have the Christian community to whom he was writing focus on greater inclusivity of all people in the body of Christ.

I believe that the Gospel of Matthew, in these six instances, shows itself to have an agenda of inclusion of diverse peoples in God's reign. Of course, the other canonical Gospels have a message of inclusion as well; for example, Luke tells the stories of the woman searching for the lost coin and the return of the prodigal (Luke 15.8–32), while John includes the story of the woman taken in adultery (John 8.2–11). The other source that I would like to highlight in discussing Jesus' ministry, however, is the non-canonical Gospel of Thomas, for I believe that it includes unique sayings and different versions of canonical sayings that mediate the gospel of Jesus for a queer milieu. For example, Thomas' Gospel states:

> Jesus said, 'Those who seek should not stop seeking until they find. When they find, they will be disturbed. When they are disturbed, they will marvel, and will rule over all.' (Logion 2)
>
> Jesus said, 'If your leaders say to you, "Look, God's imperial rule is in the sky," then the birds of the sky will precede you. If they say to you, "It is in the sea," then the fish will precede you. Rather, God's imperial rule is inside you and outside you. When you know yourselves, then you will be known, and you will understand that you are children of the Living God. But if you do not know yourselves, then you live in poverty, and you are the poverty.' (Logion 3)
>
> His disciples said to him, 'When will God's imperial rule come?' [Jesus replied,] 'It will not come by watching for it. It will not be said, "Look, here!" or "Look, there!" Rather, God's imperial rule is spread out upon the earth, and people don't see it.' (Logion 113)[34]

These three logia, or sayings, demonstrate a departure from the way Jesus is portrayed in the canonical Gospels.

The Jesus of Thomas is much more 'in your face' than the Jesus of Matthew, Mark, Luke and certainly John. This 'in your face' quality is attractive to a queer Christology, for queer theory and activism asserts that this type of confrontational, transgressive stance is necessary to effect change in today's heteronormative world. The Jesus of Thomas

---

34 'The Gospel of Thomas' in *The Complete Gospels: Annotated Scholars Version*, ed. Robert J. Miller (Sonoma, CA: Polebridge Press, 1992), pp. 305, 322, rendered in inclusive language.

encourages us to keep on seeking for what we need, but warns us that when we find what we are searching for, we will be disturbed. This is sometimes the case with civil rights: when slavery was abolished, blacks became ghettoized and their poverty skyrocketed; when women began to assert their rights, they were placated by the resulting tokenism of a few women in high-profile jobs; and when US gays and lesbians began to receive a hearing from such politicians as President Bill Clinton, they were ultimately disturbed by betrayal in the form of the military 'don't ask, don't tell' policy and the Defense of Marriage Act (DOMA).

Jesus in Thomas' gospel encourages queer readers to know themselves, with the caution that if one does not become proactive in knowing oneself, poverty is the result, and the queer person who has been inattentive to their own becoming is the source of the poverty, indeed the very bankruptcy of the queer liberation movement. Moreover, Thomas' Jesus portrays the reign of God as already present all around us, but people don't see it because they are so preoccupied in looking elsewhere. As a result, others will take advantage of God's reign (or 'imperial rule') to the exclusion of those who are inattentive. What a wonderful commentary on the requirement of all oppressed people to take care of themselves and be vigilant for their rights and prerogatives. If the oppressed do not look after themselves, they will be left 'in the back of the bus', while everyone else rides up front.

Two elements of Andrew Harvey's Christology are also instructive for a queer Christology of Jesus' ministry. The second threshold in Harvey's scheme is Jesus' temptation in the wilderness. Harvey believes that everyone who seeks to embrace the mystical Christ must go through a period of temptation, testing and wandering in the wilderness. This is certainly a part of queer experience. Jesus went into the wilderness to collect himself and was tempted by the devil. (See Matthew 4.1–11; Mark 1.12–13; Luke 4.1–13.) Those who go on a journey of self-search are often tempted by various demons. Some are ejected from their churches, families and jobs to wander aimlessly, often seeking solace at the bottom of a bottle, at the end of a coke spoon, or from the temporary lift of casual sex. Others drift from one relationship to another, seeking from another person the wholeness that they could derive from a relationship with the Christ. But as Delores Williams notes of the experience of black women, the wilderness is often the place where God meets the wanderer and helps her or him to 'make a way out of no way'.[35]

---

35 Delores S. Williams, *Sisters in the Wilderness: The Challenge of Womanist God-Talk* (Maryknoll, NY: Orbis Books, 1993), p. 108.

Lesbian Episcopal priest M. R. Riley concurs from a queer perspective:

We are a people whose entire past has been eradicated. We must dig deep, unearth it, fit the broken fragments back together as best we can, preserve it, pass it on, so that never again will one of ours be left to perish in the desert for the lack of vision.[36]

Like Jesus, queer people can find Christ in the desert of the heart, in the wilderness of coming out in a hostile world. We can cross the threshold into the promised land of our Christ consciousness.

When we do so, we, like Jesus, are prepared to encounter the threshold of transfiguration, in which we see a foretaste of what we can become – the possibility of health and wholeness, a unified community of sisters and brothers who help one another and fight for one another. Jesus was revealed in all his splendour as the Risen Christ in the Transfiguration (Matthew 17.1–13; Mark 9.2–8; Luke 9.28–36); each day, gay and lesbian people have transfigurational foretastes of our Christic becoming as we foster our self-esteem, take care of ourselves, make love, forge a partnership and perhaps even raise children – against the odds to the contrary.

While we are on that 'high', we experience in our queer Christology the triumph and joy of Jesus' entry into the city of Jerusalem on Palm Sunday (Matthew 21.1–11; Mark 11.1–11; Luke 19.28–38). Matthew tells us:

The crowds that went ahead of Jesus and those that followed kept shouting, 'Hosanna to the Son of David! Blessed is the one who comes in God's name! Hosanna to the highest heaven!' When Jesus entered Jerusalem, the entire city was disturbed, asking, 'Who is this?' But the crowds kept saying, 'This is the prophet Jesus from Nazareth of Galilee.' (Matthew 21.9–11)

As I view this story from a queer context in the contemporary world, there is one major issue. In today's world, if all people can be Christs, as I have argued throughout the course of this Christology, what does it mean 'to come in God's name'? Many queer people are anointed to

36 L. William Countryman and M. R. Riley, *Gifted by Otherness: Gay and Lesbian Christians in the Church* (Harrisburg, PA: Morehouse Publishing, 2001), p. 108.

bring good news to their own community and to the world at large, but, like the onlookers in Jerusalem, others may ask, 'Who is this who presumes to speak or act in God's name?' In answering this question, it is instructive to see how the continually shouting crowds around Jesus answered it; they said, 'This is the *prophet* Jesus.' I believe it is significant that out of all the Christological titles contained in the Gospels (Christ, Messiah, Lord, Son of God, Son of Man, etc.), 'prophet' is the form of identification selected by the crowds. This signals to me that those who 'come in God's name' are prophets, anointed to do God's work as the Hebrew prophets were, filled with a message of confrontation and judgement as those same prophets were, and ready to die for justice as prophets have been throughout time. We can call to mind recent prophets who spoke a truth that was unpleasant to hear – Abraham Lincoln, Sojourner Truth, John F. Kennedy, Malcolm X, Martin Luther King, Rosa Parks, Che Guevara, Gloria Steinem, Betty Friedan, Mohandas Gandhi, Anwar Sadat, Harvey Milk, Troy Perry, the rioters at Stonewall – many of whom have been silenced through incarceration or assassination.

From a queer perspective, the Palm Sunday story empowers us to action – collective action, like the crowds who, in partnership with Jesus, stormed the city of Jerusalem to 'act up'. Like the crowds on Palm Sunday, we must not be silenced. Like Jesus, we must accept our prophetic, Christic role to criticize, change, and replace systems and structures in Church and society that perpetuate all kinds of oppression, not just homophobia and heteronormativity. We must be in solidarity with all who struggle for equality – women, people of colour, the poor, the aged, the young, the differently abled, and those of questionable gender or sexuality. In doing so, we must constantly ask ourselves what it means to 'come in God's name', what it means to speak and to act 'in God's name'. Do we use God's name in vain, for our own violent and sinful agendas, such as those who bomb abortion clinics in God's name or fly planes into buildings in Allah's name, or advocate 'killing a queer for Christ'? Or do we use God's name to lift up the lowly as Mary envisioned in her Magnificat, to create justice and liberation as Gandhi and King advocated, and to proclaim good news and the year of God's favour as Jesus did?

This is how the life and ministry of Jesus become paradigmatic for revealing a queer Christology: he demonstrated what God was like. He solved the problem of God's true nature articulated in Hebrew wisdom literature (especially the book of Job). He showed in his person a perfect

God-consciousness and revealed in his words and his deeds the face of God – One who is with the oppressed, One who tells good news in the midst of bad, One who lifts up and carries those who are crucified by their peers. And because the people saw God in this Jesus, they called him the Son of God and, many years after his death, came to believe that Jesus himself was God. A queer Christology recognizes that when we emulate Jesus, we become sons and daughters of God and create God in our midst through the incarnation of the Christ in our bodies, minds, and spirits.

Passion, Death and Resurrection

The events of the last week of Jesus' life are well known and are recorded by all four of the canonical Gospels. (See Matthew 26.36—27.56; Mark 14.32—15.41; Luke 22.39—23.49; John 18.1—19.37.) While I do not want to overemphasize the passion and death of Jesus in a queer Christology, nor do I wish to underestimate it. Many people, myself included, prefer to concentrate on the joy and new life of Easter Sunday rather than the death and hopelessness of Good Friday. However, as Matthew Fox points out in his interpretation of Meister Eckhart's mystical theology, we must embrace the negative path before we can break free of it and enter the creative and transformative paths.[37] True creativity and authentic transformation come out of privation. Jesus had to experience a humiliating and painful death before he could become fully Christ in the resurrection. In the same way, I believe that queer people often must encounter humiliation, discrimination, physical and emotional torture, and even death in order to birth liberation for all. The Christological importance of the cross for queers is the possibility of meeting God in our pain and receiving ultimate transcendence. Two of Andrew Harvey's thresholds to experiencing the mystical Christ are Jesus' agony in Gethsemane and his death; Harvey sees these painful experiences as cathartic for Christic becoming.

We must recognize, however, that we ourselves do not always reap the benefits of our struggles; many times it is those who come after us who are gifted by our suffering. Thus, African-American poet and essayist Maya Angelou reminds us:

---

37 This is a theme in all of Fox's work, but see especially *The Coming of the Cosmic Christ*, pp. 167, 199.

When we cast our bread upon the waters, we can presume that someone downstream whose face we will never know will benefit from our action, as we who are downstream from another will profit from that grantor's gift.[38]

Is this not the very meaning of what theologians have called Jesus' vicarious suffering for humanity? I agree with Rita Nakashima Brock that Jesus' suffering and death were not willed by God, that such a view of salvation relegates God to the role of abusive parent.[39] I concur with Jürgen Moltmann and Robert Goss that God was suffering with Jesus on the cross, that God did not plan the crucifixion but could not necessarily stop it, and that our hope as Christians comes from how God reacted to the crucifixion of Jesus and reacts to contemporary crucifixions.[40]

In this regard, the interpretative moment – the hermeneutical key, if you will – for my queer reading of the crucifixion is the death of Matthew Shepard, a gay college student in Laramie, Wyoming, who was beaten, tied to a fence and abandoned to die alone in the wilderness. Eyewitnesses stated that Matthew looked like a 'scarecrow' on that fence,[41] but might he not also have looked like the crucified left by the side of the road in Roman Palestine for others to notice and learn a lesson from? I believe that Matthew Shepard is the most famous example of the crucifixions of gays and lesbians that have occurred for generations. His humiliation and suffering were meant, like the scarecrow, as a warning for queers to 'keep away' from 'decent' people, and, like ancient crucifixions, as an example to queers of what might happen if they 'flaunt' themselves on heteropatriarchal territory.

Where was God in this situation? I believe that God was with Matthew as he hung there dying – comforting him, taking away his

---

38 Maya Angelou, *Wouldn't Take Nothing for My Journey Now* (Toronto: Random House of Canada, 1993), pp. 15–16.

39 Rita Nakashima Brock, *Journeys by Heart: A Christology of Erotic Power* (New York: Crossroad, 1991), pp. 53–7. See my discussion of Brock in Chapter 6.

40 Jürgen Moltmann, *The Crucified God: The Cross of Christ as the Foundation and Criticism of Christian Theology*, trans. R. A. Wilson and John Bowden (London: SCM Press, 1974), pp. 1–5; Goss, *Jesus ACTED UP*, pp. 76–7.

41 Edward J. Ingebretsen, *At Stake: Monsters and the Rhetoric of Fear in Public Culture* (Chicago and London: University of Chicago Press, 2001), pp. 178–9. See also Beth Loffreda, *Losing Matt Shepard: Life and Politics in the Aftermath of Anti-Gay Murder* (New York: Columbia University Press, 2000); as well as the HBO film *The Laramie Project* (2002).

pain, and assuring him that God would welcome him to Godself when his suffering finally ended. However, I believe that God was present in an even more tangible way. There was something redemptive above Matthew's experience; it did not go unnoticed, as other atrocities against homosexuals have been. The horror and brutality of his death, the perpetrators' insistence that he 'had it coming' because he had 'come on' to them, and the media circus created by homophobic hatemongers at his funeral served to bring the issue of queer-bashing into the public consciousness, and some steps have been taken to preclude this from happening again.

Terrence McNally, in the introduction to the printed version of his play *Corpus Christi*, makes explicit the Christological link between Matthew and Jesus and concludes that we 'forget his story at the peril of our very lives'.[42] American studies scholar Ed Ingebretsen, in discussing the phenomenon of monsters in pop culture, has elaborated on the Christological importance of Matthew Shepard, noting that 'Jesus' short life was marked continuously by scandal, beginning with his shame-filled birth out of wedlock in a stable and ending with the ignominious death of a criminal.'[43] Shepard's grotesquely 'transfigured' body, like Jesus' own, presents a scandal and an offence to 'decent' people. The category of 'monster' has thus been created in popular culture for those whom the majority find scandalous and offensive:

> The stigma created by the interlocking legal and social taboo surrounding the homosexual body (symbolic as well as actual), extends an ironic tribute to the original scandal of Jesus – whose *sacred* body is likewise characterized by monstrosity, offense, and riddled with pain. Both are bearers of social opprobrium.[44]

We, like the women who watched Jesus' death from a distance, may emulate them by drawing closer to the graves of modern-day martyrs in order to witness the resurrection God has in store for all oppressed and marginalized people.

I agree with Robert Goss that Easter was the moment when God made Jesus queer. This is when God 'queered' or 'spoiled' the spoiling of God's Son by raising him from the dead. This is when God stirred up the status quo by vindicating the deaths of political martyrs for all time

---

42 McNally, *Corpus Christi*, p. vi.
43 Ingebretsen, *At Stake*, pp. 180–1.
44 Ingebretsen, *At Stake*, pp. 180–1.

and saying 'no' to the oppressions associated with discrimination in all its forms. In a strictly queer context, the Christ that God queered on Easter says, 'Never again!' the same way that holocaust survivors try to make some sense of that tragedy. The queer Christ not only bursts forth from the empty tomb, leaving behind the graveclothes of homophobic violence and compulsory heterosexuality, but also is resurrected in each of us as we accept our queerness – our divine birthright to imagine, to stir up, and to spoil in God's name.

As we do that, I believe that queer Christians can also emulate the mysterious figure of the Gospel of John known as 'the one whom Jesus loved' or, in popular terminology, 'the Beloved Disciple'. Who is the Beloved Disciple? There have been many theories,[45] but the final answer is that we do not know. It may have been John; it may have been Thomas; it may have been Lazarus; it may have been Mary of Magdala. Each of these possibilities has been proffered, but each is not without its problems. In my queer Christology, I see this Beloved Disciple in a different way: I choose to see the Beloved not as a historical person but as a metaphorical clue left to us by the Fourth Evangelist. The Beloved Disciple can be any person who believes that Christ has risen without having the proof at hand; the Beloved Disciple can be the queer person of faith who believes that God has a plan for her/his life and believes that there will be an end to heterosexist oppression, even though at present there seems no end in sight. For those of us who are striving to follow and become the queer Christ, the Fourth Evangelist speaks down the corridors of time: 'Blessed [fortunate; commendable] are those who have not seen and yet have come to believe' (John 20.29).

Beyond Resurrection

It is significant that, in the mystical Christology of Andrew Harvey to which I have alluded throughout my own Christology, three of the eight thresholds to the mystical Christ occur after the human Jesus' death. While it is certainly important to live our lives according to the wisdom

---

45 See, for example, James H. Charlesworth, *The Beloved Disciple: Whose Witness Validates the Gospel of John?* (Valley Forge, PA: Trinity Press International, 1995); Raymond E. Brown, *The Gospel According to John*, two volumes (Garden City, NY: Doubleday, 1966–1970); Francis J. Moloney, *The Gospel of John* (Collegeville, MN: The Liturgical Press, 1998); and Robert E. Goss, 'The Beloved Disciple: A Queer Bereavement Narrative in a Time of AIDS', in *Take Back the Word*, ed. Goss and West, pp. 206–18.

that Jesus imparted during his own path along the Christ way, it is essential that we recognize that a queer Christology must ultimately progress beyond the life of Jesus of Nazareth and into the lives of all believers – all of the 'other Christs' that Eckhart describes. According to Harvey, Christ was resurrected, ascended to God and returned in the flames of Pentecost to empower the Christian community forevermore. I agree that these three thresholds can be informative; however, I would go further into the lives of the first Christians by examining some post-resurrection events, for, after all, Christology is the apprehending of Christ by the community gathered in his name, beginning with the New Testament witnesses and progressing to today's seekers.

The risen Christ appeared to two of Jesus' followers as they walked along the road toward Emmaus (Luke 24.13–35). We are told that as they walked, Jesus joined them as Christ, but they did not recognize him; they continued to talk about their problems, their distress over what had happened to Jesus, and their disappointment that what they had hoped for had not materialized. I believe this story is paradigmatic for all of us who travel life's journey focused on our own problems and our own agendas. We are unwilling to realize that Christ walks with us because we are making our journey 'all about us'. The disciples travelling to Emmaus finally recognized Jesus 'in the breaking of the bread' (Luke 24.35), a simple, ordinary, everyday gesture that brought Jesus back into their consciousness and made them see the risen Christ. In the same way, queer people of faith can look around our daily lives for everyday miracles to be found in the ordinary parts of our daily round: the Christ is made known to us in our individual circumstances, if we will allow our eyes to be opened to the extraordinary within the ordinary. An encounter with Christ transforms our journey, 'queering' it by stirring it up and surpassing our expectations.

We can also gain nourishment for our journey from the experience of another solitary traveller whose story is told in Acts of the Apostles 8.26–40 – the Ethiopian eunuch. Here is the quintessential queer, one who is outcast on several levels: black, possibly gay, possibly intersexual or transgendered.[46] He has gone to worship at the Jerusalem temple, but is going home unfulfilled, for the Torah prohibits any male whose genitals are not intact from worshipping (Deuteronomy 23.1). He, like many queer refugees from religion, was on 'a wilderness road' (Acts

---

46 Wilson, *Our Tribe*, pp. 128–31. For a traditional interpretation, see Ben Witherington, III, *The Acts of the Apostles: A Socio-Rhetorical Commentary* (Grand Rapids, MI: William B. Eerdmans, 1998).

8.26). But the apostle Philip joins him and – in a scene that looks remarkably like a gay 'pick-up' to me – explains to the eunuch the Scriptures he is attempting to read and goes on to assure him that he may be baptized into the Christian movement.[47] Thus, this person who was marginalized on several levels becomes the first non-Jewish convert to the Christian faith. This is good news for queers! When we are taught that there is no place for us in the churches or in society, messengers from God announce to us that we have a place with the queer Christ, who breaks down barriers, who queers the structures and systems that would seek to keep people out. Like the eunuch, we can ask, 'What is to prohibit me from being baptized?' and the risen Christ, the queer Christ, speaks to our hearts and says, 'Absolutely nothing!'

Harvey makes much of the fact that Pentecost is the opportunity for everyone to have a share in the mystical Christ. I believe that every day is Pentecost for every Christian, but especially for queer followers of the Christ way. We are told that the Spirit came upon the believers and gave them the ability to speak to others in their own languages (Acts 2.1–11). I have stated previously that for me the Christ Spirit was breathed out upon us when Jesus came through the walls of fear and said, 'Receive the Holy Spirit' (John 20.22). Often, however, it is our first impulse to keep that Spirit to ourselves; the Pentecost experience, however, teaches us that this Christ Spirit cannot be contained, that, like fire, it travels fast and consumes everything in its path. The queer Christ animates his/her followers to speak to others in their own language: this tells me that there are many diverse ways to tell the Christ story and to share the Christ Spirit. There are many 'queerings' possible because of that restless Spirit that burns to be shared. There are many sub-communities within the queer community that need to be shown the Christ: bisexuals, transgendered, transsexual, intersexual, differently sexual, non-sexual, supportively heterosexual, people of leather and lace, celibate people, those into S/M and those into 'vanilla' sex, those who are single or partnered and monogamous, as well as those who are in open relationships or triads. Our God of diversity empowers us to share the queer Christ in diverse ways to diverse people in their own languages. May it be so!

---

47 It is significant that the text the eunuch is reading is Isaiah, which includes the promise of God to the eunuchs that are faithful to God that God will give them a name that shall be not be 'cut off' (as other things have been). See Gaiser, 'A New Word on Homosexuality?'

Epilogue

Has Christ Been 'Queered'?

This study has offered a new Christology to the panoply of liberation Christologies that seek to interpret the Christ figure from various social locations. The social location in this instance is sexual orientation, namely a 'queer' location, as I have defined that term – imaginative, playful, stirring up, sometimes spoiling what has already been spoiled, but always interpreting Christ through the lens of justice for all people, especially those marginalized because of their sexuality.

Have I succeeded in this endeavour? Only my reader will be able to answer that question. However, I would like to critique my queer Christology, employing the guidelines set forth by theologian Roger Haight in his discussion of constructive Christology. In suggesting what Christologies in an increasingly postmodern age should look like, Haight says:

> First, postmodernity involves a radical historical consciousness. Gone is the confidence in progress, goals toward which history is heading . . . All knowledge is local. . . . In christology a return to the historical Jesus is a sign of historical consciousness. . . . It seems clear that post-modernity demands new interpretations of Jesus of Nazareth.
>
> Second, postmodernity involves a critical social consciousness. . . . One of the marks of modernity is the turn to the subject, to universal and critical reason, as the foundation of truth. Now the human sub-ject appears to be a function of history, of social arrangements . . . The various socially mediated christologies are both a recognition of the fundamental sociality of human existence and a reaction against any reductionism. . . . Liberation christologies are a reassertion of human subjectivity and freedom, but a personal human subject-with-others, a freedom in society, and the sociality of human existence. . . .
>
> Third, postmodernity involves a pluralist consciousness. At no other time have people had such a sense of the difference of others, of the pluralism of societies, cultures, and religions . . . But postmodernity

provides an opportunity for dramatic new christological meaning. The discovery of pluralism is precisely a discovery of the 'other' . . .

Finally, postmodernity involves a cosmic consciousness. . . . We need a christology that will confirm the importance of a common humanity.[1]

Does my Christology fulfil Haight's criteria? I believe so. First, my queer Christology has demonstrated a localized knowledge, speaking from my own experience as a queer interpreter. I have been careful to reiterate that this is only one queer Christology among many that can and will be envisioned. I have looked to the historical Jesus for some information about Jesus Christ; yet, I have not limited myself to the results of historical Jesus research nor the most allegedly 'reliable' factual data on Jesus. Rather, I have been guided by my belief that 'something does not have to be factual to be true'. I have chosen to find truth not only in the 'facts' of Jesus' life but in the way he was interpreted by his followers then and now. This is true Christology.

Second, I have captured the relational quality of Jesus Christ in my Christology. I have sought to portray the importance of the Christ figure by how it is appropriated and used by a community, in this case the queer community. I have not presumed to imply a universal consciousness, nor have I accepted it uncritically from others. Ultimately, the queer view of Christ will only succeed if it is applied in community; one of the problems with what I have called 'Christophobia' is that it has isolated individuals from God who is Source, Saviour and Sustainer.

Third, I have been respectful of pluralism in my Christology. In my definition of 'Christ' in Chapter 11, I very carefully stated that I use a Christian vocabulary because my audience is the queer community that has emanated from Judaeo-Christian culture. However, I believe it was also clear that my view of Christ – human anointedness to share good news – could cross over between religions and was an idea that could function in various interfaith settings. Additionally, I believe my queer Christology has been inclusive of other types of pluralism. By examining and analysing the other liberation Christologies in Part II, I showed just how diverse the thinking is on this topic so that my own small contribution could be situated in an overall context.

Fourth and finally, I have articulated a queer Christology that can be shared among many segments of society – 'queer' or 'non-queer'. I have

1 Roger Haight, *Jesus Symbol of God* (Maryknoll, NY: Orbis Books, 1999), pp. 331–4.

not created a separatist Christology or one that is so nuanced and detailed that it will only appeal to a group of biblical scholars or queer theorists. I have intentionally sought *not* to shock, although I may have inadvertently done so, for it has been my intent in creating this Christology to appeal to the so-called 'middle-of-the-road' gays and lesbians as well as the 'cutting-edge' queers.

I have learned much on this journey, especially that the queer Christ has infused this work because I am he. As Jesus said that he and his Parent were one, so too I believe that I and the queer Christ are one. I pray that those who have read this study have encountered the Christ who meets us all in the very depths of our being – and our queerness.

Bibliography

Abraham, K. C. and Bernadette Mbuy-Beya, eds, *Spirituality of the Third World: A Cry for Life*, Maryknoll, NY: Orbis Books, 1994.

Allison, Dale C., *Jesus of Nazareth: Millenarian Prophet*, Minneapolis: Fortress Press, 1998.

Althaus-Reid, Marcella, *The Queer God*, London and New York: Routledge, 2003.

——, *Indecent Theology: Theological Perversions in Sex, Gender and Politics*, London and New York: Routledge, 2000.

Angelou, Maya, *Wouldn't Take Nothing for My Journey Now*, Toronto: Random House of Canada, 1993.

Aquino, María Pilar, *Our Cry for Life: Feminist Theology from Latin America*, translated by Dinah Livingstone, Maryknoll, NY: Orbis Books, 1993.

Ashton, John, *Understanding the Fourth Gospel*, Oxford: The Clarendon Press, 1991.

Bailey, Derrick Sherwin, *Homosexuality and the Western Christian Tradition*, London: Longmans-Green, 1955.

Batchelor, Edward, Jr, ed., *Homosexuality and Ethics*, New York: The Pilgrim Press, 1980.

Bawer, Bruce, *Stealing Jesus: How Fundamentalism Betrays Christianity*, New York: Crown Publishers, 1997.

Berkey, Robert F. and Sarah A. Edwards, eds, *Christology in Dialogue*, Cleveland: The Pilgrim Press, 1993.

Berryman, Phillip, *Liberation Theology: The Essential Facts About the Revolutionary Movement in Latin America and Beyond*, Oak Park, IL: Meyer Stone Books, 1987.

Boff, Leonardo, *Holy Trinity, Perfect Community*, translated by Phillip Berryman, Maryknoll, NY: Orbis Books, 2000.

——, *Jesus the Liberator: A Historical-Theological View*, translated by Paul Burns and Francis McDonagh, Maryknoll, NY: Orbis Books, 1993.

——, *When Theology Listens to the Poor*, translated by Robert R. Barr, New York: Harper & Row, 1988.

—— and Clodovis Boff, *Liberation Theology: From Confrontation to Dialogue*, translated by Robert R. Barr, New York: Harper & Row, 1986.

Bohache, Thomas, 'Embodiment as Incarnation: An Incipient Queer Christology', *Theology and Sexuality* 10:1 (October 2003), pp. 9–29.

——, 'Heterocolonialism Queered: Eros Comes to Church', unpublished doctoral dissertation, Episcopal Divinity School, 2007.

Bond, L. Susan, *Trouble with Jesus: Women, Christology, and Preaching*, St. Louis: Chalice Press, 1999.

Borg, Marcus J., *Conflict, Holiness, and Politics in the Teachings of Jesus*, second edition, Harrisburg, PA: Trinity Press International, 1998.

——, *Jesus in Contemporary Scholarship*, Harrisburg, PA: Trinity Press International, 1994.

——, *Meeting Jesus Again for the First Time: The Historical Jesus and the Heart of Contemporary Faith*, New York: HarperCollins, 1994.

——, *Jesus, A New Vision: Spirit, Culture, and the Life of Discipleship*, New York: Harper & Row, 1987.

——, ed., *Jesus at 2000*, Boulder, CO: Westview Press, 1997.

Bornkamm, Günther, *Jesus of Nazareth*, translated by Irene and Fraser McLuskey with James M. Robinson, New York: Harper & Row, 1960.

Boswell, John, *Christianity, Social Tolerance, and Homosexuality: Gay People in Western Europe from the Beginning of the Christian Era to the Fourteenth Century*, Chicago and London: University of Chicago Press, 1980.

Bouldrey, Brian, ed., *Wrestling with the Angel: Faith and Religion in the Lives of Gay Men*, New York: Riverhead Books, 1995.

Brawley, Robert L., ed., *Biblical Ethics and Homosexuality: Listening to Scripture*, Louisville: Westminster/John Knox Press, 1996.

Brock, Rita Nakashima, *Journeys by Heart: A Christology of Erotic Power*, New York: Crossroad, 1991.

—— and Susan Brooks Thistlethwaite, *Casting Stones: Prostitution and Liberation in Asia and the United States*, Minneapolis: Fortress Press, 1996.

——, Claudia Camp, and Serene Jones, eds, *Setting the Table: Women in Theological Conversation*, St Louis: Chalice Press, 1995.

Brooten, Bernadette J., *Love Between Women: Early Christian Responses to Female Homoeroticism*, Chicago and London: University of Chicago Press, 1996.

Brown, Raymond E., *An Introduction to New Testament Christology*, New York/Mahwah: Paulist Press, 1994.

——, *The Gospel According to John*, two volumes, Garden City, NY: Doubleday, 1966–1970.

——, *The Birth of the Messiah*, New York: Doubleday, 1979.

Browning, Frank, *The Culture of Desire: Paradox and Perversity in Gay Lives Today*, New York: Crown Publishers, Inc., 1993.

Bullough, Vern L., *Homosexuality: A History*, New York: New American Library, 1979.

——, *Sex, Society, and History*, New York: Science History Publications, 1976.

——, *Sexual Variance in Society and History*, Chicago and London: University of Chicago Press, 1976.

Bultmann, Rudolf, *New Testament and Mythology and Other Basic Writings*, translated and edited by Schubert M. Ogden, Philadelphia: Fortress Press, 1984.

——, *The History of the Synoptic Tradition*, translated by John Marsh, Oxford: Basil Blackwell, 1963.

——, *Theology of the New Testament*, two volumes, translated by Kendrick Grobel, New York: Charles Scribner's Sons, 1951, 1955.

Butler, Judith, *Gender Trouble: Feminism and the Subversion of Identity*, New York and London: Routledge, 1990.

Bynum, Caroline Walker, *Jesus As Mother: Studies in the Spirituality of the High Middle Ages*, Berkeley: University of California Press, 1982.

Carr, Anne E., *Transforming Grace: Christian Tradition and Women's Experience*, New York: Harper & Row, 1988.

Carter, Warren, *Matthew and the Margins: A Sociopolitical and Religious Reading*, Maryknoll, NY: Orbis Books, 2000.

Charlesworth, James H., *The Beloved Disciple: Whose Witness Validates the Gospel of John?*, Valley Forge, PA: Trinity Press International, 1995.

Christ, Carol P. and Judith Plaskow, eds, *Womanspirit Rising: A Feminist Reader in Religion*, New York: Harper & Row, 1979.

Chung Hyun Kyung, *Struggle to Be the Sun Again: Introducing Asian Women's Theology*, Maryknoll, NY: Orbis Books, 1990.

Clark, Elizabeth and Herbert Richardson, eds, *Women and Religion: A Feminist Sourcebook of Christian Thought*, New York: Harper & Row, 1977.

Clark, J. Michael, *Defying the Darkness: Gay Theology in the Shadows*, Cleveland: The Pilgrim Press, 1997.

——, *Beyond Our Ghettos: Gay Theology in Ecological Perspective*, Cleveland: The Pilgrim Press, 1993.

——, *A Place to Start: Toward an Unapologetic Gay Liberation Theology*, Dallas: Monument Press, 1989.

Cleage, Albert B., Jr, *The Black Messiah*, New York: Sheed and Ward, 1968.

Cleaver, Richard, *Know My Name: A Gay Liberation Theology*, Louisville: Westminster/John Knox Press, 1995.

Comstock, Gary David, *A Whosoever Church: Welcoming Lesbians and Gay Men into African American Congregations*, Louisville: Westminster/John Knox Press, 2001.

——, *Unrepentant, Self-Affirming, Practicing: Lesbian/Bisexual/Gay People within Organized Religion*, New York: Continuum, 1996.

——, *Gay Theology Without Apology*, Cleveland: The Pilgrim Press, 1993.

—— and Susan E. Henking, eds, *Que(e)rying Religion: A Critical Anthology*, New York: Continuum, 1997.

Cone, James H., *A Black Theology of Liberation*, 20th anniversary edition, Maryknoll, NY: Orbis Books, 1990; originally published 1970.

——, *Black Theology and Black Power*, 20th anniversary edition, New York: Harper & Row, 1989; originally published 1969.

——, *God of the Oppressed*, New York: The Seabury Press, 1975.

—— and Gayraud S. Wilmore, eds, *Black Theology: A Documentary History*, two volumes, Maryknoll, NY: Orbis Books, 1993.

Conn, Joann Wolski and Walter E. Conn, eds, *Horizons on Catholic Feminist Theology*, Washington, DC: Georgetown University Press, 1992.

Cooey, Paula M., William R. Eakin and Jay B. McDaniel, eds, *After Patriarchy: Feminist Transformations of the World Religions*, Maryknoll, NY: Orbis Books, 1991.

Corrington, Gail Paterson, *Her Image of Salvation: Female Saviors and Formative Christianity*, Louisville: Westminster/John Knox Press, 1992.

Countryman, L. William, *Dirt, Greed, and Sex: Sexual Ethics in the New Testament and Their Implications for Today*, Philadelphia: Fortress Press, 1988.

—— and M. R. Riley, *Gifted by Otherness: Gay and Lesbian Christians in the Church*, Harrisburg, PA: Morehouse Publishing, 2001.

Crossan, John Dominic, *The Historical Jesus: The Life of a Mediterranean Jewish Peasant*, New York: HarperCollins, 1991.

——, *The Cross That Spoke: The Origins of the Passion Narrative*, New York: Harper & Row, 1988.

Daly, Mary, *Beyond God the Father: Toward a Philosophy of Women's Liberation, with an Original Reintroduction by the Author*, Boston: Beacon Press, 1985; originally published 1973.

——, *The Church and the Second Sex, with the Feminist Postchristian Introduction and New Archaic Afterwords by the Author*, Boston: Beacon Press, 1985; originally published 1968.

Davis, Angela Y., *Women, Race, and Class*, New York: Vintage Books, 1983.

De Jonge, Marinus, *Christology in Context: The Earliest Christian Response to Jesus*, Philadelphia: The Westminster Press, 1988.

de la Huerta, Christian, *Coming Out Spiritually: The Next Step*, New York: Jeremy P. Tarcher/Putnam, 1999.

Dickey Young, Pamela, *Christ in a Post-Christian World: How Can We Believe in Jesus Christ When Those Around Us Believe Differently – or Not at All?* Minneapolis: Fortress Press, 1995.

Donaldson, Laura E. and Kwok Pui-lan, eds, *Postcolonialism, Feminism, and Religious Discourse*, New York and London: Routledge, 2002.

Douglas, Kelly Brown, *Sexuality and the Black Church: A Womanist Perspective*, Maryknoll, NY: Orbis Books, 1999.

——, *The Black Christ*, Maryknoll, NY: Orbis Books, 1994.

Duberman, Martin, *Stonewall*, New York: E. P. Dutton, 1993.

Dunn, James D. G., *Christology in the Making: A New Testament Inquiry into the Origins of the Incarnation*, second edition, London: SCM Press, 1980, 1989; Grand Rapids, MI: William B. Eerdmans Publishing Company, 1996.

Durang, Christopher, *Christopher Durang Explains It All to You: Six Plays*, New York: Grove Press, 1990.

Ehrmann, Bart D., *The New Testament: A Historical Introduction to the Early Christian Writings*, second edition, Oxford and New York: Oxford University Press, 2000.

——, *Jesus: Apocalyptic Prophet of the New Millennium*, Oxford and New York: Oxford University Press, 1999.

Elizondo, Virgil and Norbert Greimacher, eds, *Women in a Men's Church*, Edinburgh: T. & T. Clark; New York: The Seabury Press, 1980.

Ellacuria, Ignacio, *Freedom Made Flesh: The Mission of Christ and His Church*, translated by John Drury, Maryknoll, NY: Orbis Books, 1976.

—— and Jon Sobrino, eds, *Mysterium Liberationis: Fundamental Concepts of Liberation Theology*, Maryknoll, NY: Orbis Books, 1993.

Elwood, Douglas J., ed., *Asian Christian Theology: Emerging Themes*, Philadelphia: Westminster Press, 1980.

Evans, James H., Jr, *We Have Been Believers: An African-American Systematic Theology*, Minneapolis: Fortress Press, 1992.

Fabella, Virginia and Mercy Amba Oduyoye, eds, *With Passion and Compassion: Third World Women Doing Theology*, Maryknoll, NY: Orbis Books, 1988.
Ferguson, Everett, *Backgrounds of Early Christianity*, second edition, Grand Rapids, MI: William B. Eerdmans Publishing Company, 1993.
Ferguson, Russell, Martha Gever, Trinh T. Minh-ha and Cornel West, eds, *Out There: Marginalization and Contemporary Cultures*, Cambridge, MA, and London: The MIT Press, 1990.
Fone, Byrne, *Homophobia: A History*, New York: Metropolitan Books/Henry Holt and Company, 2000.
Fox, Matthew, *Sins of the Spirit, Blessings of the Flesh: Lessons for Transforming Evil in Soul and Society*, New York: Three Rivers Press, 1999.
——, *Wrestling with the Prophets: Essays on Creation Spirituality and Everyday Life*, New York: HarperCollins, 1995.
——, *The Coming of the Cosmic Christ: The Healing of Mother Earth and the Birth of a Global Renaissance*, New York: Harper & Row, 1988.
——, *Original Blessing: A Primer in Creation Spirituality*, Santa Fe, NM: Bear and Company, 1983.
Fredricksen, Paula, *From Jesus to Christ: The Origins of the New Testament Images of Jesus*, New Haven and London: Yale University Press, 1988.
Fuller, Reginald H., *The Foundations of New Testament Christology*, New York: Charles Scribner's Sons, 1965.
Funk, Robert W., Roy W. Hoover and the Jesus Seminar, *The Acts of Jesus: The Search for the Authentic Deeds of Jesus*, New York: HarperCollins, 1998.
——, *The Five Gospels: The Search for the Authentic Words of Jesus*, New York: Macmillan Publishing Company, 1993.

Gagnon, Robert A. J., *The Bible and Homosexual Practice: Texts and Hermeneutics*, Nashville: Abingdon Press, 2001.
Gaiser, Frederick J., 'A New Word on Homosexuality? Isaiah 56:1–8 as Case Study', *Word and World* 14:3 (Summer 1994), pp. 280–93.
Gamble, Harry Y., Jr, *The New Testament Canon: Its Making and Meaning*, Philadelphia: Fortress Press, 1985.
Garland, David E., *Reading Matthew: A Literary and Theological Commentary on the First Gospel*, New York: Crossroad, 1995.
Gebara, Ivone, *Longing for Running Water: Ecofeminism and Liberation*, translated by David Molineaux, Minneapolis: Fortress Press, 1999.
Gibellini, Rosino, ed., *Paths of African Theology*, Maryknoll, NY: Orbis Books, 1994.
Gillis, Chester, *Roman Catholicism in America*, New York: Columbia University Press, 1999.
——, *Pluralism: A New Paradigm for Theology*, Louvain: Peeters Press; Grand Rapids, MI: William B. Eerdmans Publishing Company, 1998.
Glaser, Chris, *Come Home! Reclaiming Spirituality and Community as Gays and Lesbians*, second edition, Gaithersburg, MD: Chi Rho Press, 1998.
Goldenberg, Naomi R., *Changing of the Gods: Feminism and the End of*

Traditional Religions, Boston: Beacon Press, 1979.

Gonzalez, Justo L., *Manana: Christian Theology from a Hispanic Perspective*, Nashville: Abingdon Press, 1990.

——, *The Story of Christianity, Volume 2: The Reformation to the Present Day*, New York: HarperCollins, 1985.

——, *A History of Christian Thought, Volume III: From the Protestant Reformation to the Twentieth Century*, revised edition, Nashville: Abingdon Press, 1987; originally published 1975.

Goss, Robert, *Queering Christ: Beyond Jesus ACTED UP*, Cleveland: The Pilgrim Press, 2002.

——, *Jesus ACTED UP: A Gay and Lesbian Manifesto*, New York: Harper-Collins, 1993.

—— and Amy Adams Squire Strongheart, eds, *Our Families, Our Values: Snapshots of Queer Kinship*, New York and London: The Haworth Press, 1997.

—— and Mona West, eds, *Take Back the Word: A Queer Reading of the Bible*, Cleveland: The Pilgrim Press, 2000.

Gramick, Jeannine and Pat Furey, eds, *The Vatican and Homosexuality*, New York: Crossroad, 1988.

Grant, Jacquelyn, *White Women's Christ and Black Women's Jesus: Feminist Christology and Womanist Response*, Atlanta: Scholars Press, 1989.

Greenberg, David F., *The Construction of Homosexuality*, Chicago and London: University of Chicago Press, 1988.

Greenspahn, Frederick E., ed., *Contemporary Ethical Issues in the Jewish and Christian Traditions*, Hoboken, NJ: Ktav Publishing House, 1986.

Gross, Rita M., *Feminism and Religion: An Introduction*, Boston: Beacon Press, 1996.

Guest, Deryn, Robert E. Goss, Mona West and Thomas Bohache, eds, *The Queer Bible Commentary*, London: SCM Press, 2006.

Gutiérrez, Gustavo, *The God of Life*, translated by Matthew J. O'Connell, Maryknoll, NY: Orbis Books, 1991.

——, *A Theology of Liberation: History, Politics and Salvation*, translated and edited by Sister Caridad Inda and John Eagleson, Maryknoll, NY: Orbis Books, 1973.

Haight, Roger, *Jesus Symbol of God*, Maryknoll, NY: Orbis Books, 1999.

Halperin, David, *One Hundred Years of Homosexuality*, New York and London: Routledge, 1990.

Hampson, Daphne, *Theology and Feminism*, Oxford: Basil Blackwell, 1990.

Harrington, Daniel J., *The Gospel of Matthew*, Collegeville, MN: The Liturgical Press, 1991.

Harvey, Andrew, *Son of Man: The Mystical Path to Christ*, New York: Jeremy P. Tarcher/Putnam, 1998.

——, *The Return of the Mother*, Berkeley, CA: Frog, 1995.

Hasbany, Richard, ed., *Homosexuality and Religion*, New York and London: Harrington Park Press, 1989.

Hays, Richard B., 'Relations Natural and Unnatural: A Response to John Boswell's Exegesis of Romans 1', *Journal of Religious Ethics* 14 (1986), pp. 184–215.

Hazel, Dann, *Witness: Gay and Lesbian Clergy Report from the Front*, Louisville: Westminster/John Knox Press, 2000.

Helminiak, Daniel A., *What the Bible Really Says About Homosexuality*, San Francisco: Alamo Square Press, 1994.

——, *The Same Jesus: A Contemporary Christology*, Chicago: Loyola University Press, 1986.

Herman, Didi, *The Antigay Agenda: Orthodox Vision and the Christian Right*, Chicago and London: University of Chicago Press, 1997.

Heyward, (Isabel) Carter, *Saving Jesus from Those Who Are Right: Rethinking What It Means to Be Christian*, Minneapolis: Fortress Press, 1999.

——, *Staying Power: Reflections on Gender, Justice, and Compassion*, Cleveland: The Pilgrim Press, 1995.

——, *Speaking of Christ: A Lesbian Feminist Voice*, edited by Ellen C. Davis, New York: The Pilgrim Press, 1989.

——, *Touching Our Strength: The Erotic as Power and the Love of God*, New York: Harper & Row, 1989.

——, *The Redemption of God: A Theology of Mutual Relation*, Lanham, MD: University Press of America, 1982.

Hick, John, ed., *The Metaphor of God Incarnate: Christology in a Pluralistic Age*, Louisville: Westminster/John Knox Press, 1993.

——, *Classical and Contemporary Readings in the Philosophy of Religion*, third edition, Englewood Cliffs, NJ: Prentice Hall, 1990.

——, *An Interpretation of Religion: Human Responses to the Transcendent*, New Haven: Yale University Press, 1989.

Hinsdale, Mary Ann and Phyllis H. Kaminski, eds, *Women and Theology*, Maryknoll, NY: Orbis Books, 1995.

hooks, bell, *Ain't I a Woman: Black Women and Feminism*, Boston: South End Press, 1981.

Hopkins, Dwight N., *Shoes That Fit Our Feet: Sources for a Constructive Black Theology*, Maryknoll, NY: Orbis Books, 1993.

Hopkins, Julie, *Towards a Feminist Christology: Jesus of Nazareth, European Women and the Christological Crisis*, London: SPCK, 1995.

Horner, Tom, *Jonathan Loved David: Homosexuality in Biblical Times*, Philadelphia: The Westminster Press, 1978.

Horsley, Richard A., *Sociology and the Jesus Movement*, New York: Crossroad, 1989.

——, *Jesus and the Spiral of Violence: Popular Jewish Resistance in Roman Palestine*, New York: Harper & Row, 1987.

—— and John A. Hanson, *Bandits, Prophets, and Messiahs: Popular Movements at the Time of Jesus*, Minneapolis: Winston, 1985.

Ingebretsen, Edward J., *At Stake: Monsters and the Rhetoric of Fear in Public Culture*, Chicago and London: University of Chicago Press, 2001.

Isasi-Díaz, Ada María, *Mujerista Theology: A Theology for the Twenty-First Century*, Maryknoll, NY: Orbis Books, 1996.

——, *En La Lucha = In the Struggle: A Hispanic Women's Liberation Theology*, Minneapolis: Fortress Press, 1993.

—— and Yolanda Tarango, *Hispanic Women: Prophetic Voice in the Church –*

BIBLIOGRAPHY

Toward a Hispanic Woman's Liberation Theology, New York: Harper & Row, 1988.
Isherwood, Lisa, *Liberating Christ: Exploring the Christologies of Contemporary Liberation Movements*, Cleveland: The Pilgrim Press, 1999.
—— and Elizabeth Stuart, *Introducing Body Theology*, Cleveland: The Pilgrim Press, 1998.

Jacobs-Malina, Diane, *Beyond Patriarchy: The Images of Family in Jesus*, New York/Mahwah: Paulist Press, 1993.
Jesus Seminar, The, *The Once and Future Jesus*, Santa Rosa, CA: Polebridge Press, 2000.
Johnson, Elizabeth A., *Consider Jesus: Waves of Renewal in Christology*, New York: Crossroad, 1992.
——, *She Who Is: The Mystery of God in Feminist Theological Discourse*, New York: Crossroad, 1992.
Johnson, Luke Timothy, *The Real Jesus: The Misguided Quest for the Historical Jesus and the Truth of the Traditional Gospels*, New York: HarperCollins, 1996.
——, *The Gospel of Luke*, Collegeville, MN: The Liturgical Press, 1991.
Jones, Major J., *The Color of God: The Concept of God in Afro-American Thought*, Macon, GA: Mercer University Press, 1987.
Jordan, Mark D., *The Invention of Sodomy in Christian Theology*, Chicago and London: University of Chicago Press, 1997.

Kähler, Martin, *The So-Called Historical Jesus and the Historic, Biblical Christ*, translated and edited by Carl E. Braaten, Philadelphia: Fortress Press, 1964; originally published 1896.
Käsemann, Ernst, *Essays on New Testament Themes*, translated by W. J. Montague, London: SCM Press, 1964.
Kelly, J. N. D., *Early Christian Doctrines*, fifth edition, New York: HarperCollins, 1978; originally published 1960.
Kim, Grace Ji-Sun, *The Grace of Sophia: A Korean North American Women's Christology*, Cleveland: The Pilgrim Press, 2002.
Kimel, Alvin F., Jr, ed., *Speaking the Christian God: The Holy Trinity and the Challenge of Feminism*, Grand Rapids, MI: William B. Eerdmans Publishing Company, 1992.
King, Ursula, ed., *Feminist Theology from the Third World: A Reader*, London: SPCK; Maryknoll, NY: Orbis Books, 1994.
Kinukawa, Hisako, *Women and Jesus in Mark: A Japanese Feminist Perspective*, Maryknoll, NY: Orbis Books, 1994.
Knitter, Paul F., *Jesus and the Other Names: Christian Mission and Global Responsibility*, Maryknoll, NY: Orbis Books, 1996.
——, *No Other Name? A Critical Survey of Christian Attitudes Toward the World Religions*, Maryknoll, NY: Orbis Books, 1985.
Koester, Craig, 'Jesus the Way, the Cross, and the World according to the Gospel of John', *Word and World* 21:4 (Fall 2001), pp. 360–9.
Küster, Volker, *The Many Faces of Jesus Christ*, translated by John Bowden, Maryknoll, NY: Orbis Books, 2001.

Kwok Pui-lan. *Postcolonial Imagination and Feminist Theology*, Louisville and London: Westminster/John Knox Press, 2005.

——, *Introducing Asian Feminist Theology*, Cleveland: The Pilgrim Press, 2000.

LaCugna, Catherine Mowry, ed. *Freeing Theology: The Essentials of Theology in Feminist Perspective*, New York: HarperCollins, 1993.

Lawrence, Raymond J., Jr, *The Poisoning of Eros: Sexual Values in Conflict*, New York: Augustine Moore Press, 1989.

Lee, Jung Young, *Marginality: The Key to Multicultural Theology*, Minneapolis: Fortress Press, 1995.

Lerner, Gerda, *The Creation of Patriarchy*, New York: Oxford University Press, 1986.

Levine, Amy-Jill, ed., with Marianne Blickenstaff, *A Feminist Companion to Matthew*, Sheffield, UK: Sheffield Academic Press, 2001.

Loffreda, Beth, *Losing Matt Shepard: Life and Politics in the Aftermath of Anti-Gay Murder*, New York: Columbia University Press, 2000.

Lorde, Audre, *Sister Outsider: Essays and Speeches*, Trumansburg, NY: The Crossing Press, 1984.

MacHaffie, Barbara J., *Her Story: Women in Christian Tradition*, Philadelphia: Fortress Press, 1986.

Mack, Burton L., *The Christian Myth: Origins, Logic, and Legacy*, New York and London: Continuum, 2001.

——, *The Lost Gospel: The Book of Q and Christian Origins*, New York: HarperCollins, 1993.

——, *A Myth of Innocence: Mark and Christian Origins*, Philadelphia: Fortress Press, 1988.

Macquarrie, John, *Jesus Christ in Modern Thought*, London: SCM Press; Harrisburg, PA: Trinity Press International, 1990.

McClendon, James Wm., Jr, *Doctrine: Systematic Theology, Volume II*, Nashville: Abingdon Press, 1994.

McFague, Sallie, *Models of God: Theology for an Ecological, Nuclear Age*, Minneapolis: Fortress Press, 1987.

McNally, Terrence, *Corpus Christi: A Play*, New York: Grove Press, 1998.

McNeill, John J., *The Church and the Homosexual*, Kansas City, MO: Sheed, Andrews, and McMeel, 1976.

Meier, John P. *A Marginal Jew: Rethinking the Historical Jesus*, three volumes, New York: Doubleday, 1991–2001.

——, *The Vision of Matthew: Christ, Church, and Morality in the First Gospel*, New York: Paulist Press, 1979.

Miller, Ed L. and Stanley J. Grenz, *Fortress Introduction to Contemporary Theologies*, Minneapolis: Fortress Press, 1998.

Miller, Robert J., ed., *The Complete Gospels: Annotated Scholars Version*, Sonoma, CA: Polebridge Press, 1992.

Mohr, Richard D., *Gays/Justice: A Study of Ethics, Society, and Law*, New York: Columbia University Press, 1988.

Mollenkott, Virginia Ramey, *Omnigender: A Trans-Religious Approach*, Cleveland: The Pilgrim Press, 2001.

Moloney, Francis J., *The Gospel of John*, Collegeville, MN: The Liturgical Press, 1998.

Moltmann, Jürgen, *The Way of Jesus Christ: Christology in Messianic Dimensions*, translated by Margaret Kohl, New York: Harper & Row, 1990.

——, *The Trinity and the Kingdom: The Doctrine of God*, translated by Margaret Kohl, London: SCM Press; New York: Harper & Row, 1981.

——, *The Crucified God: The Cross of Christ as the Foundation and Criticism of Christian Theology*, translated by R. A. Wilson and John Bowden, London: SCM Press, 1974.

Monette, Paul, *Halfway Home*, New York: Avon Books, 1991.

Morrison, Toni, *Beloved*, New York: Alfred A. Knopf, 1987.

Moxnes, Halvor., *Putting Jesus in His Place: A Radical Vision of Household and Kingdom*, Louisville and London: Westminster/John Knox Press, 2003.

Mudflower Collective, The, *God's Fierce Whimsy: Christian Feminism and Theological Education*, New York: The Pilgrim Press, 1985.

Nardi, Peter M. and Beth E. Schneider, eds, *Social Perspectives in Lesbian and Gay Studies: A Reader*, New York and London: Routledge, 1998.

Newbold, Robert T., Jr, ed., *Black Preaching: Select Sermons in the Presbyterian Tradition*, Philadelphia: The Geneva Press, 1977.

Newsom, Carol A. and Sharon H. Ringe, eds, *The Women's Bible Commentary*, Louisville: Westminster/John Knox Press, 1992.

Nissinen, Martti, *Homoeroticism in the Biblical World: A Historical Perspective*, translated by Kirsi Stjerna, Minneapolis: Fortress Press, 1998.

Norris, Richard A., Jr, *The Christological Controversy*, Philadelphia: Fortress Press, 1980.

Nugent, Robert, ed., *A Challenge to Love: Gay and Lesbian Catholics in the Church*, New York: Crossroad, 1983.

O'Collins, Gerald, *Christology: A Biblical, Historical, and Systematic Study of Jesus*, Oxford and New York: Oxford University Press, 1995.

Oduyoye, Mercy Amba and Musimbi R. A. Kanyoro, eds, *The Will to Arise: Women, Tradition, and the Church in Africa*, Maryknoll, NY: Orbis Books, 1992.

Pagels, Elaine H., *Adam, Eve, and the Serpent*, New York: Random House, 1988.

——, *The Gnostic Gospels*, New York: Random House, 1979.

Panikkar, Raimundo, *The Unknown Christ of Hinduism*, revised and enlarged edition, Maryknoll, NY: Orbis Books, 1981; originally published 1964.

Patterson, Stephen J., *The God of Jesus: The Historical Jesus and the Search for Meaning*, Harrisburg, PA: Trinity Press International, 1998.

Pedraja, Luis G., *Jesus Is My Uncle: Christology from a Hispanic Perspective*, Nashville: Abingdon Press, 1999.

Pelikan, Jaroslav, *The Christian Tradition: A History of the Development of Doctrine, Volume 5: Christian Doctrine and Modern Culture (Since 1700)*, Chicago and London: University of Chicago Press, 1989.

Perkins, Pheme, *Reading the New Testament*, second edition, New York/Mahwah: Paulist Press, 1988; originally published 1978.

Perry, Troy D., with Thomas L. P. Swicegood, *Don't Be Afraid Anymore: The Story of Reverend Troy Perry and the Metropolitan Community Churches*, New York: St. Martin's Press, 1990.

——, with Charles L. Lucas, *The Lord Is My Shepherd and He Knows I'm Gay*, Los Angeles: Nash Publishing, 1972.

Pfirman, Carl, director, 'The Confession', UCLA School of Film, Theatre, and Television, in *Boys to Men*, Jour de Fête Films, Strand Releasing, 2000.

Pharr, Suzanne, *Homophobia: A Weapon of Sexism*, Little Rock, AR: Chardon Press, 1988.

Phipps, William E., *The Sexuality of Jesus*, Cleveland: The Pilgrim Press, 1996.

——, *Was Jesus Married? The Distortion of Sexuality in the Christian Tradition*, New York: Harper & Row, 1970.

Pittenger, W. Norman, *Christology Reconsidered*, London: SCM Press, 1970.

——, *The Word Incarnate: A Study of the Doctrine of the Person of Christ*, New York: Harper and Brothers, 1959.

Queen, Carol and Lawrence Schimel, eds, *PoMoSexuals: Challenging Assumptions About Gender and Sexuality*, San Francisco: Cleis Press, 1997.

Ramsey Colloquium, The, 'The Homosexual Movement, a Response by the Ramsey Colloquium', *First Things* 41 (March 1994), pp. 15–20.

Ratzinger, Joseph Cardinal, 'Letter to the Bishops of the Catholic Church on the Pastoral Care of Homosexual Persons', Rome: Sacred Congregation for the Doctrine of the Faith, 1 October 1986.

Riggs, Marcia Y., *Awake, Arise, and Act: A Womanist Call for Black Liberation*, Cleveland: The Pilgrim Press, 1994.

Riley, Gregory J., *One Jesus, Many Christs: How Jesus Inspired Not One True Christianity, But Many*, New York: HarperCollins, 1997.

Ringe, Sharon H., *Jesus, Liberation, and the Biblical Jubilee: Images for Ethics and Christology*, Philadelphia: Fortress Press, 1985.

Roberts, J. Deotis, *Liberation and Reconciliation: A Black Theology*, revised edition, Maryknoll, NY: Orbis Books, 1994; originally published 1971.

Robinson, James M., ed., *The Nag Hammadi Library in English*, New York: Harper & Row, 1978.

——, *A New Quest for the Historical Jesus*, London: SCM Press, 1959.

Rudy, Kathy, *Sex and the Church: Gender, Homosexuality, and the Transformation of Christian Ethics*, Boston: Beacon Press, 1997.

——, '"Where Two or More Are Gathered": Using Gay Communities as a Model for Christian Sexual Ethics', *Theology and Sexuality* 4 (1986), pp. 81–99.

Ruether, Rosemary Radford, *Introducing Redemption in Christian Feminism*, Sheffield, UK: Sheffield Academic Press, 1998.

——, *Women and Redemption: A Theological History*, Minneapolis: Fortress Press, 1998.

——, *Sexism and God-Talk: Toward a Feminist Theology*, Boston: Beacon Press, 1983.

——, *To Change the World: Christology and Cultural Criticism*, New York: Crossroad, 1981.

—— and Eleanor McLaughlin, eds, *Women of Spirit: Female Leadership in the*

Jewish and Christian Traditions, New York: Simon and Schuster, 1979.

——, *New Woman, New Earth: Sexist Ideologies and Human Liberation*, New York: The Seabury Press, 1975.

——, *Faith and Fratricide: The Theological Roots of Anti-Semitism*, New York: The Seabury Press, 1974.

——, *Liberation Theology: Human Hope Confronts Christian History and American Power*, New York/Mahwah: Paulist Press, 1972.

——, *The Church Against Itself: An Inquiry into the Conditions of Historical Existence for the Eschatological Community*, New York: Herder and Herder, 1967.

——, ed., *Religion and Sexism: Images of Women in the Jewish and Christian Traditions*, New York: Simon and Schuster, 1974.

Rusch, William G., *The Trinitarian Controversy*, Philadelphia: Fortress Press, 1980.

Sanders, E. P., *Jesus and Judaism*, Philadelphia: Fortress Press, 1985.

Schaberg, Jane, *The Illegitimacy of Jesus: A Feminist Theological Interpretation of the Infancy Narratives*, New York: Harper & Row, 1987.

Schaff, Philip, ed., *The Creeds of Christendom*, sixth edition, three volumes. Grand Rapids, MI: Baker Book House, 1993; originally published 1931.

Schneiders, Sandra M., *Beyond Patching: Faith and Feminism in the Catholic Church*, New York/Mahwah: Paulist Press, 1991.

Schreiter, Robert J., ed., *Faces of Jesus in Africa Today*, Maryknoll, NY: Orbis Books, 1991.

Schüssler Fiorenza, Elisabeth, *Jesus and the Politics of Interpretation*, New York and London: Continuum, 2000.

——, *Jesus, Miriam's Child, Sophia's Prophet: Critical Issues in Feminist Christology*, New York: Continuum, 1994.

——, *Discipleship of Equals: A Critical Feminist Ecclésia-ology of Liberation*, New York: Crossroad, 1993.

——, *But She Said: Feminist Practices of Biblical Interpretation*, Boston: Beacon Press, 1992.

——, *Bread Not Stone: The Challenge of Feminist Biblical Interpretation*, Boston: Beacon Press, 1984.

——, *In Memory of Her: A Feminist Theological Reconstruction of Christian Origins*, New York: Crossroad, 1983.

——, ed., *The Power of Naming: A Concilium Reader in Feminist Liberation Theology*, London: SCM Press; Maryknoll, NY: Orbis Books, 1996.

——, ed., *Searching the Scriptures, Volume One: A Feminist Introduction*, New York: Crossroad, 1993.

Schweitzer, Albert, *The Quest of the Historical Jesus: A Critical Study of Its Progress from Reimarus to Wrede*, translated by W. Montgomery, New York: Collier/Macmillan, 1968; originally published, 1906.

Scroggs, Robin, *The New Testament and Homosexuality: Contextual Background for Contemporary Debate*, Philadelphia: Fortress Press, 1983.

Sedgwick, Eve Kosofsky, *Epistemology of the Closet*, Berkeley: University of California Press, 1990.

Segovia, Fernando F., *Decolonizing Biblical Studies: A View from the Margins*, Maryknoll, NY: Orbis Books, 2000.

Segundo, Juan Luis, *An Evolutionary Approach to Jesus of Nazareth*, edited and translated by John Drury, Maryknoll, NY: Orbis Books, 1988.

——, *The Historical Jesus of the Synoptics*, translated by John Drury, Maryknoll, NY: Orbis Books, 1985.

Sheehan, Thomas, *The First Coming: How the Kingdom of God Became Christianity*, New York: Vintage Books, 1986.

Shellenberger, David, *Reclaiming the Spirit: Gay Men and Lesbians Come to Terms with Religion*, New Brunswick, NJ, and London: Rutgers University Press, 1998.

Sjöo, Monica and Barbara Mor, *The Great Cosmic Mother: Rediscovering the Religion of the Earth*, New York: Harper & Row, 1987.

Smith, Morton, *Jesus the Magician: Charlatan or Son of God?* New York: Harper & Row, 1978.

Sobrino, Jon, *Christology at the Crossroads: A Latin American Approach*, translated by John Drury, Maryknoll, NY: Orbis Books, 1978.

——, *Jesus Christ Liberator: A Critical Christology for Our Time*, Maryknoll, NY: Orbis Books, 1978.

—— and Ignacio Ellacuria, eds, *Systematic Theology: Perspectives from Liberation Theology*, Maryknoll, NY: Orbis Books, 1996.

Society of Biblical Literature, The, *The HarperCollins Study Bible*, New Revised Standard Version, New York: HarperCollins, 1993.

Soehnlein, K. M., *The World of Normal Boys*, New York: Kensington Books, 2000.

Sölle, Dorothée, *Beyond Mere Obedience: Reflections on a Christian Ethic for the Future*, translated by Lawrence W. Denef, Minneapolis: Augsburg Publishing House, 1970.

Song, Choan-Seng, *Jesus, the Crucified People: The Cross in the Lotus World, Volume I*, Minneapolis: Fortress Press, 1996; originally published 1990.

——, *Jesus in the Power of the Spirit: The Cross in the Lotus World, Volume III*, Minneapolis: Fortress Press, 1994.

——, *Jesus and the Reign of God: The Cross in the Lotus World, Volume II*, Minneapolis: Fortress Press, 1993.

——, *Third Eye Theology: Theology in Formation in Asian Settings*, revised edition, Maryknoll, NY: Orbis Books, 1990; originally published 1979.

Spencer, Daniel T., *Gay and Gaia: Ethics, Ecology, and the Erotic*, Cleveland: The Pilgrim Press, 1996.

Spong, John Shelby, *Resurrection: Myth or Reality? A Bishop's Search for the Origins of Christianity*, New York: HarperCollins, 1994.

——, *Born of a Woman: A Bishop Rethinks the Birth of Jesus*, New York: HarperCollins, 1992.

Stemmeler, Michael L. and J. Michael Clark, eds, *Constructing Gay Theology*, Las Colinas, TX: Monument Press, 1991.

——, *Homophobia and the Judaeo-Christian Tradition*, Dallas: Monument Press, 1990.

Stevens, MaryAnne, ed., *Reconstructing the Christ Symbol: Essays in Feminist Christology*, New York/Mahwah: Paulist Press, 1993.

Stone, Ken, ed., *Queer Commentary and the Hebrew Bible*, Cleveland: The Pilgrim Press, 2001.

Stuart, Elizabeth, *Just Good Friends: Towards a Lesbian and Gay Theology of Relationships*, London and New York: Mowbray, 1995.

Sugirtharajah, R. S., ed., *Asian Faces of Jesus*, Maryknoll, NY: Orbis Books, 1993.

Sullivan, Andrew, *Virtually Normal: An Argument About Homosexuality*, New York: Alfred A. Knopf, 1995.

Swidler, Arlene, ed., *Homosexuality and World Religions*, Valley Forge, PA: Trinity Press International, 1993.

Swidler, Leonard, 'Jesus Was a Feminist', *The Catholic World* (January 1971), pp. 177–83.

—— and Paul Mojzes, eds, *The Uniqueness of Jesus: A Dialogue with Paul F. Knitter*, Maryknoll, NY: Orbis Books, 1997.

Talbert, Charles H., ed., *Reimarus: Fragments*, translated by Ralph S. Fraser, Philadelphia: Fortress Press, 1970.

Tamez, Elsa, *The Scandalous Message of James: Faith Without Works Is Dead*, translated by John Eagleson, New York: Crossroad, 1992.

——, ed., *Through Her Eyes: Women's Theology from Latin America*, Maryknoll, NY: Orbis Books, 1989.

Terrell, JoAnne Marie, *Power in the Blood? The Cross in the African-American Experience*, Maryknoll, NY: Orbis Books, 1998.

Tessier, L. J., *Dancing After the Whirlwind: Feminist Reflections on Sex, Denial, and Spiritual Transformation*, Boston: Beacon Press, 1997.

Thébaud, Françoise, ed., *A History of Women in the West, Volume V: Toward a Cultural Identity in the Twentieth Century*, Cambridge and London: The Belknap Press of Harvard University Press, 1994.

Thistlethwaite, Susan Brooks, *Sex, Race, and God: Christian Feminism in Black and White*, New York: Crossroad, 1991.

—— and Mary Potter Engel, eds, *Lift Every Voice: Constructing Christian Theologies from the Underside*, revised and expanded edition, Maryknoll, NY: Orbis Books, 1998.

Thompson, Mark, ed., *Gay Soul: Finding the Heart of Gay Spirit and Nature*, New York: HarperCollins, 1994.

——, *Gay Spirit: Myth and Meaning*, New York: St. Martin's Press, 1987.

Townes, Emilie M., ed., *A Troubling in My Soul: Womanist Perspectives on Evil and Suffering*, Maryknoll, NY: Orbis Books, 1993.

Tracy, David, *Blessed Rage for Order: The New Pluralism in Theology*, New York: The Seabury Press, 1978.

Trible, Phyllis, *God and the Rhetoric of Sexuality*, Philadelphia: Fortress Press, 1978.

Vaid, Urvashi, *Virtual Equality: The Mainstreaming of Gay and Lesbian Liberation*, New York: Anchor Books/Doubleday, 1995.

von Campenhausen, Hans, *The Formation of the Christian Bible*, translated by J. A. Baker, Philadelphia: Fortress Press, 1972.

von Kellenbach, Katharina, *Anti-Judaism in Feminist Religious Writings*, Atlanta: Scholars Press, 1994.

Wainwright, Elaine M., *Shall We Look for Another? A Feminist Rereading of the Matthean Jesus*, Maryknoll, NY: Orbis Books, 1998.

Walker, Alice, *In Search of Our Mothers' Gardens: Womanist Prose*, Orlando, FL: Harcourt, Brace, and Jovanovich, 1983.

Warner, Michael, *The Trouble with Normal: Sex, Politics, and the Ethics of Queer Life*, New York: The Free Press/Simon & Schuster, 1999.

Weidman, Judith L., ed., *Christian Feminism: Visions of a Just Humanity*, New York: Harper & Row, 1984.

West, Cornel, *The Cornel West Reader*, New York: Basic Civitas Books, 1999.

——, *Prophesy Deliverance! An Afro-American Revolutionary Christianity*, Louisville: Westminster/John Knox Press, 1982.

Wilken, Robert L., ed., *Aspects of Wisdom in Judaism and Early Christianity*, Notre Dame, IN: University of Notre Dame Press, 1975.

Williams, Delores S., *Sisters in the Wilderness: The Challenge of Womanist God-Talk*, Maryknoll, NY: Orbis Books, 1993.

Williams, Robert, *Just As I Am: A Practical Guide to Being Out, Proud, and Christian*, New York: Crown Publishers, Inc., 1992.

Williams, Walter L., *The Spirit and the Flesh: Sexual Diversity in American Indian Culture*, Boston: Beacon Press, 1986.

Wilmore, Gayraud S., *Black Religion and Black Radicalism: An Interpretation of the Religious History of Afro-American People*, second edition, Maryknoll, NY: Orbis Books, 1983.

Wilson, Nancy L., *Our Tribe: Queer Folks, God, Jesus, and the Bible*, New York: HarperCollins, 1995.

Wilson-Kastner, Patricia, *Faith, Feminism, and the Christ*, Philadelphia: Fortress Press, 1983.

Witherington, Ben, III, *The Acts of the Apostles: A Socio-Rhetorical Commentary*, Grand Rapids, MI: William B. Eerdmans Publishing Company, 1998.

——, *The Jesus Quest: The Third Search for the Jew of Nazareth*, Downers Grove, IL: InterVarsity Press, 1995.

——, *Jesus the Sage: The Pilgrimage of Wisdom*, Minneapolis: Fortress Press, 1994.

——, *The Christology of Jesus*, Philadelphia: Fortress Press, 1990.

Witvliet, Theo, *The Way of the Black Messiah: The Hermeneutical Challenge of Black Theology as a Theology of Liberation*, translated by John Bowden, London: SCM Press; Oak Park, IL: Meyer Stone Books, 1987.

Wondra, Ellen K., *Humanity Has Been a Holy Thing: Toward a Contemporary Feminist Christology*, Lanham, MD: University Press of America, 1994.

Woods, Richard, *Another Kind of Love: Homosexuality and Spirituality*, Chicago: Thomas More Publishing, 1977.

CPSIA information can be obtained
at www.ICGtesting.com
Printed in the USA
JSHW060317180723
44941JS00003B/15